BRUSHWORK *for the* OIL PAINTER

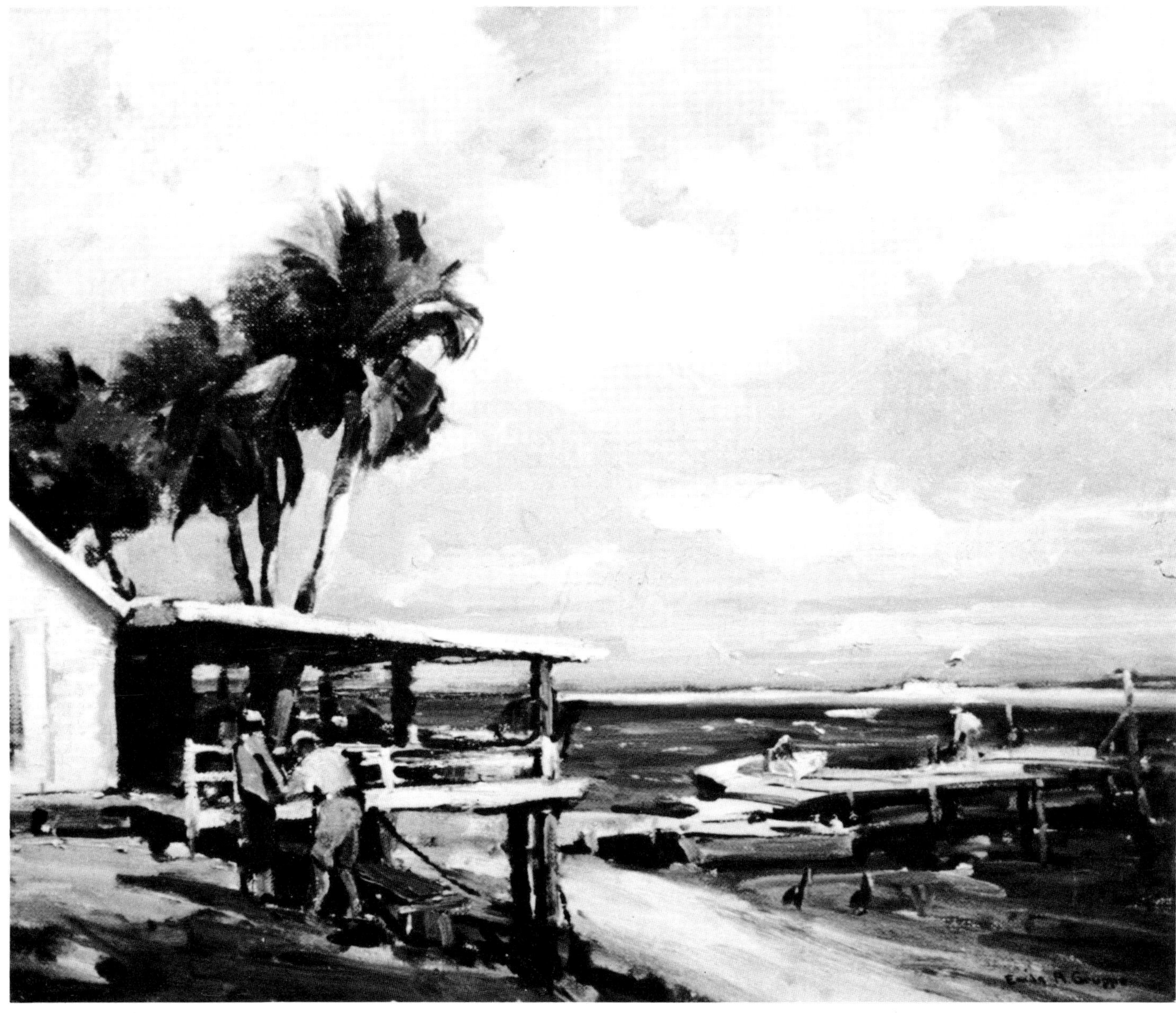

Going Fishing
oil on canvas
25″ × 30″ (64 × 76 cm)

Florida is known for its flatness and the breadth of its skies. So why not emphasize these qualities? The long stroke of the distant beach suggests the flat landscape. And this movement is echoed by the nearby landing and boats. Part of the fun of the painting is to see how *few* strokes are needed to suggest the wharf.

The top of the wharf is a few flat strokes—with five dark lines to suggest planking. The pilings are simple verticals. The lighter ones are painted first; then the darker are added. Notice how they connect to the dark line under the wharf and thus form a single shape. Each light and dark stroke is different. The reflections are a jumble of horizontal slashes. Pelicans suggest the tropical nature of the place: a blob for the body, a vertical for the neck, and a light diagonal slash for the bill.

BRUSHWORK *for the* OIL PAINTER

By Emile Gruppé/Edited by Charles Movalli

WATSON-GUPTILL PUBLICATIONS/NEW YORK

I dedicate this book
to my wife, Dorothy,
and to my two children,
Robert and Emily.

First published 1983 in New York by Watson-Guptill Publications,
a division of Billboard Publications, Inc.
1515 Broadway, New York, N.Y. 10036

Library of Congress Cataloging in Publication Data
Gruppé, Emile A., 1896–1978.
Brushwork for the oil painter.
Rev. ed. of: Brushwork. 1977.
Bibliography: p.
Includes index.
1. Brushwork. 2. Painting—Technique.
I. Movalli, Charles. II. Title.
ND1505.G78 1983 751.45 83-12461
ISBN 0-8230-0526-7

Distributed in the United Kingdom by Phaidon Press Ltd., Littlegate
House, St. Ebbe's St., Oxford

Manufactured in Japan
1 2 3 4 5 6 7 8 9/88 87 86 85 84 83

ACKNOWLEDGMENTS

I would like to thank Don Holden and David Lewis, who originated the idea for this book, and Charles Movalli, who photographed and organized it.

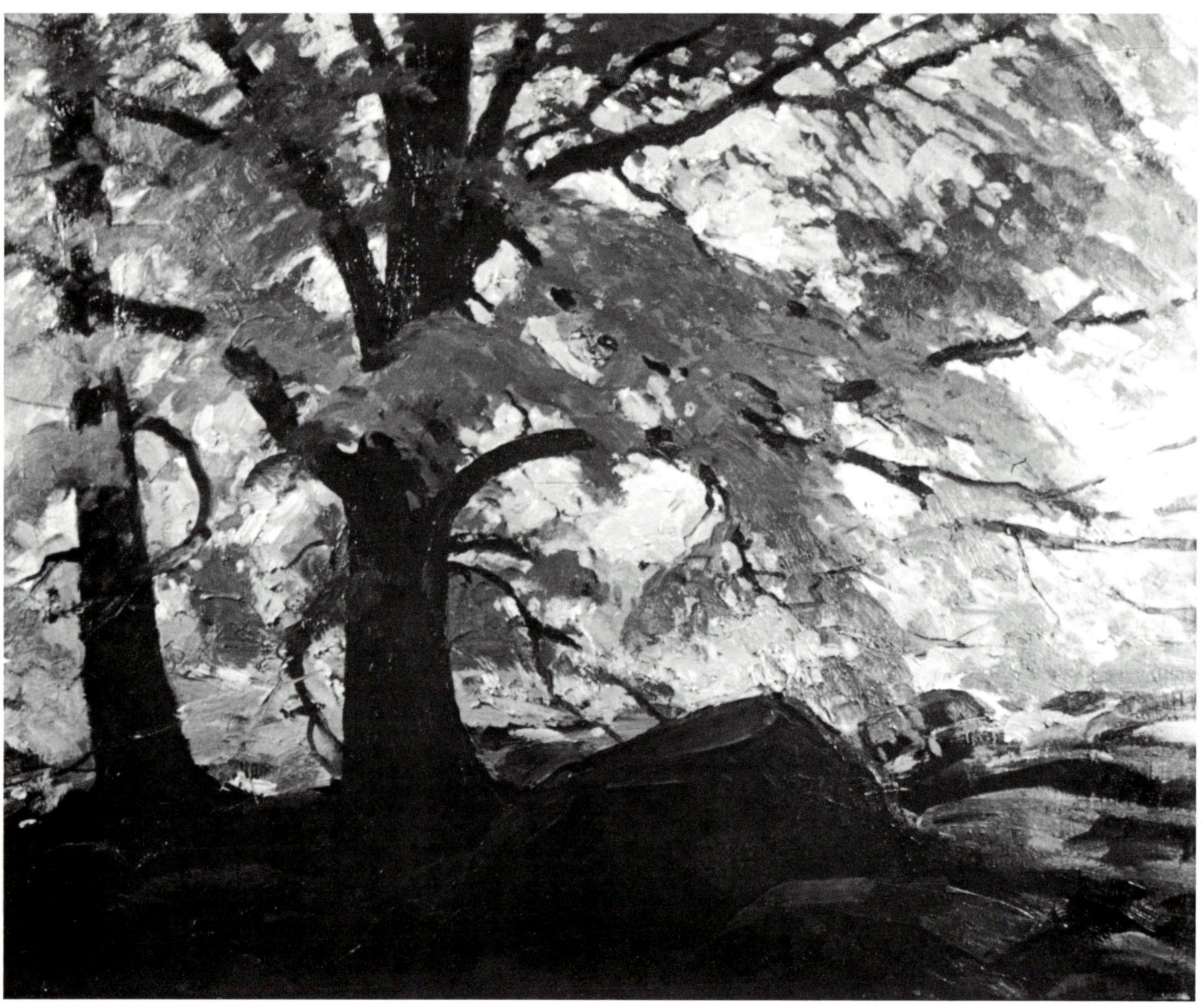

Rocks and Trees
oil on canvas
30″ × 36″ (76 × 91 cm)

The sun is directly in back of the trees, silhouetting them and giving an interesting and colorful character to their fall leaves. The leaves have a strong texture, but they're painted in big clusters with individual strokes visible only at the edges. Sometimes the leaves are painted into the wet sky. Sometimes the sky is painted into the mass of wet leaves. A clump of leaves cuts across the center of the tree and unites the foliage on either side of it. Probably the most important element in the picture is the small tree on the left. It fills the left side of the canvas and forces your eye toward the main interest: the long horizontal branch on the right and the leaves that obscure it.

CONTENTS

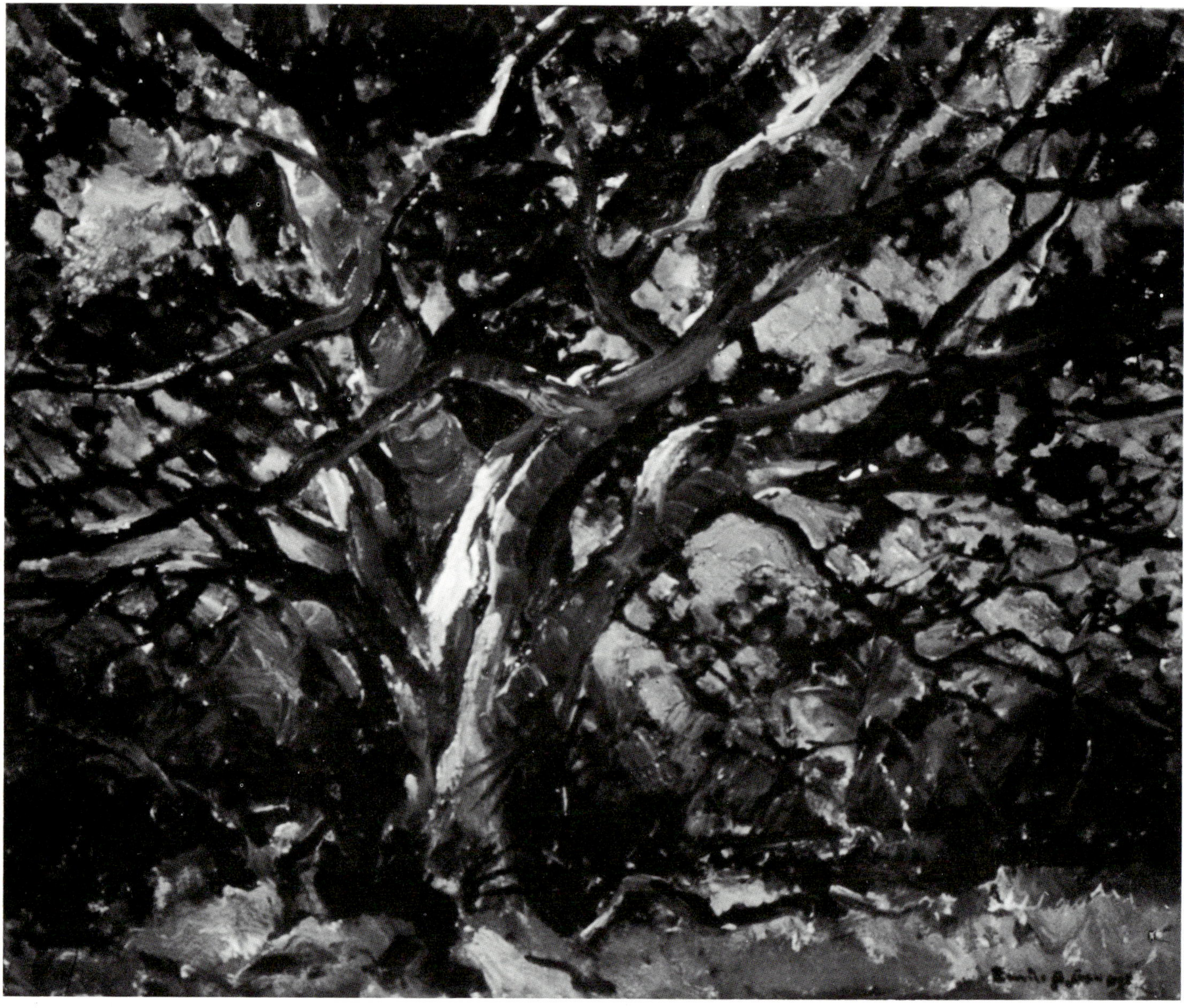

The Banyan Tree
oil on canvas
25″ × 30″ (64 × 76 cm)

This is my kind of subject. As a kid, I studied with John Carlson, one of the greatest of all tree painters, and he taught me to look for the character of the tree and to exaggerate it, much as you would exaggerate the stance of a model in a life class. Here I like the way the strong movement of the branches to the right is balanced by a less pronounced, but equally powerful movement of the trunk to the left.

The branches and leaves silhouette against the sky. There's a slight difference in color within this silhouette—but not a difference in value. Squint at the page, and you'll see how the section forms a single, large unit.

In the distance, there's no need to distinguish branches from leaves by a change of color. The flat mass serves as a foil to the more varied branches in front of it. Within the mass, a few lines suggest branches. The delicacy of these lines accentuates the massiveness of the nearby branches. Without them, the tree would be too heavy in appearance. The lines add a hint of playfulness.

INTRODUCTION

Few things are as interesting as a good, descriptive brushstroke. It's full of character—not only that of the subject, but of the painter too. It has personality. It's also analytical. Seeing a well-placed stroke, you sense the intellect of the painter. And that's a satisfying sensation. When you look at a Cézanne, for example, you can almost *feel* him thinking.

For some reason, the public often equates loose painting with sloppiness. A watercolorist friend of mine who works in a very free style once told me that a student said he joined her class because he couldn't draw and thought her style would be a good one to emulate! He didn't understand that expressive brushwork is based on sound drawing ability. Every stroke counts: the right size stroke, of the right value and color, in the right place. You're after the significant facts of nature. You have to look with a sharp eye, ask questions, and draw conclusions.

LINE VERSUS MASS. There seem to be two basic kinds of painters: those who work in line and those who work in mass. Fine draftsmen tend to work in a linear way, enjoying their skillful ability to draw the details of a scene—and that kind of work has its appeal. When I was a student, I saw a great painting by Eugene Speicher. It was of an old guide. His legs were crossed and you could see the soles of his shoes—and the nails—and the *rust* from those nails! I heard that he had paid a $100 posing fee—in the days when models worked for fifty cents an hour. So you can see the kind of effort he put into his pictures. They were terrific!

But I decided early in my career that that wasn't for me. My background probably played a part in my decision. My father was my first teacher. He was a tonal painter who had learned his technique from years of conversations with artists in Holland. And so I started by admiring the tonalists, men who were almost exclusively concerned with the value relationships among the masses in a picture. The subtler the values, the better. They loved gray days, fog, moonlight—the sort of moods that their hero, Whistler, also loved to paint. Since it was important to gauge my tones correctly, I worked very thinly, slowly adjusting my values.

Properly done, tonal pictures were full of that mysterious something called "quality." They were wonderfully beautiful. But they didn't have much sparkle. In a big show, a tonal painting would hardly be seen—particularly if it was near one with lots of color. It just wasn't decorative.

I wanted a fuller range of values in my pictures—and more spunk. I wanted them to look good from any place in a room and to have an impact, the minute you looked at them. Part of this feeling may also have resulted from changes in my palette. The tonalists weren't interested in strong color. Nor did they use the bright pigments we have now. In fact, some of them weren't even available. I still remember the first time I got my hands on the new cadmiums. I'd been using chrome colors till then, and the brilliance of the new paint astounded me. That brilliance, in itself, almost demanded a more vibrant way of painting.

I was also lucky to see and hear painters like the great Robert Henri. As a kid, I'd be amazed at the way he did a head. One stroke for an eye—bang! Then another for the chin. He was a master. And when his pictures were finished, they'd look more like the person than the person! I remember one of an Irish street kid. He was laughing and had large front teeth, with a big space between them. I loved those paintings.

As a result of all these factors, I've never been inclined to do a "portrait" of a bit of peeling paint on a wall. Instead, I see the landscape in terms of large units and big relationships. And once I've stated those relationships, I've usually had my say. Of course, I like texture too—the look of a pile of leaves, jumbled rocks, and rough bark. But where some painters see the leaves first and then work them into a pile, I see the *pile* first and am happy if I can get the effect *without* even painting the leaves. The *pile* is what counts.

My old instructor, John F. Carlson, once told his students that when he painted birches, he tried to make the viewer think of "nudes dancing on a hillside" first—then he worried about the details of the actual tree. That's the right attitude: It keeps you from getting lost in unessential details. Look at the Oriental artists. They take two or three objects and make a world of them, while we take all of Yosemite—and make nothing of it!

Here's an outdoor set-up, ready for use. A collaps-

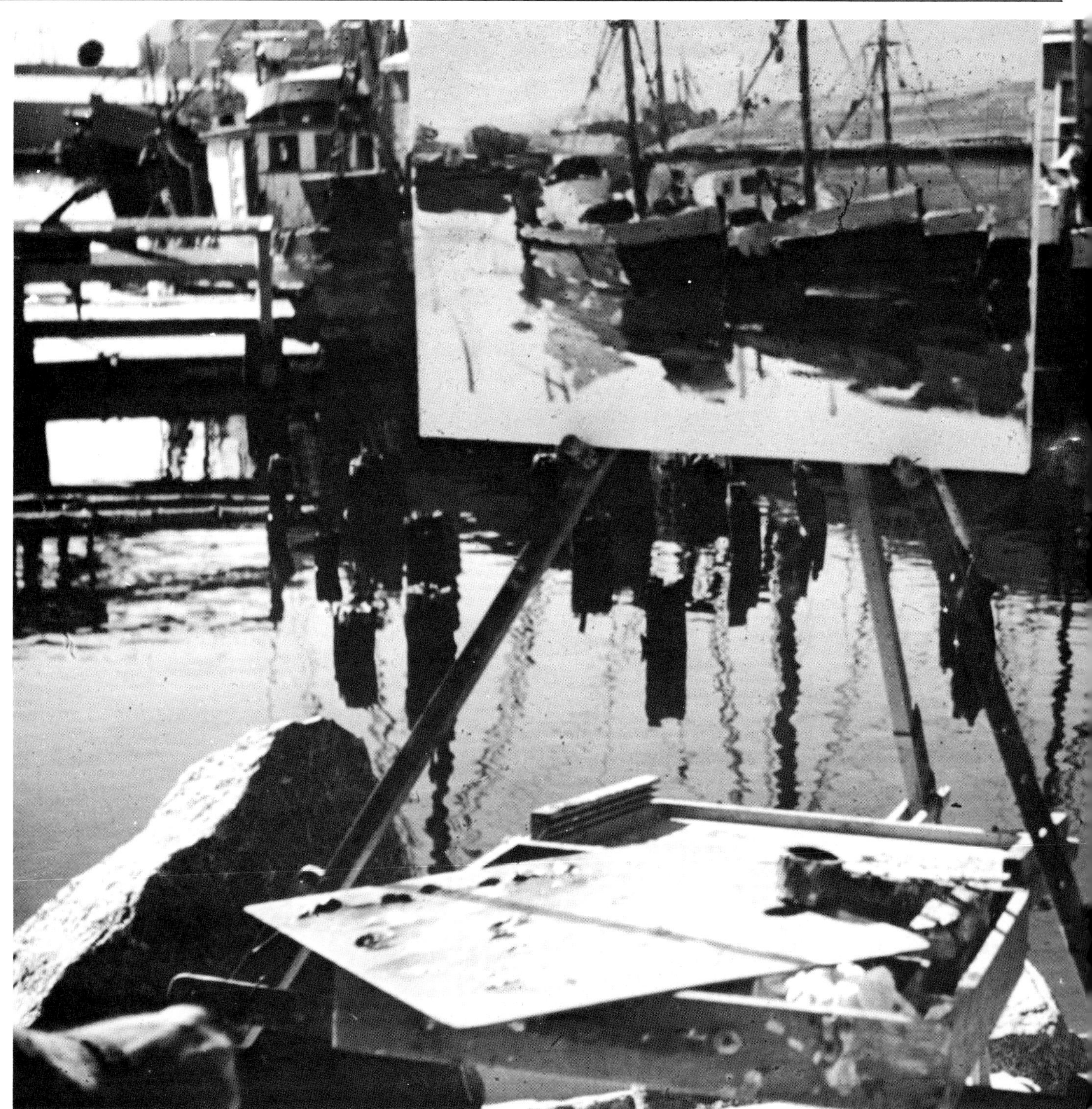

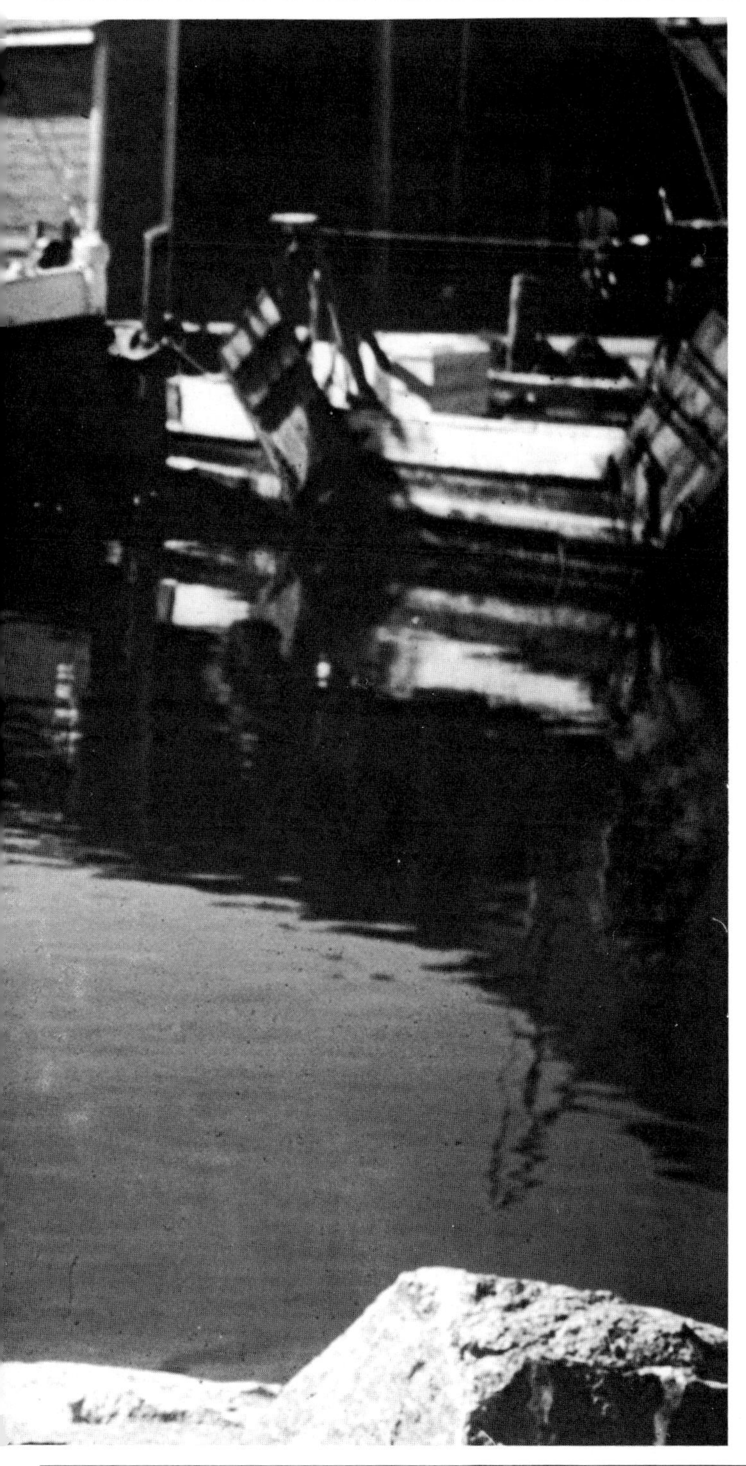

ible wooden easel holds the open paintbox. (The top is "broken" so it lays perfectly flat.) The palette lies across the box, the colors ranged on the farthest side. There are rags inside the box for cleaning the brushes. Because the canvas is white, keep it in shadow. It's hard to paint on a canvas that's hit by the sun—you can't tell how dark your darks are. You can keep your palette in the sunlight, though, so you can see the colors you mix. The wooden palette will absorb some of the light so it doesn't glare in your eyes.

Some of these brushes are used and some are relatively new. There aren't many small ones—and there are no round brushes or sables. They're all "flats," with long bristles to hold plenty of paint.

MATERIALS

Before we look at specific brushstrokes, let's look at some suggested painting materials. Remember, these materials may not be the best ones for you—you may prefer others. And no particular brand of paint or brushes can make a painter. What's important is how you *think* about painting, not what you use. When you develop a style, your method and materials will follow of their own accord.

WOODEN PALETTE. I suggest using a dark wooden 20″ × 24″ (51 × 61 cm) palette. It's easy to carry, since it fits neatly into the paintbox. A white palette might catch the light of the sun and throw a glare into your eyes. When you paint outdoors, you want as few distractions as possible. The old-timers took endless precautions in this area. I've seen photos of the great Spanish painter Sorolla at work on the beach. He'd set his gear on a black tarpaulin and surround himself with umbrellas and screens—all to keep reflected light from influencing his work.

MEDIUM. The medium I use is a mixture of one part stand oil to five parts turpentine. Stand oil is a thickened linseed oil. Since it's already predried, it makes a quick-drying medium. It takes the place of the damar varnish that some people use. I don't put any varnish in my medium. It breaks down the paint and "blooms" after a while, giving the picture a milky cast. Of course, this bloom can be eliminated by a restorer, but I prefer to avoid the problem altogether.

Since stand oil is bleached, it won't revert to its original yellowish hue like linseed oil. However, if the whites in your finished picture *do* yellow, you can try bleaching them by putting the canvas in the sun for fifteen minutes. Some painters bleach a painting in this way before sending it to a show. It restores the snap to the highlights. Of course, sometimes this yellowing is good—it gives the picture a mellow look. It all depends on what you like.

Since I work wet-in-wet, I need to use a lot of medium. It acts as a lubricant and lets me glide one area of paint over another. Anyone who has watched me paint knows how my brush drips with medium as I go from the cup to the palette.

I use only one large cup of medium when I paint. I don't have a second filled with turpentine. There's a lot of turpentine in my medium already, and when it mixes with the paint on the brush, it thins the paint a bit. You can even use the medium like turpentine, dipping the brush in it and then wiping it off on a rag. But just touch the brush to the medium. Don't swirl the dirty brush in it. That will cloud the medium and the dirty residue will creep into your other mixes.

CANVAS. There are many kinds of canvas available. I prefer linen canvas, made in Belgium and oil-primed. It comes in a long roll. To make it easier to handle, you can figure out what sizes you need and then cut the roll into smaller segments with a band saw. This canvas is fairly thick, with little give to it. After it's stretched, it *stays* stretched. Cotton has a tendency to sag—and, as a result, is better left for student work.

Oil-primed canvas looks somewhat yellow when you first unroll it. In fact, you can tell oil-primed canvas by this yellow tinge. You can fix that, however. If you leave the piece around for a day or so, it will bleach out on its own. I like its whiteness and work directly on the untoned canvas. The white adds luminosity to the colors because light shines through the paint and bounces off the white ground.

I like a rough-weaved canvas with a good tooth. A smooth canvas wouldn't make sense for my type of painting: I go for the big color spots and don't worry about detail. A smooth canvas is more useful for portraits, where modeling and subtle modulations count. But when you paint outdoors, there isn't much modeling needed because the sun flattens things out. If you've never painted outdoors, though, you don't need expensive canvas. Cheap canvas panels—canvas backed with cardboard—are fine for practice. You might even try Upson board, a heavy cardboard, and coat it with acrylic gesso. At first you can start small, with 8″ × 10″ (20 × 25 cm) or 12″ × 16″ (31 × 41 cm) sizes. You can cover them easily, and they won't intimidate you. Then, as you gain experience, you can switch to larger canvases. I prefer the squarer sizes—16″ × 20″ (41 × 51 cm), 20″ × 24″ (51 × 61 cm), 25″ × 30″ (64 × 76 cm)—because oblong canvases dictate to you, while a square canvas can be made to look either long or tall, depending on how you arrange the composition.

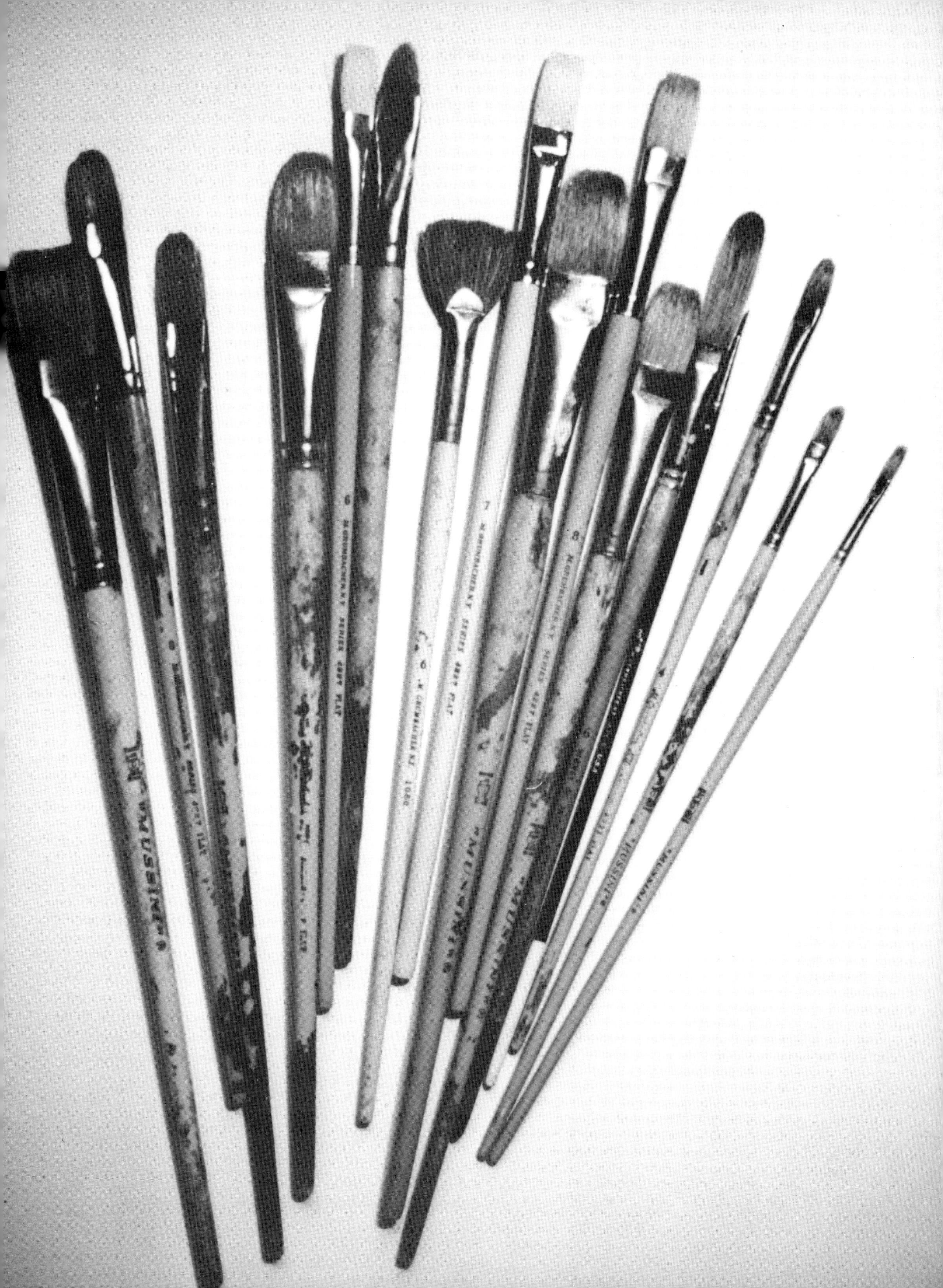
MUSSINI

CHARCOAL. I use soft vine charcoal to draw the design on the canvas. Some people start arranging the composition on canvas with paint. But I think designing the composition is the most important part of painting, and I want to be able to remove lines and shift masses with minimum difficulty. If I'd painted on the design, I'd need turpentine to wipe it off the canvas. On the other hand, soft charcoal can be brushed off with only a rag.

PIGMENTS. I recommend that you buy the best pigments you can afford. Never stint on materials. And put out plenty of paint too, so you won't have to keep reaching into your box as you work. My rule of thumb is: Put out twice as much paint as you think you'll need—and then *use it all!*

I use a "limited" pure-color palette. Because it's so simple, however, such a limited palette can sometimes be hard to master. It takes time to learn what it can do. Briefly stated, it's built on the primary colors—a warm and cool version of each primary. Each tubed pigment has only two of the three primaries in it. For example, ultramarine blue—a reddish blue—has no yellow in it, while cadmium lemon yellow—a greenish yellow—has no red in it. No tubed color is absolutely perfect, but it's important to select colors that are as close to pure primaries as possible, for colors made of all three primaries—like umber, sienna, or black—are dull and dirty (or muddy) the palette. The first chart lists my colors and their components.

Primary Hues in Palette Colors

Palette Colors	Red	Yellow	Blue
Ultramarine blue	x		x
Phthalo blue		x	x
Cadmium red deep	x	x	
Rose madder	x		x
Cadmium lemon yellow		x	x
Cadmium yellow deep	x	x	
Orange	x	x	

I arrange my colors on the palette for maximum mixing efficiency. I keep all the colors at the top of my palette and put white in the lower half of the palette. That way, most of the space is left for mixing. I arrange—and mix—my colors as shown in the second chart on the facing page.

COLOR ARRANGEMENT AND MIXING. This is how my mixing system works. If you want to mix a green, the purest one is made of yellow and blue, with no adulterating (or neutralizing) red. So if I want to get a pure green, I choose the blue and yellow that contain qualities of *only* blue and yellow—in this case, phthalo blue and cadmium lemon yellow. That way, the mixture remains intense. But if I'd wanted to mix duller greens, I'd use the blues and yellows that have red in them, say, ultramarine blue and cadmium yellow deep. That way, I'd get a mixture of all three primaries—a more neutral or duller mix.

Try to avoid overmixing on the palette. If you want a green, for example, dip into a yellow and blue, mix it quickly on the palette, and then put it directly on the canvas. If you then want to add yellow to the green, don't mix it on the palette. Work the yellow directly into the color on the canvas. This is more direct, gets more intense color, and often leads to interesting accidental color mixtures too.

Beating the White. There's a ritual I always perform before starting to paint: I whip up my white paint. I first saw this done years ago at a demonstration given by the famous illustrator Dean Cornwell. When he'd finished, he said he'd done the hardest part of the job. When I whip up the white, I put medium into the paint first, then mix it with a knife, stopping when it has the consistency of mayonnaise. Of course, if your white paint is very oily to begin with, this step isn't necessary. But if your paint comes out of the tube hard, you have to do something to soften it. Otherwise, you have to break it down to add color to it, and that leads to overmixing.

BRUSHES. I suggest using a "flat" brush, a long-bristle brush that holds plenty of paint. The "brights" (short-bristle brushes) are good for portrait painters who need crisp, blocky strokes to define the planes of the head. But scrubbing the paint on canvas quickly wears brushes down to that size—so why buy half a

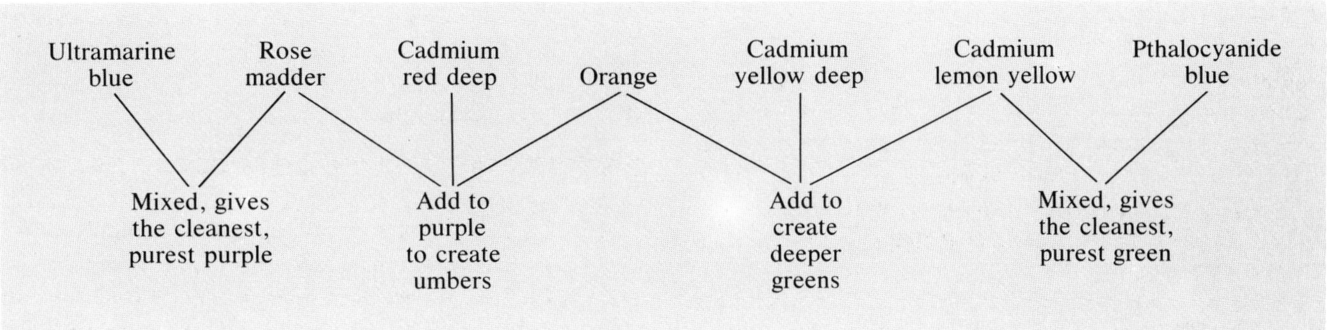

brush? Oddly enough, the Europeans once bred a special breed of pig, just for use in brushes. Their bristles had a natural taper. But World War I took care of them. The people ate them all! Nowadays, the bristles are *sanded* to a taper. You've probably noticed the result. Since the end of the bristles have been damaged, they always hold a ghost of color, even after you've cleaned the rest of the brush.

Choose a brush that isn't too soft, one that has some spring to it. This type of brush responds to the touch. You can push down hard for a wide stroke or lightly pull the brush over the canvas for a drybrush effect. Whenever you choose a brush, pick the biggest one you can, sizes like 12, 10, and 7. Smaller brushes are good for signing your name—or maybe picking your teeth. I had a student years ago who'd decided at the last minute to take a painting trip. He borrowed his mother's paint set, but it was full of little brushes. We were working down by the ocean when I first saw his brushes. I grabbed them, told him he wouldn't be needing those anymore, and tossed them out to sea. Then I gave him a few of mine to use till he bought some of a decent size.

I use many brushes when I work—maybe 15 or 16 brushes outdoors, and I reserve special brushes for my lights and darks and for my warms and cools. But once the complement is on the brush—if, for example, I'm working with red and get some green on it—I stop using it for the rest of that painting session. You'll have to thoroughly clean the brush before you can get clean color again. Since I dislike holding a bunch of dirty brushes in my hand, I use my box as a brush holder. This is how: When I buy the paintbox, I break off and remove the metal support that holds the top at a right angle to the palette. That support is left over from the days when people painted with the paintbox on their laps and put panels in the slits on the top. Now with the top lying flat, I can rest my brushes in it as I work. (My students never seemed to like this method, though. They always had a handful of brushes, and when I went to talk to them, either they or their neighbors would get paint on me. But I solved that. After awhile, I learned to sneak up on them, so I could "disarm" them before giving my critique!)

Brush Care. When you get a new brush, first soak it in kerosene. The paint won't accumulate in the ferrule so easily. Use kerosene to clean your brushes too. It's oily, and that's good. After all, the bristles had oil in them when they were on the hog! If you don't use your brushes every day, give them a good washing with Ivory soap.

Sometimes paint stiffens in a brush. When that happens, add a cup of Fels Naptha to half a cup of boiling water. Take the mix off the stove before putting the brush in. (A student of mine boiled the soap and the brush together, cooking the bristles. They curled up on either side of the ferrule!) After you've swirled the brush in the solution, wash it again with kerosene and the paint should come out. Then rinse it with clean water and lay it on a table to dry. Of course, there may be all kinds of new products by now that could clean your brush just as well—but this is the method I've used for the last 60 years.

A Word about Sable Brushes. I don't recommend sable brushes. They don't pick up enough paint—and

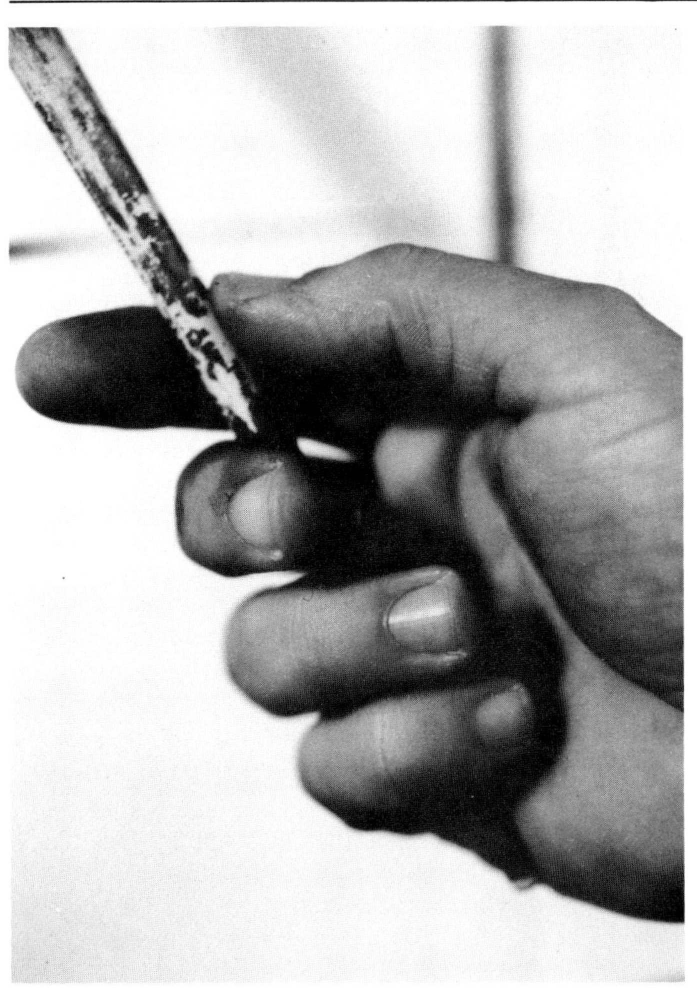

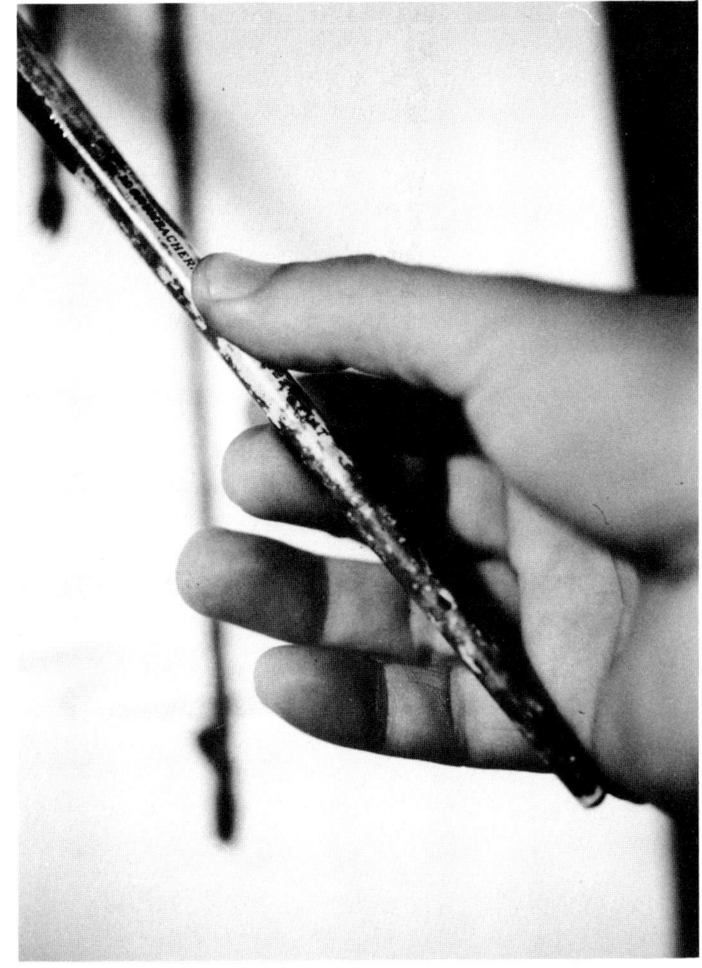

they're too floppy. They wear out fast too. They're better for watercolors, for paintings that depend on a lot of thin washes, and for the old-fashioned-type academic paintings, where every walnut-sized head had to have carefully drawn features.

PALETTE KNIFE. I rarely use the palette knife for painting, but mainly for scraping colors off my palette or the canvas. I used the knife when I painted in Provincetown with the famous teacher, Charles Hawthorne. He wanted us to think about spots of color instead of detail. Unfortunately, the knife leaves a lot of edges where dirt can accumulate. In fact some of my old knife paintings are so covered with dust that they look like batiks!

Occasionally, a knife is useful for making the edge of a rock or for pulling together areas that are too broken and busy. But too much use of a palette knife can also make your work look stiff. I've seen marines where the water, painted with a knife, looked like it was made out of curduroy!

HOLDING THE BRUSH. There are three ways to hold a brush. The least effective is to hold it like a pencil. That's the most "comfortable" method for the beginner, but it makes painting a matter of finger and wrist movement.

I believe a stroke should involve the whole arm, if not the whole body. So I think that the proper way to use a brush is to cradle it inside the fingers of your hand, holding it in place with the thumb (see first photo). This enables you to have a good, firm grip, and it brings the full arm into play. Now hold the brush near the end and extend your arm its full length as you paint. That will keep you a few feet from the canvas and let you see how it's developing *as a whole*. When you hold the brush like a pencil, you crowd the canvas and get lost in the individual parts.

If you need to make a more delicate stroke, hold the brush in the same manner, but use only your thumb and forefinger (see second photo). This loose grip makes a gentle but steady stroke because less arm tension is conveyed by two fingers than by all five. The grip is especially good for straight, upright lines. Students always have trouble with them, making them wobble all over the place.

To make a straight vertical line, hold the end of the brush between your thumb and forefinger and place the bristles at the top of the proposed stroke. Then let the brush drop of its own accord. Let gravity and the brush do the work.

To paint thin, twisting lines—like those on the branches of a tree—hold the brush the same way, but twist it as you move. That makes the line vary in width and value. As you get to the end of the branch, flip the brush off the canvas and draw the line to a fine point.

It would be helpful if I could tell you just how much or how little pressure to use when making a stroke, but I can't. You'll have to rely on common sense and experience. However, there are some general rules: The more you press, the wider the stroke will be and vice versa. If you work wet-over-wet, pressure will mix the color layers. On the other hand, with a light touch and plenty of paint and medium as a lubricant, you can run one color over another without disturbing the bottom layer. Self-restraint also plays a part. When you want to lay one color cleanly over another, you have to be satisfied with the first attempt. Touch the area a second time, and you'll begin to mix the layers of pigment.

None of this is a problem if you're a painter who works in stages, letting everything dry between each step. But since I do most of my work outdoors, I have to finish in two or three hours. I have no time to let things dry—and I wouldn't want to. I *like* working one wet color over and into another wet color. That means I'm never sure how a stroke will turn out. And that uncertainty is part of the fun of painting. As I often tell my friends, I paint for my own amazement!

PAINTING PROCEDURE

Before we look at specific brushstrokes, let's review the general painting procedure. Despite the "roughness" of this style, you can work fairly methodically. Almost everything you paint—whether it's a landscape, a marine, or the figure—can develop along the lines of the following example.

Begin with your darks. They're the shadows, the part of the scene that changes the fastest. These initial darks are *thin*—save the heavier paint for later. Just follow the old maxim, "Load your lights and stain your darks."

Once the darks are established, search for the light areas. Whenever possible, tie your light shapes together—and your dark shapes too. See them as two big, separate—but interconnected—patterns, like parts of a poster. You can always add subtleties later. At the beginning, always paint things in the broadest possible way.

Working in this manner, rapidly cover the canvas. Once the raw canvas is eliminated, you can see the lights and darks more accurately. They're hard to gauge at the beginning because almost everything looks dark against the white canvas—and nothing looks light! But by the end of the picture, you will usually have to restate some of your darks and add highlights to the most strongly lit areas.

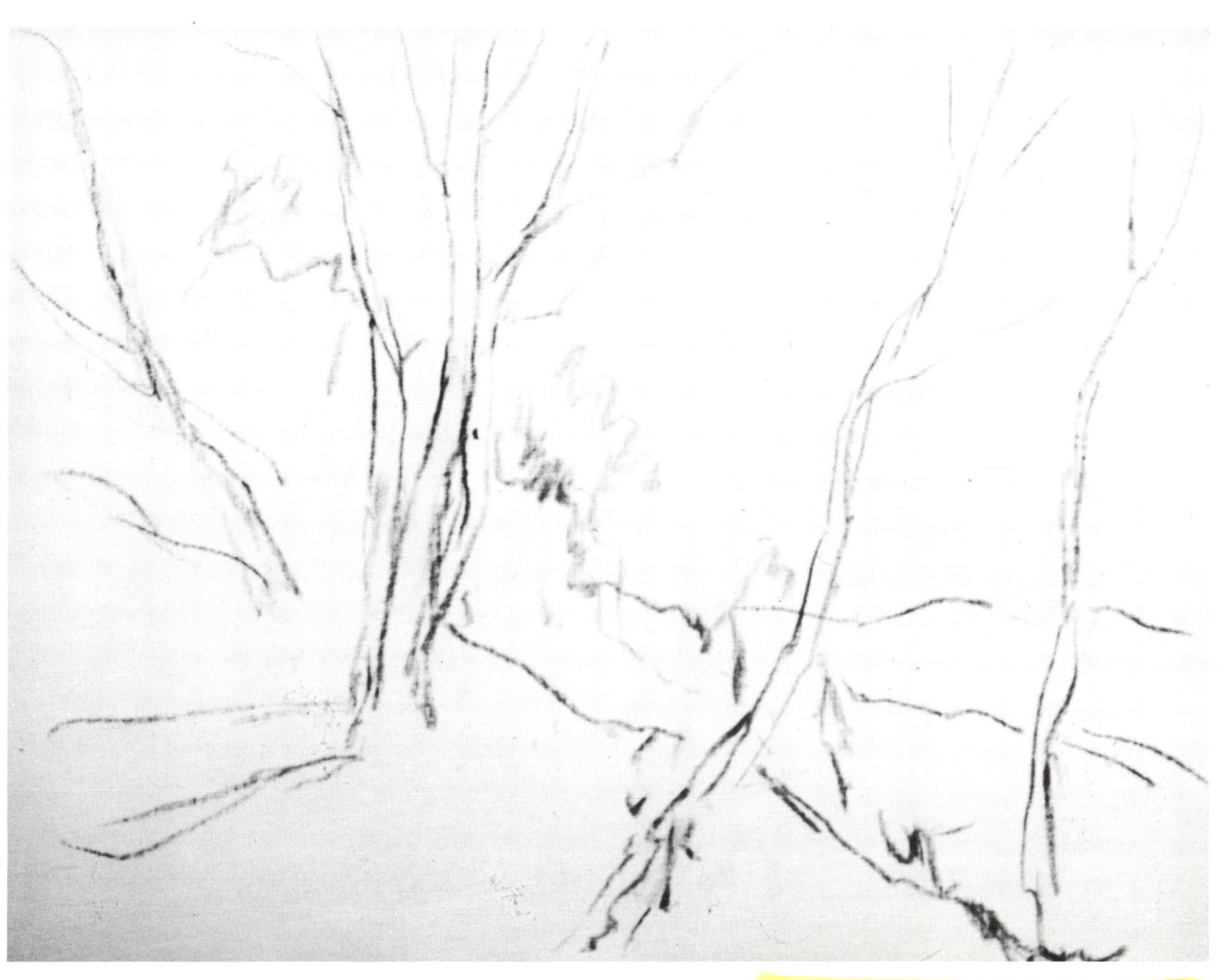

STEP 1. Never hurry when drawing the design. The design is the key to the painting. I often tell students who've already been drawing on the canvas for fifteen minutes and are ready to paint that what they need is *another* fifteen minutes. Not to draw bricks or branches, but to consider how best to place their big shapes. A well-designed picture paints itself.

As you draw the trees, think of them as units: a central group of three, with subordinate groups on either side. You're after the *movement* in the trees. You don't want them to look like telephone poles. Emphasize their height by keeping the background mountain low. (Imagine the mountain higher, and you'll see how it diminishes the trees.) Also, let the shadows fan to the sides, away from the central light source.

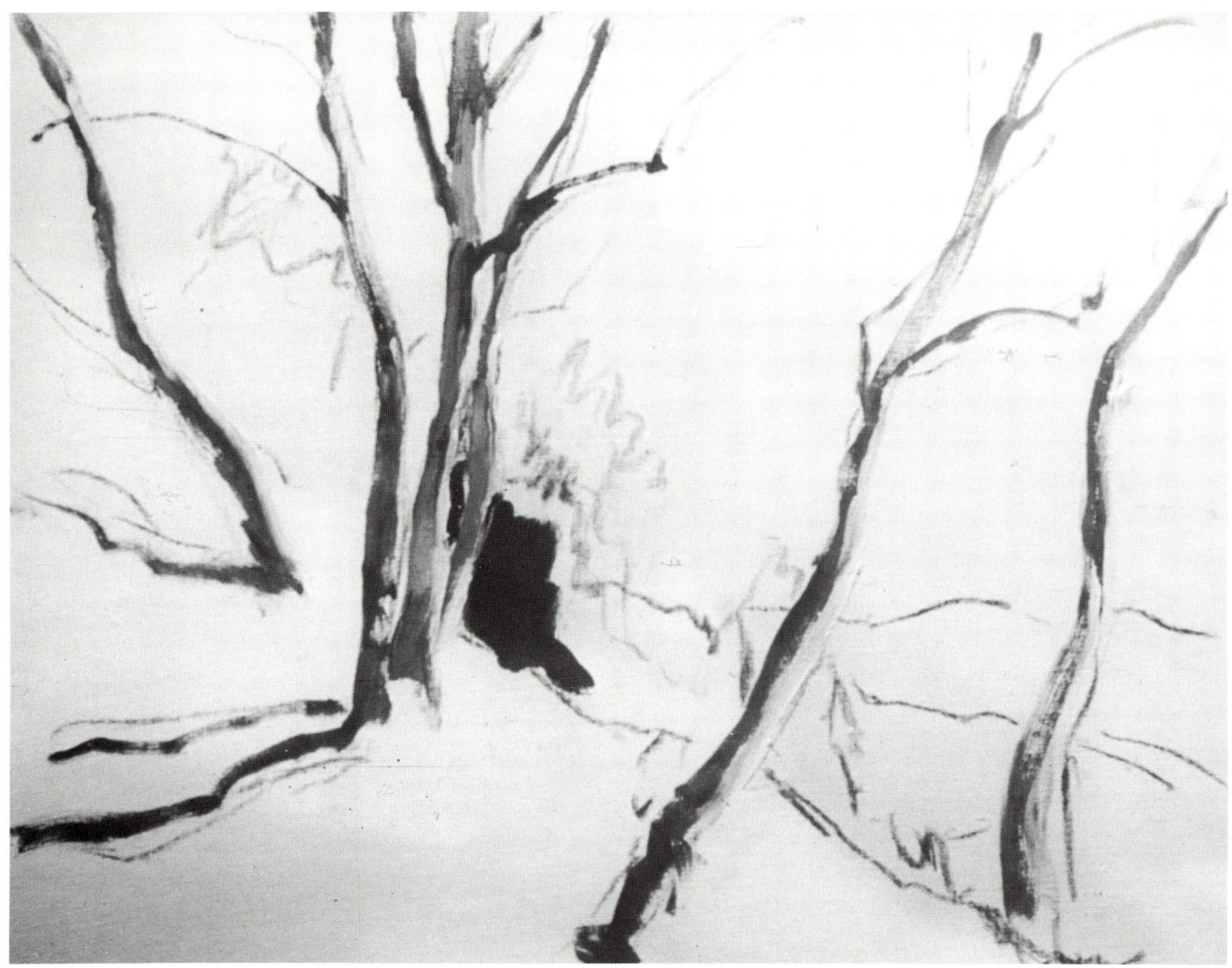

STEP 2. Start with the trunks of the principal trees. They're important shapes and you want to describe their silhouette against the sky. Choose a reddish-purple tone—on the warm side—because the trees catch reflected light from both the land and each other. Then paint the shadows as you did the tree trunks. Don't think in terms of tree and shadow, but rather of the *single shape* the two make together. After all, they're both darks.

Once the darks are established, put a highlight on the tree (white and a touch of yellow). That's the lightest light. Next to it, place the darkest note—the background evergreens. That accent makes the shadowed birches look relatively light by contrast. Now, having determined the darkest accent and the lightest light, you can work *between* these two extremes in the rest of the painting.

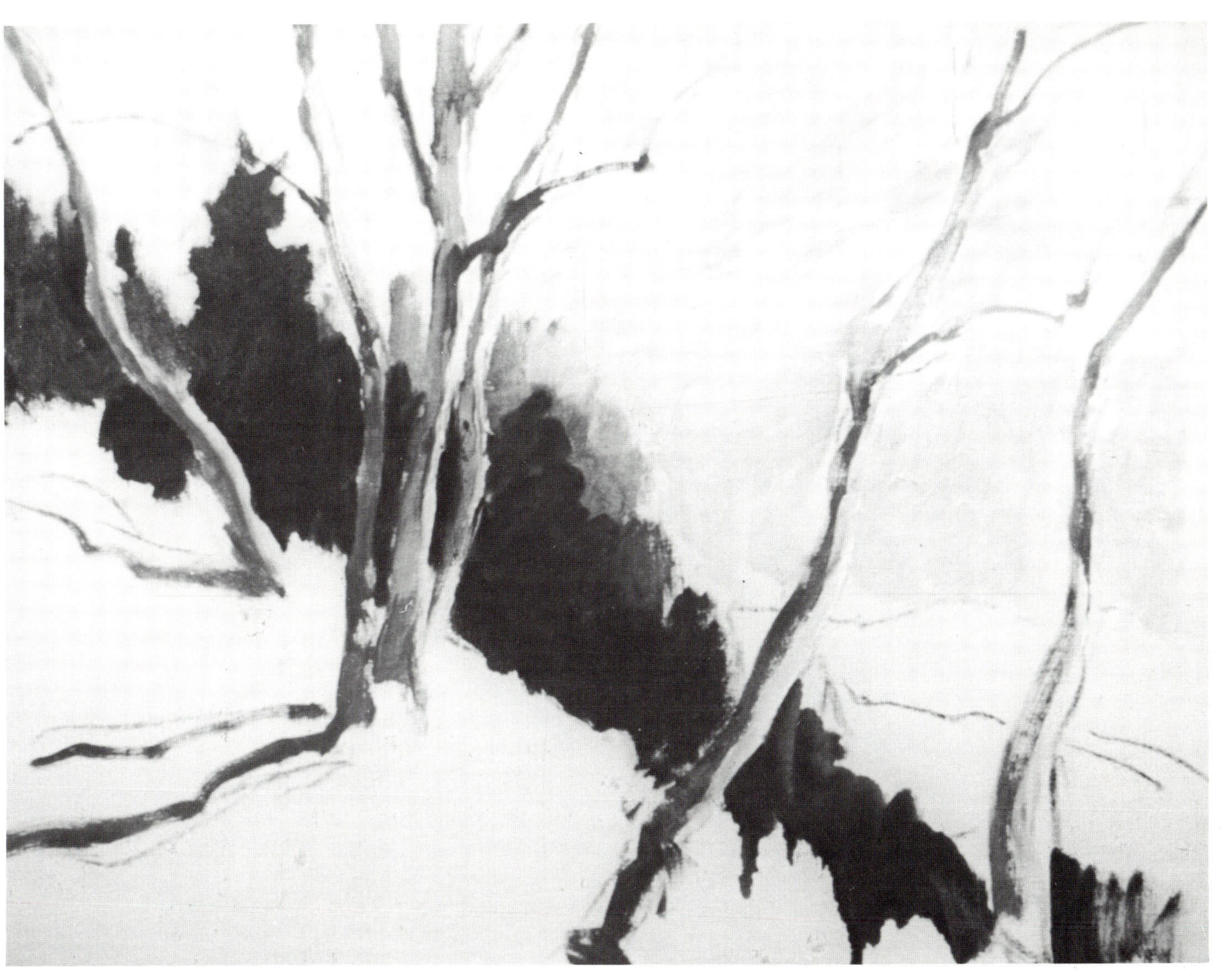

STEP 3. Now block in the rest of the evergreens. Can you see how *light* the birches look? The red in these evergreens gives them their rich, dark color (ultramarine blue and cadmium yellow deep). Block them in with broad strokes to suggest their large masses. Let them form a single dark unit behind the birches. Then add red and yellow to suggest the sunlit branches behind the evergreens.

Since you're looking into the light, the sky is very warm. Paint it thickly, with lots of warm color in it. The orange sky establishes a color harmony in the picture. You've used all the secondary colors: green in the pines, purple in the birches, and orange in the sky. This range of warm *and* cool color keeps you from going color-blind. If the picture were all warm, you'd get *used* to the warmth and make the whole picture too hot. The same thing happens when you use too many cool colors.

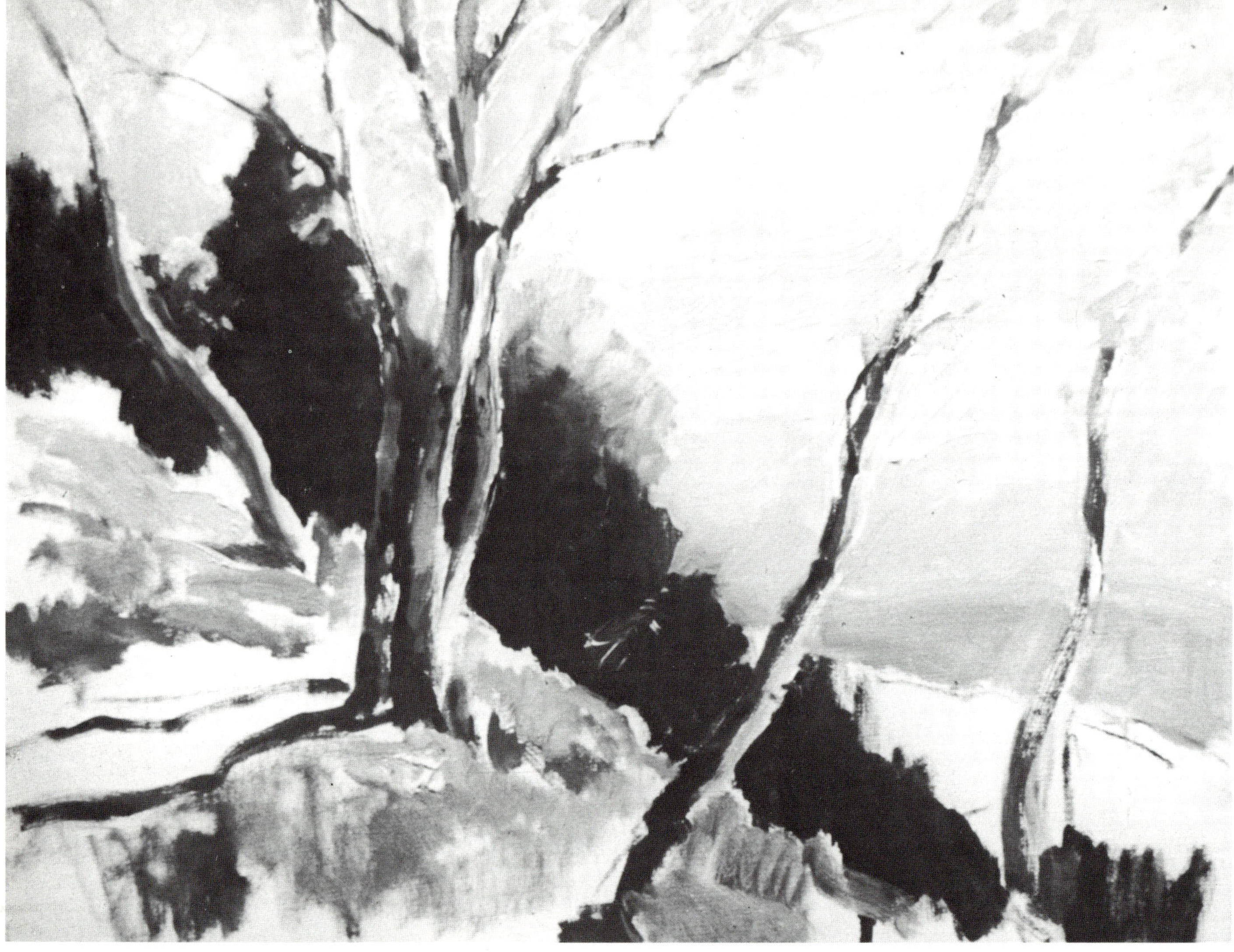

STEP 4. Establish the distant mountain with purple, adding a hint of the warmer phthalo blue to pull it forward. At the horizon, atmosphere piles up, giving the area a red-purple cast.

Overhead, the sky is warmer—a greenish tone mixed with phthalo blue and lemon yellow. It is also warmer near the sun. Then, as it moves away from the light, it becomes gradually cooler. You can show this by adding ultramarine blue to the part of the sky farthest from the sun. To understand why you should do this, study the color chart in the chapter on *Materials*. As you move away from the sun, the sky has less yellow in it and more of the duller red, as the phthalo blue gives way to ultramarine blue.

Now paint the birch leaves. Against the sky, the leaves are painted with cadmium yellow and a touch of red. Use full-intensity color. It's easy to kill color but hard to brighten it up. Add phthalo blue to the shadow side of the evergreens. The dark, intense blue adds to the richness of the shadows.

Then put a raking light from the sun in the foreground. Use rich reds, yellows, and greens to suggest dead leaves and bushes and cooler strokes to indicate rocks. Finally, add warm reflected light to the central tree. Break up the bark with dark lines and paint cool color into the upper part of the trunk where the cool overhead sky reflects into it.

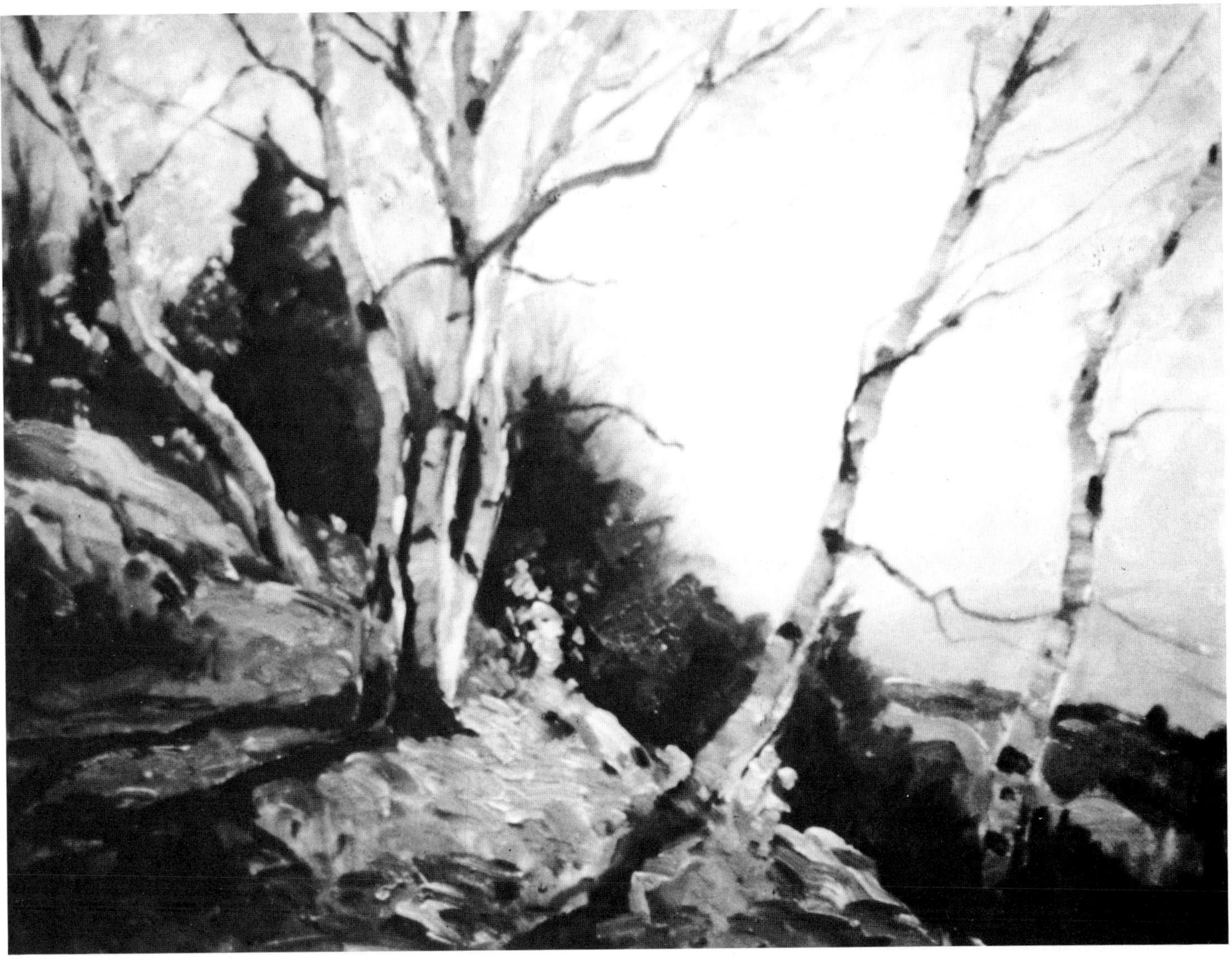

Birches and Pines
oil on canvas
16" × 20" (41 × 51 cm)

STEP 5. Darken the tree shadows with ultramarine blue and red. They fall across a warm surface, so in places add more red to the mix. Since the heaviest concentration of leaves is at the base of the trees, load the paint on there. Use blue strokes to show where the cool sky reflects onto the earth.

Put strokes of light green at the edges of the evergreens to indicate where the foliage catches the light, but leave the center of the evergreens dark, since no light can penetrate the mass of needles. You can anchor the main trees with dark spots of green moss at their base, but the other trees should be handled differently. The less important tree on the far right, for example, disappears into the distant pines.

The bright, warm, yellow of the bush moves it forward, pushing the background back. By placing it near the coolest part of the evergreen, you can heighten this effect. You can also use contrasting color effects elsewhere. For example, you can make the sky seem more brilliant by adding a few slashes of pure white and paint the foreground leaves as complementary reddish masses in shade, with yellow highlights and spots of pure white to suggest a glare.

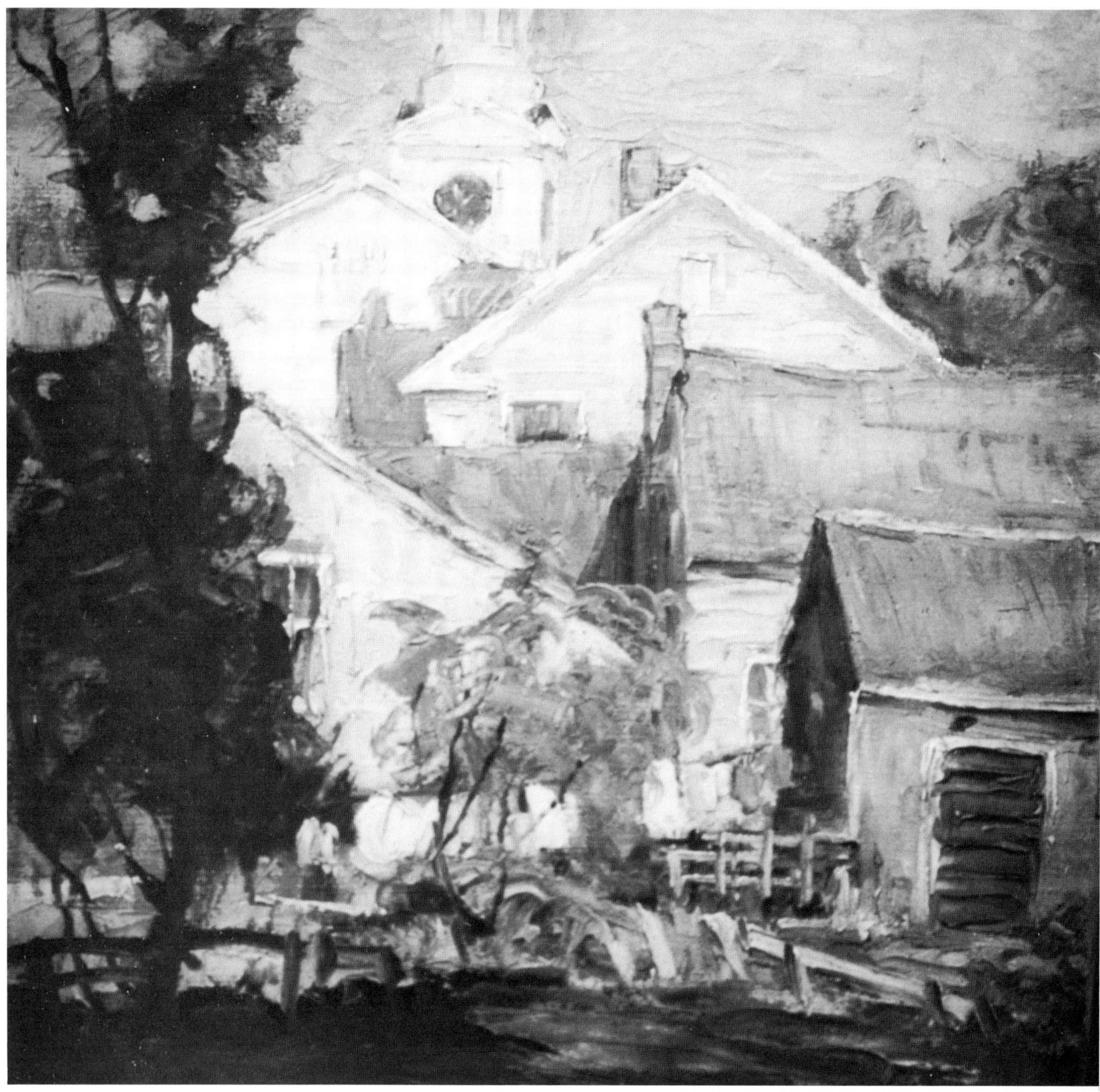

Rockport Backyards
oil on board
12″ × 12″ (31 × 31 cm)
Collection of Mrs. Dorothy Gruppé

When I studied with Charles Hawthorne in the 1920s, he made us use palette knives so we wouldn't put in a lot of detail. This picture dates from that period. I like the way the houses overlap: there isn't a single complete roof in the picture, just sides and gables. I emphasize the height of the distant steeple by bringing it out of the picture and by paralleling its upward movement with that of the dark foreground tree, the sides of the buildings, and the upright chimneys.

Thick foreground strokes suggest the flatness of the land. This horizontal movement is echoed and reinforced by the lines of the nearby fences. In contrast to the flat land, the nearest buildings and hanging clothes are painted with vertical strokes. The slanting roof is suggested by strokes that move in the same diagonal direction. Long diagonal strokes indicate the ends of the gables. These diagonals keep the picture from being dominated by horizontal and vertical lines. They also add vitality to the composition. The sky is a series of flat, horizontal strokes. These strokes emphasize the upward thrust of the steeple.

BASIC FUNCTIONS OF THE BRUSHSTROKE

Always try to find the stroke that best describes what you feel about a particular subject. After all, you want to communicate quickly and directly with the viewer—in a broad and simple way. The direct approach lets you tell the story with a minimum of digressions. In addition, each stroke says something about the subject. Remember, look twice and paint once! First study the subject, and figure out where you want to place it on your canvas. Then look a second time, checking for its characteristic angles and curves. And finally make your stroke. By that time, you should know what you're after. This directness is especially important if you're painting outdoors. Then you have to work fast, and so you need a technique that records facts quickly and concisely.

Years ago, I painted with one of my old instructors. We stopped along a road at sunset. He thought it was too late and too cold to paint—but I jumped out and did a quick canvas, 25″ × 30″ (64 × 76 cm). I can still remember his slapping his head as I came back to the car and turned the picture toward him. "You don't paint pictures," he said. "You write them—each stroke is descriptive!"

People wonder how I can paint so broadly, yet still know that the picture will look "realistic" from a distance. There isn't any mystery to it. As I work, I try to get the general shape of the subject and, more important, its correct value—its lightness or darkness, how it would look if you took a black-and-white photo of it. If you get the *values* right, almost anything will look good from a few feet back.

One way to get the right value is by squinting your eyes—especially when you work outdoors. That pulls shapes together and simplifies values. Look for the big pattern and paint it as simply as possible. Don't count strokes, but remember that one stroke states an idea more clearly than four or five. Multiple strokes blunt your point, and the picture becomes like a story with too many words in it. That's why Charles Hawthorne made his students use a knife. We had to ignore the unimportant details. I remember that at the time I worked with Hawthorne, my father would sometimes suggest I carry my pictures a bit further. But that wasn't to my taste. And I don't think it was to his either. I once *did* a picture full of detail; he walked by, took one look, and said, "Too much for the money!"

The most important thing to know about brushstrokes is when to use them—and when not. Brushstrokes can be intoxicating. And I know that part of my appeal as a teacher over the years comes from the fact that students are fascinated by the way paint is put on canvas. They have a hard time doing it. Anybody who paints with assurance seems like a magician! Then, when they get some confidence themselves, it's easy for them to overdo it. They put strokes everywhere. But there's a difference between slapping paint on the canvas and putting it in the right place. What counts is your feeling about the scene. What does the scene "say" to you? And what kind of stroke most expresses that feeling?

Don't let my ideas get in the way of your personal development. Just use what makes sense to you. In other words, the way I paint a branch, leaf, or reflection is my own personal solution. But in showing you the thinking *behind* the stroke, I may give you some insight. Remember, when you paint loosely, you're not just throwing paint on canvas, hoping it will land in the right spot. Each time you make a stroke, you have to think. You have to know what you want to say.

Students think "perfection" is the greatest art. But who can draw the perfection of nature? If you really want perfection, you could spend your whole life on one picture. You'd never get in every detail. There'd always be more to do. From that point of view, it doesn't matter if you stop halfway to perfection—as even the most accomplished draftsman does—or a quarter of the way. I stop when I've said what I want to say. What counts is the statement. When I go to a gallery, I don't look at the details of the paintings there. I want the pictures to *do* something to me. I want to feel what the painter felt. But if all the edges and brushstrokes are hard and cold, I move away. I might as well be looking at a photograph.

Let's look at this study for a mural. Since it's very roughly and economically painted, it shows the bare bones of the method I'm describing. It also contains the three basic functions of brushstrokes: to contribute to the overall *design* of the painting, to *describe* individual objects, and to show the *relationships* among these objects.

Panorama of Gloucester
oil on canvas
16" × 24" (41 × 61 cm)

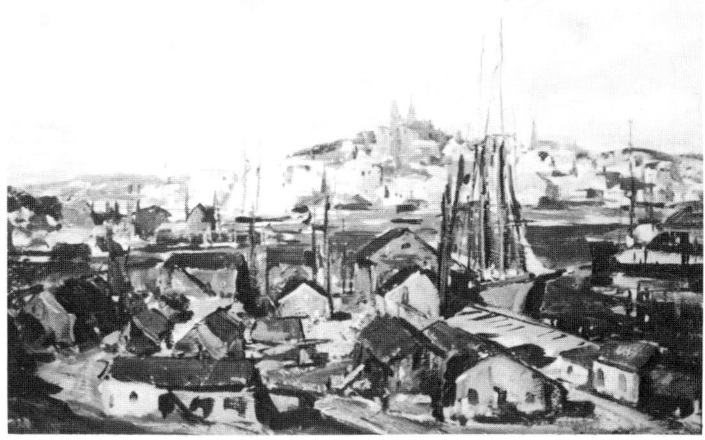

Viewed abstractly, this painting is composed of horizontal and vertical strokes, balanced by diagonals, and contrasting concave and convex forms. That's the essential *character* of the objects in Gloucester harbor. Now the amount of "description" you decide to add to this abstract analysis is up to you. Some people like to add a lot; others, not as much.

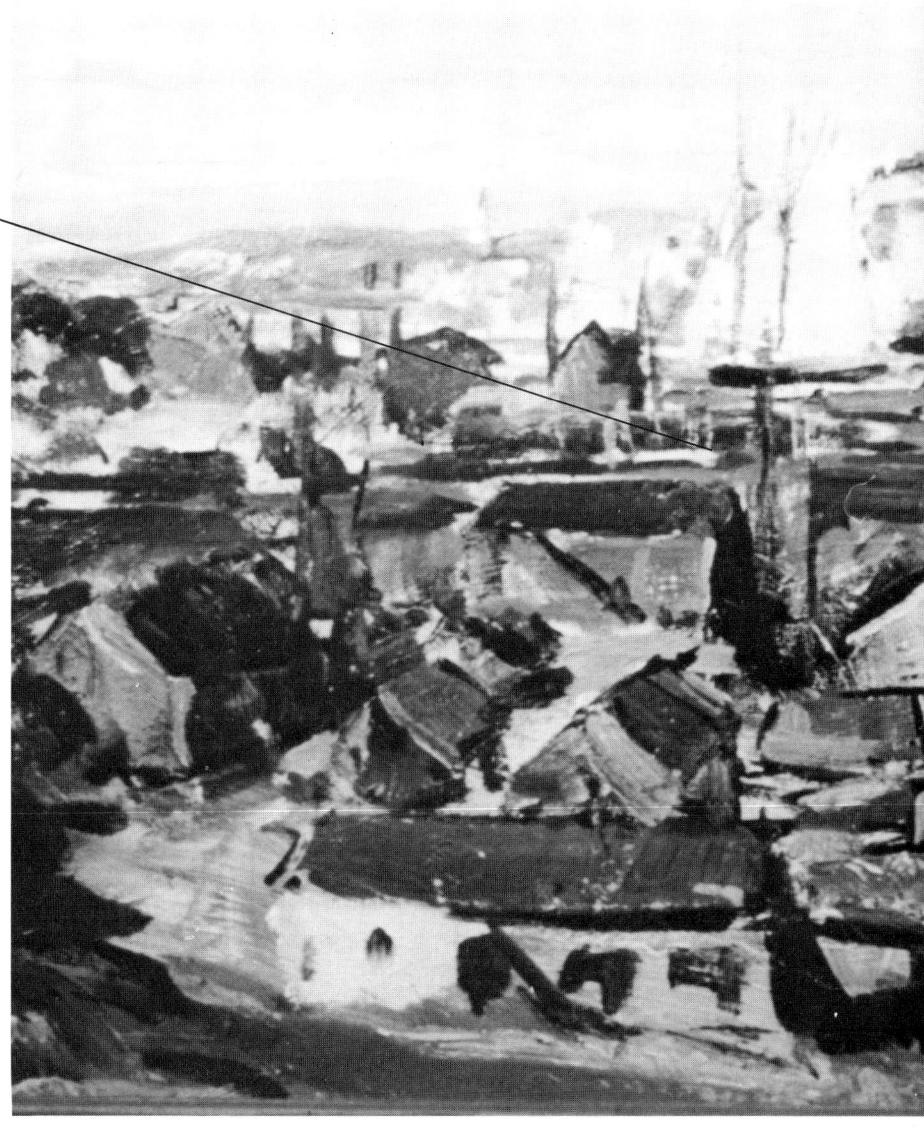

The dominant shape of the canvas and composition is horizontal—to emphasize the breadth of the harbor. This horizontal character is echoed by the horizontal strokes in the water, by the line of the distant docks, and by the flat shapes of the background boats.

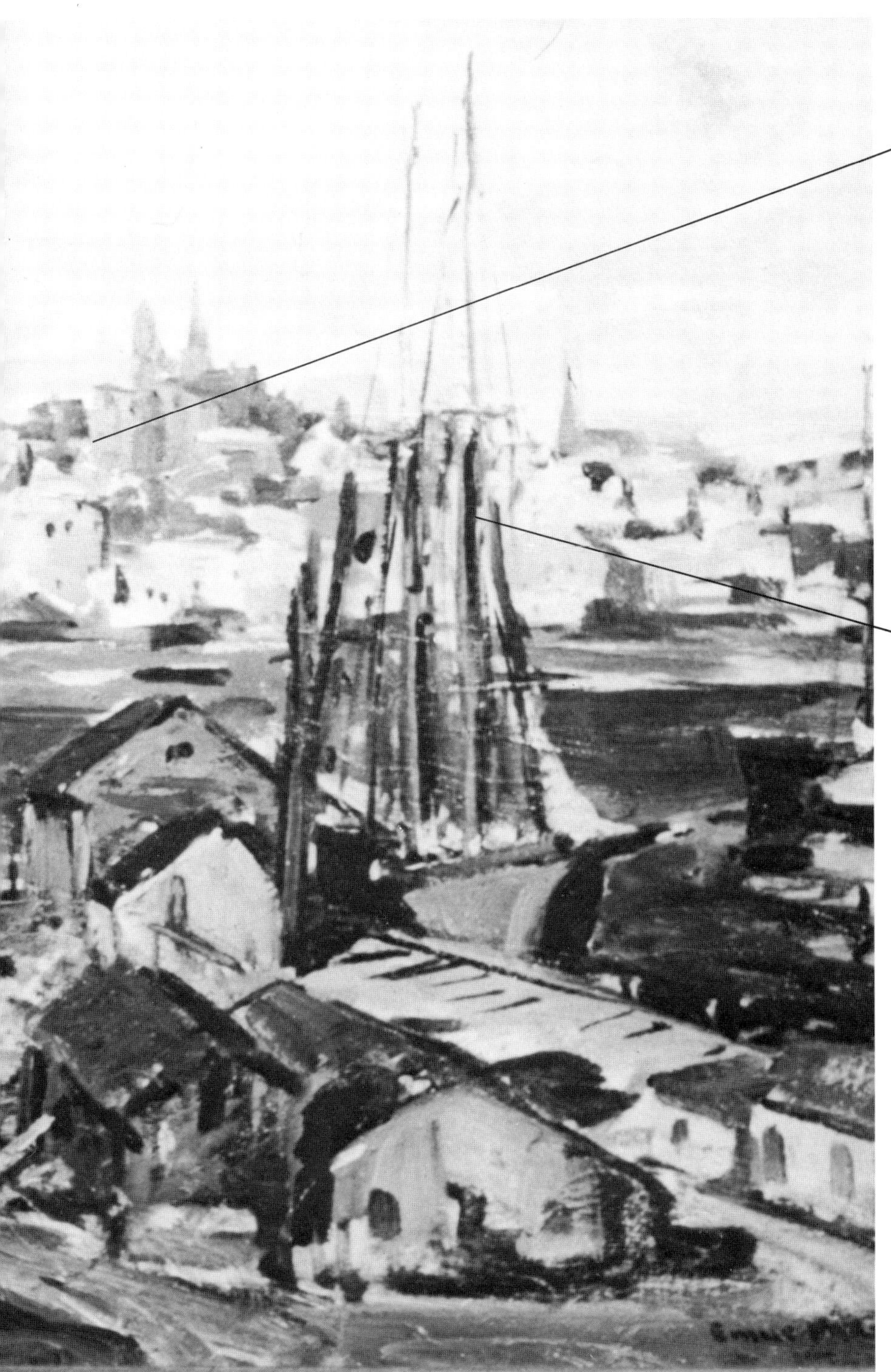

Notice how the rounded strokes of the distant hill contrast with the sharp triangular forms of the foreground buildings—and how the concave strokes of the overhead clouds emphasize the convex shape of the hill itself. One movement of the brush is played against another. You can sense this contrast and you're intrigued by it—even though you may not know why.

The upright strokes of the ships' masts are contrasted against these dominant horizontals. These masts are very simply painted: no ropes, no wires, no pulleys. They're just a few, quickly drawn verticals. But you understand the shorthand. You also subconsciously know that the verticals help balance the picture. You're thus relieved by their presence and you don't miss the lack of detail. Have you seen pictures that were full of detail—but so unbalanced that you felt uneasy looking at them?

Descriptive Strokes

A brushstroke should tell you about an object's form, what it's doing, if it's rhythmical, flowing, angular, or rounded in character. Such details as windows, doors, or doorknobs add nothing to the final statement. They just break up the big shapes and make it hard to understand them. Maybe in a different picture such details might be of interest, but not in this one. Here only the buildings' forms—oblongs, squares, and triangles—are important. These simple geometric shapes suggest a cluster of shacks and warehouses.

The nearby water is untextured. That's because the harbor water's most important characteristic is its *flatness*. So don't worry about ripples, highlights, and reflections. There isn't room for them; and if you did paint them, they'd detract from the buildings.

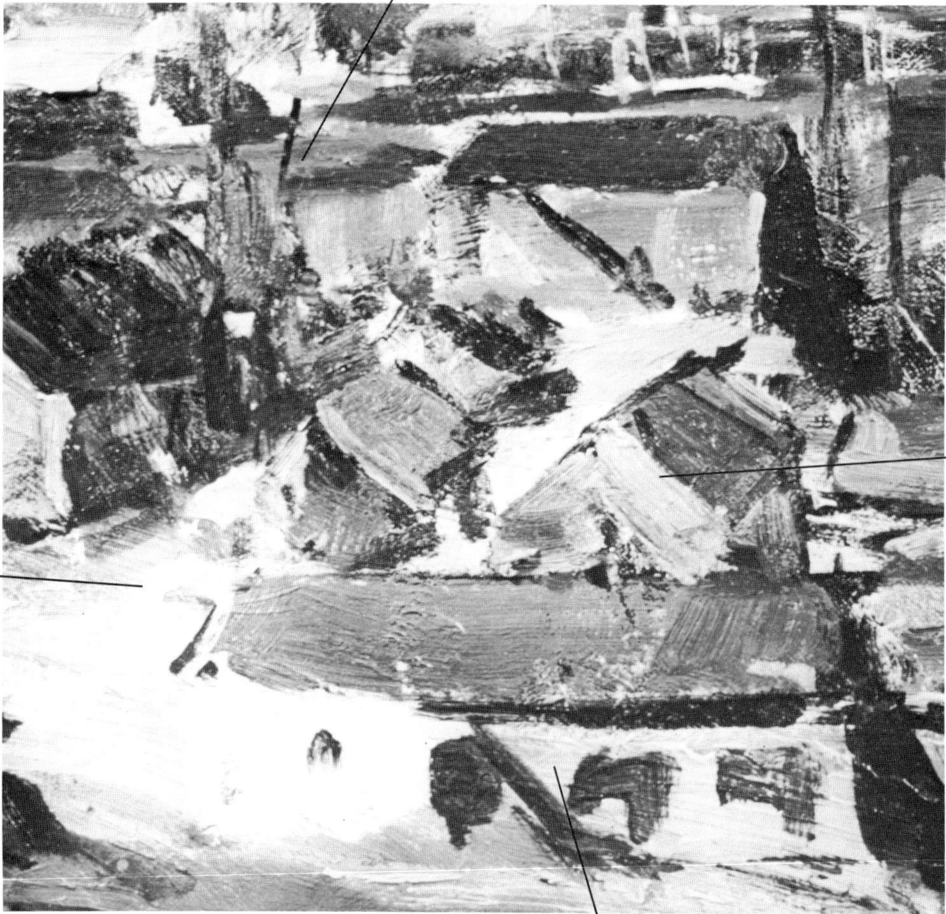

The background red building is surrounded by trash, nets, and junk—a mishmash with no dominant edges. Because of that, in this area, the brushstrokes are smudged. The idea is that you know something's there, but neither you—nor I—know what it is!

The sharp lines in the buildings are arbitrary—just a few diagonal strokes to suggest background roofs. There are few real lines in nature, but these buildings are man-made and the lines are useful to exaggerate the sharpness of the architecture.

In the foreground building, there are two thick horizontal strokes. You can even see the marks of the brush hairs. Notice that the strokes are made only *once* and they're not brushed smooth. These marks suggest the shingles on the side of the wall.

In order to paint loosely and give a sense of the whole, you can't describe *everything* without emphasis or choice—you'd end up with an etching rather than a painting. A painter is interested in the relationships among objects, not a precise reproduction of a scene. Nothing exists in isolation.

One of the most obvious relationships among objects is their position in space—how they fit into the perspective of the picture. Let's see how it's done.

The distant hills almost vanish into the sky. They're painted with strokes that are thinner than those used in the clouds. The clouds are nearer to us and are hit by the sun. They are painted heavily—with "impasto" brushstrokes—to separate them from the more thinly painted sky. Think of it this way: The sky is atmosphere, just air, while the clouds are objects. Therefore texture of the clouds is crucial to creating perspective. Cover them, and you'll see how the hills begin to come forward.

This headland and town are perhaps a half mile away. The buildings are thinly painted, light in value, and composed of small strokes and soft edges. In addition, their color is much less vibrant than that of the nearer buildings.

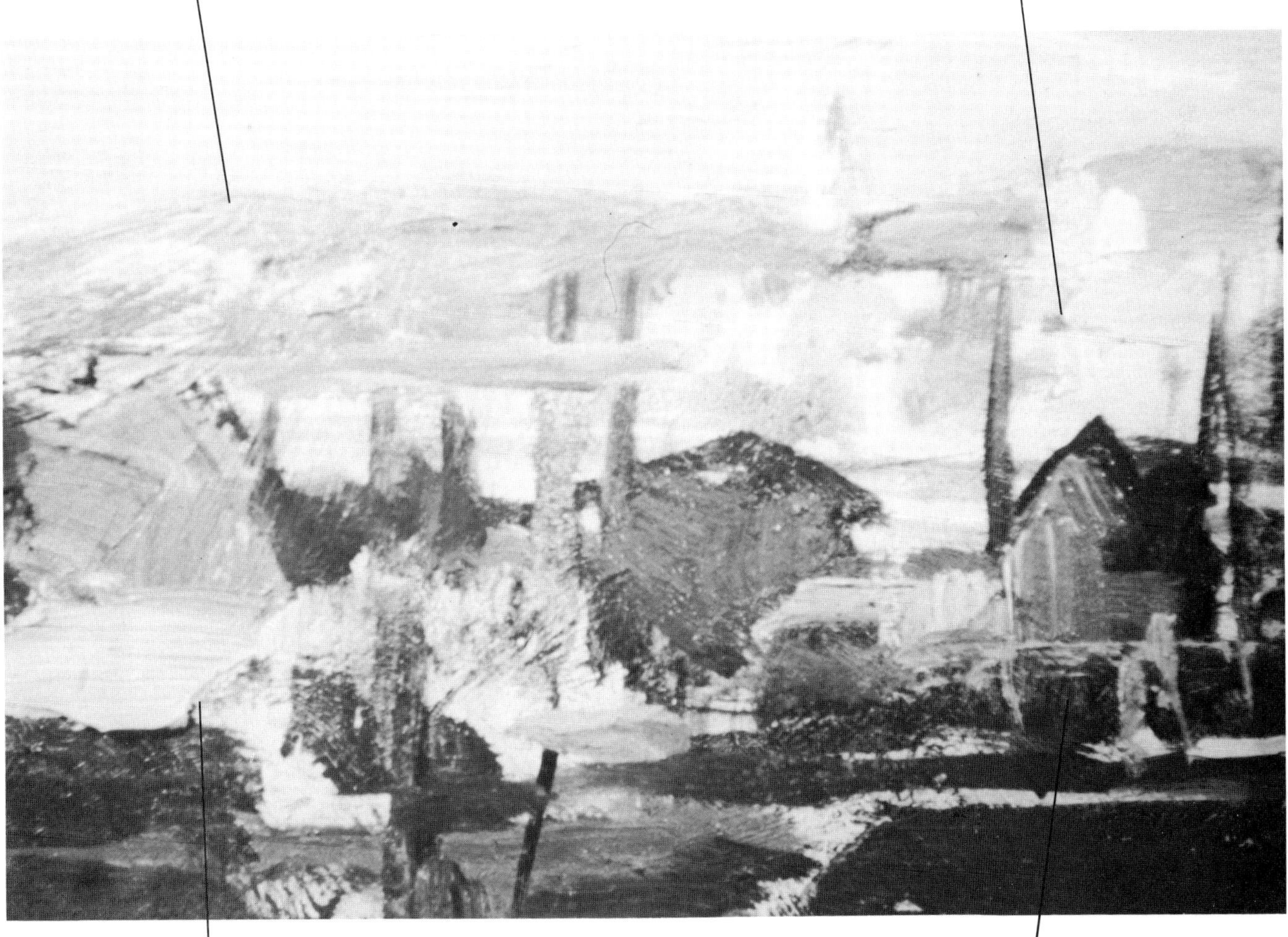

The foreground buildings are dark, heavily painted, and composed of a few large strokes. They also have sharp edges. As a result they look close to you.

This vertical dark stroke offers an important clue to perspective. It overlaps the background and emphasizes how light and distant it is. It also "cancels" the background, making it seem less important, and draws your eye to the nearer buildings.

Pattern and Opposition

Objects that are close together also have important interrelationships. When you look at a scene, don't look at individual objects. See them as a mass and try to figure out the characteristics of that mass.

The distant buildings have a broken, staccato rhythm. You can emphasize this quality by painting them with a series of simple geometric strokes: a diagonal slash, a few right angles, and an occasional dark blob.

To emphasize the angularity of the buildings, the mass of distant trees is painted with a big, curved stroke. Cover this stroke, and you'll see that the buildings lose some of their sharpness. One stroke explains another.

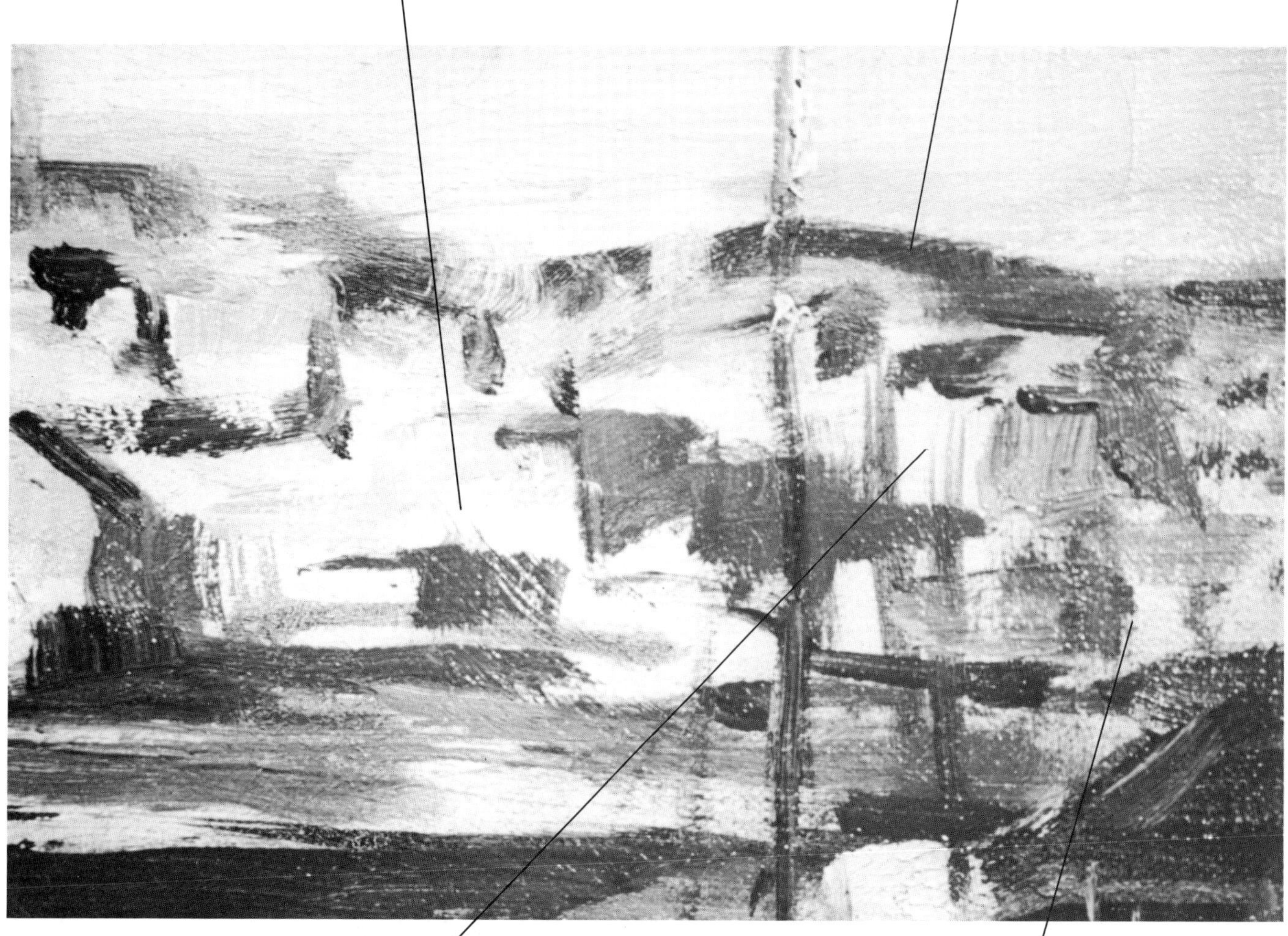

The white of the buildings is just the raw canvas with a few thin, pink washes here and there of transparent and luminous paint. By contrast, the darks are thicker and more opaque, increasing the luminosity of the neighboring areas.

At the actual site, a strong light washed out most of the details, though, if you looked hard enough, you could see windows and chimneys. But such details have nothing to do with the all-important rhythm of the buildings, so they are left out. Instead, organize your few descriptive strokes into big light and dark units.

Strokes can help make meaningful exaggerations—exaggerations that emphasize your feeling for the subject. For example, I've always been impressed by the fact that Gloucester is built on a hill. Since I like the effect, I often exaggerate it, making the hill taller than it is in reality. This isn't a lie. The exaggeration makes the place look *more* like itself.

One way to emphasize the height of the town is to use a lot of vertical strokes. Notice, for example, the towers on top of the hill and the shadows that run down the sides of the buildings.

You can also introduce other subtle horizontals—here, the flat roofs of the buildings and, especially, the important horizontal of the overhead cloud bank.

Since the bright, orange-red building catches your eye and leads you toward the top of the hill, you can ensure its attraction by adding a dark vertical shadow and a few random dots for windows. In contrast, the windows of the nearby buildings are much less noticeable—one edge blurs into another. They are deliberately lacking an identity because they're just a setting for the main structure.

To make these verticals seem even taller, you can introduce some strong, contrasting horizontals: the dark line of the wharf and the slashes of green, white, and purple that indicate boats in the harbor. These lines also add a feeling of activity. Cover them up and you'll see that the hill doesn't look quite as high.

BRUSH TECHNIQUES

Now that we've seen a few of the ways the stroke can work in a single painting, let's look at some technical aspects of the subject—how you use brush and paint to get specific effects. But before starting, let me emphasize that what's important is not how I make each stroke. That's a personal, almost unconscious process. It's more important to understand the *thinking* behind each stroke.

It's this thinking that makes the picture. I remember when I was a student in Charles Chapman's illustration class in New York. We dressed an Italian model like an Indian, and I worked on one figure in the corner of a huge canvas. I must have been planning a massacre. The great western illustrator Harvey Dunn was behind me, waiting to go to lunch with Chapman. He must have been frustrated by my slow, directionless approach, for he finally came over and asked, "What do you think you're doing?" Then he took my brush and painted a tremendous Indian—in about a minute—with feathers all over the place. It took up most of the canvas and made me see that when you want to say something—say it!

I had a similar experience some years later with John F. Carlson, when I took him to one of my favorite painting spots. I pointed downstream, explaining the best composition; but he turned his back and painted upstream. I thought he was crazy. Yet when I came back a few hours later and saw what he was doing, I realized that *I* was the one who had been looking in the wrong direction. Carlson seized on the rhythmic, angular movement of the creek and exaggerated it with great effect. Distracted by the confusing details, I'd missed the design possibilities of the subject.

Carlson was looking at the subject as a painter—rather than a passive observer. He knew how to glance at a scene, how to catch and hold his first emotional reaction to the spot. That's real painting. With practice, experimentation, and the study of the artists you most admire, you'll eventually arrive at your own technique. Then you won't need me or anyone else to tell you how to paint. No teacher can give you a viewpoint. That's up to you!

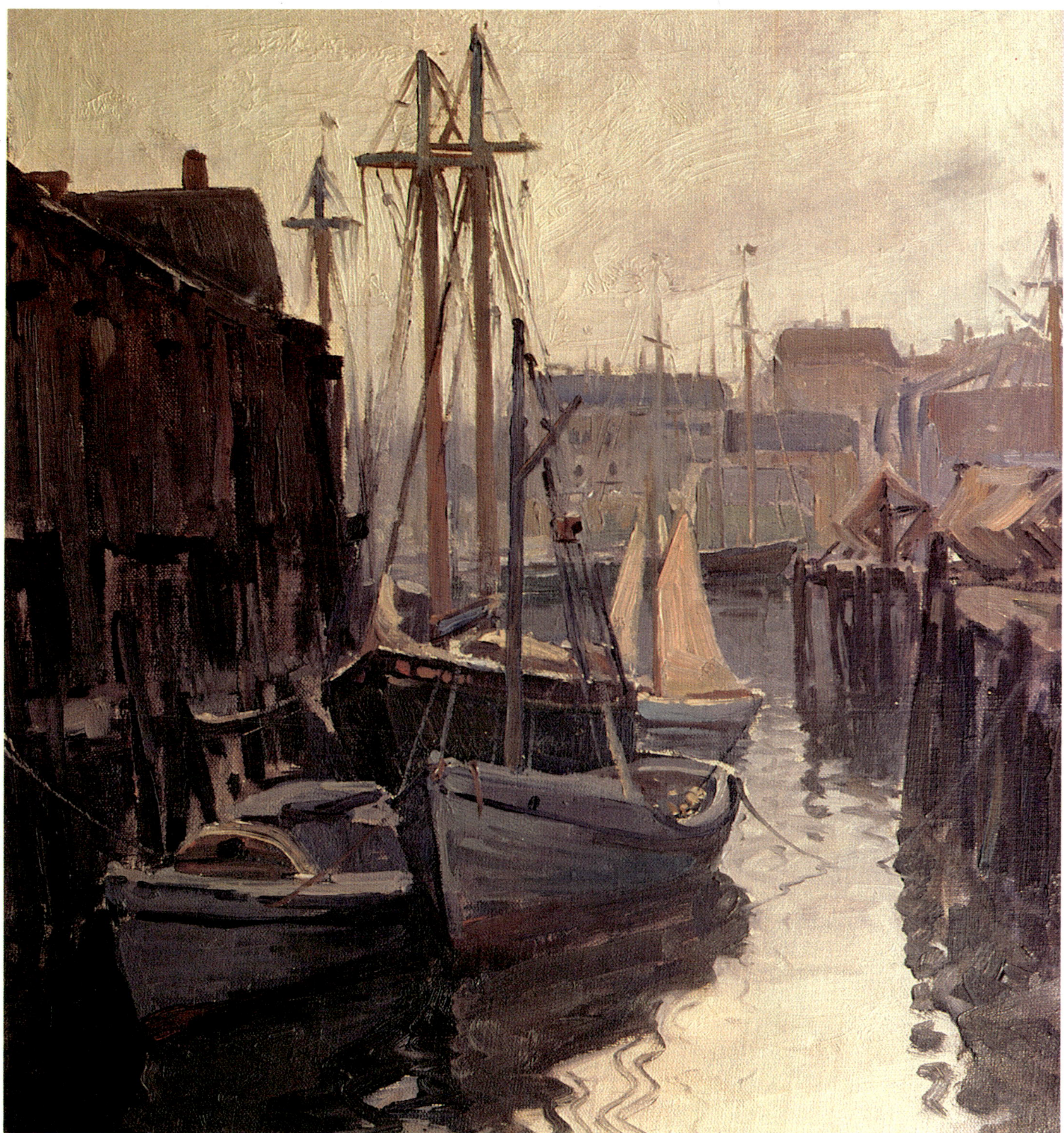

Early Morning
oil on canvas
18″ × 20″ (46 × 51 cm)
Collection of Mrs.
C. Richard Clark

This is a picture of Gloucester in the old days. Since the picture is an intimate one, I want you to stay in the foreground. Cover the sail with your finger, and you'll see how your eye suddenly rushes into the background. The cozy inlet suddenly opens up, spoiling the effect. The buildings and pilings were first stained on the canvas. Into this stain I worked thicker paint for individual pilings and boards. Where the stain shows through, it suggests discolored planks and open places under the wharf. Dark horizontal and vertical accents describe the different directions of these boards. Diagonal strokes on the nearby boats follow the line of the planking that makes them up. Horizontal strokes in the water suggest broken reflections. In the distance, horizontal strokes become the roofs of buildings. The sail of the small sailboat keeps you from going into the distance.

Wet over Wet

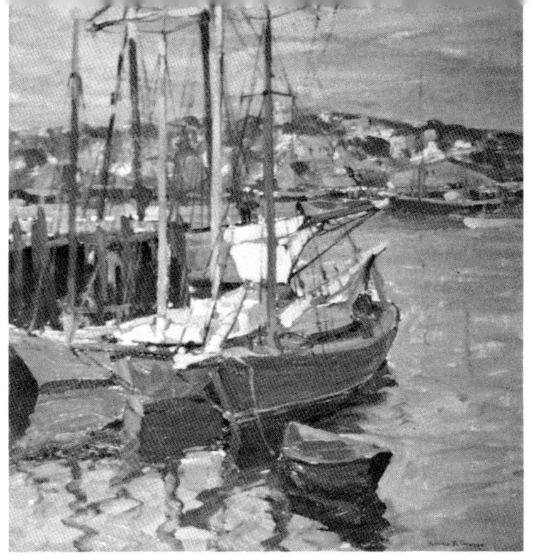

Rocky Neck
oil on panel
20" × 16" (51 × 41 cm)

Look at the way the boats are clustered together here. You have to look *through* them to see the distant, sunlit schooner. Since the canvas is relatively small, each stroke counts. In the foreground, large areas of color describe the main objects. You can see how flatly the boats are painted. Since these masses are simple, you can break up the foreground and background without confusing the viewer. The breadth of the foreground boats also adds a feeling of distance and perspective to the painting—the big areas contrast with the small strokes in the distant hill. Notice the interesting, irregular shapes of the white areas that cluster near the middle of the painting.

To emphasize the sunlit mast, you should paint the dark pilings very simply. As you can see, they're just a stain here, with some opaque strokes added to suggest the areas under the wharf.

After the cabins are painted, the furled foreground sail is added wet over wet. I want one layer to stay on *top* of the other, with no mixing. So I use one stroke, without too much pressure and with lots of medium as a lubricant. You can't adjust the stroke once it's made; the paint would mix with the undercoat and you'd lose the clarity of the form. You have to be right the first time. I planned this sail from the start. The shadows behind the sail bring it out even more by contrast. Then adding a few lines of rigging makes the foreground stronger and helps obscure the background boat.

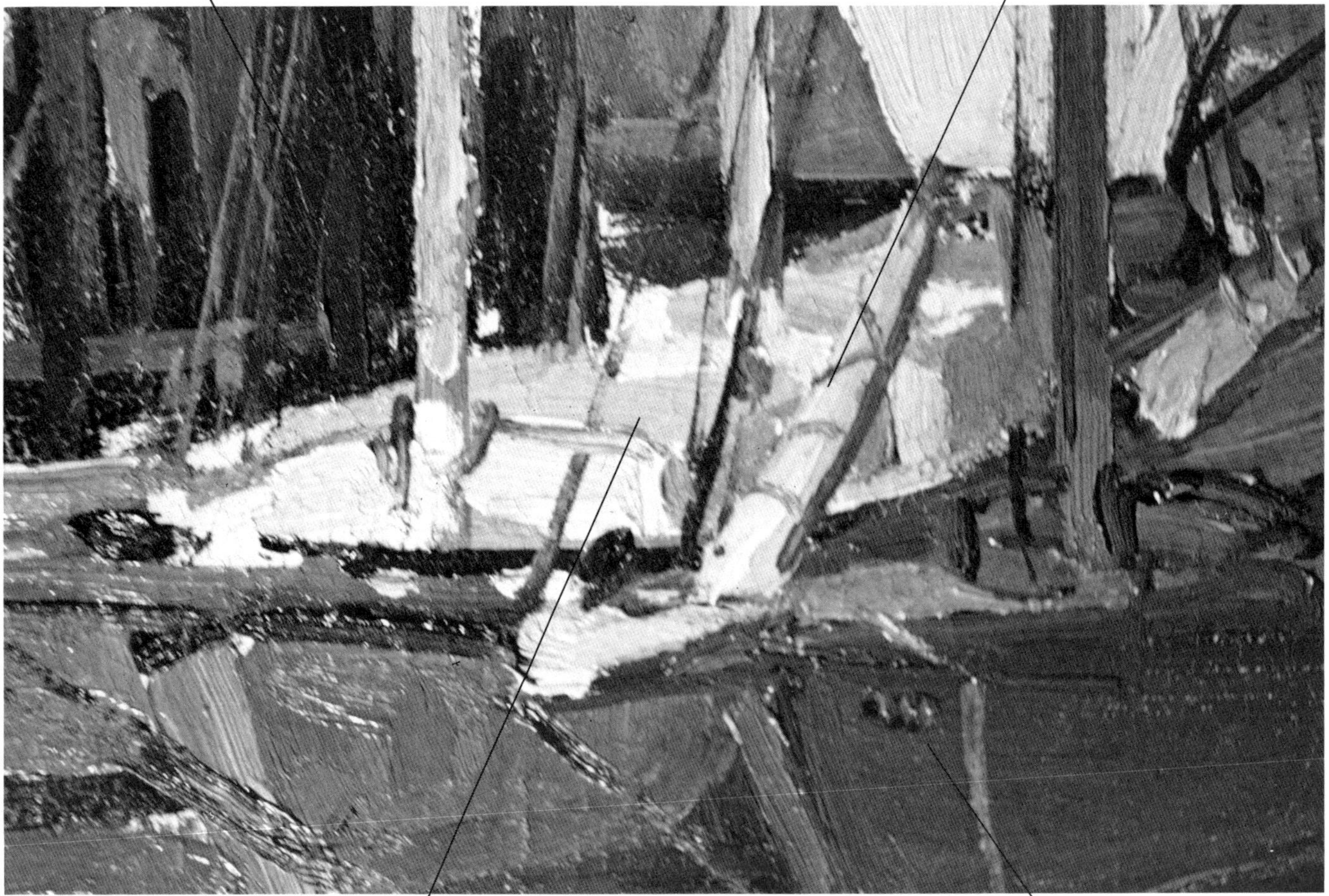

The cabins receive a strong blast of sunlight. In fact, everything is so bright that even the cabins' shadows are light in value, and color is reflected into them from the nearby boats and decks. In reality, these cabins had doors, moldings, lights, and all sorts of details. But here they are handled as just simple masses: a horizontal stroke for a side, a vertical stroke for a shadow.

Since the subject is the *decks* of the boats, you should keep the hulls very simple—describe them with just a few big brushstrokes. To add some interest to these areas, you can vary the strokes, using both horizontal and vertical ones.

Wet into Wet

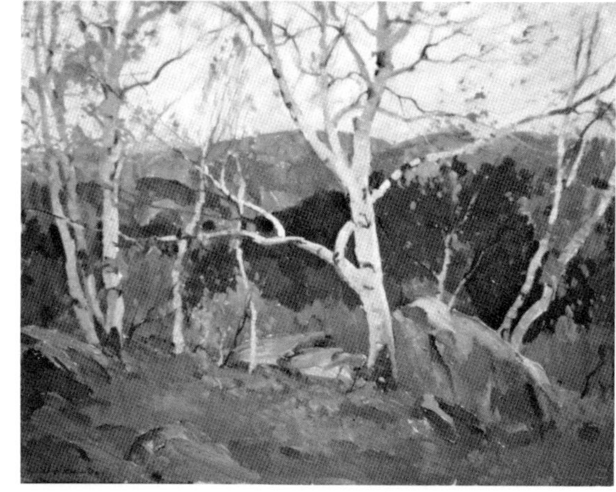

Autumn
oil on canvas
25″ × 30″ (64 × 76 cm)
Collection of
Robert Gruppé

In this cluster of trees, notice the way one dominates while the others twist and turn to escape its branches. Because it's a gray day and there are no strong value contrasts, much of the modeling is eliminated. For example, the distant evergreens are painted fairly flatly as an untextured foil to the birches. The distant mountain is also simple in shape and color. Notice how the main tree *is* the composition: its branches reach out of three sides of the picture.

As in the previous illustration, use a light touch and plenty of paint and medium when painting this birch. It will keep the brush from picking up the paint below and keep your colors fresh. Note that the upper part of the tree is especially clean and white. By lifting the brush off the canvas as you paint the foliage toward the center of the tree, you can suggest that the trunk is surrounded by leaves. This also keeps you from feeling that the birch is pasted onto the background.

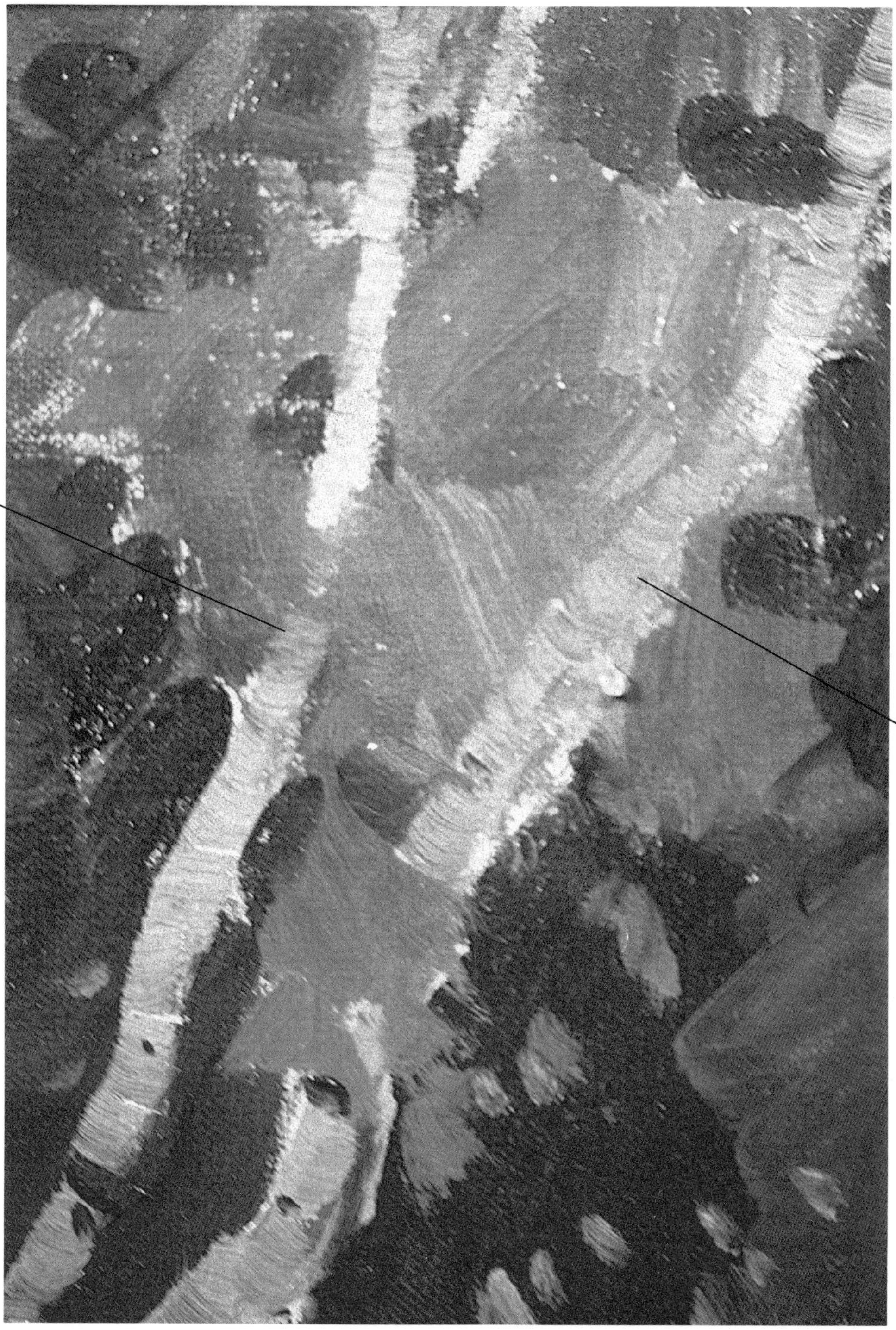

Whenever two similar objects are side by side, it's a good idea to emphasize one and subordinate the other. Since this birch tree isn't very important, I use less pigment to paint it than I do the main birch. Also, I don't clean the brush quite so well before I load it with fresh paint, so the color is duller. Unlike in the previous painting, I now *want* to intermix color layers wet in wet. So I push down a bit harder on the brush. The strokes pick up some of the darker undercoat, the colors mix, and the tree fades into its surrounding. One economical stroke creates shape, value, and texture!

Painting around Objects

I was struck by the size of this church. It reaches beyond the top of the canvas, while the houses farther down the road are all small in comparison. The distant trees are painted flatly and become more and more simple as they recede. In the distance, they form a single large mass. The large tree in front of the church was an important part of the picture—and the tower was difficult to draw. This part of the painting required a bit of preplanning to paint.

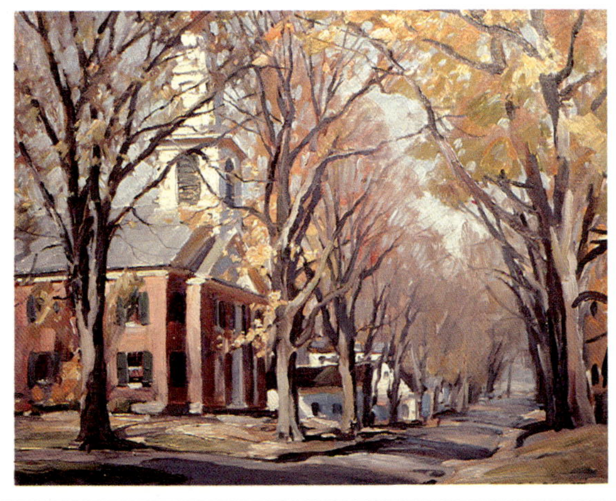

Deerfield Church
oil on canvas
25″ × 30″ (64 × 76 cm)

The safest way to paint the tree and tower is to wash in a suggestion of where the tower will be and then use the thicker paint to establish the foliage and the movement of the principal branches. If you paint the tower first and then draw the tree over it, a mistake in the branches would force you to redo everything.

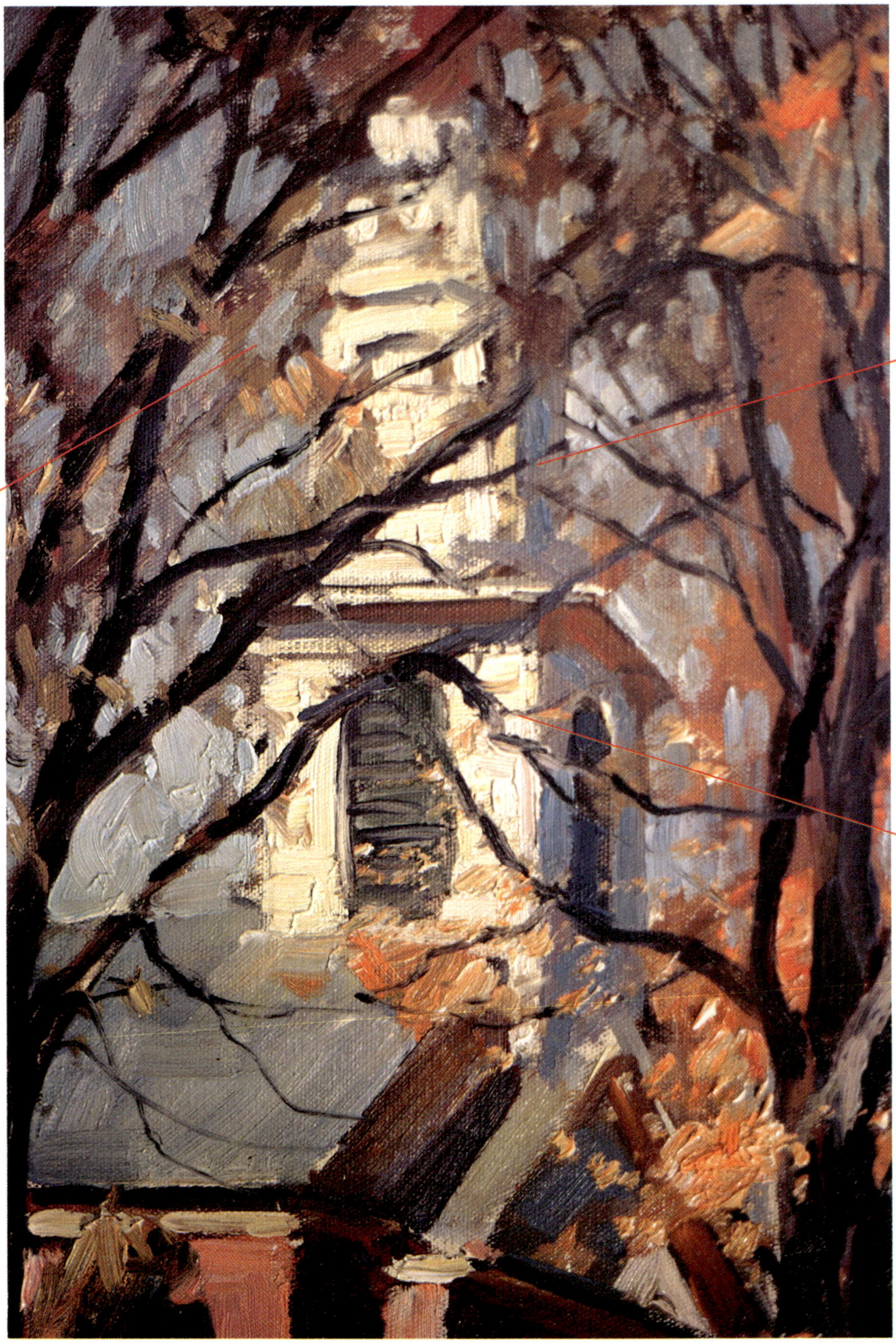

A small brush is used to "knit" the tower around the tree with a series of upright and horizontal strokes. The preliminary wash has dried in by this time and isn't a problem. You can see some of it still showing through under the eaves. The sky is painted like this too. In some places, I accidentally painted out parts of the branches and didn't bother to restate them.

I finish the job of painting tree over tower by taking a small brush and running a few thin, dark branches over the tower, thus making my method (of painting the tree first) a little less obvious.

Painting around Objects

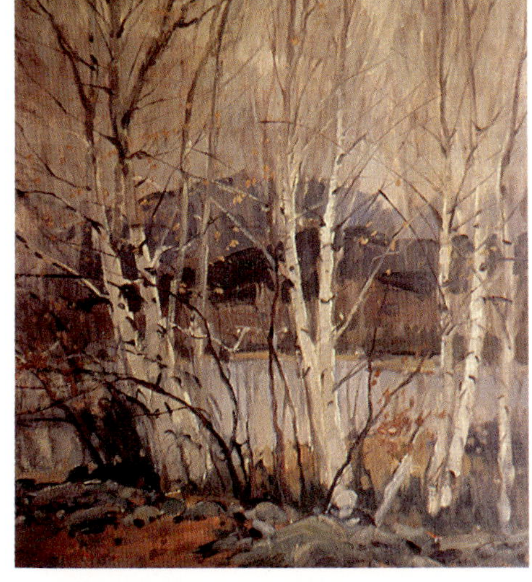

Gray Day Birches
oil on canvas
24″ × 20″ (61 × 51 cm)
Collection of Mrs.
Cathryn Nugent Gibbs

On a gray day, color and value relationships are very subtle. This picture is painted thinly, with lots of stains. The picture consists of nine birches, but the center group has the cleanest color and is accentuated by the nearby darks, so you see it first. The other trees are subsidiary to it. Things become less defined as you move toward the edges of the canvas.

Once the lightest and darkest areas—your full range of values—are established, you can paint the middle tones. This midtone is painted with vertical strokes of varying value. The direction of the strokes suggests growth. The shifts in value suggest individual trees. A few light branches are run over the area later.

Place the birch trees first because their movement is the key to the picture. Then roughly stain the area around them. After the trees are developed, you can paint the background *over* the stain, which by now is dry.

The dark, massed strokes of the evergreens help to emphasize the white tree trunks of the birches. Painting around the tree also helps improve its shape.

Here the dark bush is blocked in first; then the lighter water is painted around it. The light color occasionally mixes with the darker, creating a blur that's just right for the fuzzy contour of a bush.

Line

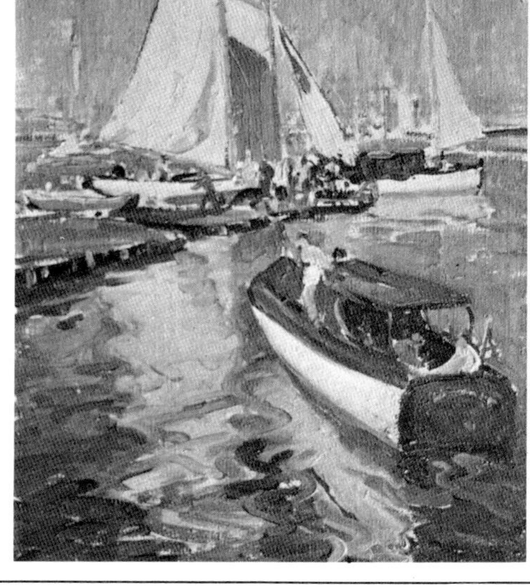

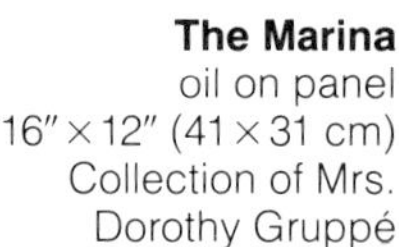

The Marina
oil on panel
16" × 12" (41 × 31 cm)
Collection of Mrs.
Dorothy Gruppé

This is a quick sketch of a marina near my studio. I was particularly struck by the brilliantly lit cluster of sailboats. You can see how I use the foreground boat to direct your eye toward them. In general, I avoid using a lot of linework, since I'd much rather get my effects through masses of color. But sometimes line adds an interesting, decorative quality to a picture.

Contrary to my usual practice, I outlined the sail with paint first and then filled in the areas. One of the reasons the outlining works is that the strong blast of light has eliminated the need for much modeling. The outline has thus exaggerated a flatness that is already present in nature.

A few upright slashes suggest distant sailboats.

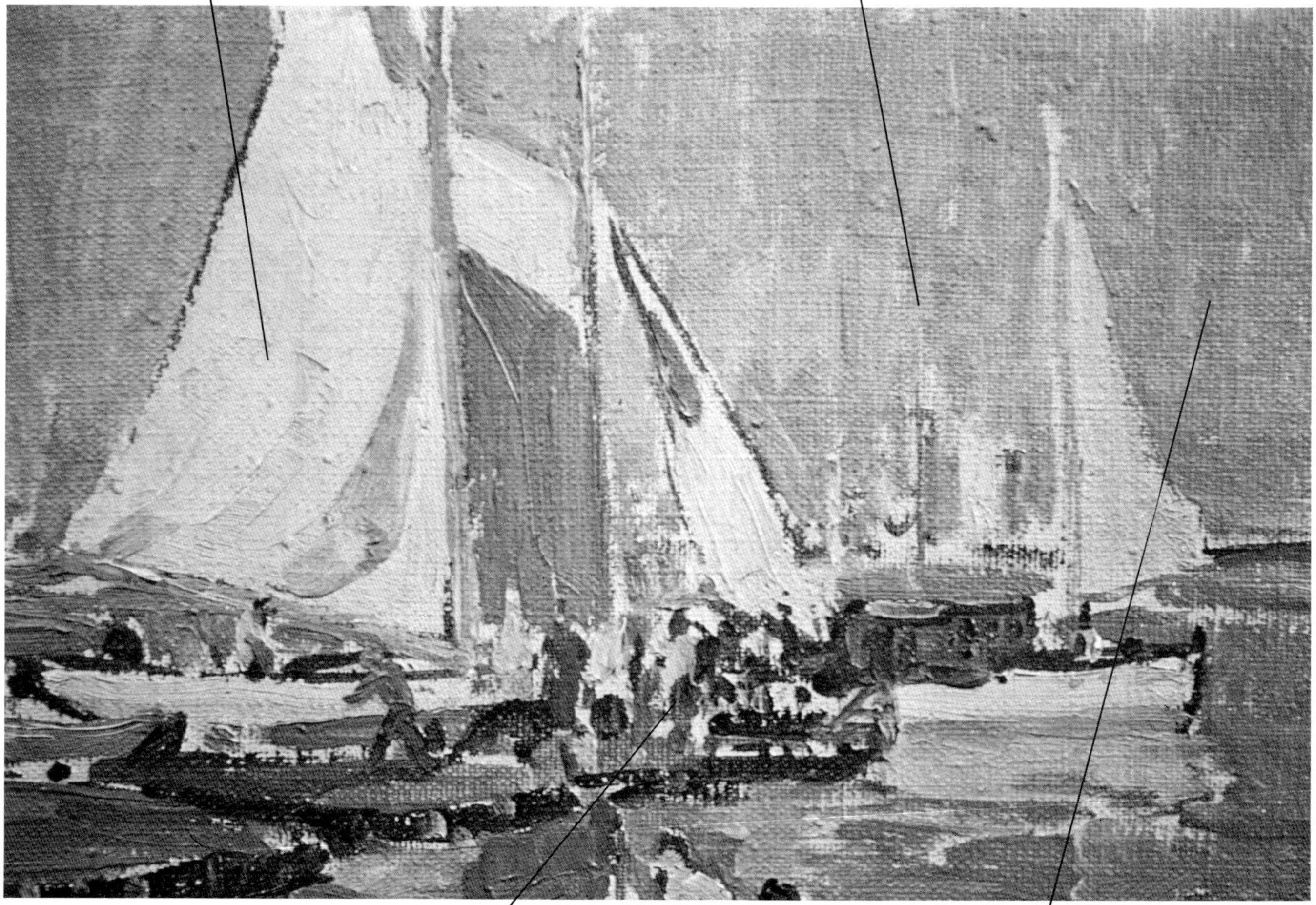

There's lots of lines here. The hulls and even parts of the wharf are all outlined.

The linear abstract quality is repeated in the sky—a series of purple, pink, and green bands. Normally, you'd blend the divisions between these bands, but here the lines match the rest of the painting, so I left them.

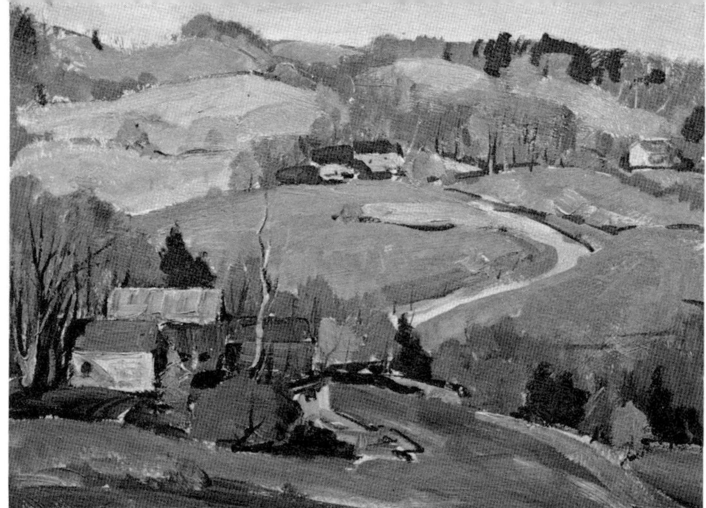

Autumn Hills
oil on canvas
16″ × 20″ (41 × 51 cm)

I like the way the land at this site comes up at us and then goes down into the valley and up into the mountains. These irregular movements are interesting to look at. I emphasized the foreground farm, with the background buildings and trees as "dessert." The distant farm is very simply stated; and the trees are even more abstract: a series of uprights, triangles, and dots.

In contrast to the previous example, this time the big areas of color are massed in first. Again, they're flatly painted because the sun is hitting them head-on, which elminates most modeling. Once the main masses are established, linear touches add some description.

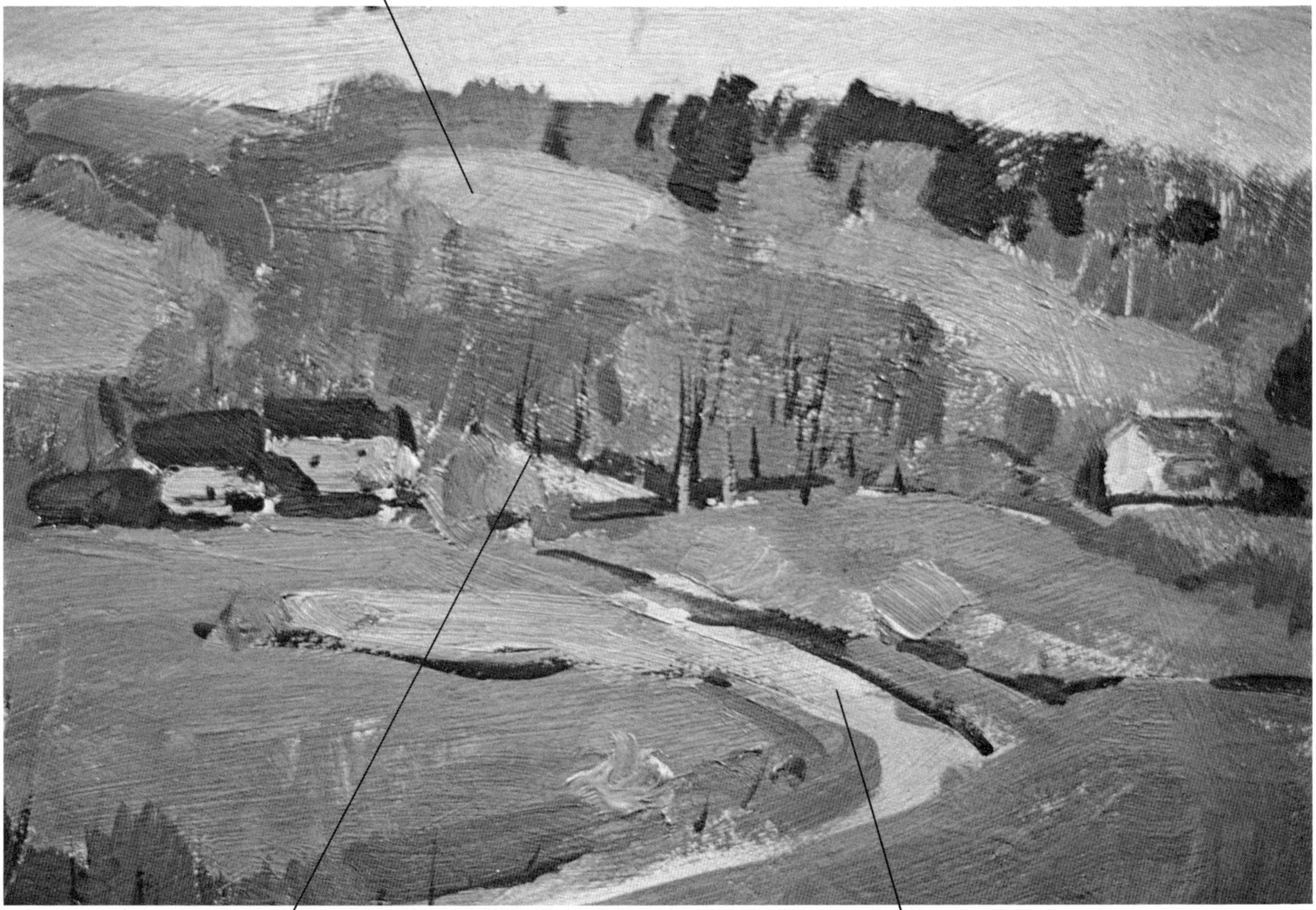

A few upright lines suggest trunks, while the dark lines at their base indicate cast shadows. These lines also tie the trunks together as a unit.

The road is painted first. Then a dark curved line is added to emphasize its upward movement. A few dark lines also suggest irregularities in the hillside.

Staccato Strokes

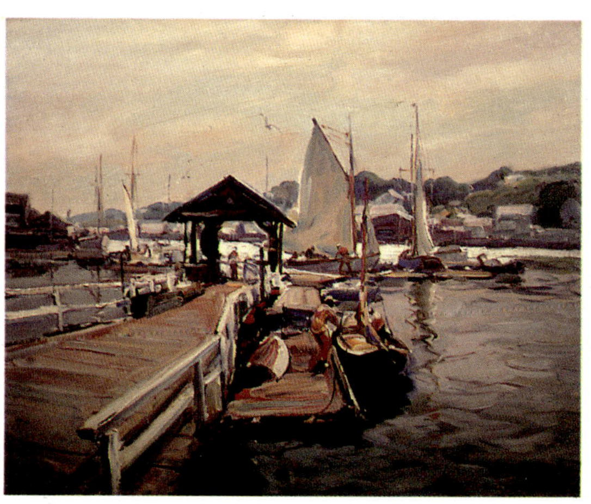

Floating Dock
oil on canvas
25″ × 30″ (64 × 76 cm)

The wharf, foreground floats, and dories all point forcefully toward the cluster of backlit sailboats. All this activity is accentuated by the contrasting quiet mass of water on the right. The distant hill slants toward the boats, while the upright sails act as a staple, tying water, background, and sky together. To emphasize the lightness of the sail, I place a dark shed directly in front of it. The darkness of the shed also helps push the lighter boats and hills into the distance. Cover the shed, and you'll see that the picture loses some of its force. The background is painted with a series of choppy staccato strokes, strokes that don't detract from the huge, simply painted masses of the wharf and the sail. Instead, the small strokes make these forms look more expansive and forceful.

The shadows on the distant pilings or the roundness of the sailboat are not important. Instead, a broken stroke is worked back and forth to establish the feel of the basic character of the subject. The sailboat, for example, is reduced to just five strokes: a horizontal, a vertical, a slash for a highlight, and two quick, long verticals. That's all you need to describe it. More detail would obscure its point as an accessory to the story, not the main subject. There's no virtue in telling the viewer more than he or she needs to know.

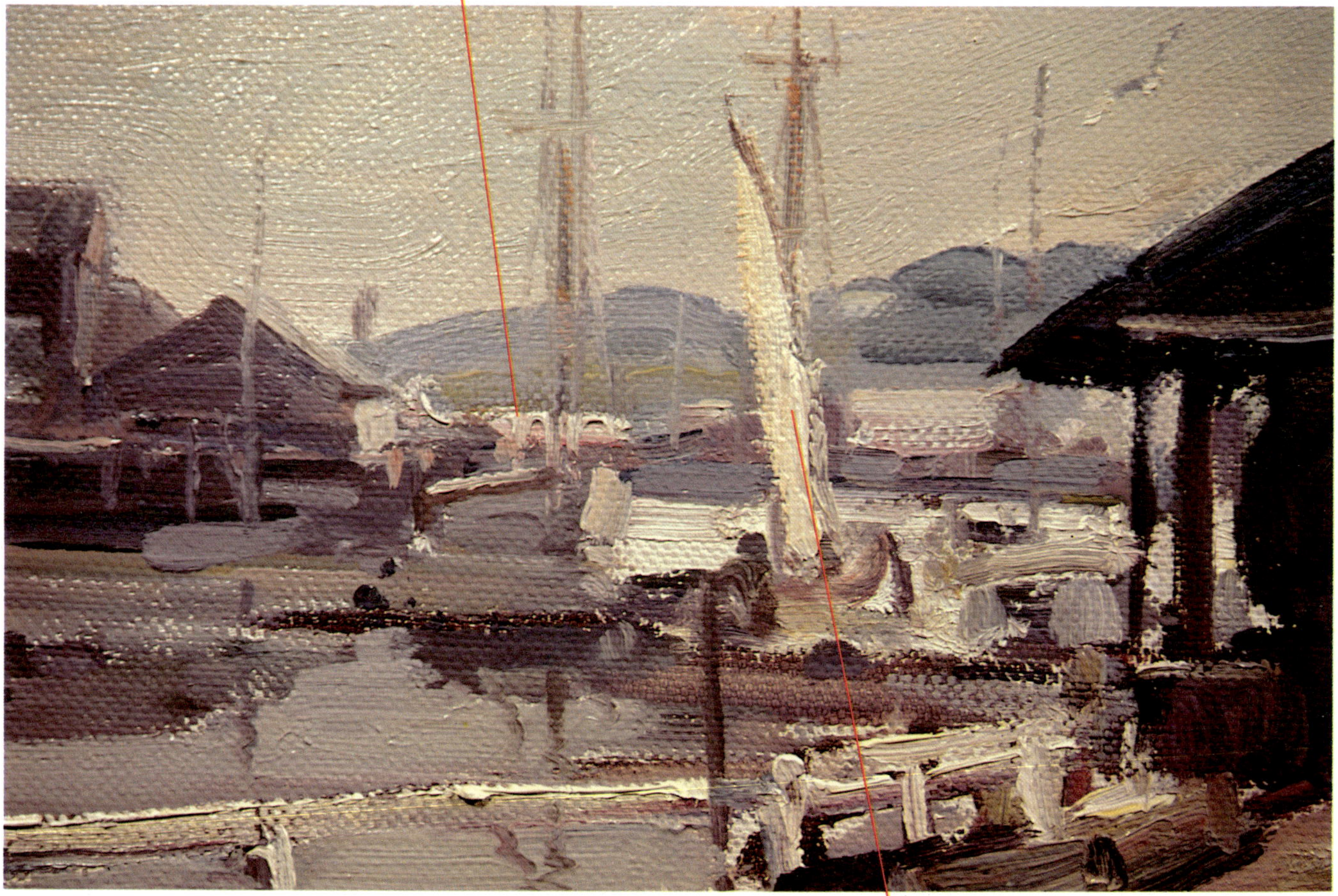

The long upright stroke of the sail differs from the other strokes, and because it is so different, it stands out and dominates this subsidiary part of the building. Near it, a few rough strokes suggest parts of other moored vessels.

Staccato Strokes

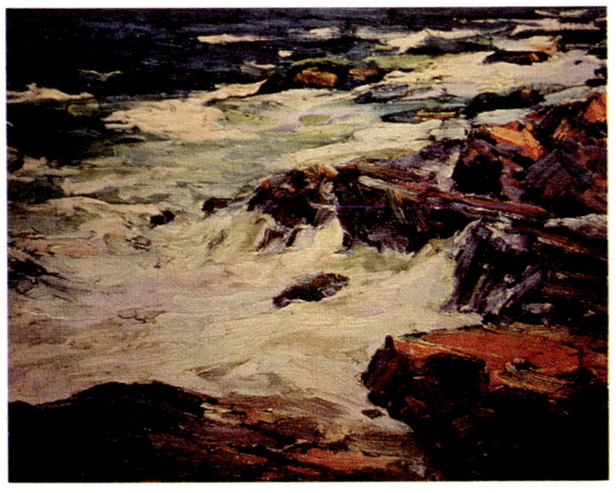

Rocky Shoreline
oil on canvas
30″ × 32″ (76 × 81 cm)

I've always liked this surf. It has a broken, rhythmic quality that's typical of this stretch of coastline. There is no big wave in the picture, so you don't get nervous looking at it and waiting for it to come crashing down. Instead, there's just white water. You can sense its movement as you look at the picture. The painting looks natural and doesn't have what I call the "smell" of the studio.

In the distance, horizontal strokes suggest the flatness of the water and of rocks, rounded by the ocean. These flat strokes emphasize the angularity of the foreground rocks.

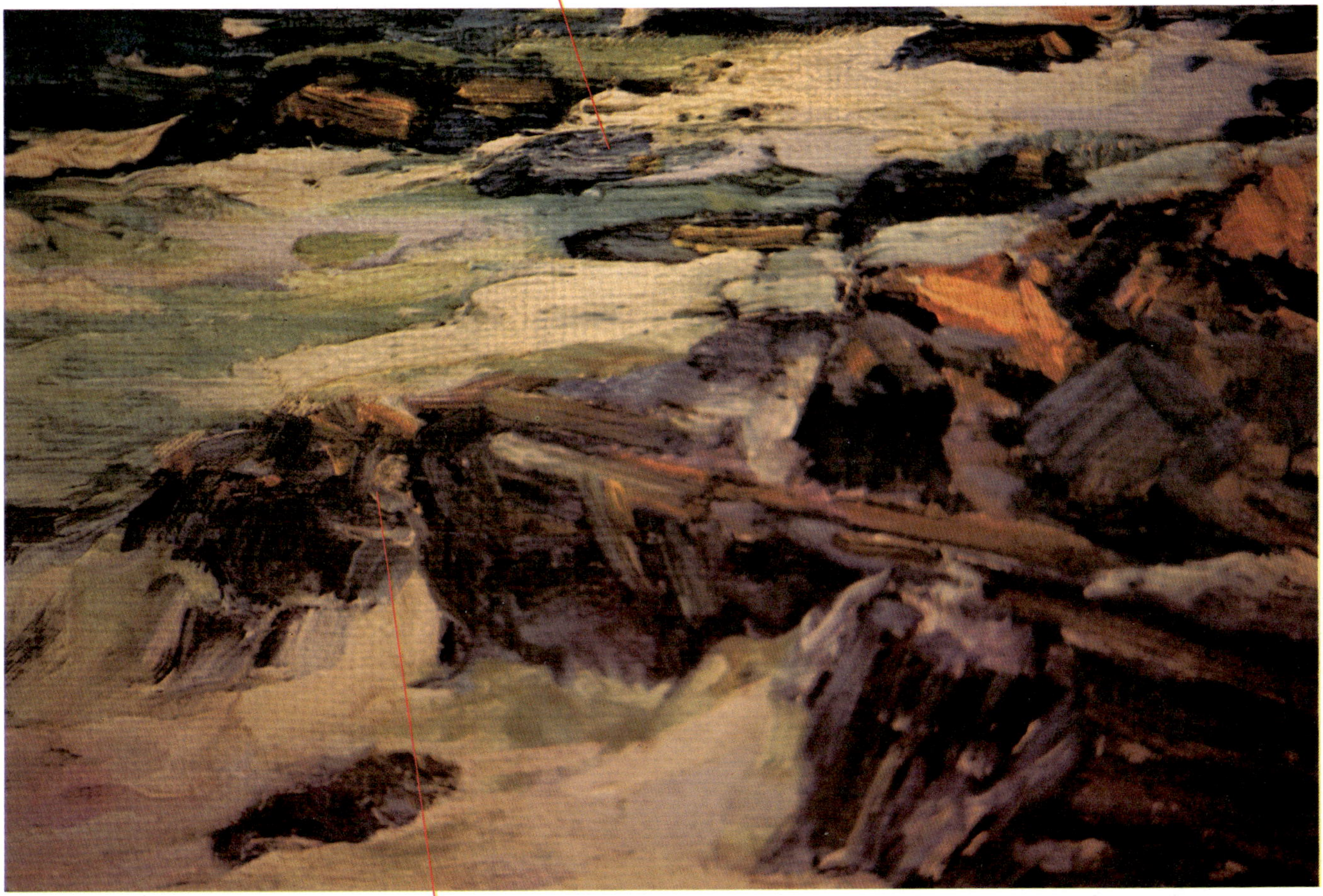

The rocks are painted with the same short, staccato strokes as in the previous picture; but, in this case, the horizontals and verticals give way to more angled strokes. Although the stroke is the same, the static quality of the previous illustration is replaced by one of dynamic activity. Each choppy stroke says something about the rocks: a facet catching the light, a wet reflecting area, a sharp crevice, or a high-and-dry spot, dark and crisp.

Painting Pines: Jagged Stroke

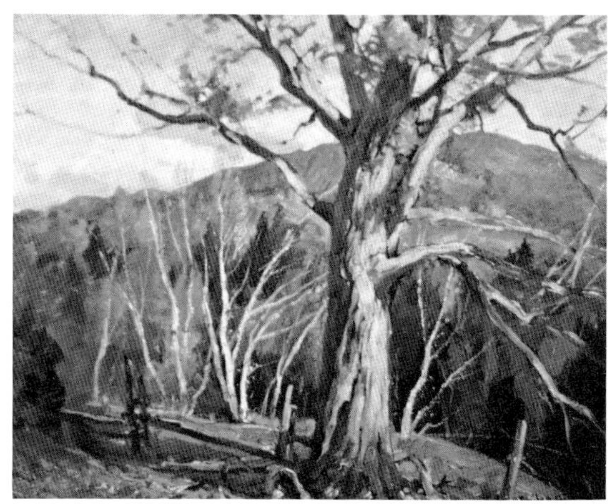

The Edge of the Pasture
oil on canvas
25″ × 30″ (64 × 76 cm)

This composition is full of interesting counterpoint. The fence goes one way, the mountain the other. The maple leans toward the right, the birches toward the left. The central tree is clearly the dominant one. As in many of my compositions, I haul this tree out to all three sides of the canvas. I like this feeling of bigness, of a tree so large and alive that you can't contain it on the canvas. Both this painting and the facing one describe distant pines. But each group is painted with a different kind of stroke.

The background foliage is a series of quick diagonal strokes. The angle of the stroke is varied to indicate the movement of the branches.

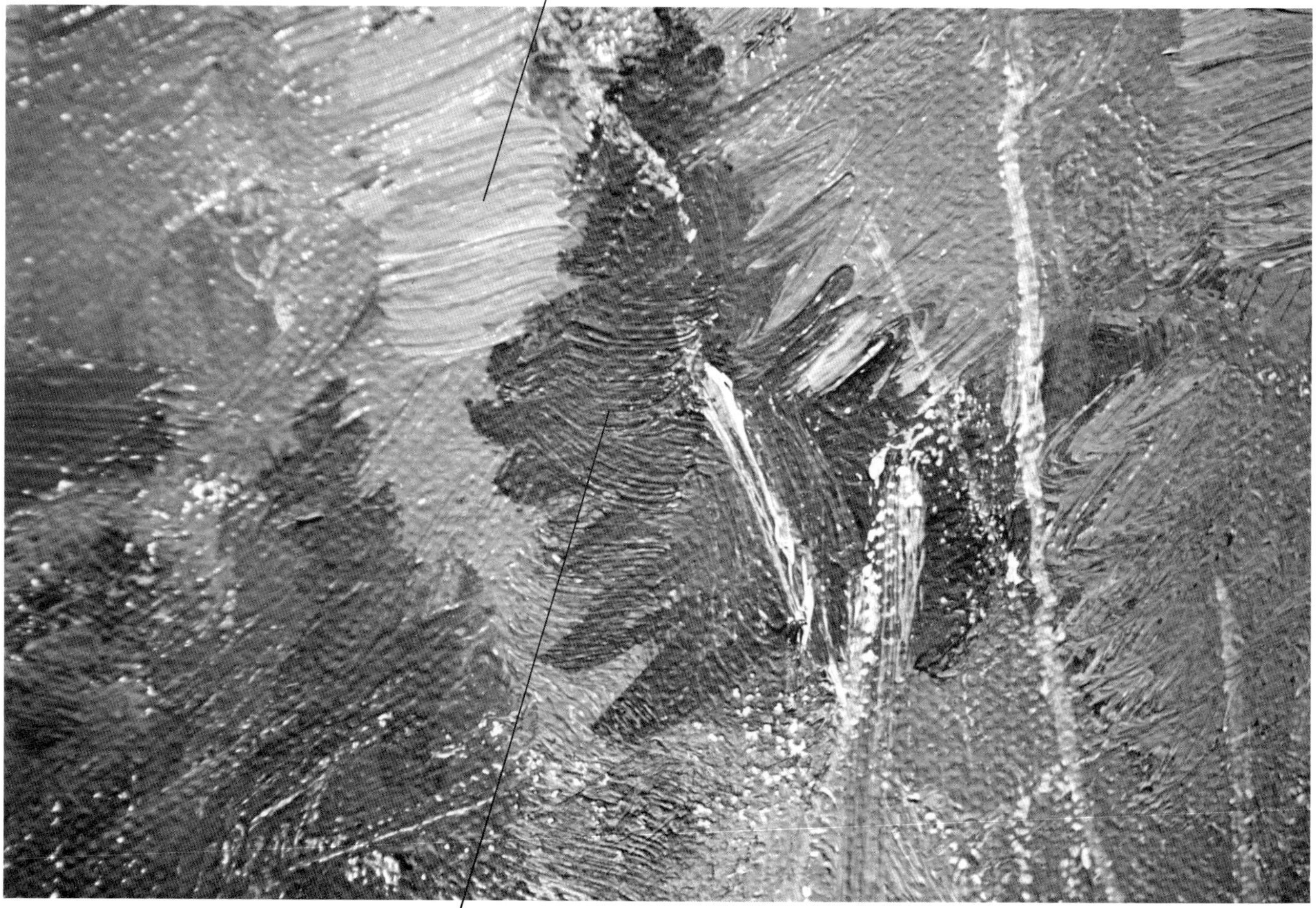

The diagonal stroke works so well that you can paint the distant evergreen similarly: a short stroke for the top, with wider ones beneath it. Then proceed to paint the larger evergreen the same way. To save time, use two long, zigzag strokes, fanning out the shape while working. Close up, you probably don't think this squiggle would "read" as a fir tree. But in the complete picture, it looks quite realistic. With the nearby pines defined, you can read some of that definition into the more abstract strokes.

Painting Pines: Dotted Stroke

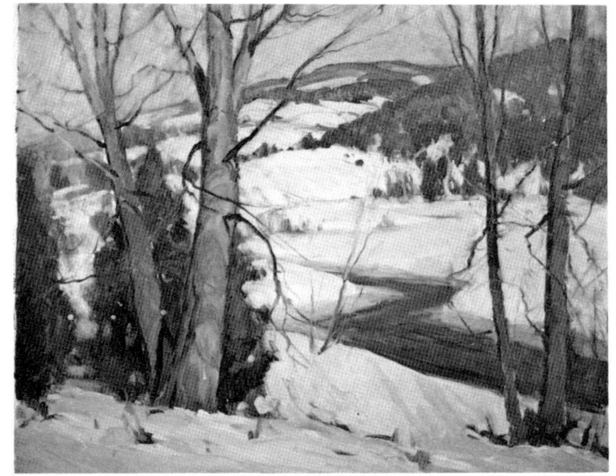

Day's End
oil on canvas
25″ × 30″ (61 × 76 cm)

In this picture of a stream and distant mountains, the cluster of pines on the left are fairly detailed and you can see color changes and a suggestion of swooping, pointed branches. The background pines are much more summarily handled. On the facing page a jagged stroke suggests a distant unimportant pine, hidden by foliage. Here the snowy background makes the distant trees stand out as an interesting pattern. A different stroke and a more complicated mix of stains and impasto are needed to describe this varied pattern.

After roughly staining the area where the pines would be, paint in the snow, bushes, and suggestions of cool shadows. Here and there, leave a bit of canvas to avoid painting into the dark preliminary stain.

Once the snow patches are established, add darker strokes to suggest distant pines. The trees are so far away that their broken edges can't be seen. They form simple shapes against the snow: dots the width of a single brushstroke. A few of the strokes are painted into the wet snow.

Texture

Mending the Nets
oil on canvas
30″ × 25″ (76 × 64 cm)
Collection of the Sawyer Free Library
Gloucester
Massachusetts

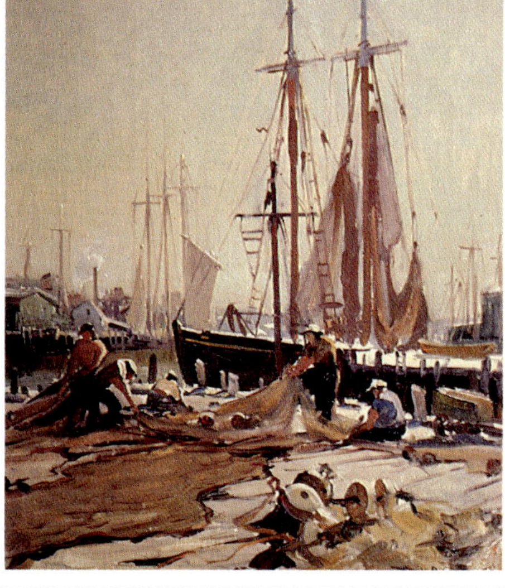

This painting is a study in different textures. The flatly painted foreground net leads you into the picture and acts as a relief from the active brushwork that describes the men, ropes, and the round cork floats. To the left of the wheelbarrow, one big stroke represents a nearby piling. Directly above it, however, the background pilings are represented by just eight brushstrokes. Because of the difference in stroke size, you sense how far away the area is.

The distant net is thinly painted. This thinness makes the net look transparent and luminous, as if the sun were shining through it. Bristle marks again suggest webbing. A few dark lines enhance the effect. Dots stand for distant corks.

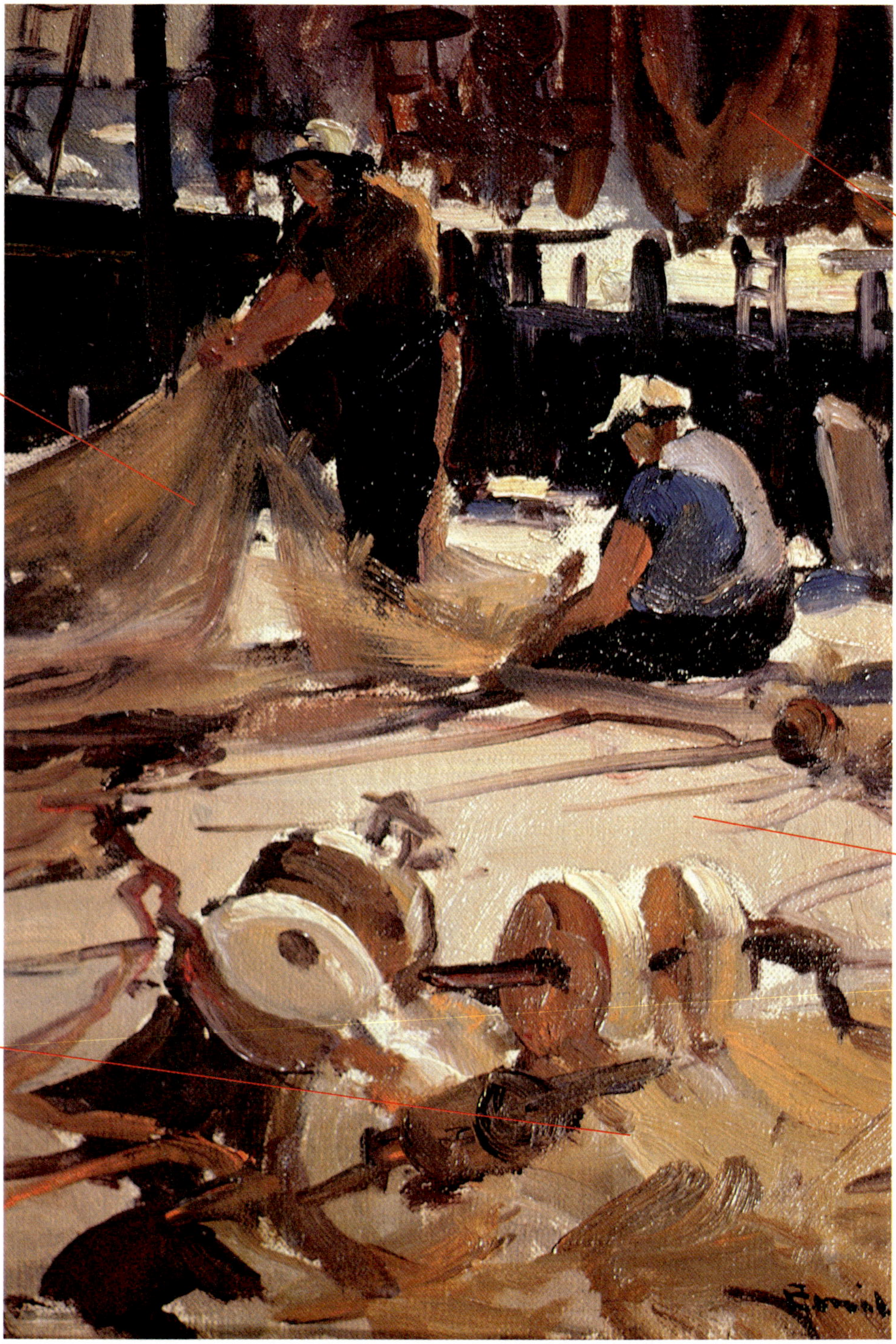

The hanging nets in the background have little texture in them because they have been painted with flat, concave strokes. You can see the progressive elimination of detail, moving from the foreground to the background.

The jumbled foreground net is close to us, and we can see its irregularities because different, contrasting strokes suggest the disorder. The strands of thick paint represent the webbing of the net. The cork floats are more smoothly painted. The orange in the shadows shows the effect of reflected light. These corks are big—almost as large as the distant workers—and this large shape enhances the sense of foreground.

To emphasize the texture of the nets, paint the wharf in a flat, untextured way. Planks are suggested by a few short lines.

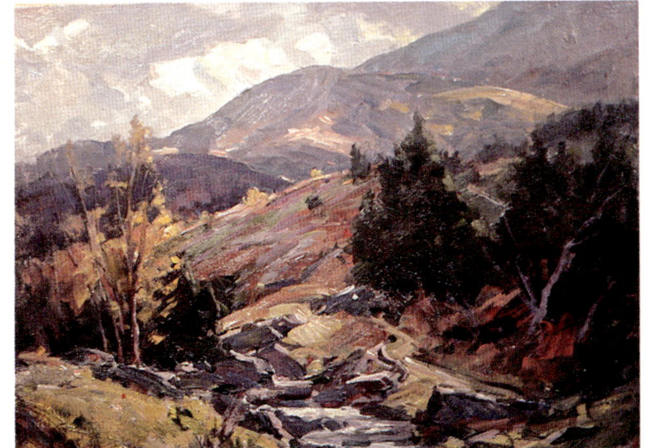

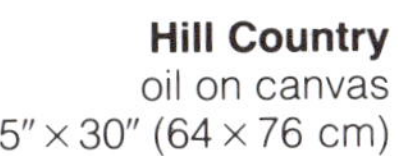

Hill Country
oil on canvas
25″ × 30″ (64 × 76 cm)

The roughness and irregularity of this spot made a strong impression on me. It has a bigness that I try to capture in the roughness of my strokes. The day is ominous, and there's a powerful bulging of the earth as it works its way toward the mountain and the cloud-filled sky. To enhance the bigness of the scene, I haul the mountain out of the top of the painting. You sense you're in a valley and that the mountain must go up for another thousand feet. Cover the mountain, and you'll see how tame the landscape becomes.

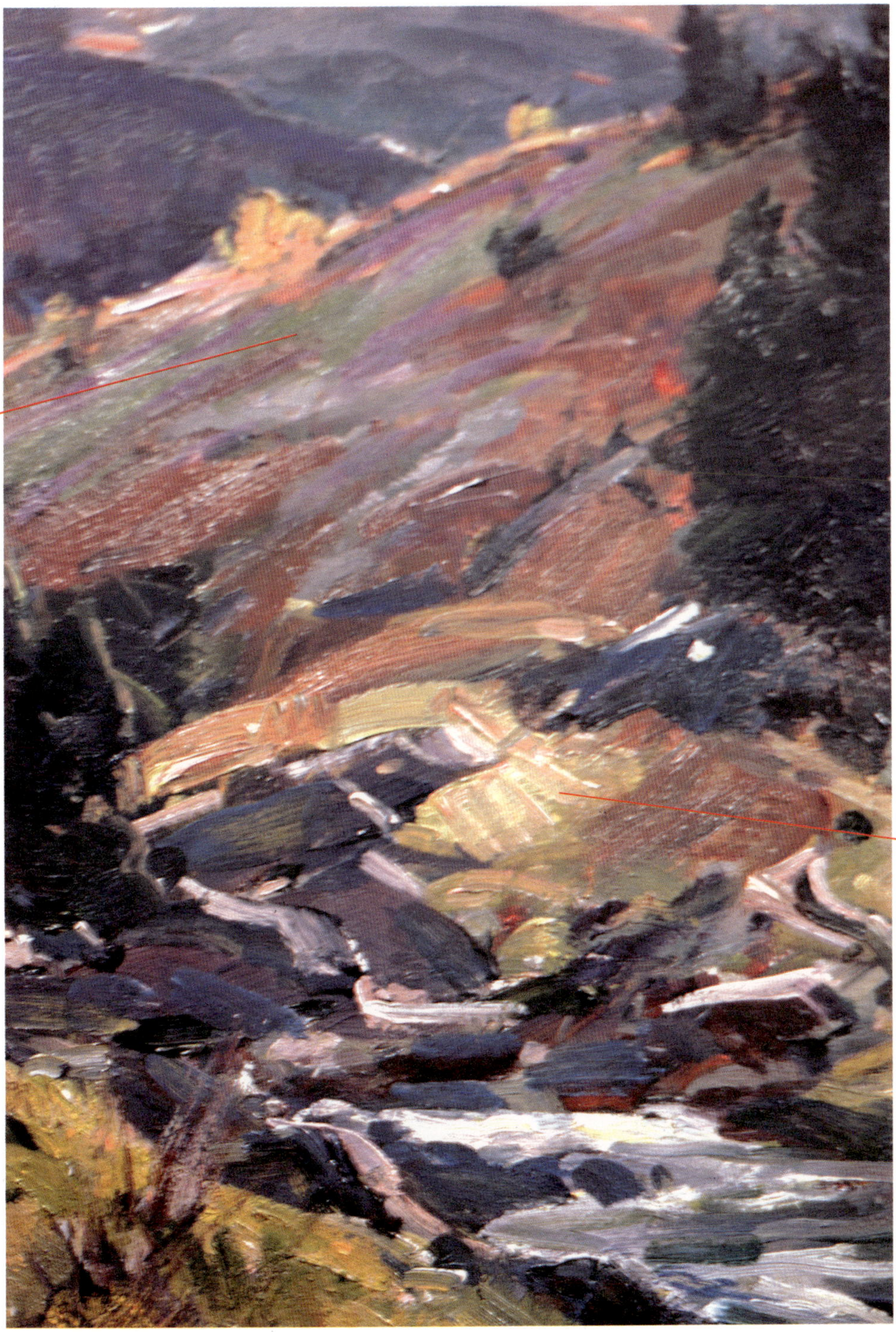

To emphasize this broken texture, paint the nearby hill with thick, rounded strokes and exaggerate the color. The rich reds and yellow contrast with the complementary purples of the rocks. A few scattered dots add snap to the landscape.

Don't waste time on crevices in the rocks or pebbles in the stream. The rock mass is reduced to a pattern of heavily painted, sharp, angular strokes: light masses against dark ones, with little concern for subtle halftones.

Scumble: Branches

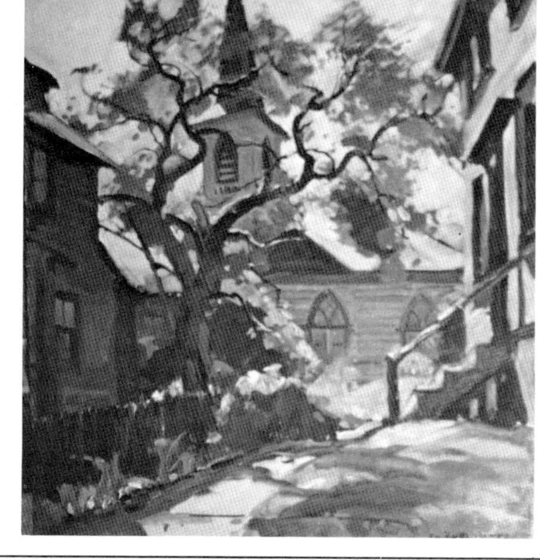

Rockport Church
oil on canvas
30″ × 25″ (76 × 64 cm)

The exuberant movement of the tree contrasts with the angularity of the nearby buildings. Their strong uprights and points make the tree seem especially lyrical. Backlighting emphasizes the strong silhouettes. To create a sense of foreground, pull the nearest building out of the top of the picture. You will notice that the perspective lines of both structures drive you toward the lively tree. Although I usually like to use a lot of paint, this picture gave me a chance to work with a stain.

First stain the area of spring growth a dull reddish-purple. Since little medium is used, the area has a drybrush look. You can see where white canvas shows through the individual brushmarks. This thin, broken texture suggests branches and new growth; they break up the light of the sky without completely obscuring it. The white bits of canvas look like glisten on branches and leaves. This effect is a "happy accident," which happened as I moved the brush.

Against the sky, the tree remains a stain. Give it definition by economically running a single dark branch across it and adding a dot for a leaf. The eye then imagines all kinds of nonexistent details.

Lay thick strokes of green paint over the stain—they represent the heavier, more developed masses of leaves. But don't show any individual leaves.

Cut the stain to shape by painting the sky into it. The heavy, opaque sky color enhances the transparency of the branches.

Scumble: Sky Holes

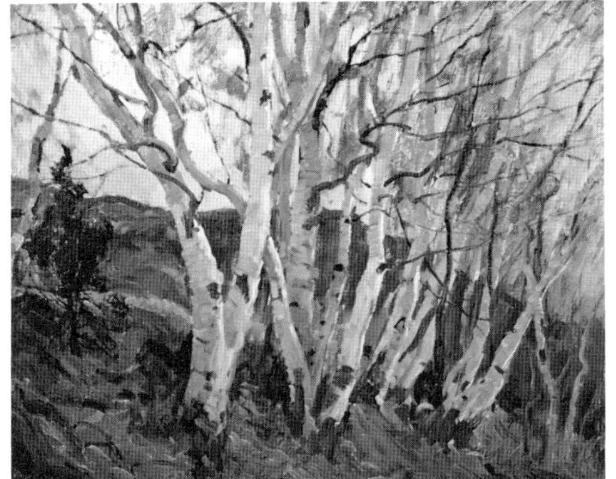

Hillside Birches
oil on canvas
30″ × 36″
(76 × 91 cm)

This is one of my favorite painting spots. It looks like it's in the middle of the woods, but, in reality, it's beside a main road, busy with passing trailer trucks. Notice the way the trees twist and dance. The dark notes at the bottom of the birches tie them to the ground. The intensely dark evergreen on the left establishes the foreground. The spaces between the trees are darkened by innumerable little branches. The sun bounces off these branches; and the rays, criss-crossing each other, create a broken, mysterious tone. My teacher, John F. Carlson, always said that it was impossible to paint one of these skyholes too dark.

Leaves appear the nearer the trees are to us. There are *no* leaves in the distance, nor any individual branches.

To suggest the numerous branches, scumble in a dark, warm color behind the birches. The specks of canvas look like bits of bright sky. To add interest, vary the value of the scumble and paint it thicker in some places than in others. Also vary the direction of the strokes.

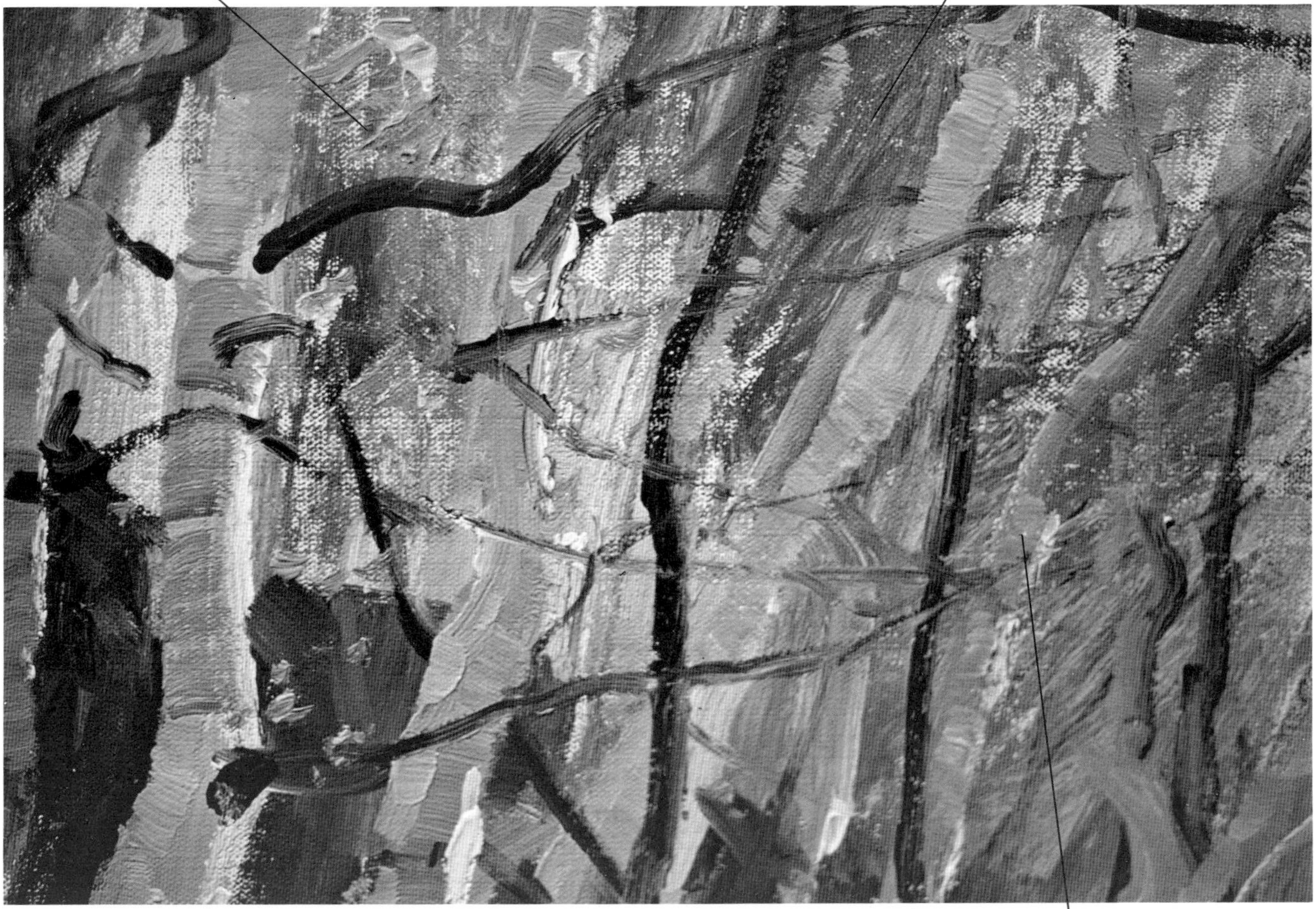

The distant birches are painted into this scumble and pick up some of its color. They look like they're disappearing into the jumble of intertwining branches.

Scumble: Buildings

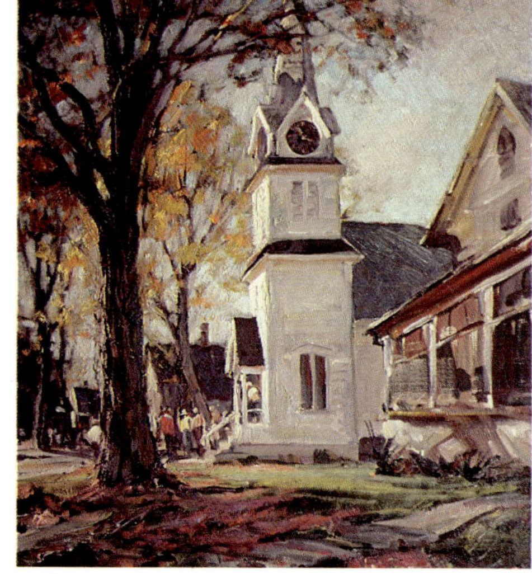

Village Sunday
oil on canvas
25″ × 30″ (64 × 76 cm)

I was impressed by the dignity of the church steeple against the sunlit sky. To emphasize the feeling of height, I chose an upright canvas and echo the vertical lines of the church in those of the nearby house and trees. The shadow side of the church isn't especially dark; it catches a warm reflected light from the ground and from the side of the house in the foreground. I greatly exaggerate the perspective of the house, using it to force you toward my center of interest.

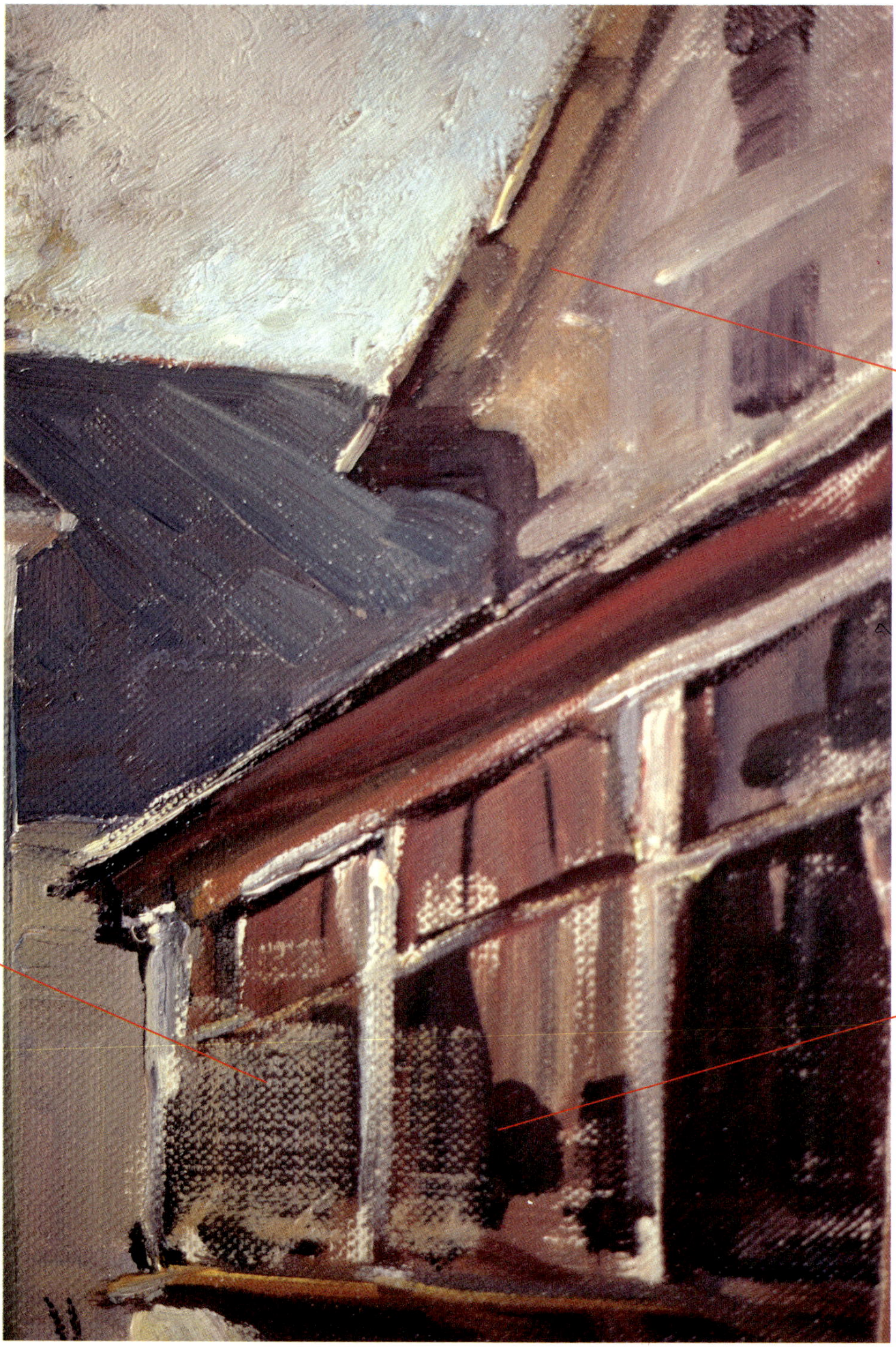

Leave the warm, transparent stain under the eaves. It looks luminous, so why use more paint? A few thick strokes suggest the boards that make up the side of the house.

Use a dark stain to show the structural supports of the porch and to suggest its shadowed interior. Once the shadow has been set up, quickly add some light vertical strokes. Use little medium and hardly touch the canvas. The texture of the canvas looks like the glittering surface of a screen.

First use a warm, reddish tone to show the light shining through the porch and glistening on the screens. Bits of uncovered canvas look like distant highlights.

Scumble: Distant Trees

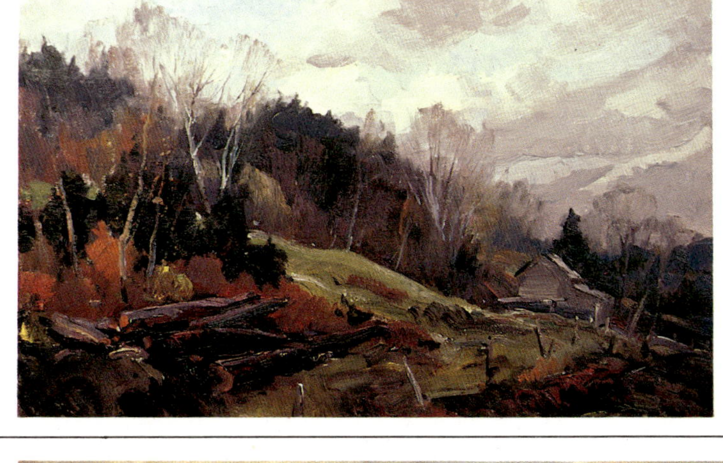

Mountain Pastures
oil on canvas
25″ × 30″ (64 × 76 cm)

This site conveys a sense of the expansiveness of the countryside, especially the big sky over the bulging field. The small house and trees enhance the bigness of the scene. Much of the drama of the scene comes from the contrast of the steeply drooping hillside and the upward moving sky.

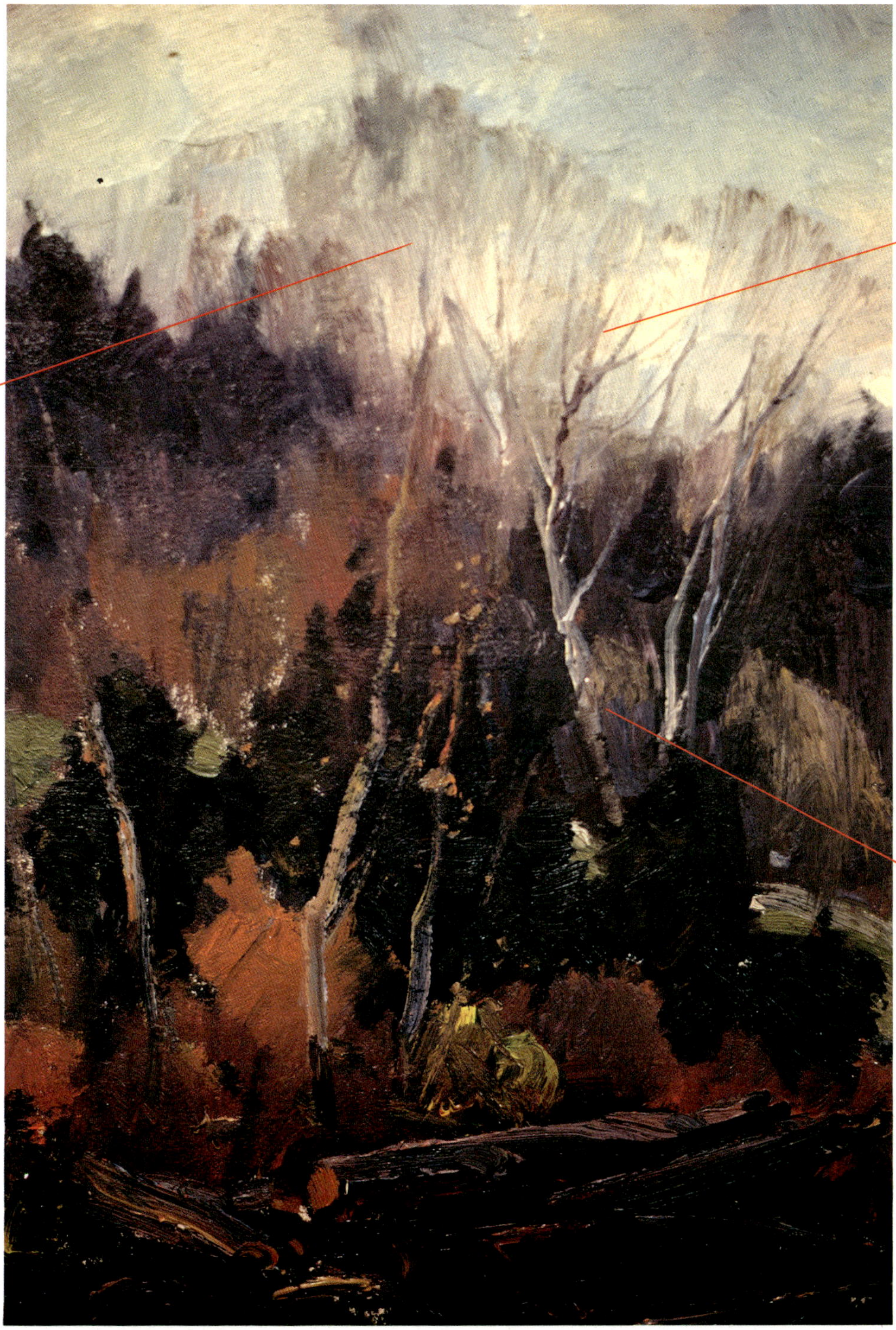

After you paint the thick, light sky, pick up some darker paint on your brush, but be sure not to add too much medium. Place the tip at what will be the outer edge of the tree branches and draw it down slightly using very little pressure. You can almost count the strokes as you work the brush against the sky in a fan-shaped pattern. The thickly painted sky comes through the brushmarks like skyholes!

Having established the mass, use a smaller brush to draw a few branches. A dozen are enough to suggest a hundred. If I tried to draw every branch, I'd still be at it. And even if I succeeded, you'd still see only a blur when you stepped back from the canvas. So why bother?

Drag the branch color down into the distant pines, breaking them up as they near the birches. If this area had been left dark and sharp, you wouldn't know whether to look at the evergreens or the tree trunks. Obliterating the evergreens gives prominence to the birches.

The Wash: Distant Hills

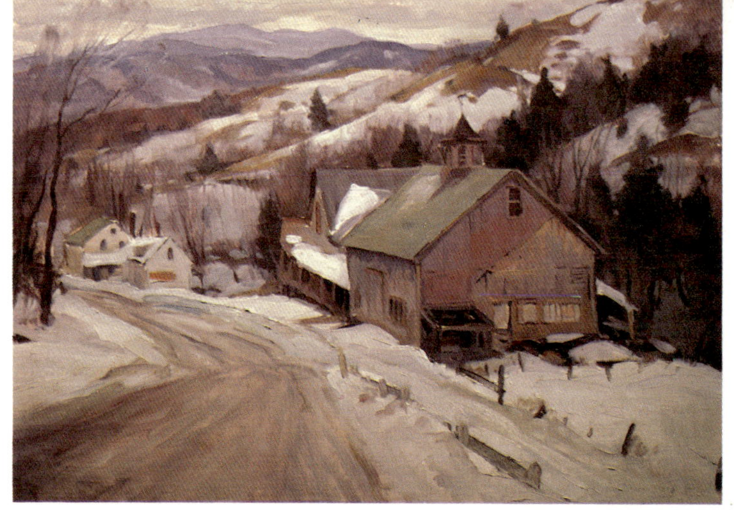

Mountain Road
oil on canvas
30″ × 36″ (76 × 91 cm)

In this picture of a gray day in the mountains, changes in scale are used to lead you into the valley. The large barn is contrasted with the small homestead; the nearby hill to the mountainous distances; the large tree on the left to the shorter trees near the white house. Note especially the near side of the barn. An addition has been removed, leaving a line of pale paint. That's the kind of detail you can only find outdoors; you could never make it up in the studio.

Paint the heavier masses of snow into this stain. At the edges of these masses, pick up some of the hill color to suggest the beginning of a thaw. The stain also colors the snow patches in a variety of "accidental" ways. The shifts of color suggest thick and thin areas of snow. The thinness of the stain here emphasizes the weight of the snow cover.

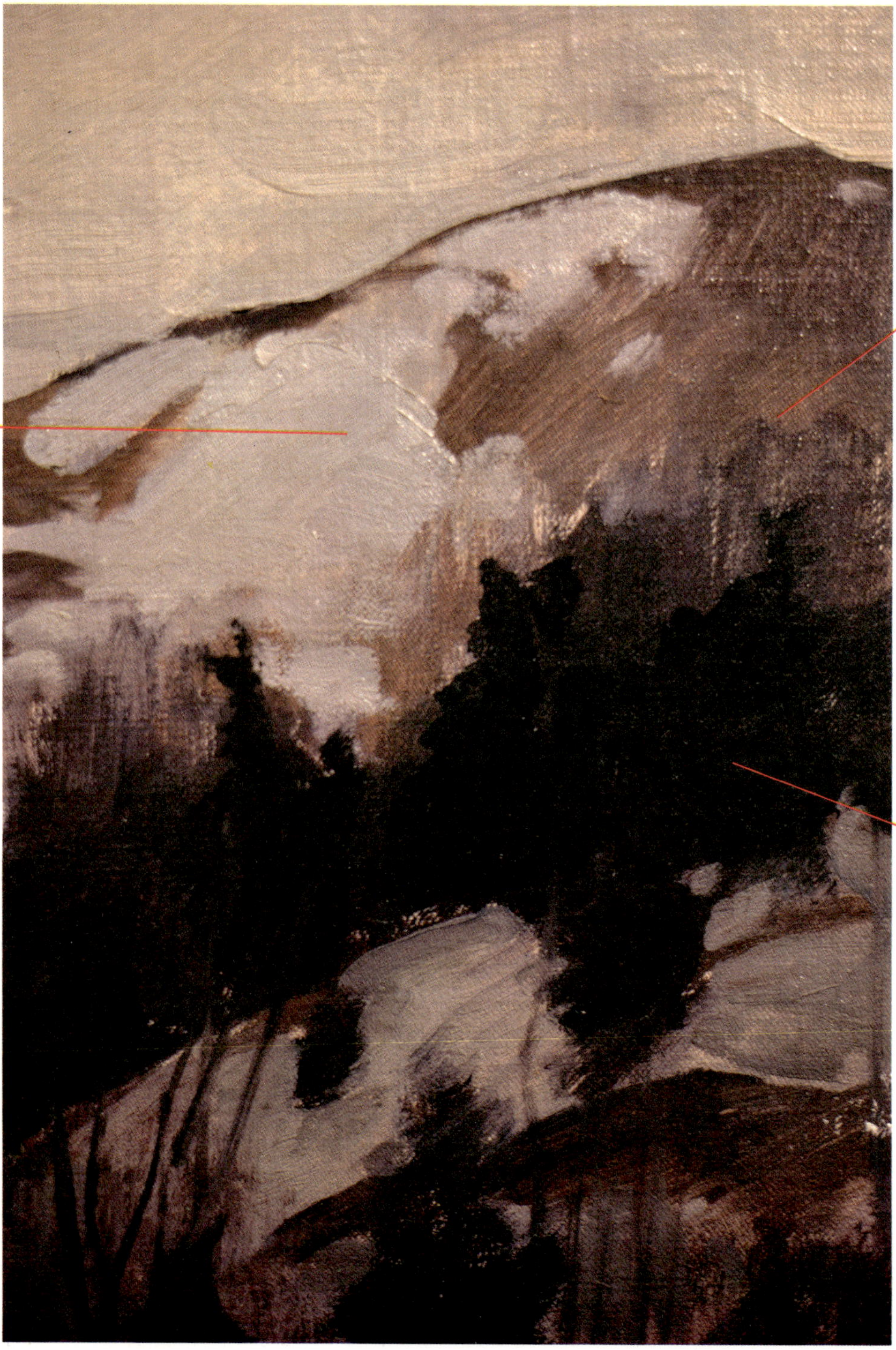

While blocking in, you can use a wash both for the mountains and for the slightly darker stain that suggests the distant pines.

Paint darker accents into the original evergreen stain. Where the stain shows through, it suggests masses of deciduous trees. Place these accents irregularly to create the impression that some evergreens are in front of distant trees and some behind them.

The Wash: Nearby Trees

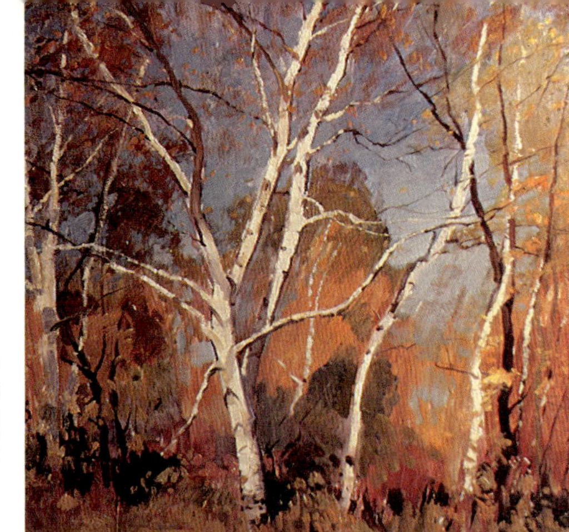

Hillside Birches
oil on canvas
20″ × 18″ (51 × 46 cm)
Collection of Mr. and Mrs. Alfred Movalli

The trick in this picture is to simplify the masses of foliage so they don't overpower the more important, lyrical line of the birch trees. The long, twisting branches enhance the delicacy of the subject. Pay particular attention to the way the central branches move toward one another, almost touch, and then shoot off in different directions. This often happens in nature, and capturing it adds a truthful note to the picture.

The sky—not quite as thickly painted as the birches—cuts into the area of stain and shapes it. Keep the sky flat, so it doesn't challenge the trees.

The distant foliage is a simple, warm stain. It's very thin and barely covers the canvas. In fact, if you swipe it with a cloth, it will make it even thinner and more transparent—creating the shimmer you feel when the sun hits masses of branches and dead leaves.

Once you have the thin stain down, work the much more thickly painted birches into it. You can see the brushstrokes of the white paint.

Add the branches last. They're broken notes, disappearing into nearby foliage or catching glints from the sun that make them sometimes visible, sometimes invisible against the background. The nearby leaves are thickly painted. This texture makes them look close to you.

The Wash: Smoke

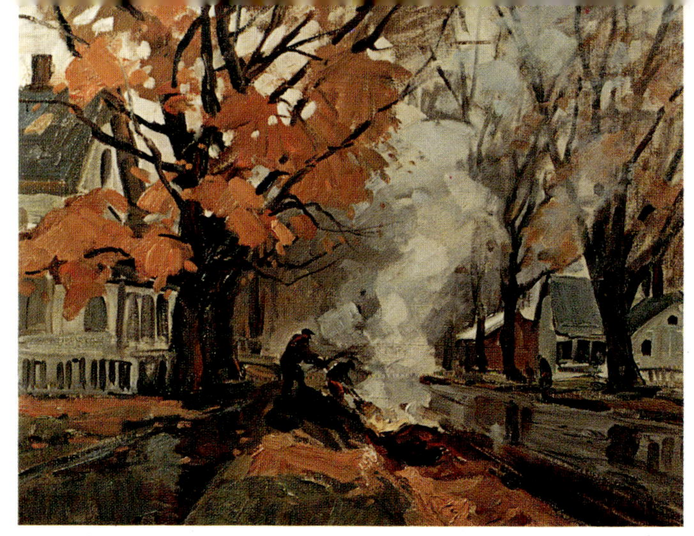

Burning Leaves
oil on canvas
18″ × 20″ (46 × 51 cm)

This scene was painted after a rainfall. The wet, burning leaves sent up billows of smoke. After a cold drizzle, it's nice to see a fire. And the smoke makes a fine color note in the composition: Its coolness contrasts with and accentuates the warm yellows and oranges of the fall foliage.

Take some of the dirty color on the brush and work a few strokes of it into the lighter areas of smoke, again suggesting a transparent area.

In the distance, the trees and houses become a thin stain. Block it in, leaving the canvas blank for the area of smoke.

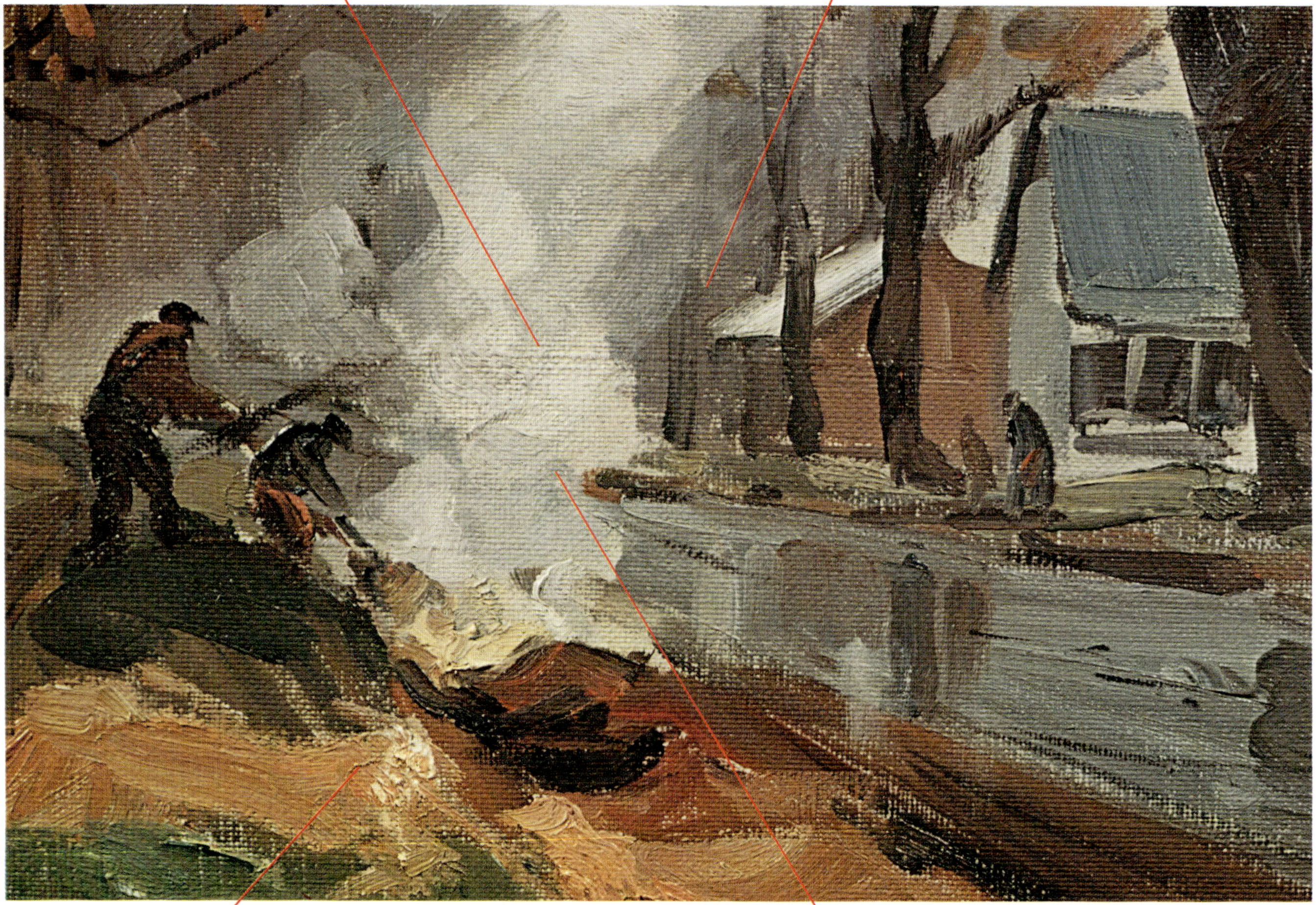

Accentuate the washy quality of the smoke by using an impasto in the immediate foreground. These heavy strokes suggest piles of fallen leaves.

When you add the equally thin smoke, pull it over and into the surrounding dark paint. The light diagonal strokes mix with the dark underpainting to suggest transparent puffs of smoke.

The Wash: Atmosphere

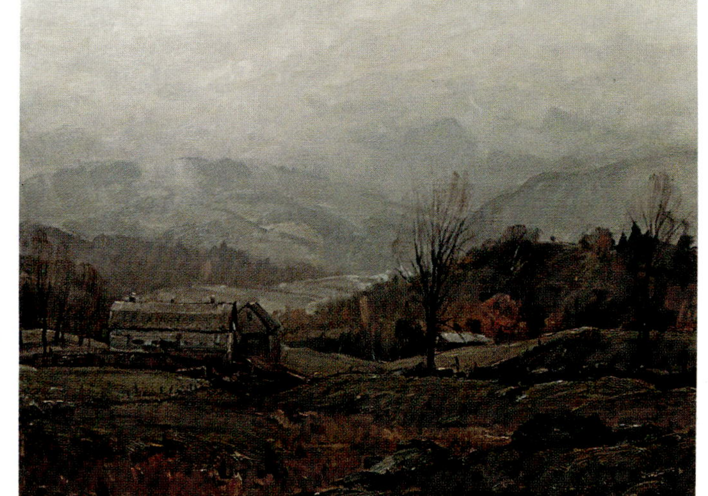

Foggy Day, Vermont
oil on canvas
25″ × 30″ (64 × 76 cm)

In this vast, atmosphere-filled valley the fog pulls together the distant values. The small buildings and trees not only emphasize the largeness of the scene; they also give some dark foreground notes. The heavily painted rocks and grass add weight to the foreground.

Use thicker paint for the whiffs of fog, brushing it over the edges of the topmost mountain. The strokes are concave and move upward, as would actual, wind-driven fog.

After staining the whole area with a midtone, work the darker mountain shapes into it.

Although this area is close in value, you can still tell the difference between maples and pines. The maples are blunt, upright strokes. The pines are darker and more pointed.

The Wash: Distance

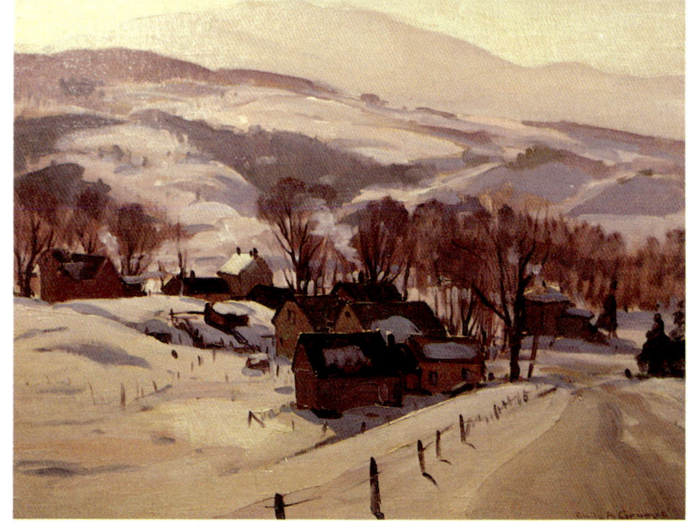

Mount Mansfield
oil on canvas
25″ × 30″ (64 × 76 cm)

Stain a warm tone behind the distant trees. Wash this area in and later add dark trunks and the hint of branches.

Paint snow over some of the stain. You can see the drybrush effect above the center of the trees. Catching the tooth of the canvas, the paint leaves a ragged edge that looks like distant snow peeping through the branches. It's important to take advantage of such an accidental development—a large part of "talent" is the ability to appreciate and utilize just such painting accidents.

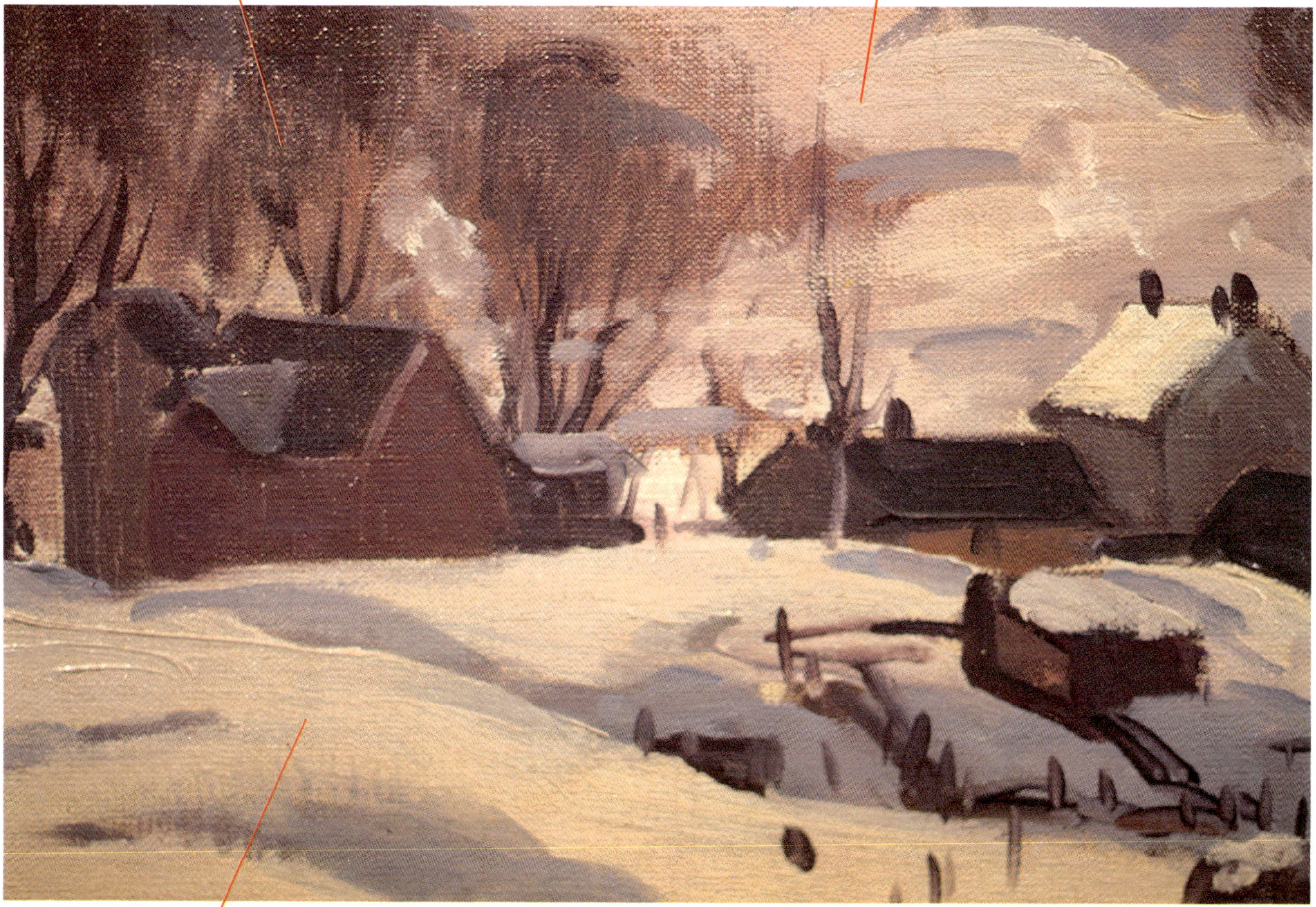

The foreground snowcover is painted thickly; the ridges of paint catch the light and emphasize the nearness of the area.

Note how the village was dwarfed by the nearby foothills and the great mountain. When a subject is backlit, there's a minimum of modeling, and we're left with a series of big silhouettes. Texture is not especially important, and a stain can be used to good effect.

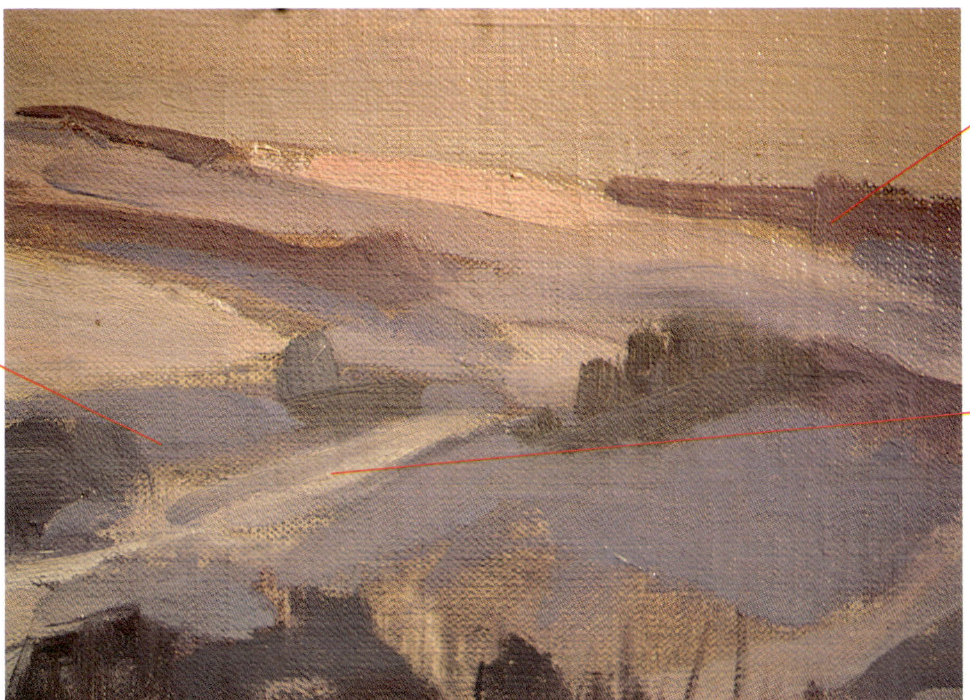

The farthest areas are painted very simply, with little brushwork within each mass. This flatness contrasts with the weight of the foreground buildings and pushes the foothills back in space.

Gray-green uprights suggest distant evergreens, while masses of purple stand for bushes and trees. Traces of the original stain look like branches and shrubs.

First stain the entire mountain reddish-brown. You can see the wash peeping through everywhere. Then work snow masses over it—some a clean white, others a cool gray. These flat, unmodulated masses show the lay of the land.

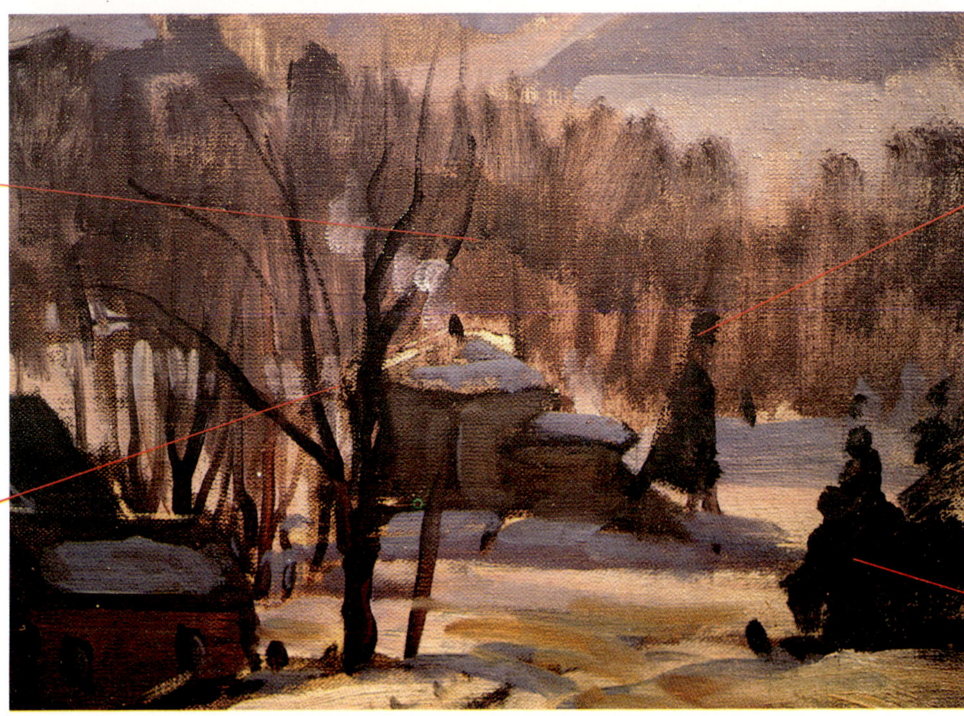

The warm color is first brushed on thinly. Work a series of upright strokes into this, hardly moving the brush as you lay it on the canvas. You can see the imprint of the end of the brush.

An up-and-down squiggle suggests a group of trunks. The stroke is like a series of interconnected Ws. Be careful not to cover the original stain. Light and luminous, it looks like distant sunlit branches and bushes.

A carefully drawn tree explains the impressionistic background. But even this tree is far from neat: Some of the branches don't even connect with the trunk.

A couple of thick, opaque evergreens accentuate the transparency of the washes.

The Wash: Foreground

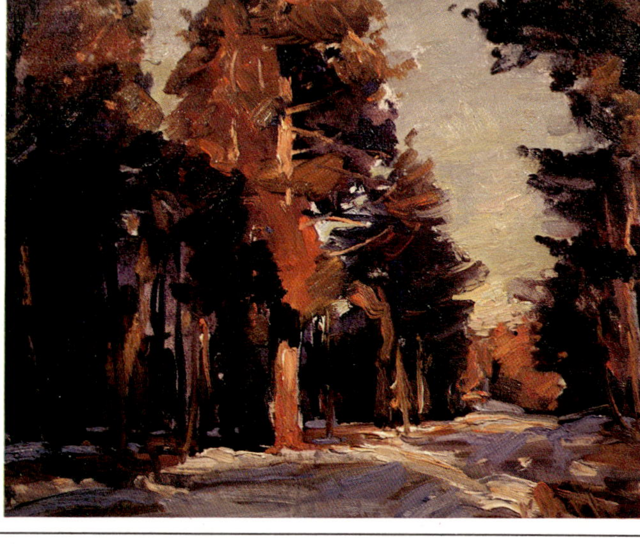

End of the Day
oil on canvas
18″ × 20″ (46 × 51 cm)
Collection of Charles Movalli

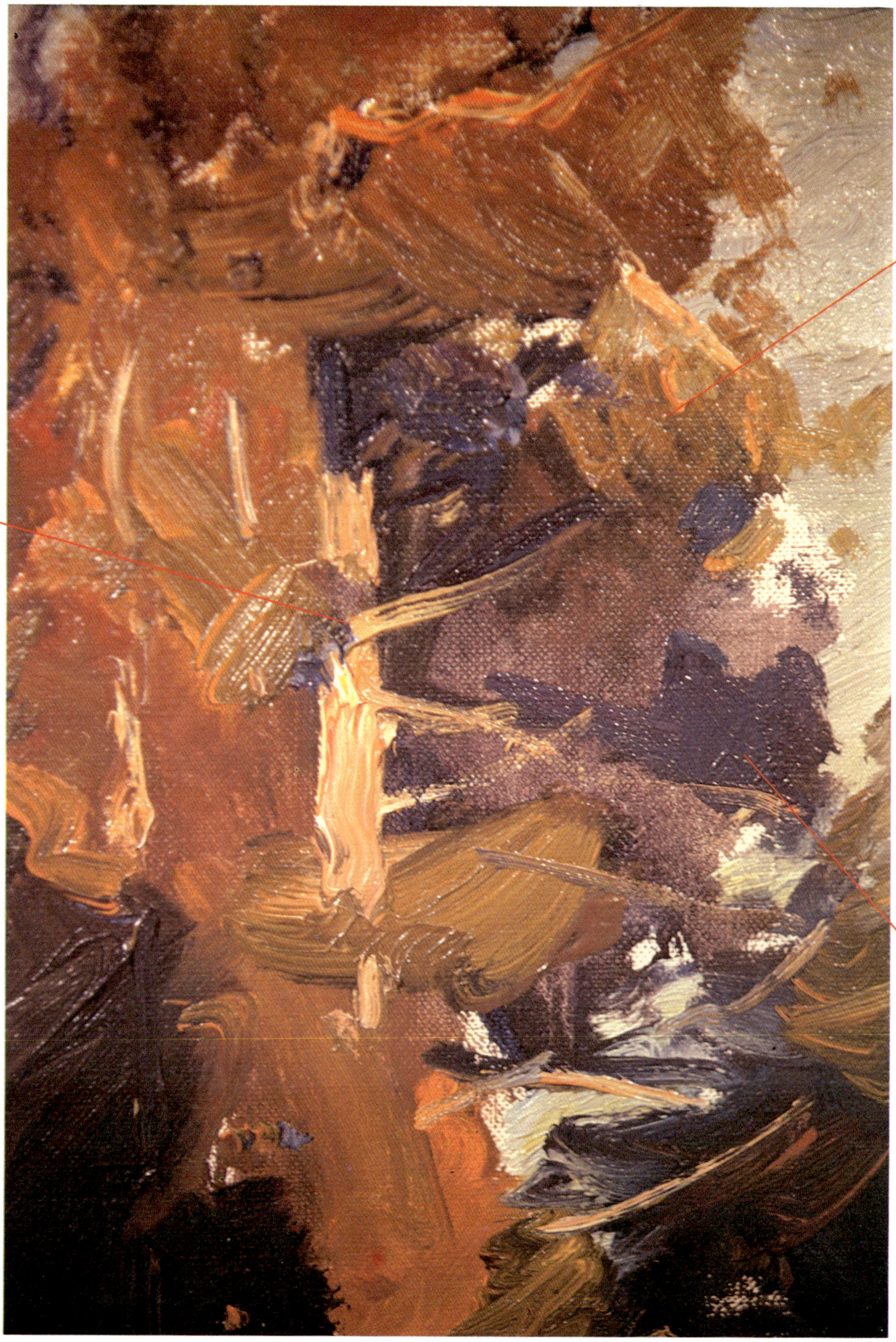

After blocking in the shadow area, add some darker, more opaque notes. But be sure to keep a lot of the original stain.

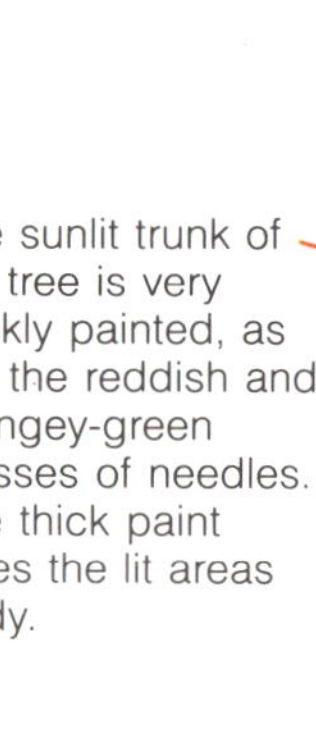

The sunlit trunk of the tree is very thickly painted, as are the reddish and orangey-green masses of needles. The thick paint gives the lit areas body.

The shadow area, on the other hand, is a purplish stain. Such a shadow is like a cup of black coffee: You can see your spoon in it even though it looks dark.

This picture was done at the end of a day's painting. After I'd worked all afternoon and was heading home, I saw this brilliant effect. Since the effect was a fleeting one, I had to work fast and make maximum use of a painterly shorthand: stains and impasto, big strokes and little.

The darks are so thinly painted that the tooth of the canvas is clearly visible. Here the stain is thin; as I move away from this spot, the stain covers the canvas more effectively.

Add warm highlights over the stain. They suggest distant trees catching the sun.

Here the stained and opaque areas become very abstract. If you saw this detail in a gallery, you'd think it was a painting by one of the "moderns." The stain still serves for the shadow area. To emphasize it, add a few opaque strokes.

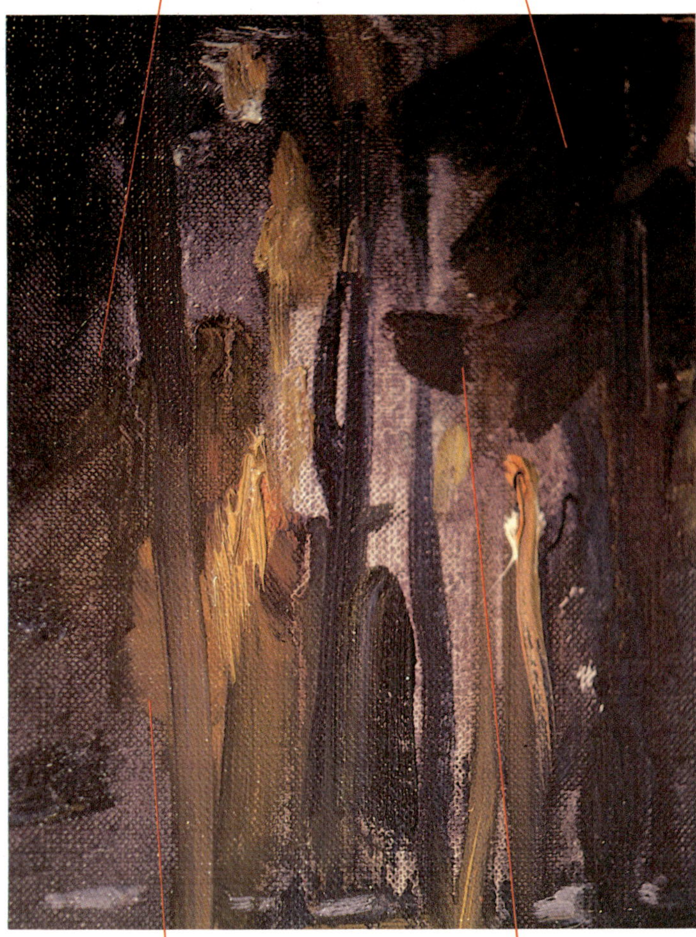

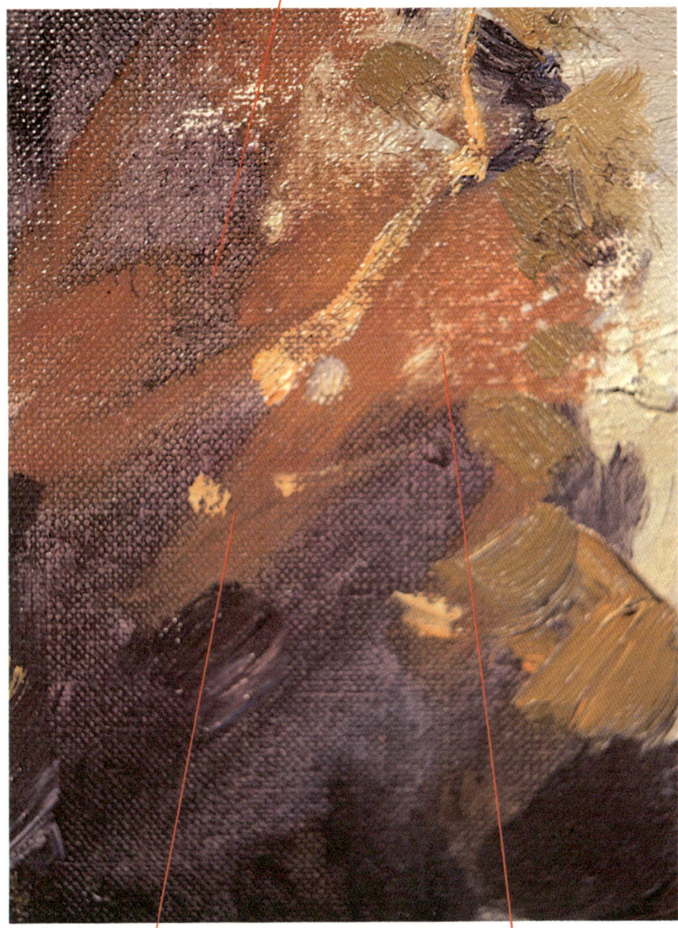

Opaque darks hint at distant trunks, while a dot or two adds interest and suggests something in the distance.

A few dark, opaque strokes indicate clumps of drooping needles.

A few short, warm, ochrish strokes suggest the branches. Dots indicate areas where most of the branch is shadowed while small segments occasionally catch the light.

The brilliantly lit evergreens are suggested by thinly painted orange areas with a touch of green impasto. They're less forceful than the masses near the center of interest.

Mood: Strength

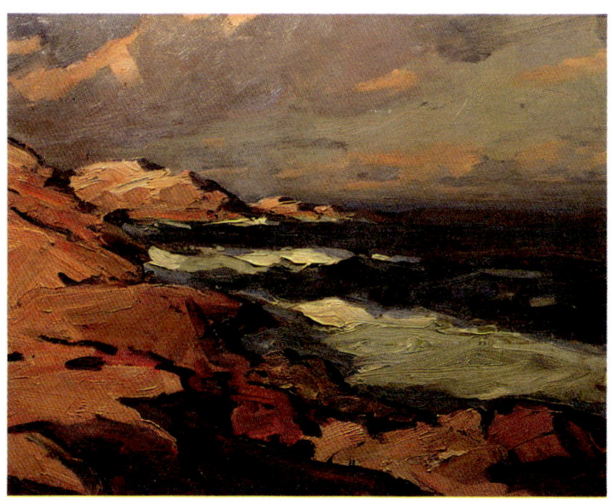

The Backshore
oil on canvas
25″ × 30″ (64 × 76 cm)

This is a large painting, but it was painted with the simplicity of an 8″ × 10″. Late in the day, the sun is low in the sky and hits the rocks with a strong blast of light. As you've seen, strong outdoor light takes the modeling out of objects. It's not like painting a still-life in the studio, where the relatively weak light lets you experience the roundness of things. The sun breaks nature into three simple units: lights, darks, and midtones. This simplicity often gives great dignity to a subject: In this case, it enhances the monumentality of the rocks and ocean.

The ocean is a dark mass of blue. Greenish water is churning in the foreground, while waves are represented by heavily impastoed globs of white. Subtlety is sacrificed to monumentality.

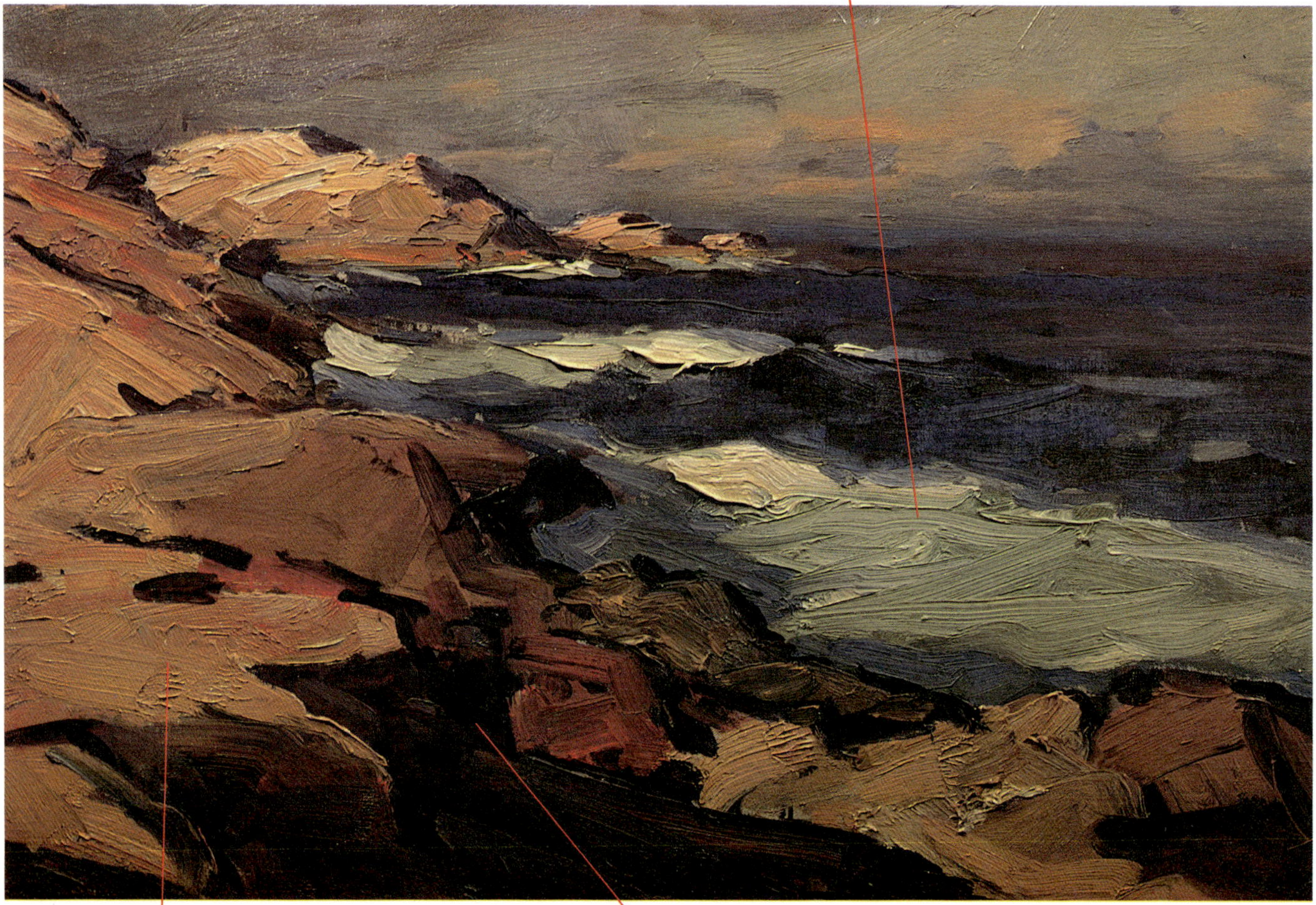

Although the rocks are fissured by thousands of crevices, you can feel their simplicity and weight and paint them that way. You can see how little modulation there is within them. Don't worry about "atmospheric perspective." It's a clear day: Why shouldn't the background rocks be almost as strong as those in the foreground?

The shadowside of the rocks is indicated by bold dark lines. The distant shadows are equally forceful.

Mood: Festival

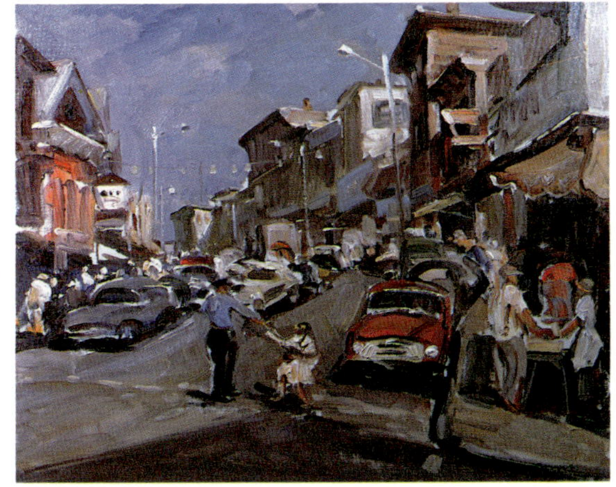

Sidewalk Bazaar
oil on canvas
25″ × 30″ (64 × 76 cm)

This painting is completely different from the preceding one. My hometown has an annual fair, and I painted it one year in a free outdoor demonstration—my contribution to the festivities. What struck me was the life and activity of the street. Simple masses wouldn't have worked here, so I emphasized the different textures of the cars, people, and buildings. I wanted a happy feeling, one that fit my mood as I tried to paint with a hundred onlookers jostling my elbow.

There were perhaps three or four dots in the preceding painting because the playfulness that such dots often add to a picture wouldn't have been appropriate. Here, the dot is a theme: You can see it in the cars, in the lights across the street, and especially in the heads of the milling crowd.

In the preceding painting, reflected light is played down in order to emphasize the massiveness of the forms. Here, note the way the light reflects off the street and buildings and bounces into the shadows. You can actually see the broken, multicolored strokes.

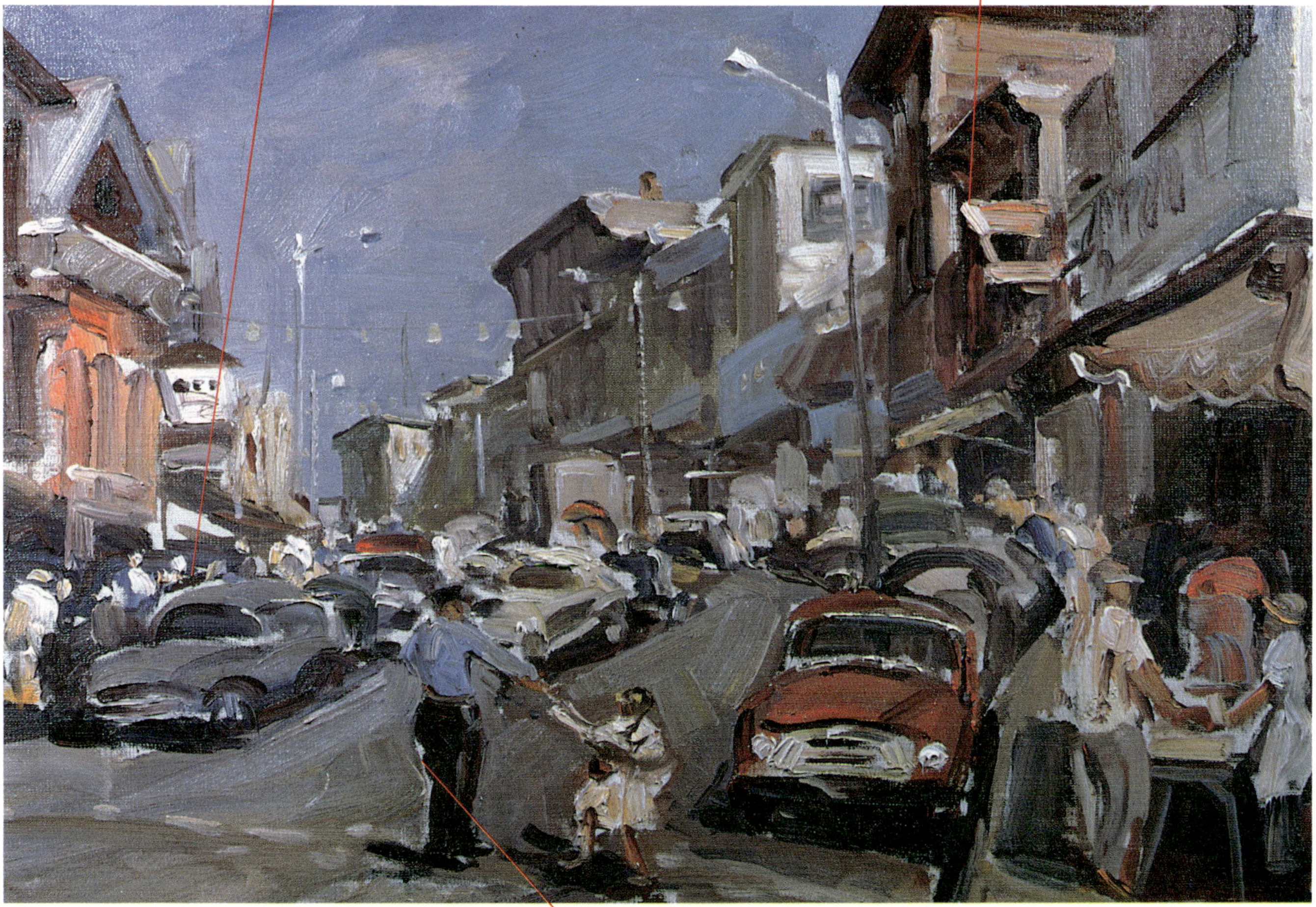

Almost no canvas shows through in the previous painting: Uncovered canvas would break up the forms. Here, to express the idea of lively, broken forms, it's necessary to leave unpainted canvas around the figures, for example, as well as the edges of the buildings.

Mood: Static

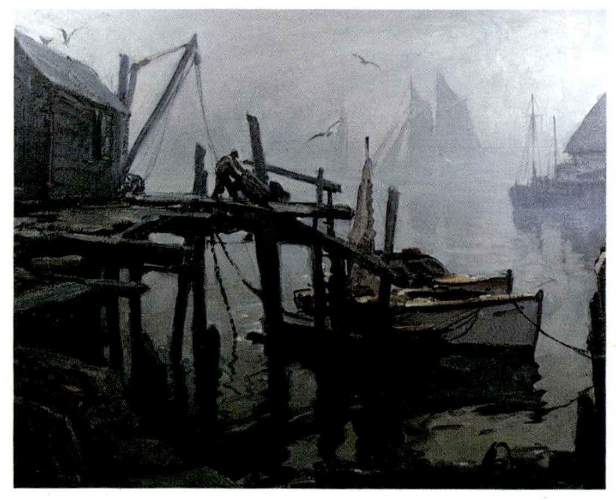

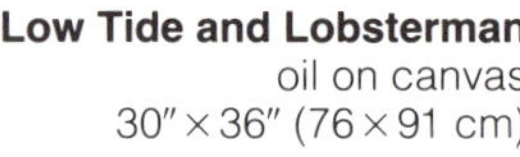

Low Tide and Lobsterman
oil on canvas
30″ × 36″ (76 × 91 cm)

This foggy day picture tells what happens under a dock, especially in the pilings, their angles, and the spaces between them. What's important is the solemnity of the scene—its stillness and dignity. The lighting adds to the effect: It creates simple silhouettes against a bright background. The strong verticals enhance the quiet, relatively static mood.

The shapes are painted flatly, with the building, wharf, and rocks all a similar grayish color. They're wet and reflect the color of the sky.

The background shapes are large and simple. Boat and buildings form a unit, with only a stroke or two to separate objects.

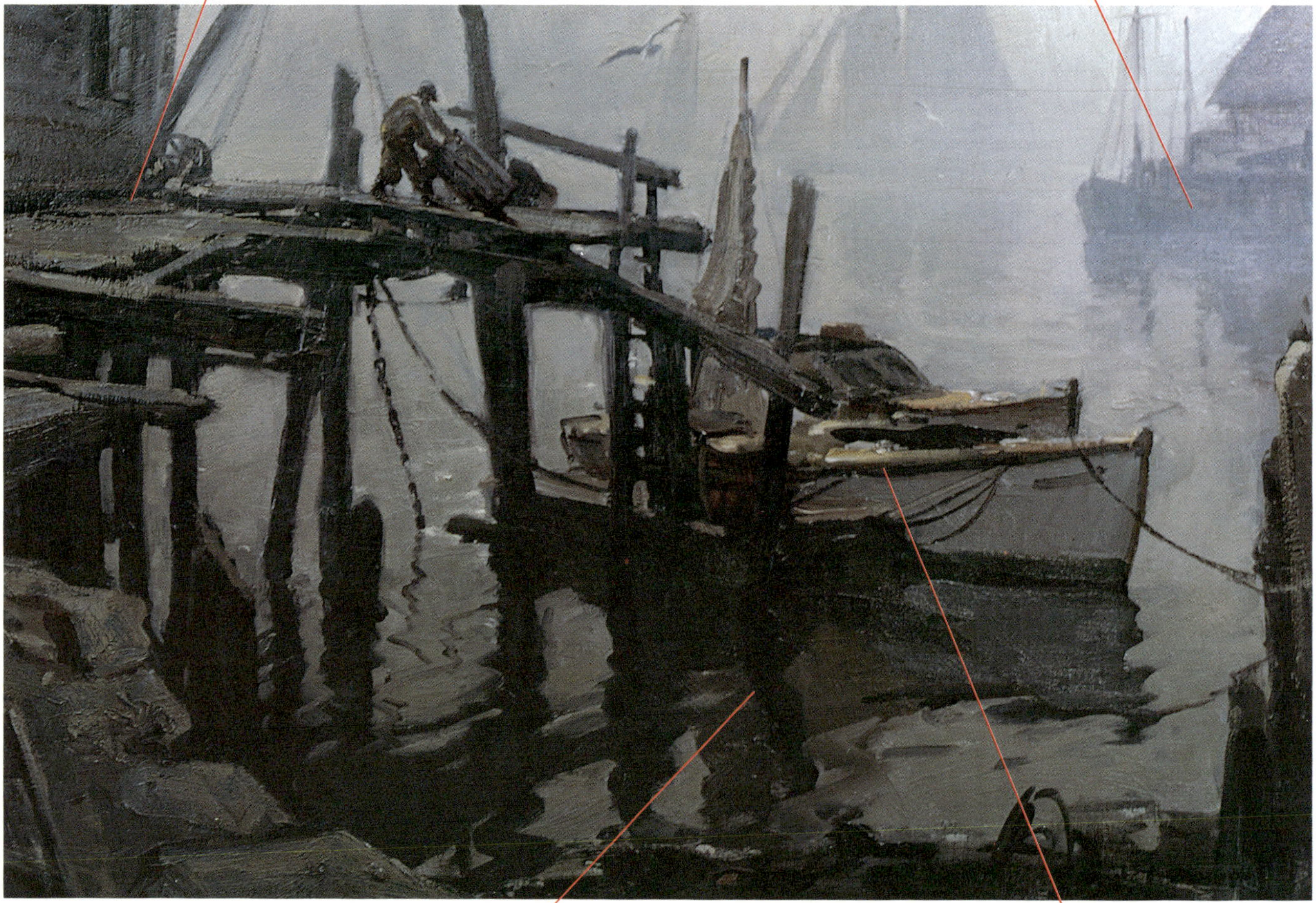

The reflections are fairly flat. Students usually try to paint every break in a reflection, but that's impossible. The general movement is more important. In a picture like this one, busy reflections would destroy the mood.

In these flatly painted boats, the color is on the decks—a few touches of warm orange. These are the *only* really warm notes in the painting. The touches add interest to the foreground and, by contrast, emphasize the cooler, more lavender colors of the buildings and water.

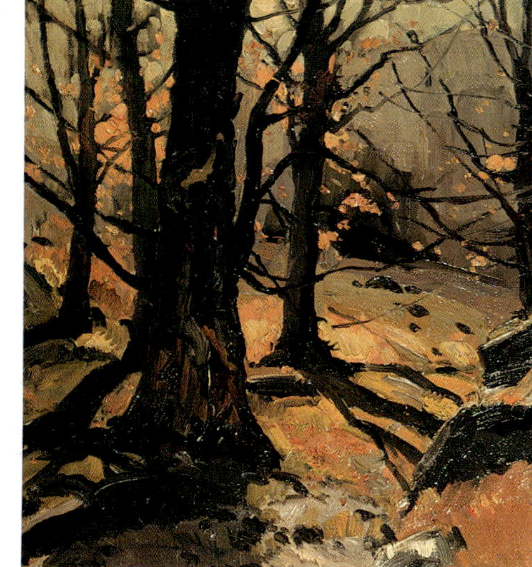

Fall Woods
oil on canvas
20″ × 18″ (51 × 46 cm)

In some ways, this scene is similar to the preceding one: the background is the brightest area, and all the foreground elements are silhouetted against it. Otherwise, the mood is completely different. The color scheme alone sets the pictures apart. One is full of subtle, cool grays; the other of brilliant reds, greens, and purples. The day has a festive quality. It's like a party, with dancing trees and balloons for leaves.

The mass of dead leaves in the foreground is painted with up, down, and wriggling strokes. The only twisting stroke in the previous painting was in the water. Here, the swiggling stroke adds a feeling of life. It appears not only in the grass, but also in the branches and the bark of the tree.

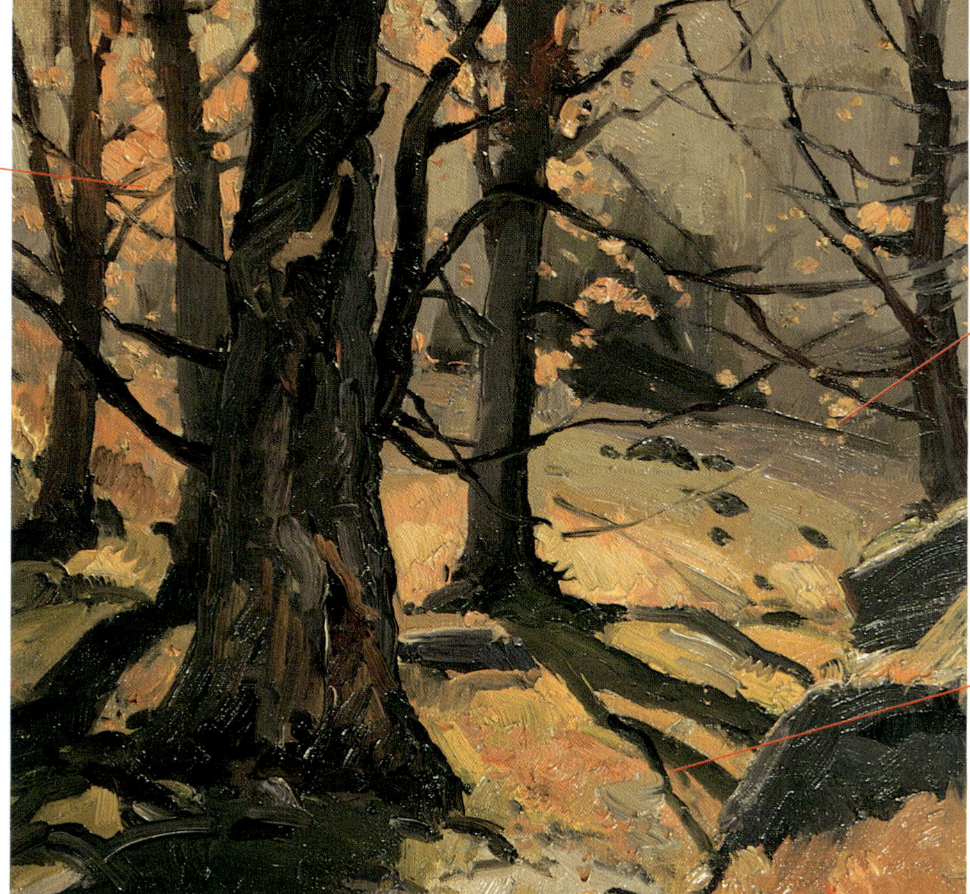

A flatter, more diagonal stroke takes over as we move back in space; the lay of the land becomes more important than the small dead leaves that cover it. Dark dots suggest distant rocks—a stroke that is echoed in the foreground and in the leaves overhead. They add to the scene's festive feelings.

The previous painting was dominated by upright lines. This painting has a swaying movement. Nothing is static: Even the shadows twist and break as they move irregularly over the land.

Mood: Sunny Day

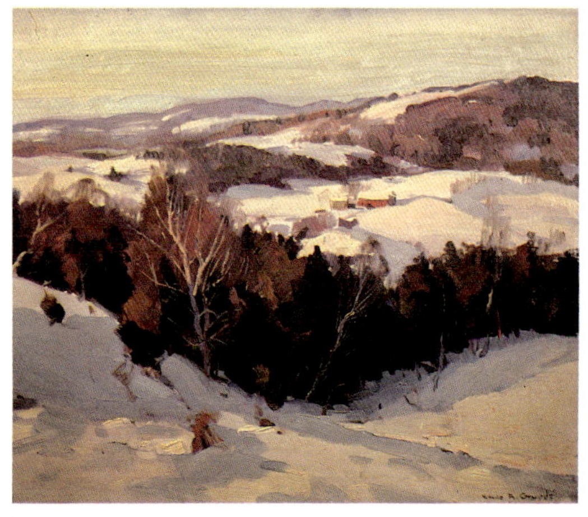

Dairy Country
oil on canvas
25″ × 30″ (64 × 76 cm)

In this as well as the next painting, note how the patches of snow-covered fields work their way up into the mountains. This kind of land formation adds to the interest of farming communities and makes them fun to paint. In the foreground, a swirling shadow leads you to the principal birch tree and up its brilliantly lit trunk to the distant mountains. The tree acts as a bridge, helping you get over the impenetrable mass of pines.

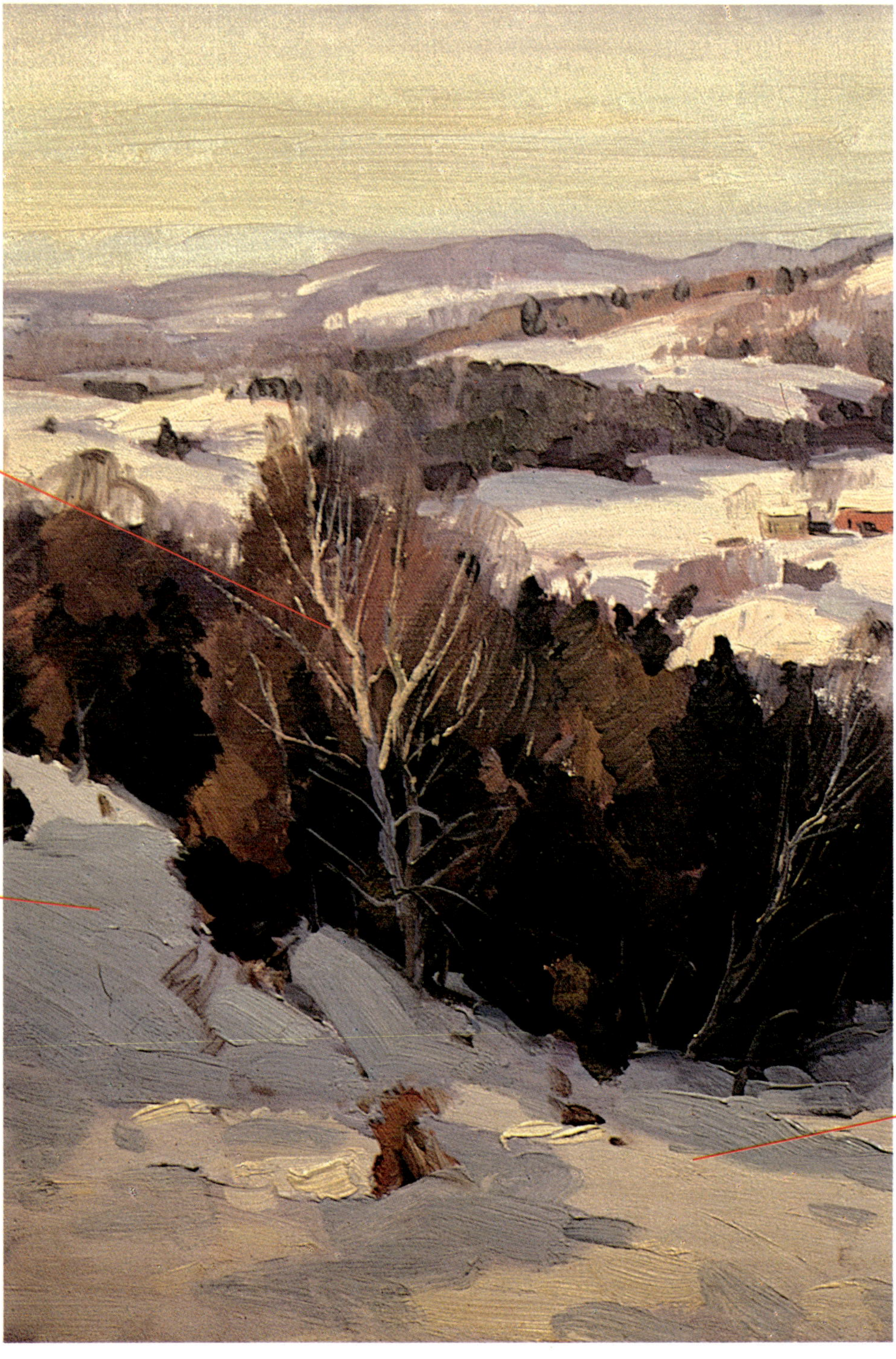

Use equally heavy paint when describing the sunlit trees. Paint the mass of evergreens first, and then pull the birch tree over them, making sure to get the birch right on the first try.

Although there's a lot in this book about staining shadows, the darks here are painted very thickly—you can see how the strokes follow the contour of the hill. The heavy, opaque feeling of the snow demands a similarly rich shadow.

Load the paint on the sunlit snow, working in long, broad strokes. They help you feel the weight of the snow on the land. Use broken strokes to suggest shadows and irregularities in the snow cover.

Mood: Gray Day

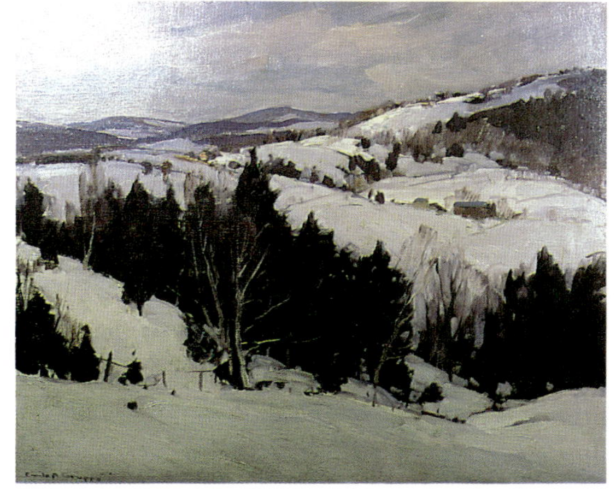

Dairy Country: Gray Day
oil on canvas
25″ × 30″
(64 × 76 cm)

On a gray day, the same site takes on a much more sober look. The scene is reduced to a black-and-white pattern: dark trees and mountains against the light sky and snow. Strong warm and cool contrasts are lacking, and although the picture is painted heavily, it doesn't suggest the rich textures that you feel in the preceding painting. There's also a compositional change. Since the brightly lit birch can no longer be used as a bridge into the distance, a break in the trees has been introduced on the lower right. Your eye slides past the birch, down to the opening, and then up the mountain. A fence helps direct you to this open spot.

There are also less value changes in the painting. The pines are dark, for example, but the snow is gray in comparison, and even the birch is a relatively dark value. To express the quiet of the scene, make the birch and the pine behind it straighter than in the preceding painting.

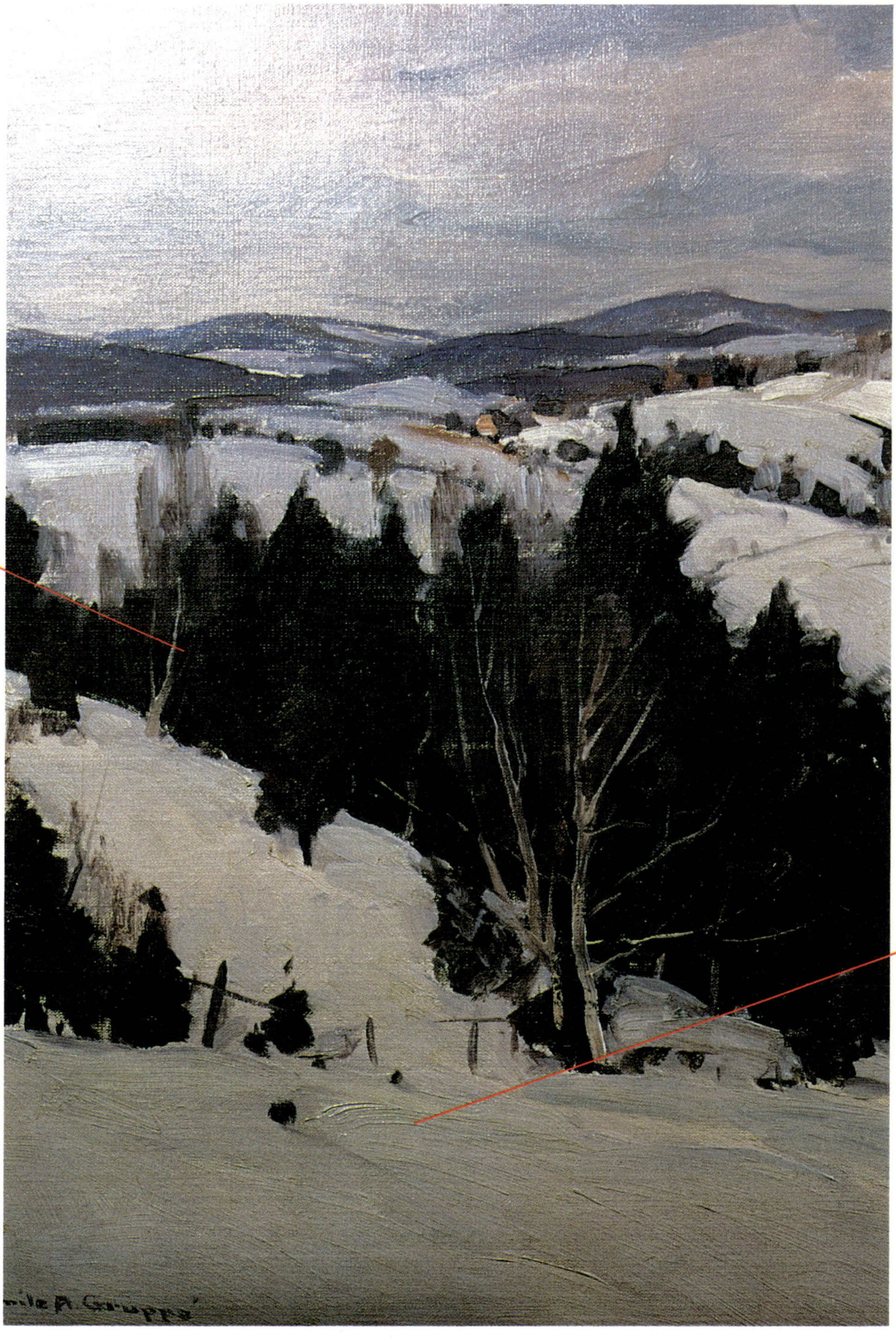

There's no broken brushwork in the foreground. A broad, less obvious stroke emphasizes the flatness of the land.

Rhythm

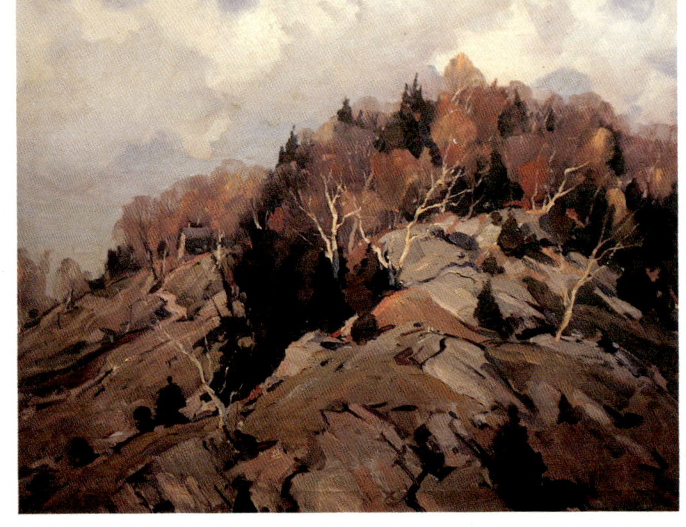

Rocky Hillside
oil on canvas
30″ × 36″ (76 × 91 cm)

The ground is also painted with a variety of strokes, but these are less noticeable: The rocks are what count.

In contrast to the rocks' blunt, angular strokes, add a few dark lines to suggest twisting, curved breaks in the rock.

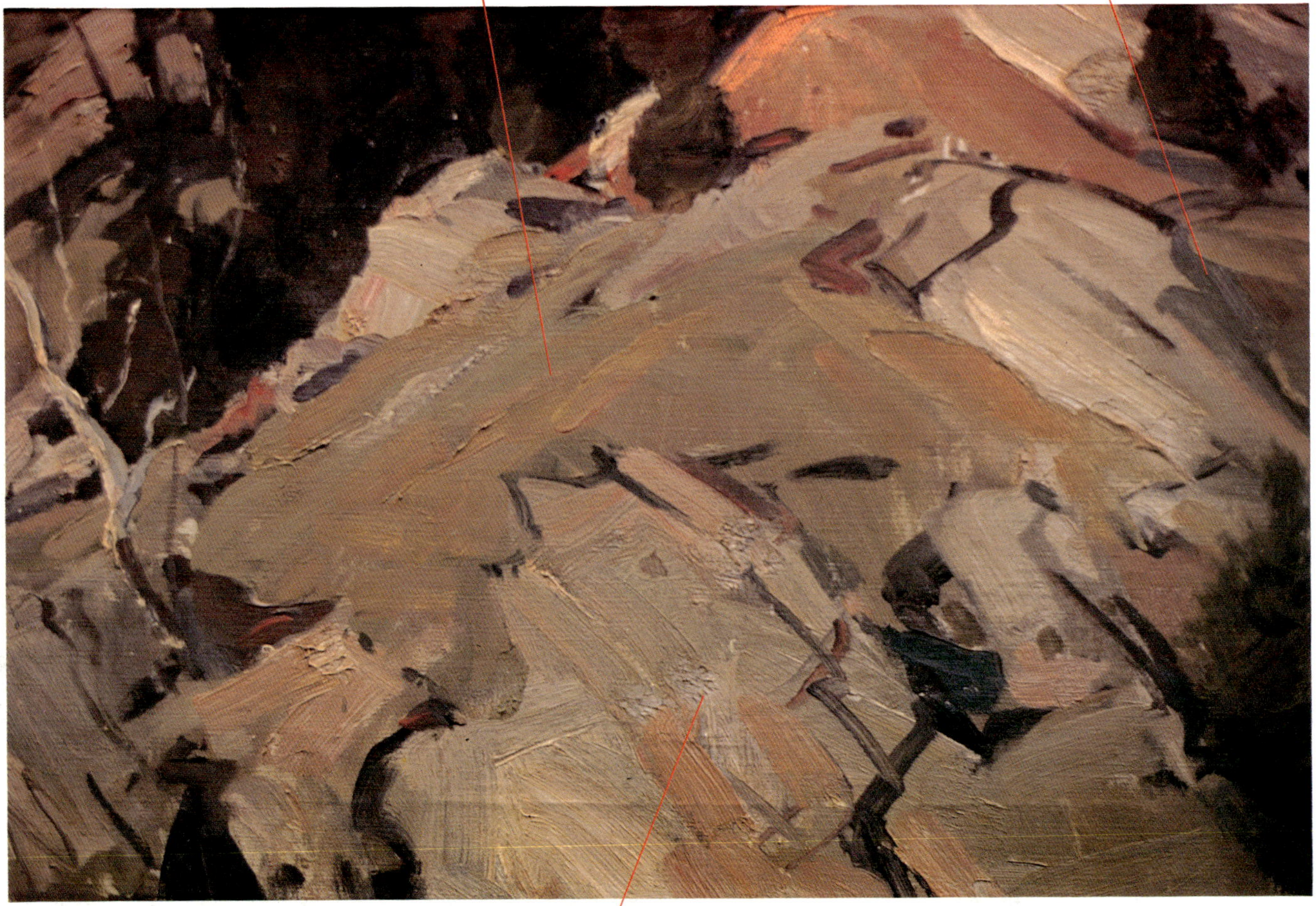

The rocks move diagonally, but there's a variety of brushstrokes within the masses. The rock on the left is relatively textureless: A few dark lines show how it slants. The center rock is made of strokes that move in a contrasting direction. The heavy, orange stroke suggest weight, texture, and the effect of the sun.

There's always a strong rhythm running through the landscape. Try to find these important, large movements—the "leading lines" of the subject—and emphasize them. Even exaggerate or distort them if you feel that will tell a better story. Here, what's exciting is the movement of the rocks up the hillside. These angular, staccato notes contrast with the rounded, lyrical shapes of the trees and clouds. You can *feel* these oppositions as you look at the painting.

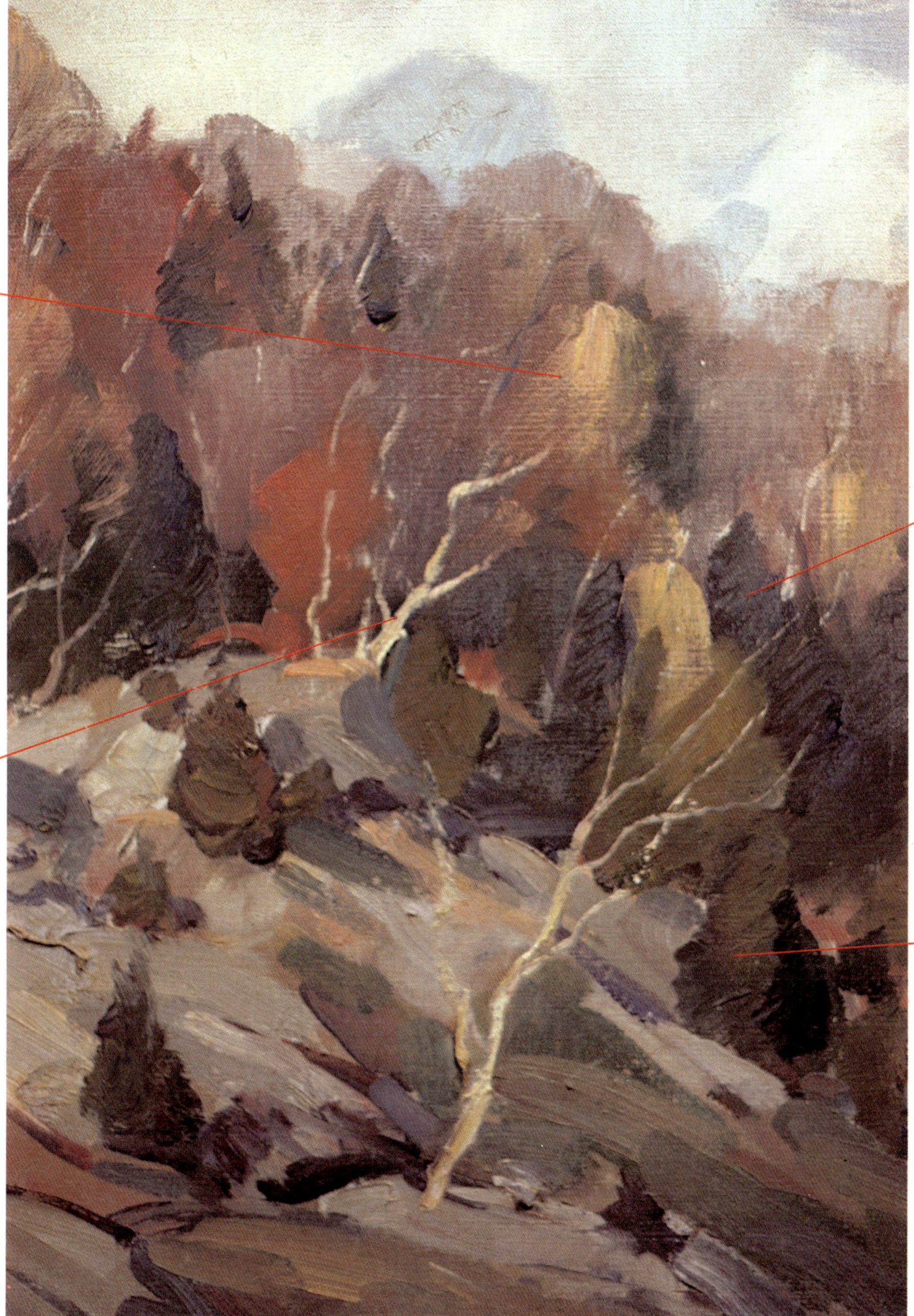

The trees behind the birch are painted with a blurred stroke to make sure the birch would stand out. Squint and you'll see how simple this distant mass is.

Far back, the rocks and grass become simple slashes of color.

The birches are another lyrical note. To emphasize their delicacy and grace, paint only the most important branches. The trees slant in a way that counterpoint the long, diagonal strokes of the ground and nearby rocks.

Notice the contrast between the pointed pines and the rounded shapes of the nearby trees. If you play up the sharpness of the evergreens, these dark, opaque spots emphasize the swaying movement of the trees. Cover these evergreens with your hand, and you'll see that the distance loses much of its effect.

Textures

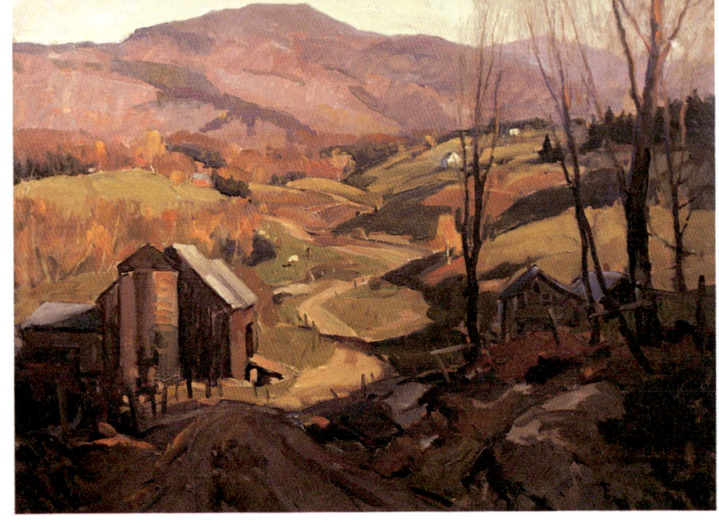

The Farm in the Valley
oil on canvas
30″ × 36″ (76 × 91 cm)

In contrast to the rocks, the grass and bushes are painted with upright strokes. Don't bother to show either blades of grass or twigs and stems in the bushes. That kind of detail would make the foreground too interesting; instead you should look *over* the foreground and into the distance.

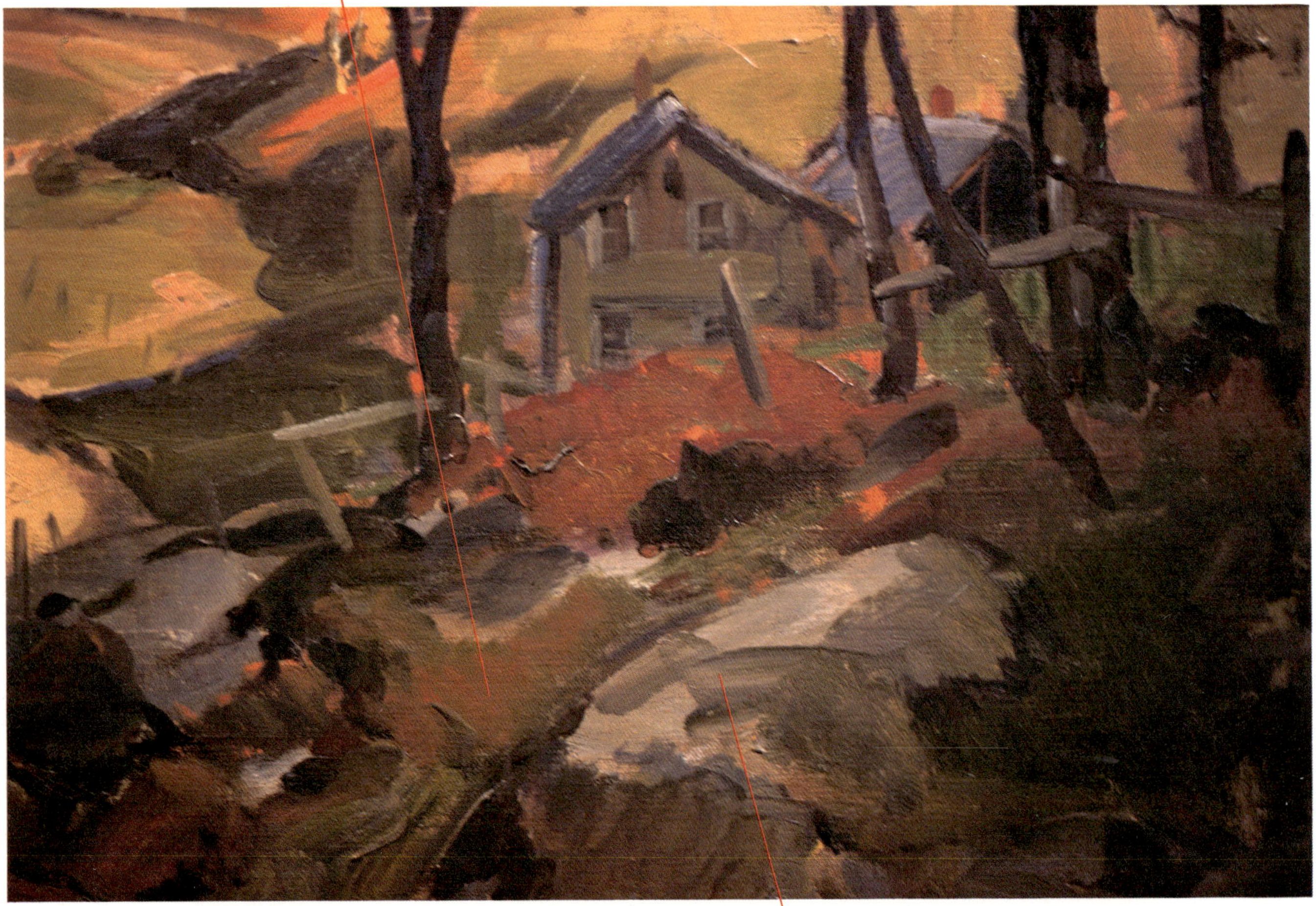

The most texture is in the foreground, where large, broad, diagonal strokes suggest boulders. A few dark lines emphasize their rounded, slanting shapes.

In this panoramic scene, note how the shadowed foreground, late in the day, accentuates the brightly lit distance. Frank Brangwyn, the great English muralist, always used this device with great effect. The dark nearby trees emphasize the sense of distance. They overlap the lightest, most distant part of the landscape.

The distance is thinly painted. A wash of color gives it a luminous glow.

Paint dark shadows into the mountain. The nearest shadow mass is irregular in shape; you sense that trees cut in front of it, though you don't have to bother to draw them. The shadow is painted *over* the stain, but it looks like it's in back of it!

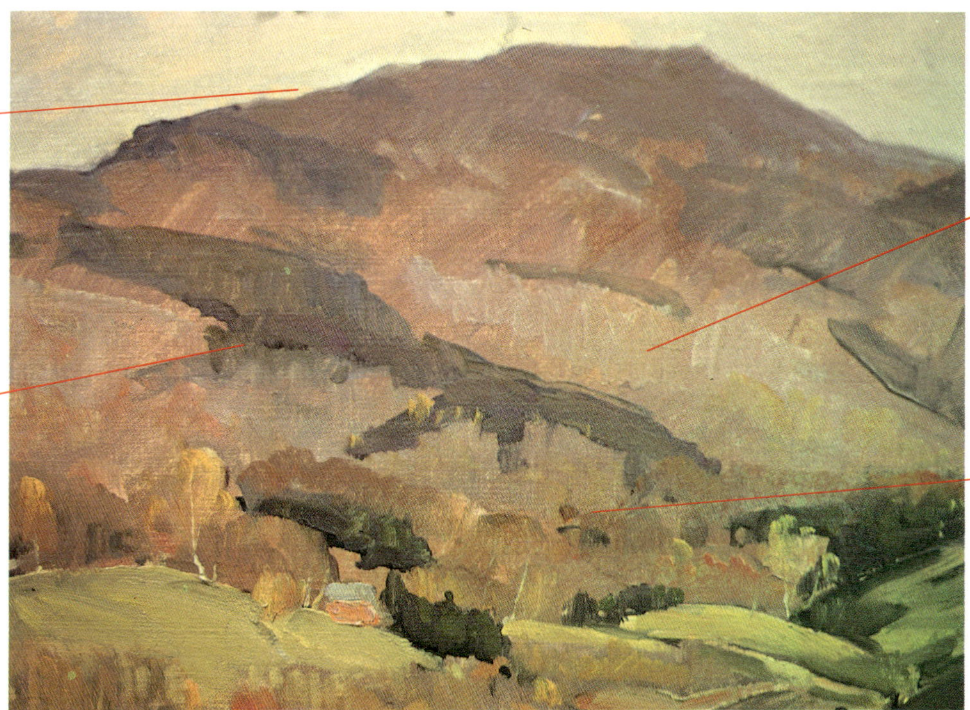

Work into the stain with a similar color, but add white to give the area opacity and make it seem closer.

The foothills are closer to us and so richer and thicker in color. There's a hint of a yellow tree, and a few strokes to indicate distant tree trunks. You see those few strokes and *imagine* a hundred more.

To show the height of the silo, paint it with three upright strokes: One stroke shows where the light hits; another where the silo goes into shadow; and another where light reflects into it from the surroundings. Eight short strokes explain the horizontal ribbing that holds the silo together.

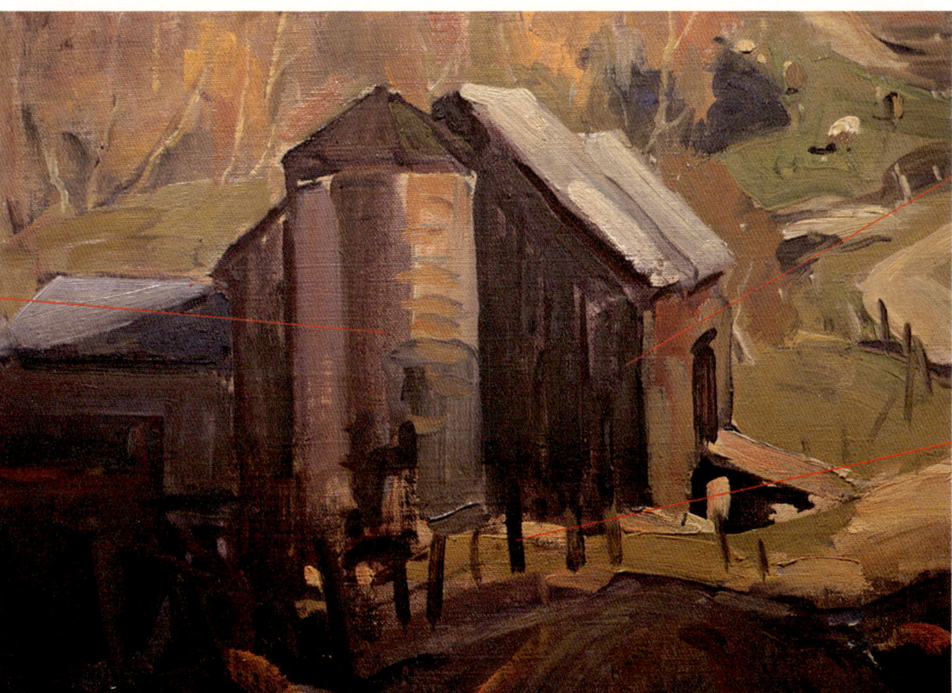

The barn is made of upright boards. First stain the building; then work vertical strokes over the stain. Although the front of the building is made of similar boards, the sunlight obliterates detail. A few strokes of color are enough. Dark lines sharpen up the architecture.

The posts get smaller as they recede. Recognizable strokes in the foreground, they're just light dots in the distance. Pull the nearest posts into and over the barn, making them part of that important mass.

BUILDINGS

When you paint buildings, think first of their *character*. They're man-made objects and are in geometric contrast with the natural surroundings—with the rolling hills and the rounded shapes of nearby trees. Stress this angular structure. If something obscures these characteristic shapes, remove the obstruction. The viewer wants to see how the building is put together; otherwise you'll confuse him or her.

When you paint buildings, either paint them small, so they become part and parcel of their surroundings, or paint them big. If you want to stress their size, run them right off the canvas. Be careful not to divide the canvas equally between buildings and landscape; the viewer won't know what you're trying to paint.

I prefer to do *groups* of buildings. When you paint a single structure, there's a danger the picture will be too specific. If the viewer isn't familiar with the building, he or she might not be interested in your painting. I'm reminded of the commissions I get to paint a person's house. The picture is of great interest to the homeowner—but to no one else.

When you paint houses, paint what you see. Distant buildings are textures. If you try to "copy" them, your background won't be a background: It'll be a collection of houses. Also try to sense the history of your buildings. They weren't built yesterday. See where they sag, where a new board replaces an older one, where the roof and the walls have been weathered and battered.

Keep scale in mind too. Your largest buildings should be in the foreground, with the smaller ones in the distance. At a site, there may be a one-story structure near you and a three-story one in the background. They look the same size. But don't paint them that way. You'll confuse the viewer, who expects buildings to get smaller as they recede. If you don't give the expected clues, he or she won't understand the spatial relationships of the picture.

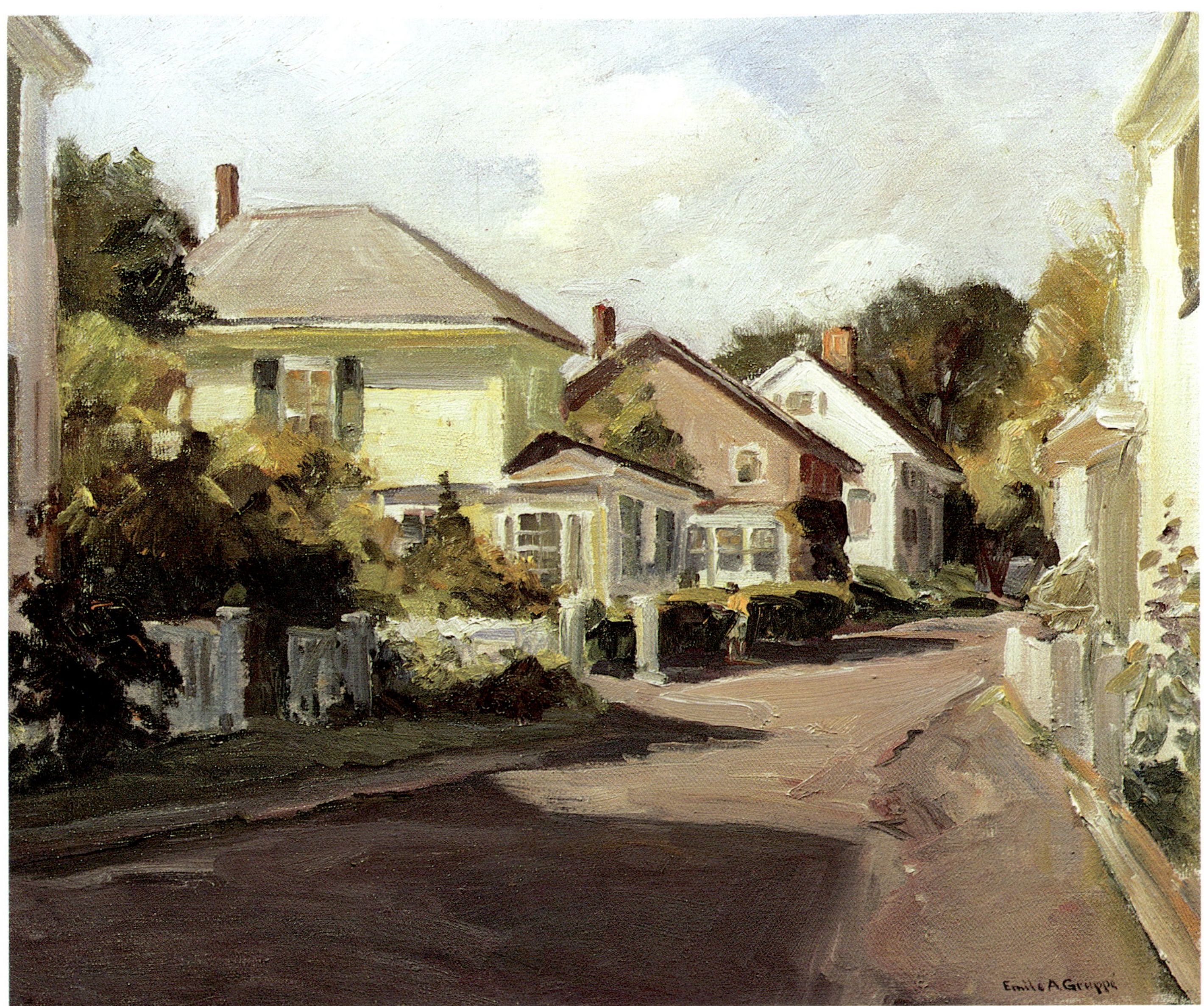

Rockport Street
oil on canvas
25″ × 30″ (64 × 76 cm)

Painters often find the summer a hard time to paint: it's too green. Here, all the green areas are underpainted with cool purples and warm oranges. Green is worked into this underpainting, thus modifying it and keeping it from being too vivid. The house in the distance is pure white. The nearer one has yellow in it; the yellow brings it forward. The foreground shadow has cool strokes within it; they show where the sky affects it. The distant shadow is dark and sharp. Since it's so far back, we can't look into it and see subtle shifts of color. The brown house makes the picture. It separates the light houses and accentuates the whiteness of the one in the distance.

Buildings: Backlit

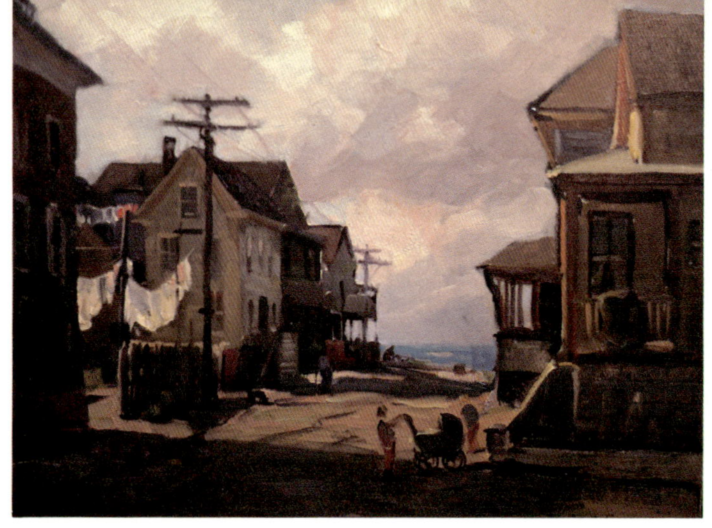

The Fort
oil on canvas
20″ × 24″ (51 × 61 cm)

The late afternoon sun throws dark shadows across the road and hits the hanging clothes with a strong blast of light. The buildings are dark silhouettes against the sky. The simple life of these people is suggested by the wash, the figures working in the distancc, and the kid pushing the baby carriage in the foreground. The large buildings come out of either side of the canvas. You feel as if you're *among* them, standing in the middle of the foreground shadow.

Vertical strokes suggest doors and windows. The upper windows catch the warm color of the surrounding sky. Each window is different: a light and dark stroke, a small light stroke with a hint of dark beneath it, a single dark stroke.

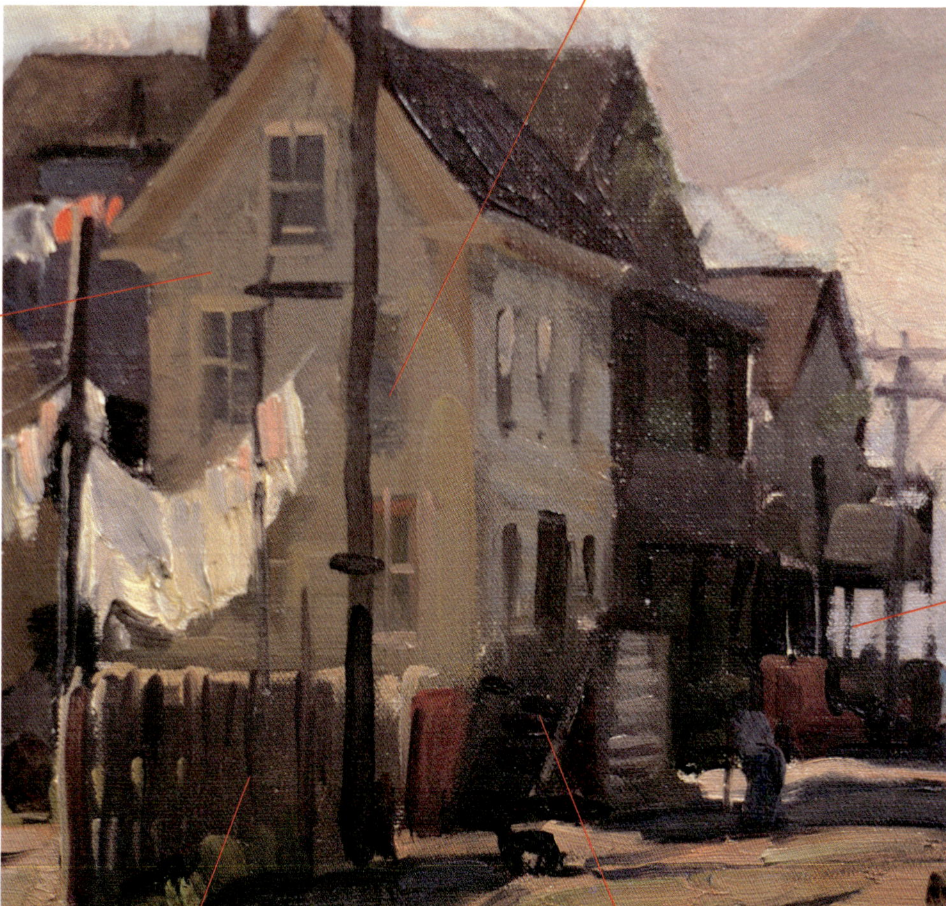

The house is cooler on the street side, where it catches color from the sky. The side facing us gets warm reflected light from the fenced-in courtyard.

Posts hold up a two-story porch. You see these strokes and imagine the other architectural details.

The fence is a dark stain, with a few dark uprights to suggest posts. An irregular highlight separates the fence from the house.

The stairs are a dark mass: Horizontal strokes suggest steps and a diagonal slash is a railing.

Buildings: Frontlit

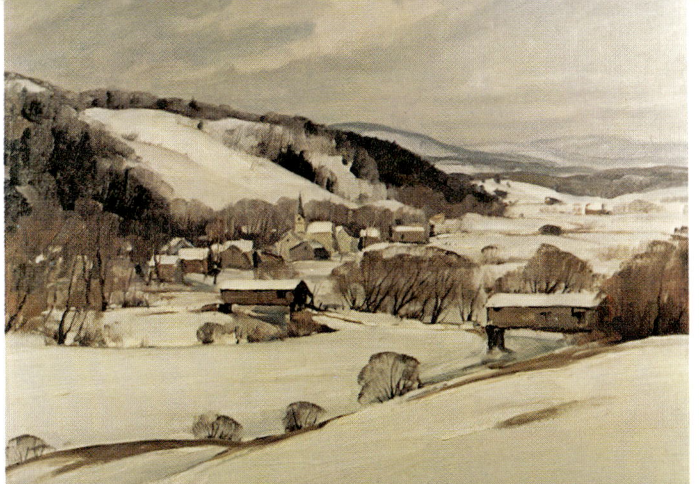

Town of Cambridge
oil on canvas
30″ × 36″ (76 × 91 cm)

Look at the way the town nestles in the valley, surrounded by bulging hills and mountains. It was painted much as it was. Were I to do the picture again, I'd make the hills even more rounded and imposing. Everything is tied together by a brown, ochrish color. You can start at the lower left and follow this color through the picture.

Overlap some of the buildings, so you know where they stand in space. Don't paint buildings like toy soldiers, all in a row.

Trees accent the white roofs and form a simple, *untextured* backdrop. A few thin fanning strokes suggest trunks.

The buildings are an interconnected group, with only a few free-standing structures. Horizontal and vertical strokes tell the story. A dot suggests a window.

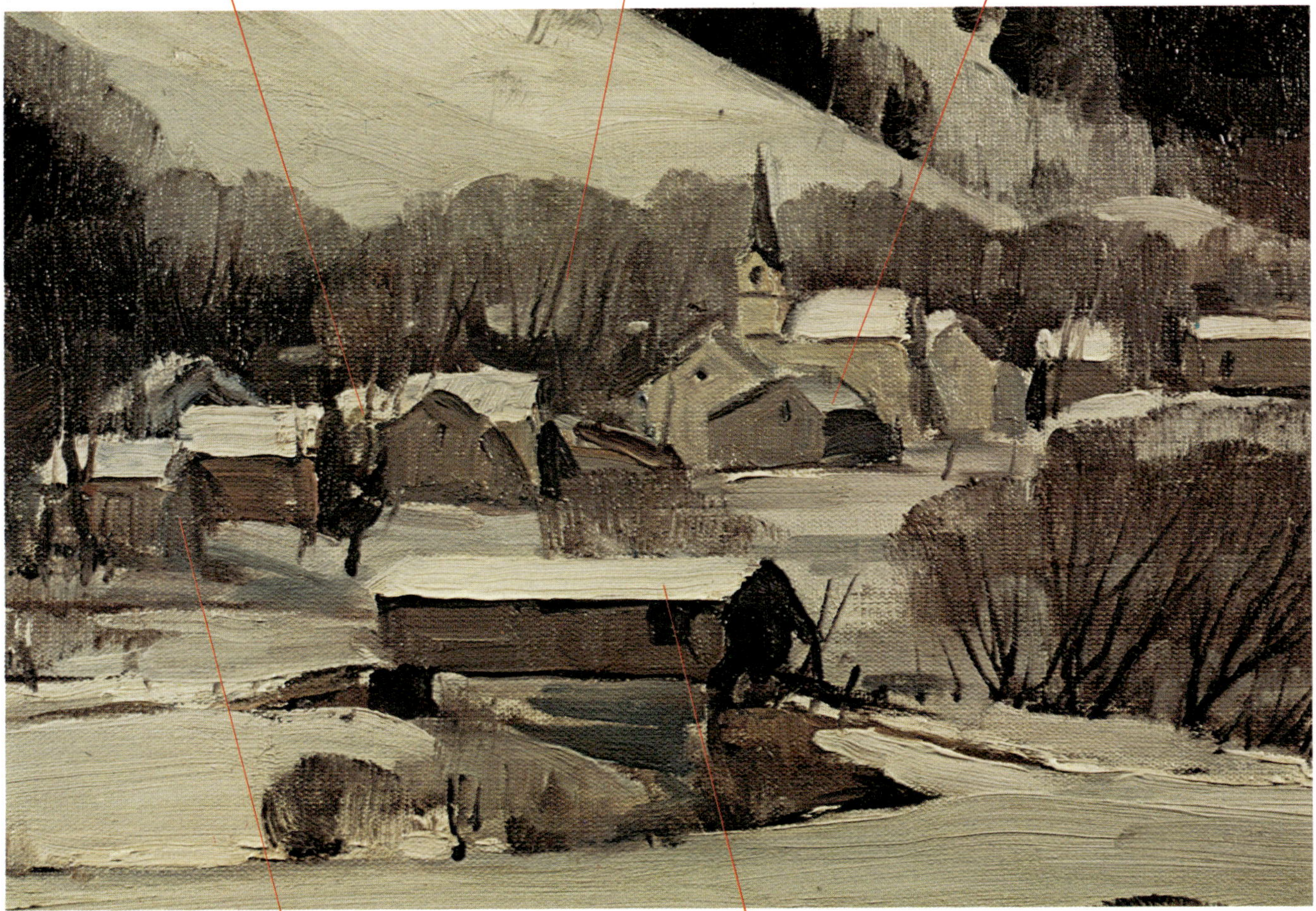

Dark strokes accent the sunlit sides of the buildings—the slanting lines tell you the direction of the sun.

The snow on the buildings is brighter than that on the ground. It's at an angle and catches more of the sun. It's also richly painted to give it added impact.

Farm Buildings

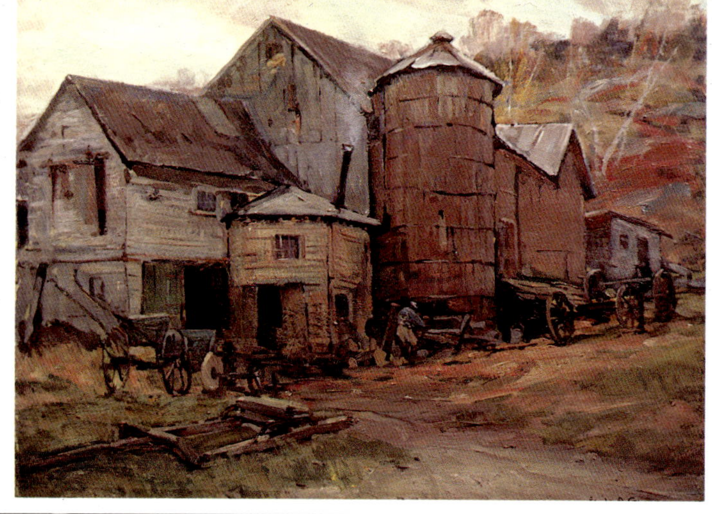

The Old Farm
oil on canvas
30″ × 36″ (76 × 91 cm)

The distant wagon is more simply treated. The wheels, for example, are thin strokes—with just a few spokes to suggest structure. Ten strokes of different sizes and values do the trick.

The wooden sides of the building are a few horizontal strokes worked over a flat underpainting. The window is very simply handled: a few bits of trim hint at its complicated structure.

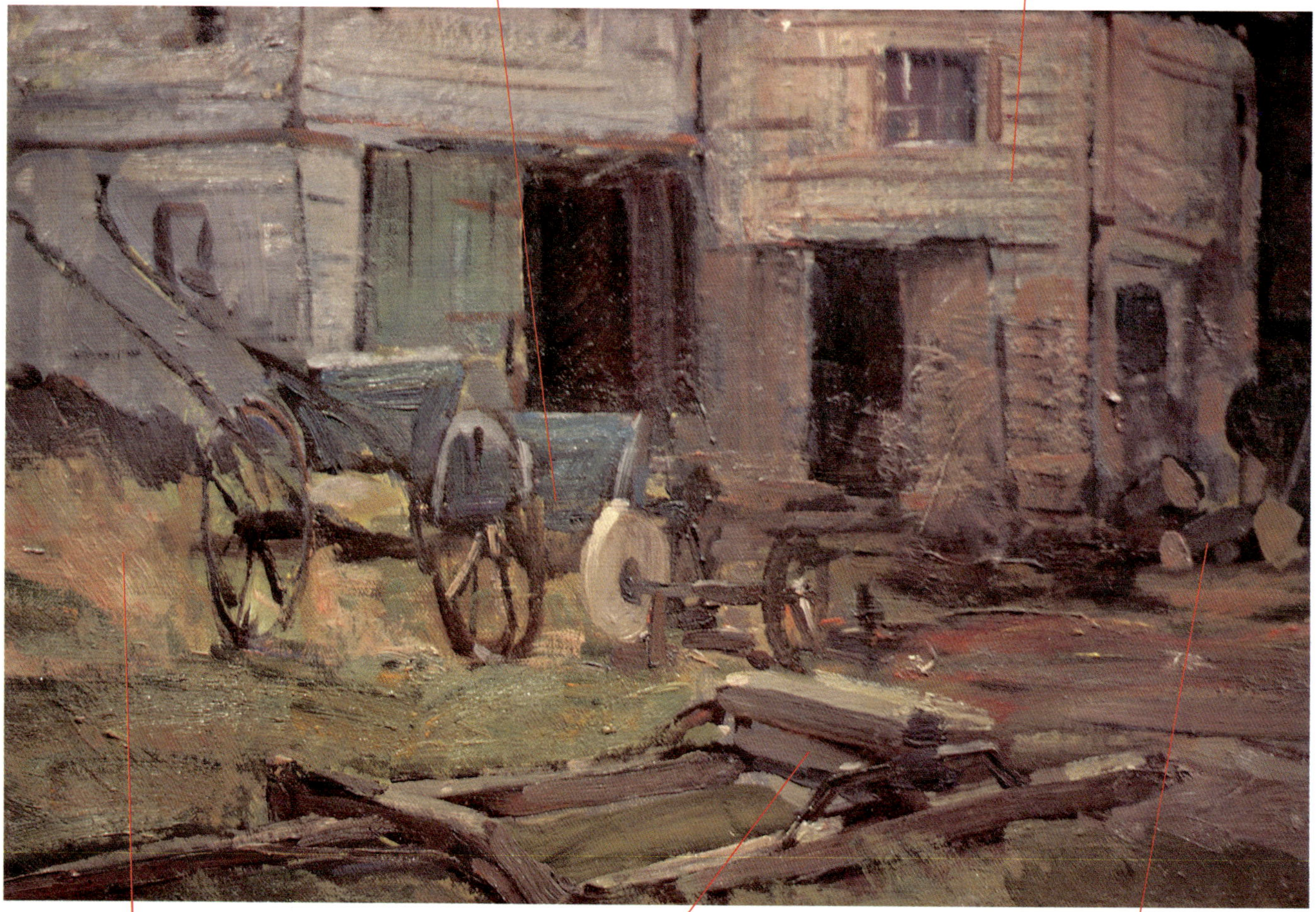

So that it doesn't detract from the wheels, the surrounding grass is painted flatly, with only the slightest hint of texture.

Since the foreground sled is near us, it's painted with a certain amount of detail. Each stroke suggests the direction of a piece of wood.

The wagon is further emphasized by the fact that you can't see where the building and land meet. There's just a series of broken, interlocking strokes, rather than an edge that might challenge the lines of the wagon.

To emphasize the bulk of this huge barn complex, make it fill most of the canvas. As a result, there's room to show its interesting structural details. Because you're close to the building, the perspective of the roofs is exaggerated; that makes you feel as if you're looking *up* at the massive structure. The sled and pieces of farm equipment all overlap the barn and are tied to it. You're not distracted by a lot of small, isolated objects.

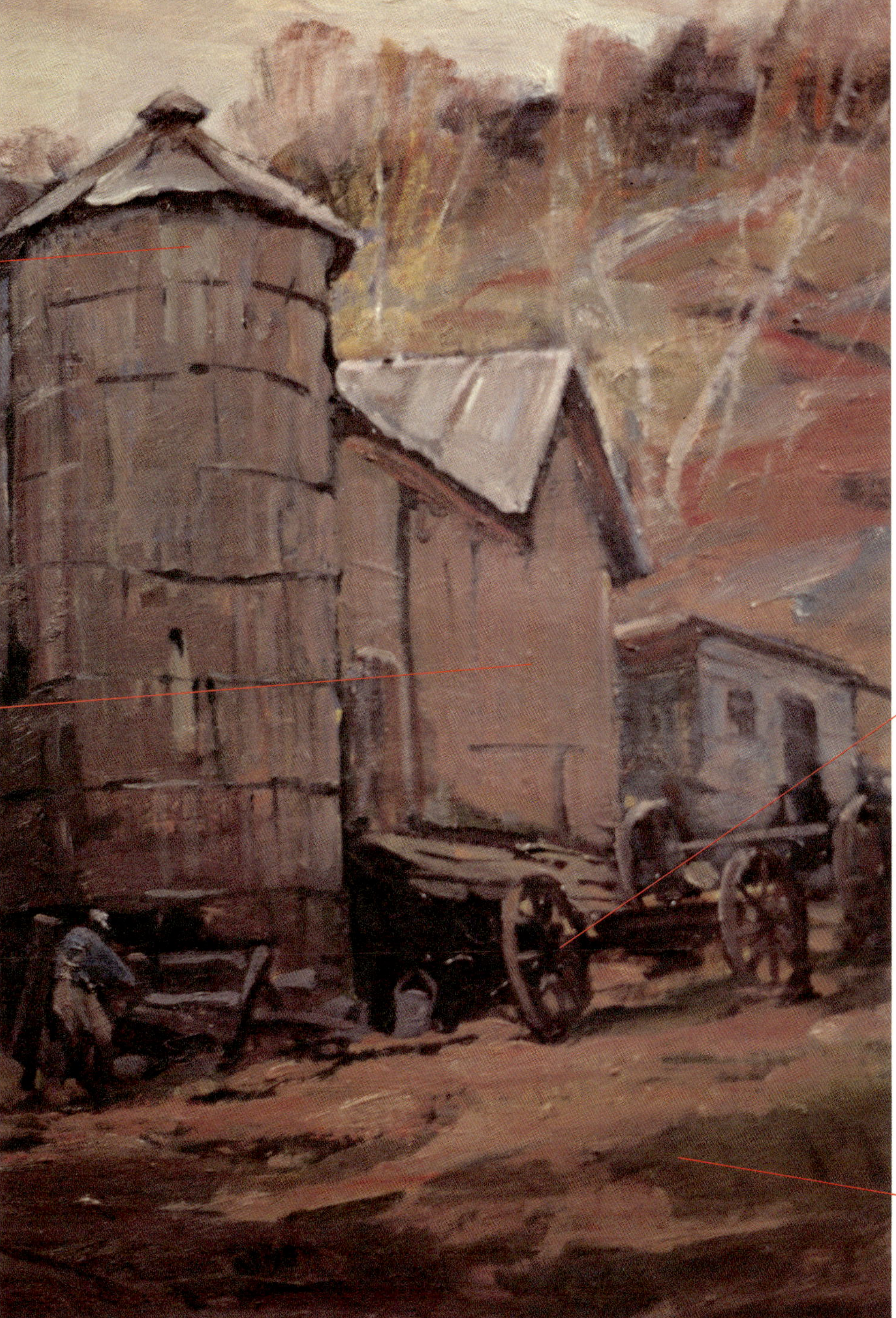

The silo has a strong vertical character; but individual boards occur only toward the side and top. By keeping the rest simple, you give the structural strokes a chance to speak.

In the distance, you don't see texture. The building is painted flatly, with a few subtle shifts of color to make it interesting. Since this area is flat, you can also see the contrasting texture of the silo more clearly.

The wheel nearest you is a circle: light against the dark shadow and dark against the light areas. A few short strokes suggest spokes. Since this wheel is down with some care, don't bother with the one to its left: it disappears into shadow.

To emphasize the textures of the implements and the buildings, keep the foreground grass flat.

Buildings On a Clear Day

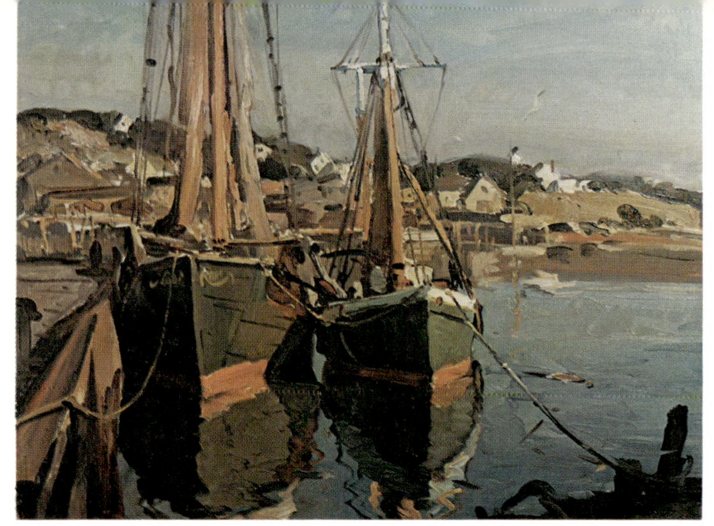

At Dock
oil on canvas
25" × 30" (64 × 76 cm)
Collection of Mr. and Mrs. Philip Shapiro

To emphasize the size of the boat near the dock, you can run its mast out of the picture. The mast of the smaller boat is inside the design. This mast explains the one beyond the frame and lets you gauge how tall it must be. Ropes are used to tie the boats to the wharf, to each other, and to the foreground pilings. The rope unifies the design. On the right, for example, it keeps you from escaping to the distant water and leads you toward the center of interest.

The afternoon light makes the distant houses stand out sharply. Paint them with correspondingly thick and juicy strokes of paint. The trees are crisp and dark. The closest building has a window and the hint of a door.

On the hill, the buildings are so far away that you can't see individual windows. The strokes summarize the buildings as simple triangular and oblong shapes.

The angular shapes of the houses are contrasted with the more rounded shapes of the trees. When the edge of the trees mixes with the color of the sky, it suggests the blurring effect of atmosphere.

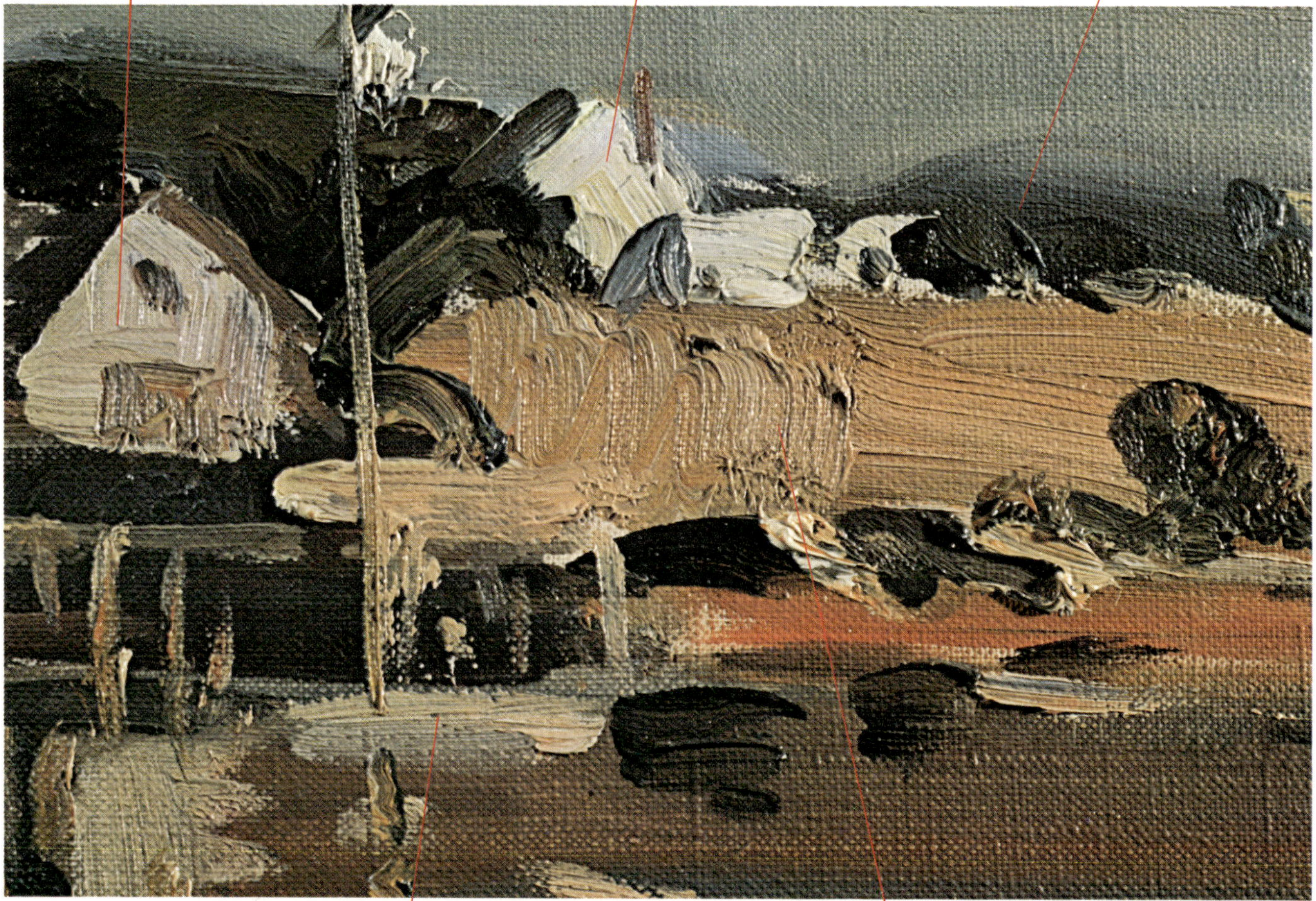

The hull of the sailboat is a horizontal stroke. The wharf is a dark stain over which are run a few broken verticals.

The field of yellow grass is thickly painted, but its warm color is neutralized by cool veils of atmosphere.

Buildings: On a Hazy Day

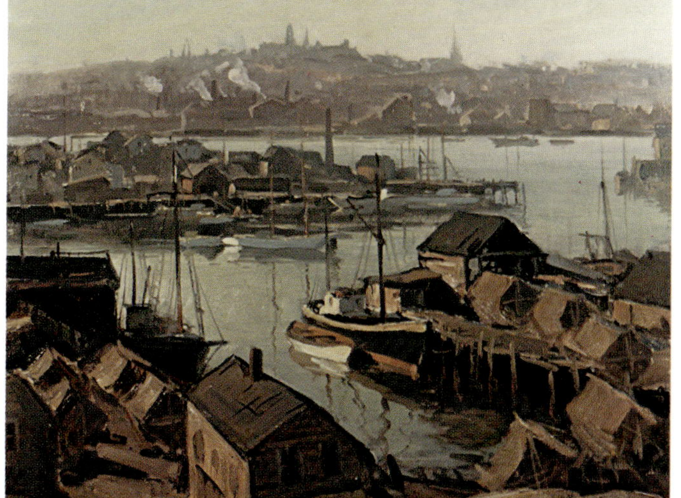

Panorama of Gloucester
oil on canvas
30″ × 32″ (76 × 81 cm)

A hazy day adds great depth to a scene. The nets on the right point you into the picture and step you up to the sunlit dragger and seine boat. The shadowed building and boat on the left accent the brighter objects on the right. Echoes of the foreground white reappear in the middle distance. The land masses are held together by the masts of the boats: They act as staples, connecting foreground to middle distance and middle distance to background.

Steam from the gas works adds vitality and interest to the area—you feel you're looking at a living city, not a ghost town. Lift the brush from the canvas to make the more transparent areas of smoke.

The hazy atmosphere makes all the buildings and trees into a large, cool mass. Paint it broadly and as a *unit*. You see it, but aren't distracted from the more important parts of the picture.

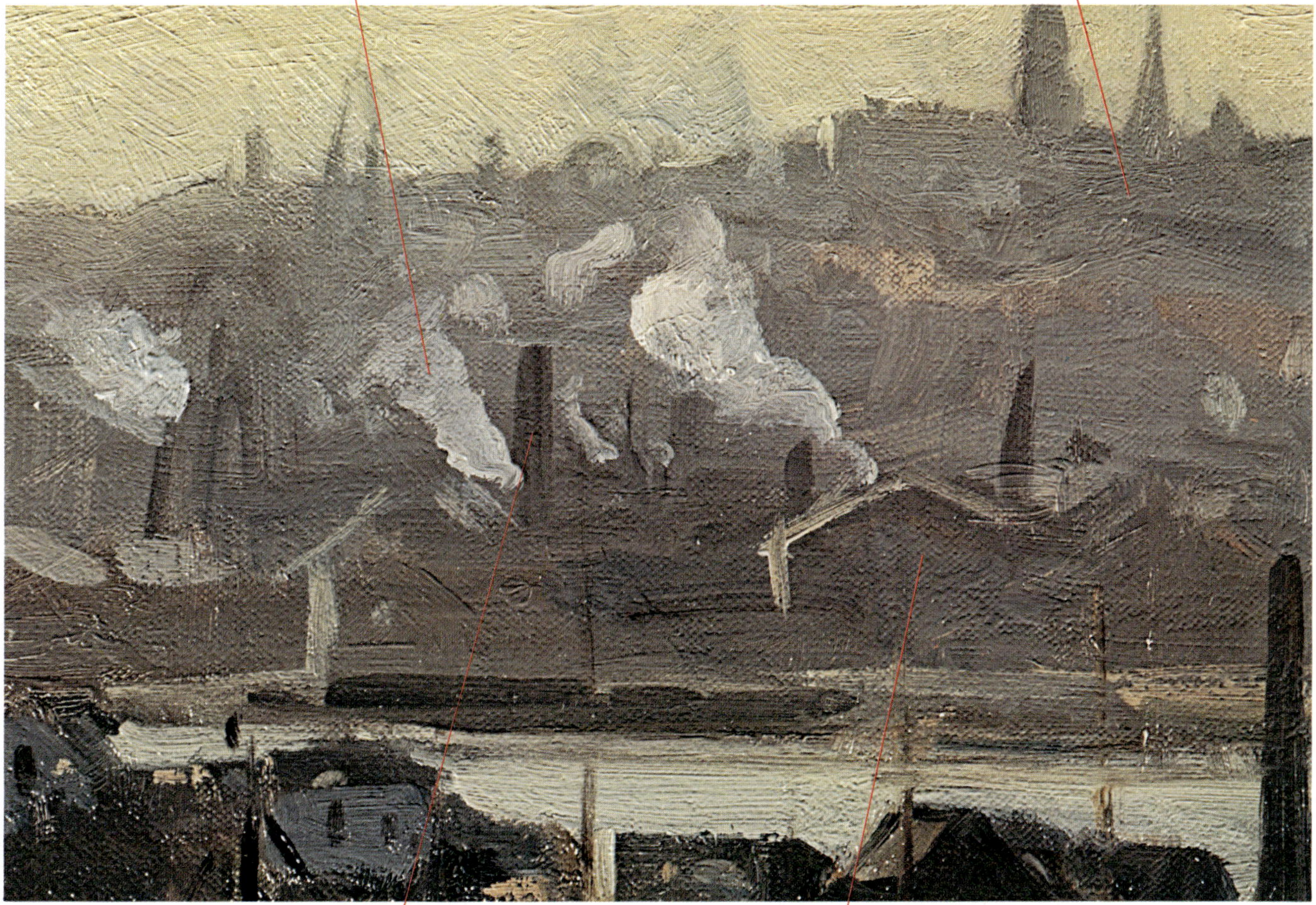

Dark uprights suggest chimneys.

Work over the mass with thin vertical and diagonal lines. The strokes represent the sides and roofs of buildings catching the sun. Don't bother to indicate the shadow sides—you can't see them at this distance.

Buildings: In Sun

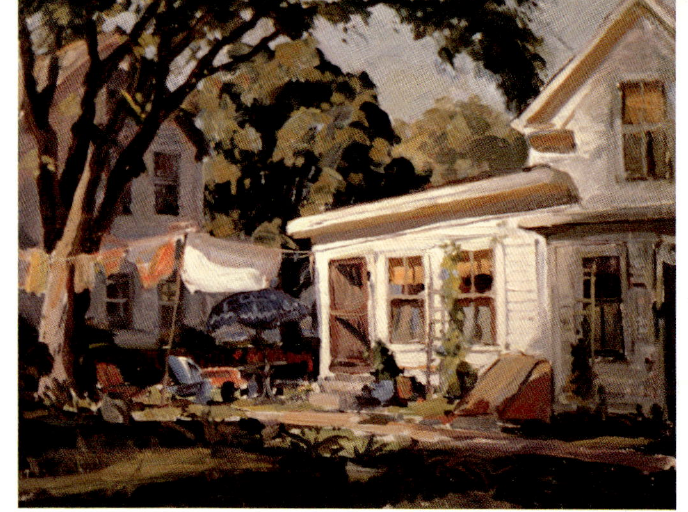

The Back Yard
oil on canvas
25″ × 30″ (64 × 76 cm)

The bright sun hits the building and makes the wash jump out from the shadowed background. The light is further enhanced by the dark overhanging foliage and the rich foreground shadow. Strong notes of red balance the dominant greens.

Each window has a yellow shade; but interest is added by pulling this one lower than the other.

The sun on the building is so strong that the clapboards and sills are eaten up. These dark lines are actually shadows cast by the thick paint.

Sun streams through the other window and makes the interior warm and light.

The dark note makes you feel as if you can look inside the house.

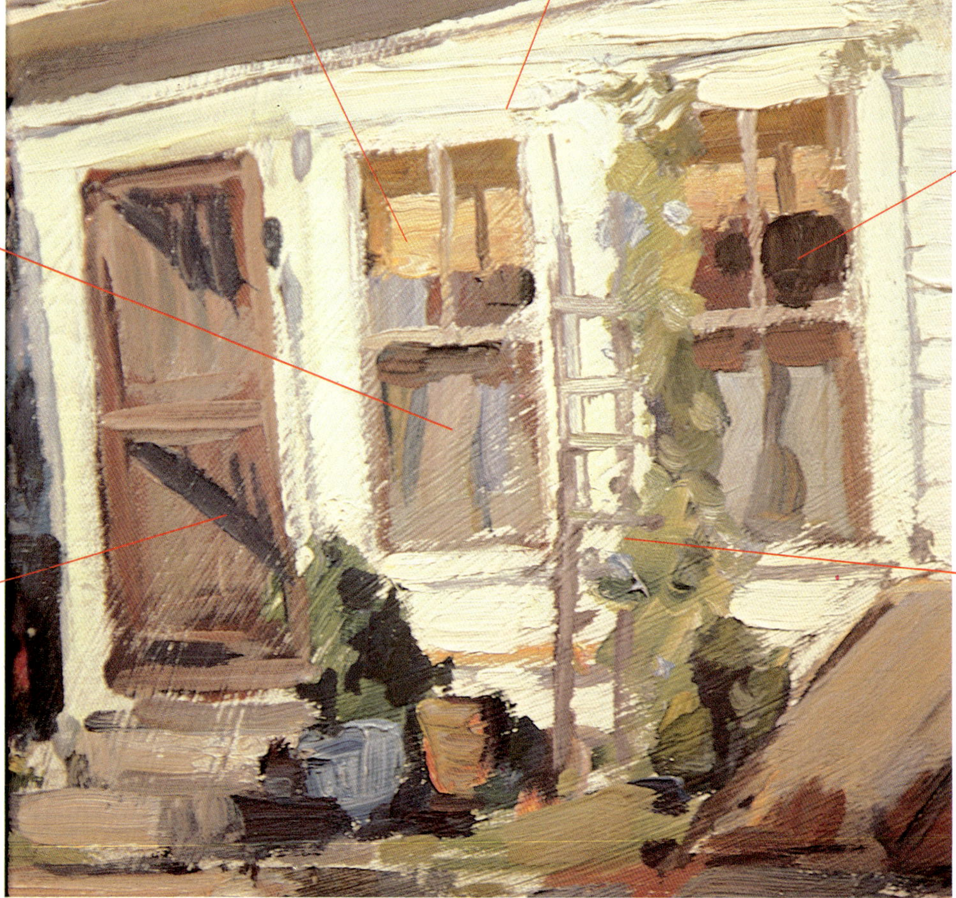

The door is first stained a reddish color. Broken darks suggest parts of the frame. Diagonal slashes make you feel that the door is ajar.

Only *one* complete window is necessary here. Use the trellis to obscure the other.

Buildings: In Shade

Shadows
oil on canvas
25″ × 30″ (64 × 76 cm)

This is an experimental picture. I try to see how *dark* I can make the shadows—and still get away with it. The distant tree trunks are almost black—as is the foreground shadow. The strong contrasts make the picture an effective decoration, which you can see a mile away. The subject is the cast shadows and the way they fall across the houses.

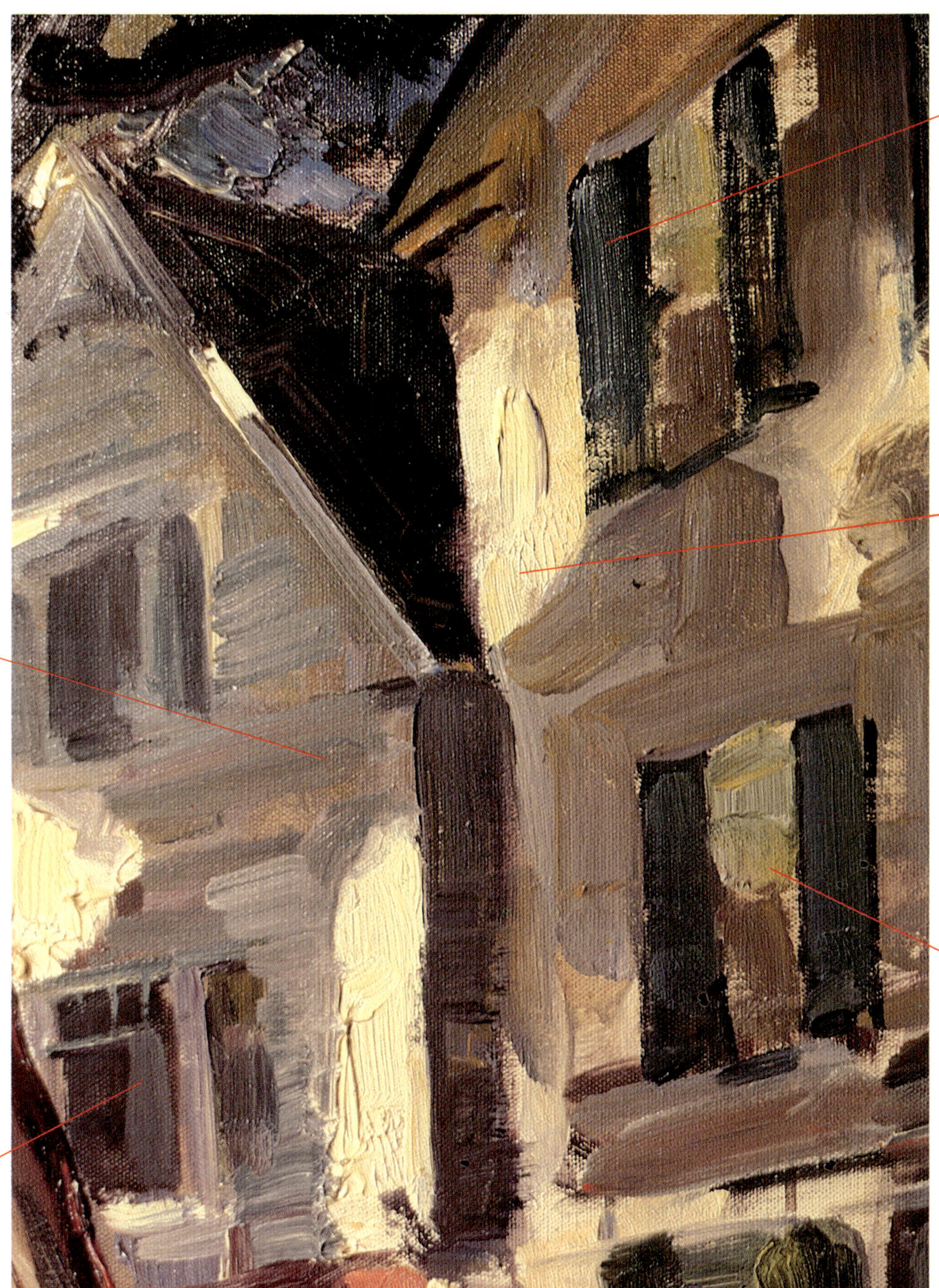

Stain the shadows a dull reddish-purple. The original stain shows through some of the heavier overpainting.

In the shadows, horizontal strokes suggest the wall's wooden siding. This texture explains that of the building on the right which you can paint more simply.

Place warm highlights—the brilliant light again obliterates any small shadows. The splashes of sun step you down toward the trees.

Leaves don't block the light as effectively: A suggestion of warm sun creeps into the shadow. The road also reflects warmth into the side of the house.

Near the tree, the heavy trunk blocks the warm light from the sun and the shadow is blue. The sky color predominates.

Buildings Near and Far

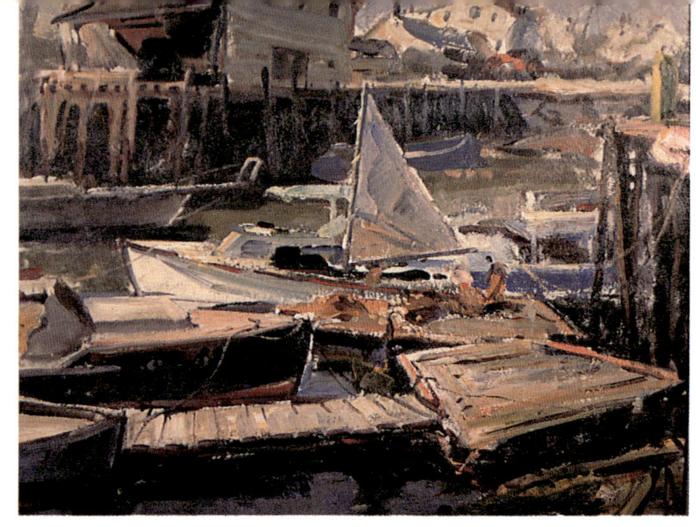

Lobster Fleet
oil on canvas
30″ × 36″ (76 × 91 cm)
Collection of the
Cape Ann Savings Bank
Gloucester
Massachusetts

The distant buildings are painted very simply. Upright strokes show the building in light; a diagonal stroke suggests the dark roof.

A few dots give scale to the buildings.

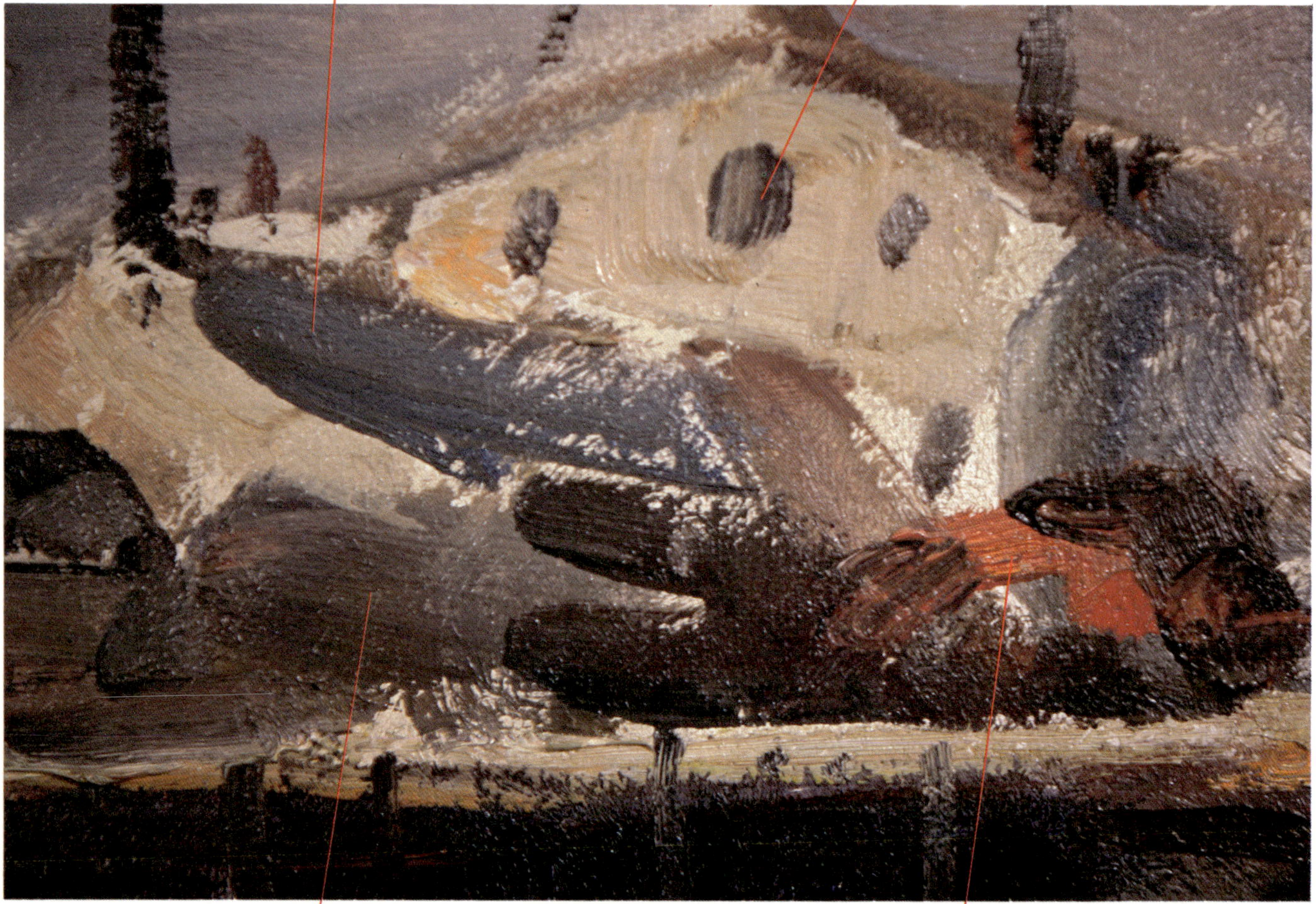

The piles of debris near the building are just a lavendar stain. Raw canvas acts as a highlight.

A red dot describes a piece of equipment. This note brings some of the rich foreground color into the background.

In this painting everything is said as briefly and simply as possible. The triangular sail states the theme: Such pointed shapes reappear everywhere. Since it's dead-low tide, we look down on the scene. That creates angles and slanting lines that lead you into the composition. The result is the kind of "designy" picture that often appeals more to painters than to the general public.

The small telephone pole gives scale to the area.

The background buildings are very rough. You can suggest them with a few irregular blobs of color.

Dots stand for chimneys and windows.

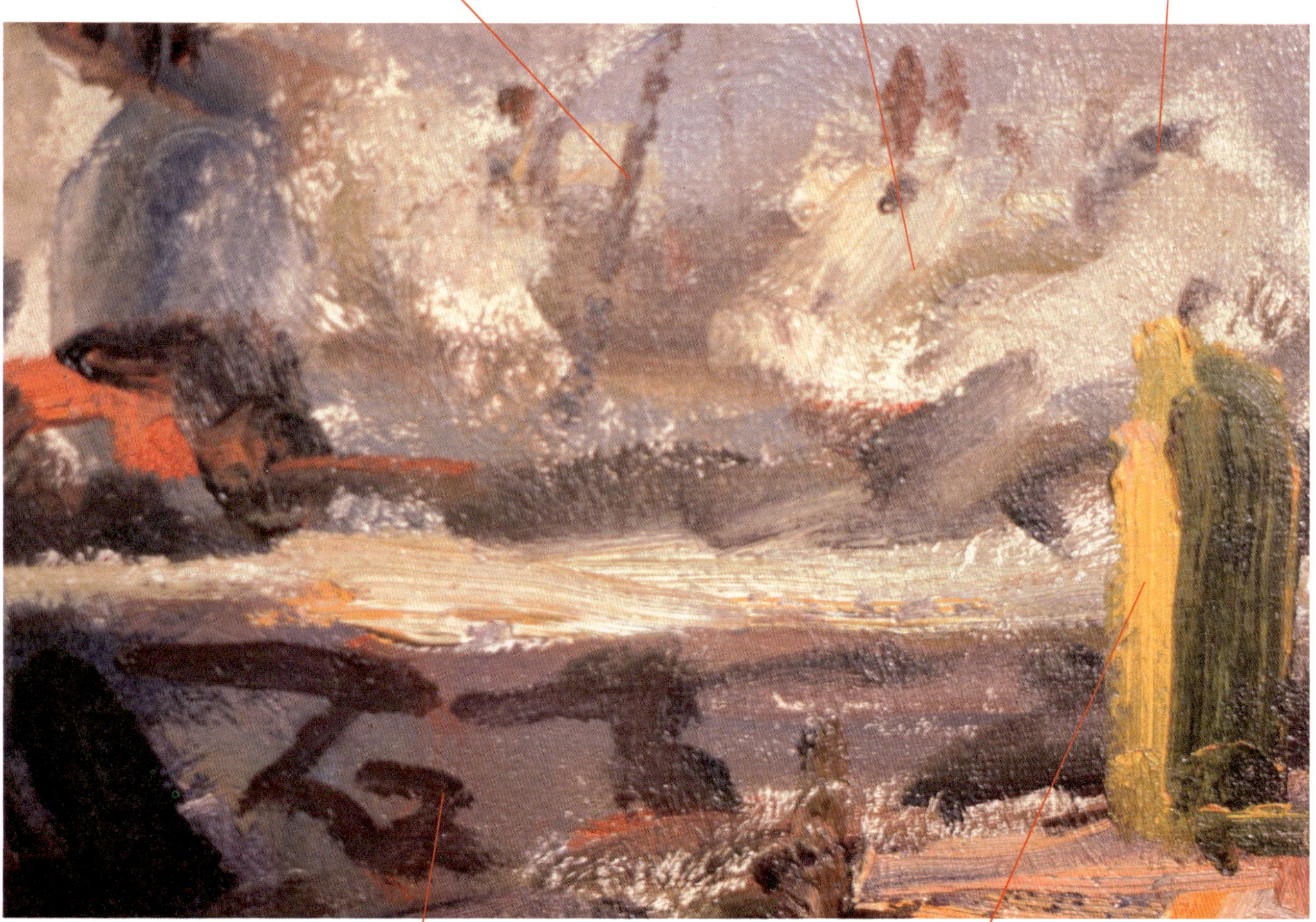

The retaining wall is a gray stain; a corkscrew stroke suggests a shadow cast by the stones.

To keep the material in the background, put a yellow pump in front of it. In the complete picture, you look at this pump and the nearby wharf—not at the distant buildings.

THE HARBOR

It takes time to understand how boats look. When I began painting them, my proportions were never right. So I talked to fishermen to find out how boats worked. I made countless studies of individual schooners and draggers. Eventually, I began to see where the cabin goes and where the masts belong. I saw the ropes that keep the mast from falling forward, backward, and to the sides. And I began to sense how the shape of the boat was related to its particular job. You start by mechanically copying the facts; then you begin to feel the character of the boat: its lightness or heaviness, its strength or fragility. Once you know the subject, you can begin to take liberties.

As a good example of how to think about boats, look at a sailboat on the horizon. At first, students draw the billowing sail and then work hard to paint the small boat beneath it. Eventually they learn to stress the important part: the sail. A sailboat is like a butterfly: You see the wings—and never notice the little worm they're attached to.

Be decisive when you draw boats. Either pull a mast right out of the picture—or keep it clearly within the composition. Don't have it just kiss the top of the frame, so it looks as if it's dangling from it. I usually keep my masts inside the design; that way the viewer sees the whole boat and better understands how it's constructed. If I do pull one or two out, I keep others in. The ones inside the picture explain those beyond the frame. Similarly, when I pull all the masts out, I try to reflect the full mast in the water. The reflections then tell you what's happening outside the canvas.

In order to scale the boats properly, place the masts first; the design they make against the sky is usually the most important part of the picture. Then draw the hulls to fit them. I like to make the masts tall—students rarely give them enough play. Students also tend to make their ships too big. Instead of a composition, they end up with a portrait of a boat.

Always keep scale in mind as you work. If you want a boat to look big, keep everything around it small—people, buildings, pilings. A small dory next to a large ship scales the whole design.

Paint only what interests you at a particular moment. Do a panoramic view of the harbor one day; make a close study of a ship on another. Above all: Learn to look for the character of your material. When I'd take students to the wharves, boats would pull out halfway through the lesson. But nobody would notice. They were all too busy moving paint around on the canvas. They had stopped looking—and studying.

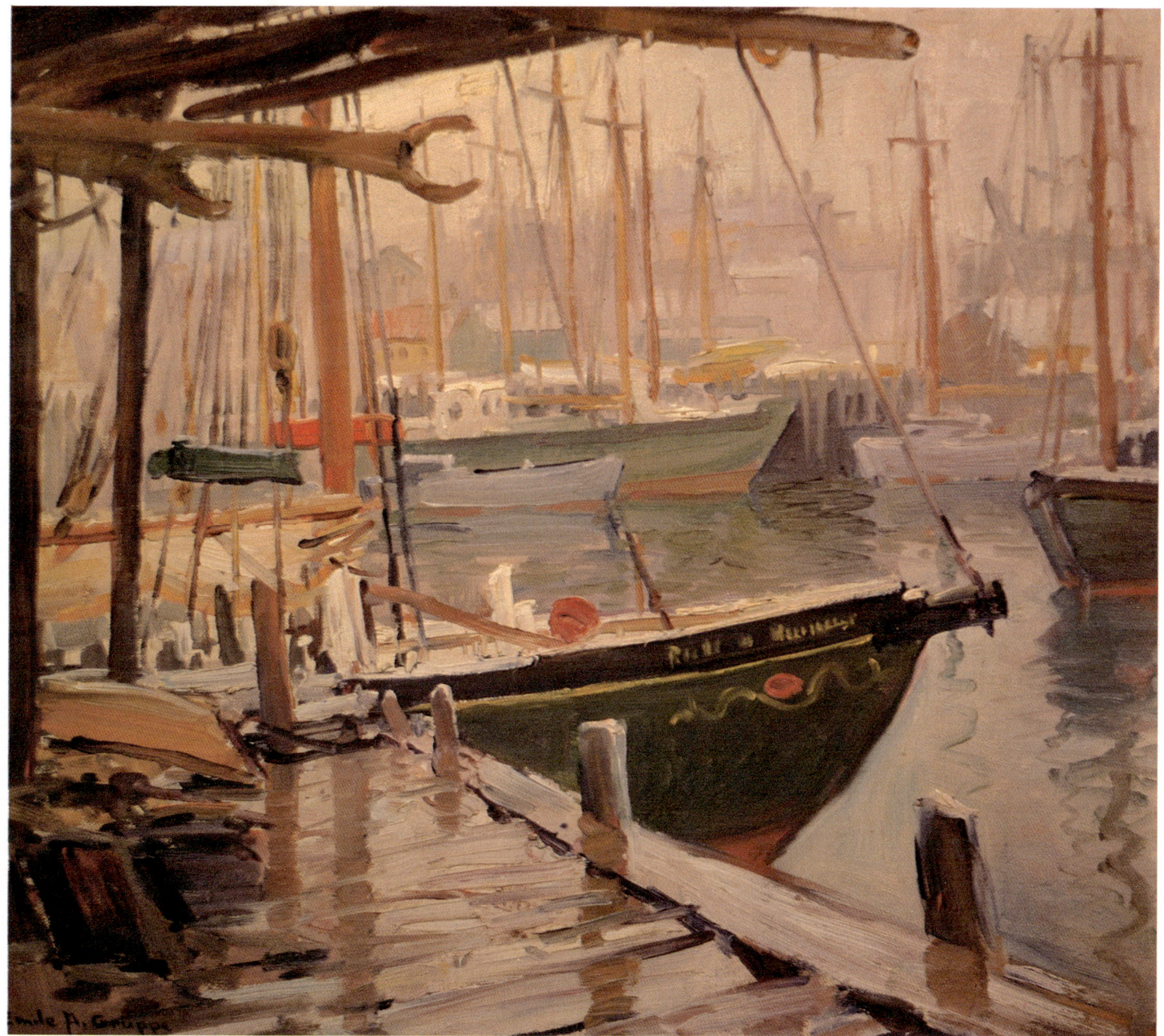

Painting in the Rain
oil on canvas
18″ × 20″ (46 × 51 cm)
Collection of
Mrs. Cathryn
Nugent Gibbs

This was painted during a rainstorm. The water running over the dock prevented it from drying out. Thus the reflections are unusually clear. The value of the wet wharf is lighter than that of the nearby water. To emphasize this sheen, place dark strokes along the board that runs the length of the wharf. These shadows are larger in the foreground and smaller in the distance. The sheen is painted with diagonal strokes that parallel the direction of the boards themselves. As you move back along the wharf, these strokes become less pronounced. The reflections are a series of short, dark strokes, going in the same diagonal direction as the water. Occasionally some of the light color is pulled through a reflection, suggesting a break in the water's surface. The dock has just a skim on it, and there's little motion to the water—that's why the reflections are so straight. Overhead, a few strokes suggest a roof. They make you sense that you're protected, so you feel comfortable.

Wharf

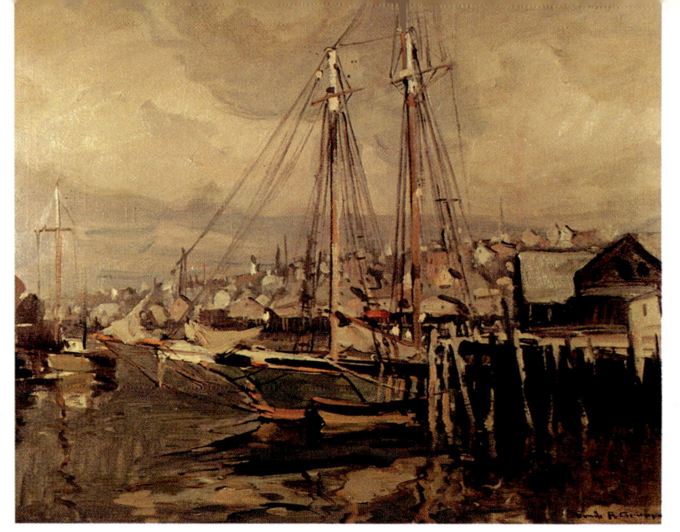

Late Afternoon
oil on canvas
25″ × 30″ (64 × 76 cm)

The sun is low in the sky and all upright planes receive a warm blast of light. Even the distant white houses are fairly strong in color. I sacrifice the sky, making it fairly dark so the lights will show up. It should reflect darkly in the water. The clouds counterpoint the downward movement of the distant hill.

The dark water brings out the light, hanging sails. These sails are painted as flatly as the hulls of the boats.

The brilliant stroke of red comes up against the distance and helps throw it back in space. Compare its vividness with the duller reds of the background buildings.

The white of the trim is echoed in the buildings and pulleys. These strokes keep the trim from being an isolated color spot.

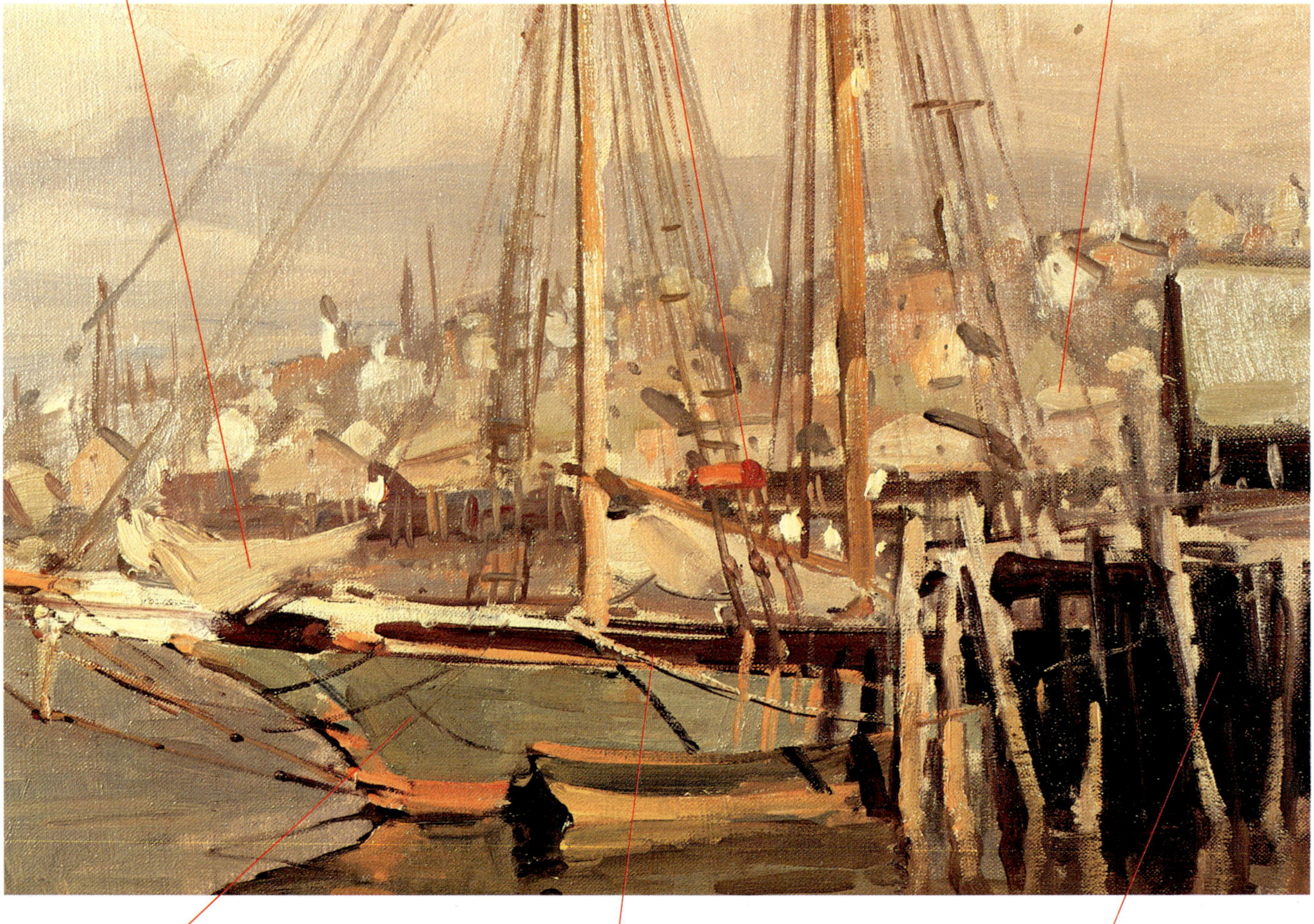

The brightly lit boats are flatly painted; there's only a hint of modeling. Did you guess that the dory is just three strokes of color?

The blackish trim is important; its intensity throws the town back in space and places the green boat clearly in the foreground.

The wharf is the most interesting part of the picture. Stain it first; then work the light pilings over it. Pilings and dock are the same color. They move in and out of the shadow, giving the area an elusive, mysterious feeling.

Pilings

The Green Boat
oil on canvas
25″ × 30″ (64 × 76 cm)

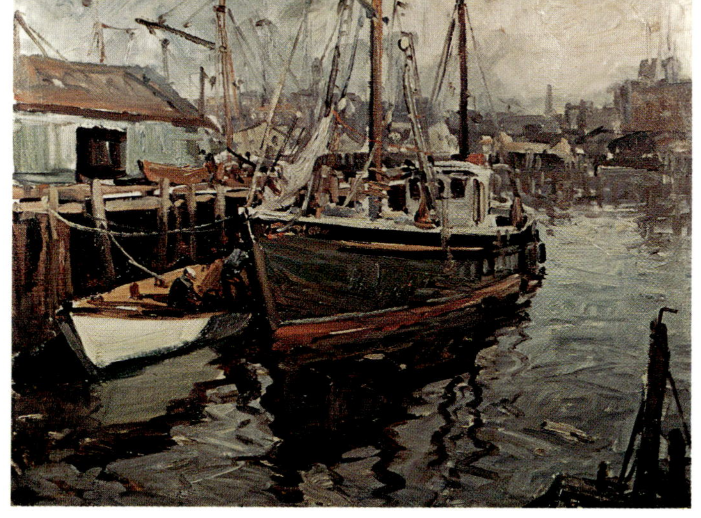

The site draws you to it by the way the lines of the white boat and the off-white sail echo each other: They create a sweeping upward movement. This line is counterpointed by the downward curve of the gunwale of the green fishing boat. To suggest the activity of the harbor, paint both the foreground water and the distant buildings with short choppy strokes.

The dock is first stained a warm color. Over that, work the more heavily impastoed pilings. Add their light tops when you paint the horizontal line of the wharf.

The sail is modeled like clay. Don't bother to paint individual folds; the strokes of the brush do that for you.

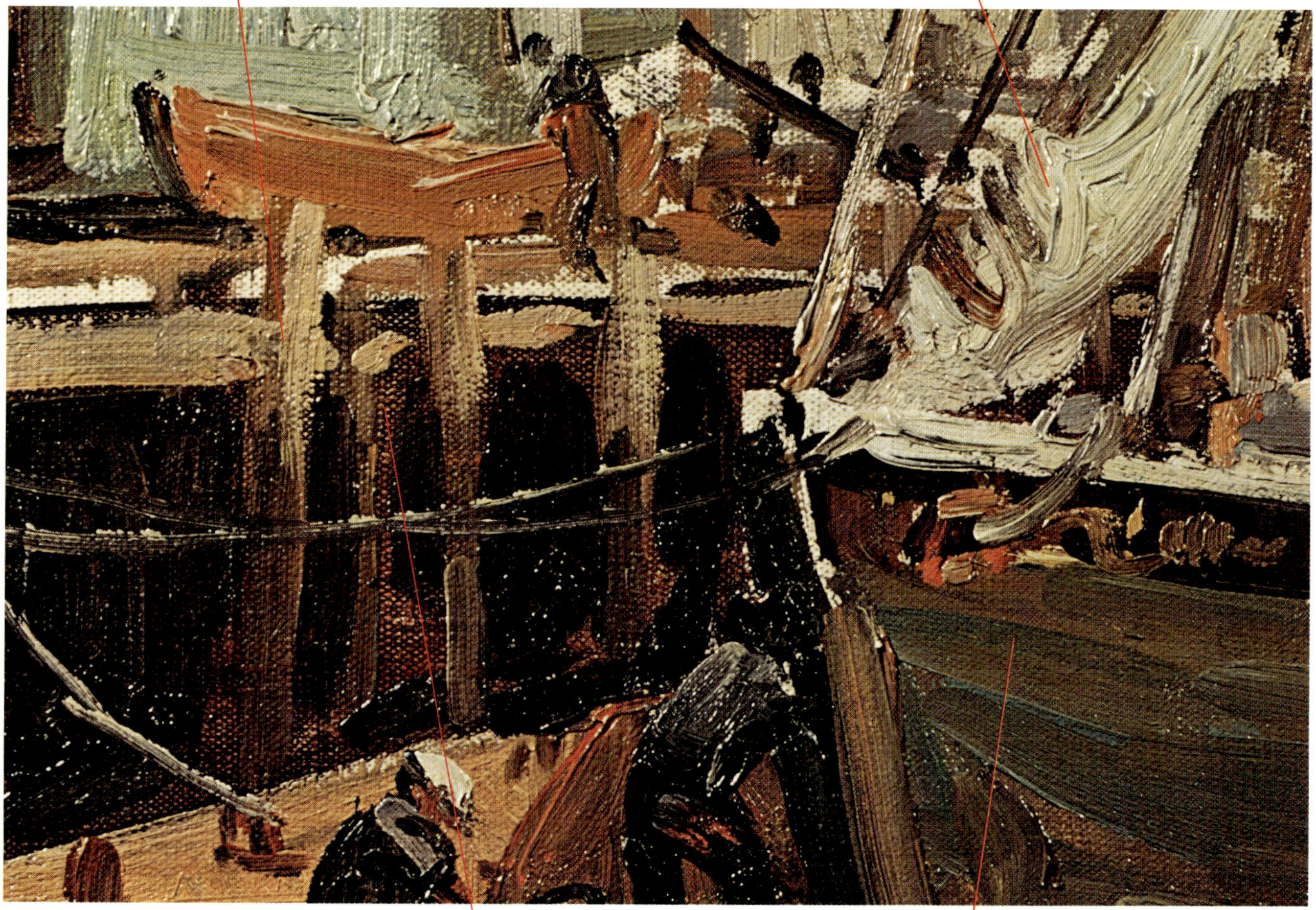

Use more opaque color between the pilings. Some of the stain shows through, suggesting spots where light works its way under the wharf.

Diagonal strokes describe the planking on the green boat. A few yellow squiggles suggest ornament on the bow.

Nets

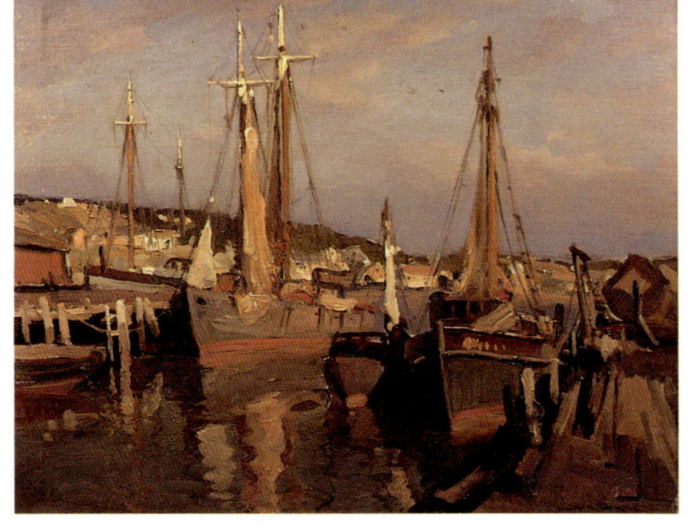

Smith Cove
oil on canvas
25″ × 30″ (64 × 76 cm)
Collection of Mr. and Mrs. Roger Curtis

The low-lying sun creates strong lights and shadows. It's a clear day, and the distant hills are dark against the sky. They form a foil to the sunlit masts and hanging nets. Your eye moves across the cluster of foreground boats to the group on the left. The clouds are dark compared with the brilliant white crosspieces. Keep the sky low in value to emphasize the brightness of the boats.

"Sculpt" with the paint. The hanging nets are concave strokes, with the brushmarks looking like broken creases.

The distant mass of trees is almost devoid of brushstrokes.

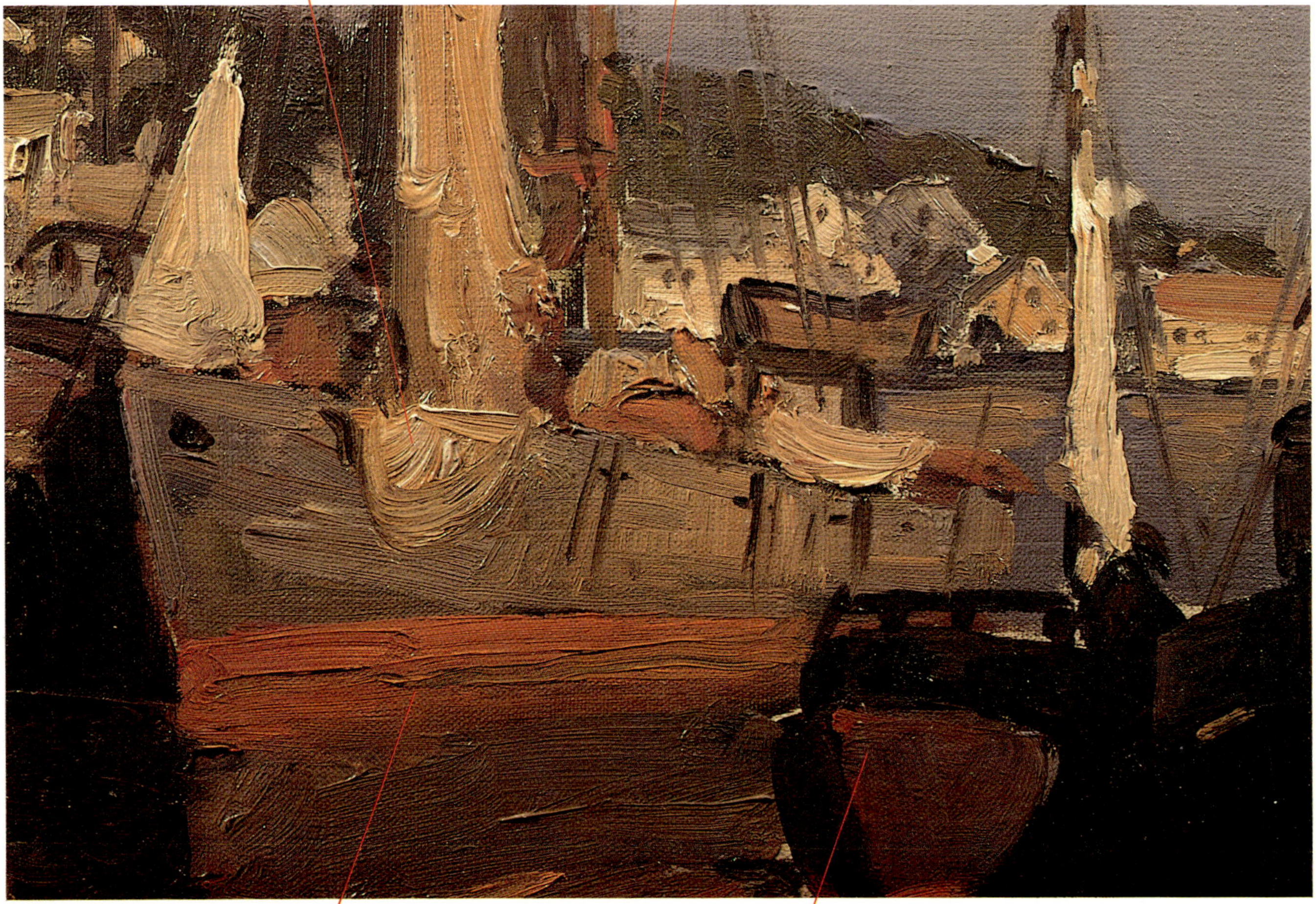

The boat and its reflections are painted with horizontal strokes.

The foreground boats are a simple lead-in. Don't bother to show where one ends and the other begins. The most informative stroke in the mass is the slash of orange. It defines the form, without my having to draw the entire shape of the hull. It also adds interest to what might otherwise be a lifeless area.

Junk

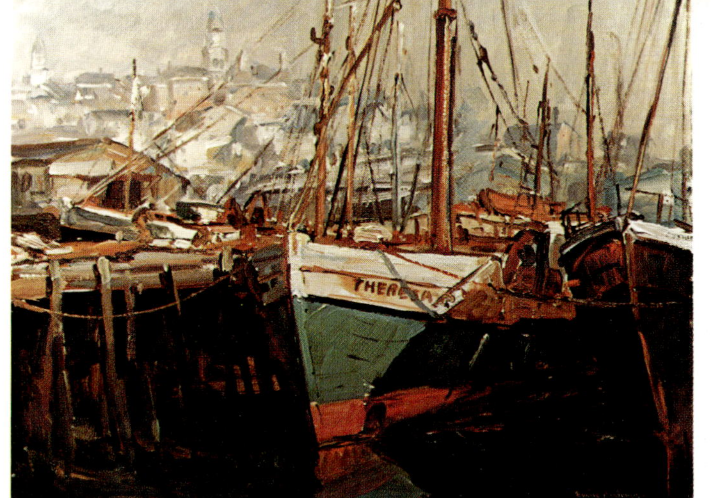

Boat Study
oil on canvas
25" × 30" (64 × 76 cm)

The green dragger dominates the composition. Since the boat is huge, pull its mast out of the top of the painting. The foreground rigging forms a screen; you look through it to the hazy but brilliantly lit buildings in the distance.

Placing the mass of the white cabin first, paint darker lines into and over it.

The brightly lit boat reflects warm light into the shadow of the dark hull. State the added warmth with bold strokes of red.

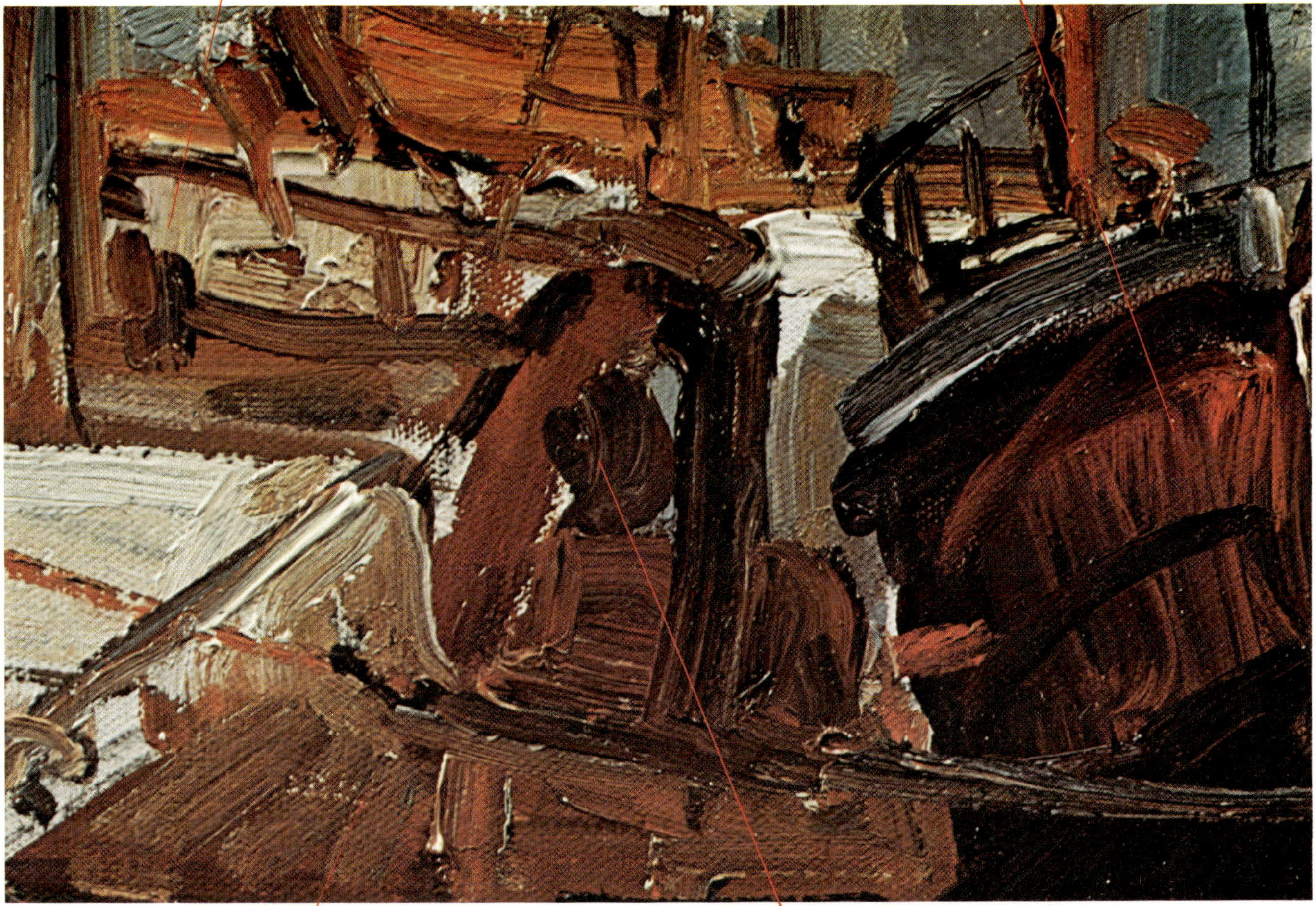

A rusty area is defined by a series of diagonal and horizontal strokes.

The complicated mass of equipment is rendered in terms of textures. A few quick strokes suggest winches, pulleys, and a distant dory. You see these strokes and *imagine* more details than could be drawn.

Boats: Close up

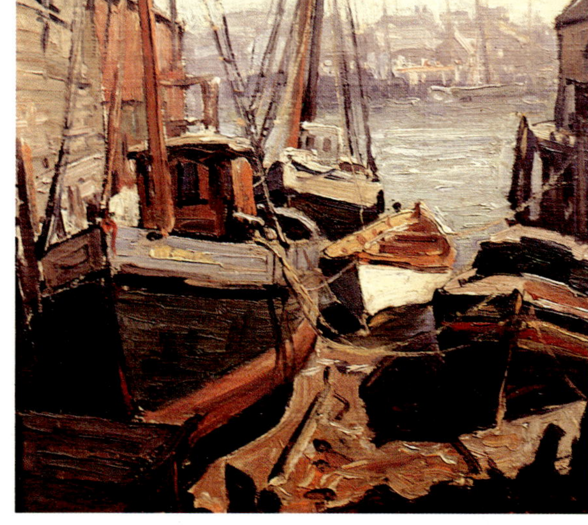

Low Tide
oil on panel
12″ × 12″ (31 × 31 cm)
Collection of
Mrs. Dorothy Gruppé

The white seine boat is the center of interest. A few thin strokes define the gunwhale; horizontal slashes suggest seats; a few vertical strokes indicate interior supports.

The deck is a warm ochrish stroke, as is the top of the cabin. The cabin has windows, of course, but they're a distraction so omit them.

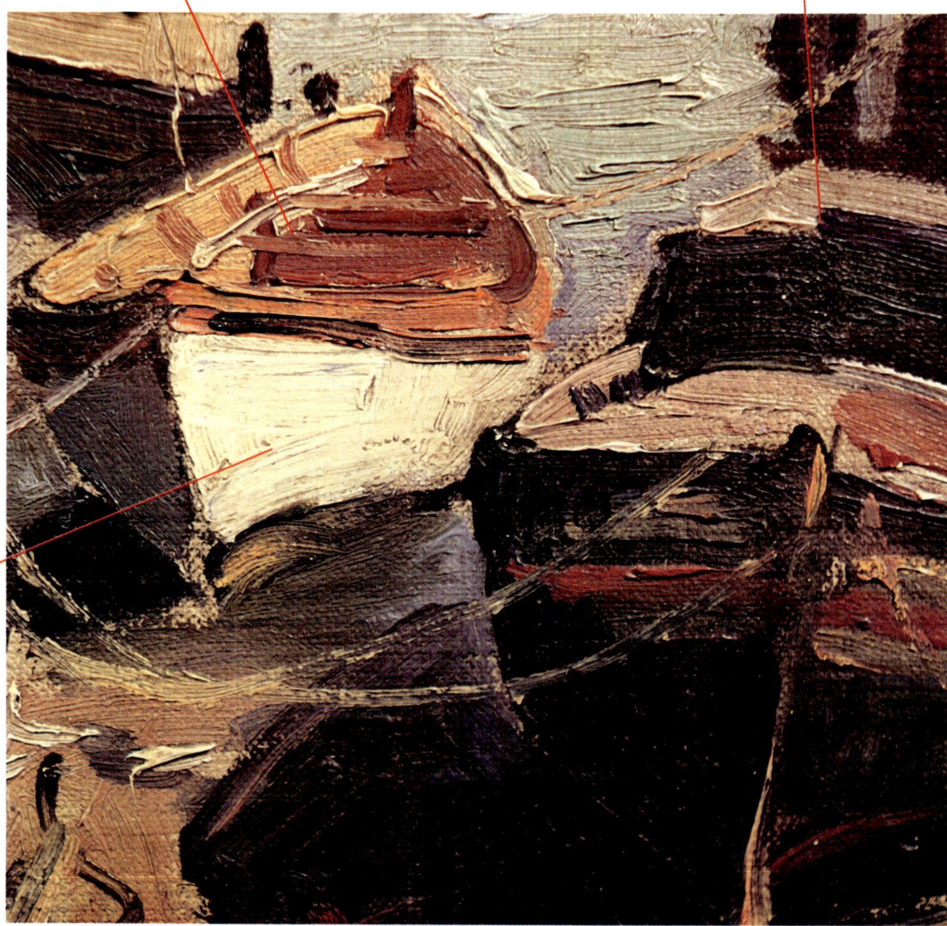

The heavy strokes of white paint follow the tapered bulge of the dory's sides.

What makes this kind of view?—a variety of colors, shapes and angles. In order to emphasize the intimacy of the scene, make everything big: The buildings and masts go out of the top of the picture. You're surrounded by the elements of the painting. The overlapping shapes of the boats also lock you into the foreground.

The horizontal planking contrasts with the vertical movement of the cabin. This rich, thick stroke of orange is painted over the dark cabin stain.

These two windows are much smaller than the foreground ones. That's a perspective clue: The difference in the size of the stroke adds depth to the picture.

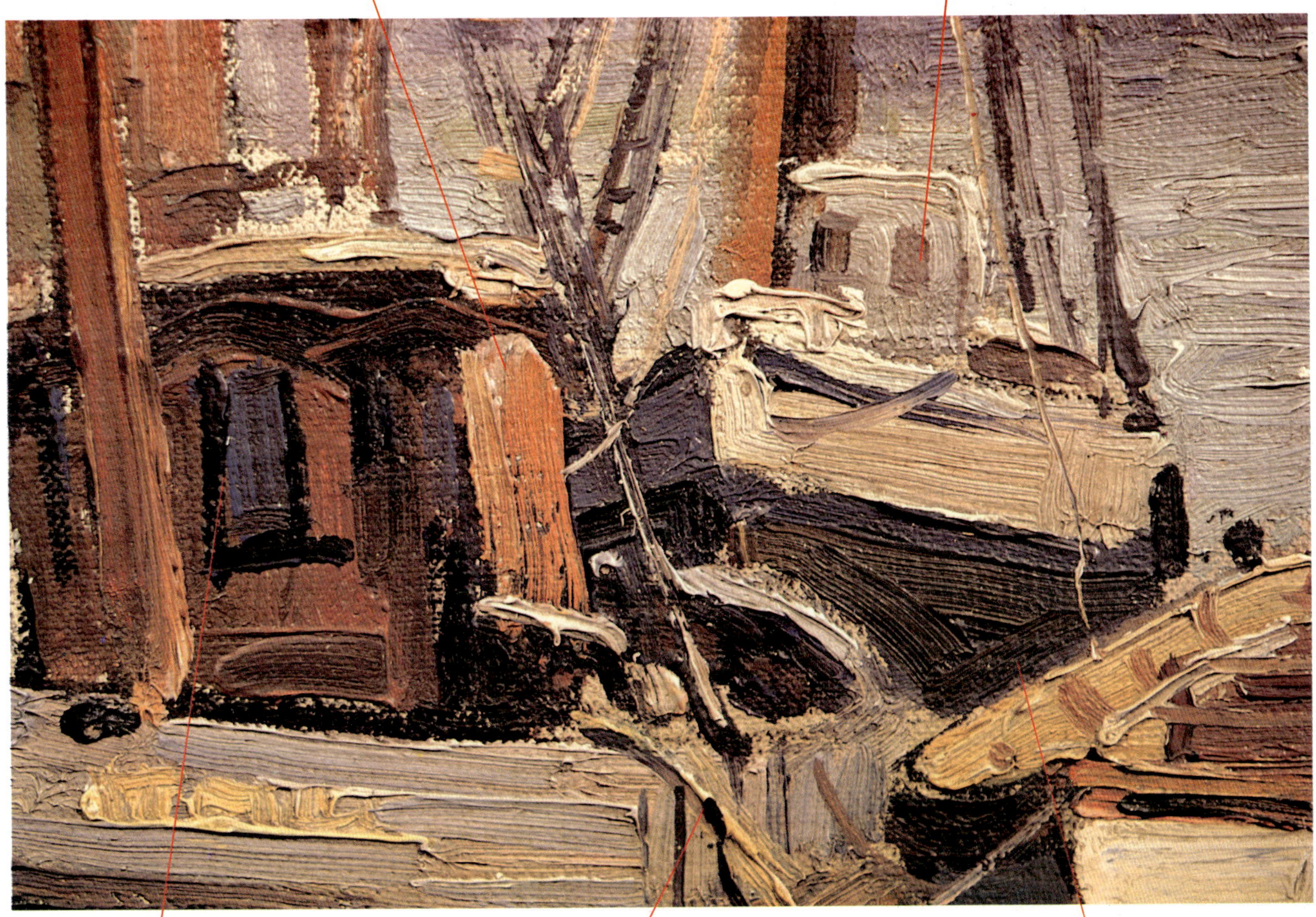

The foreground window is purple, which was outlined with dark paint. There are three windows, but I smudge one and cover the other with a mast. Only *one* counts.

Strong diagonal strokes show the planks that make up the gunwhale.

Delicately curved lines accentuate the bluntness and force of the nearby verticals and horizontals.

Boats: Middle Distance

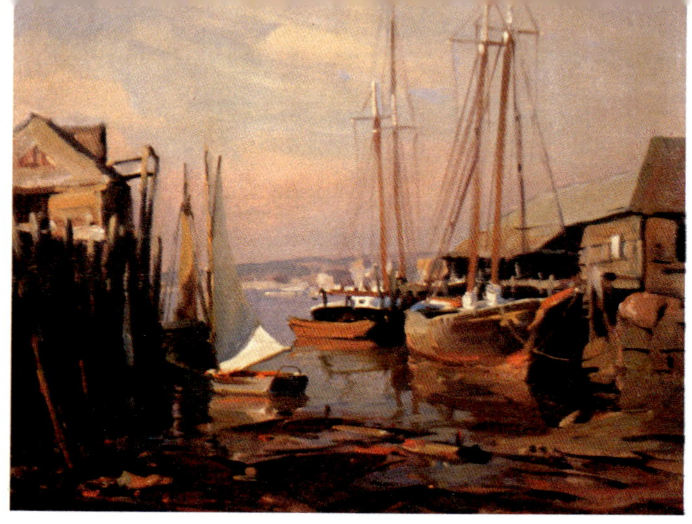

The Sadie Noonan and the Wentworth
oil on canvas
25″ × 30″ (64 × 76 cm)

Play up the textures of the main boat by painting the other boats more flatly. The dory, for example, is just a few strokes of orange paint, with a line to suggest a plank. The schooner behind it has no modeling at all.

Two diagonal slashes suggest the planking on the bow of the schooner. A few thin strokes in the opposite direction describe the curve of the schooner as it nears the water.

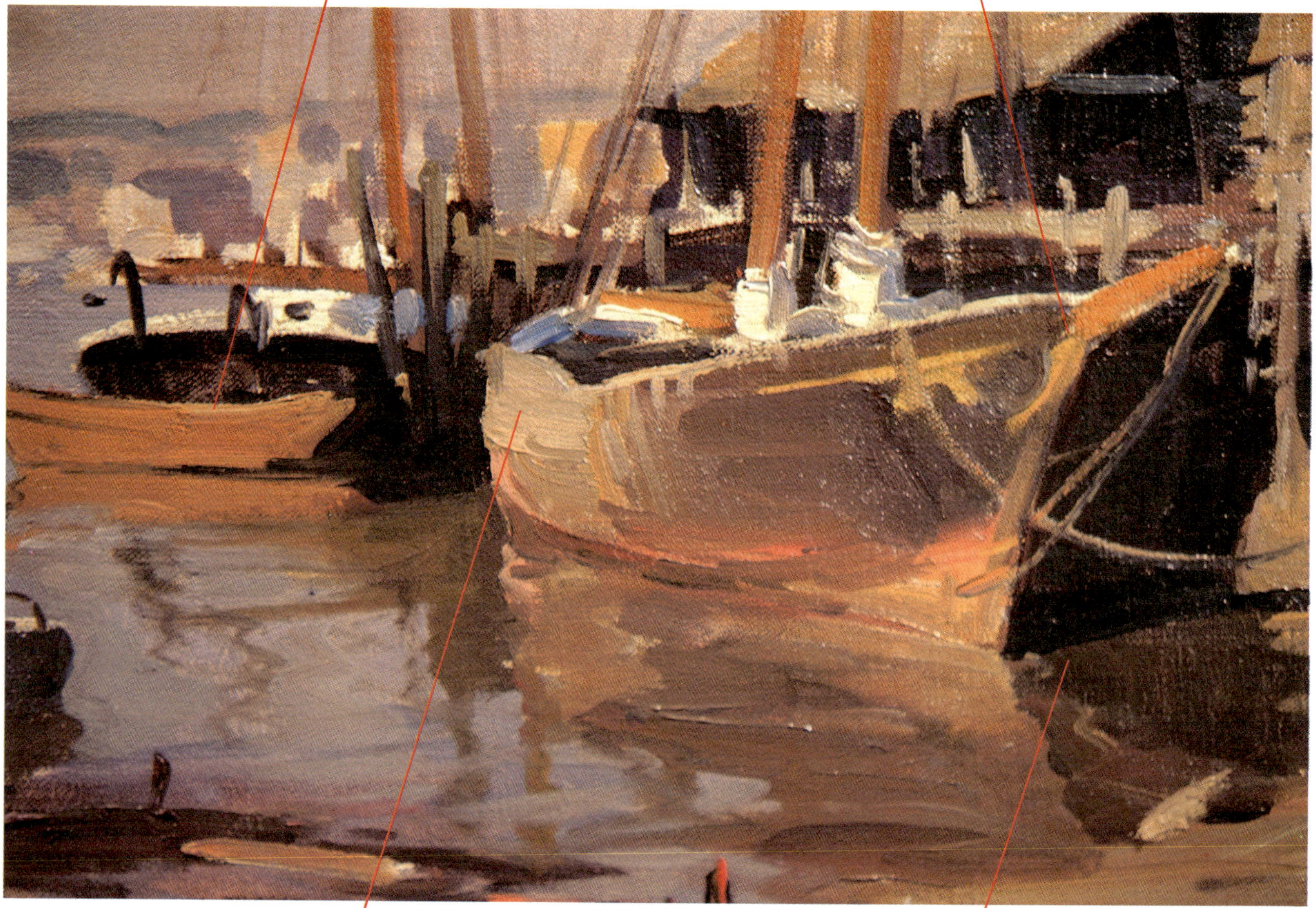

At the stern, the boat catches a glare from the sun; the modeling is largely obliterated. There're just a few strokes of light color.

Keep the shadows dark and simple, forcing your eye to the sunlit boats. The reflections, for example, are just warm notes with a few horizontal strokes to suggest the surface of the water.

Note the way the schooners nestle against the pier. The mud forms an interesting pattern as it angles toward the large boats. Probably the most important single stroke in the picture is the diagonal line at the extreme bottom left of the design. It adds interest to the pilings by breaking their dominant up-and-down movement. It also counterpoints the line of the schooner's leaning masts.

The pilings are painted flatly—their color goes right up into the side of the building.

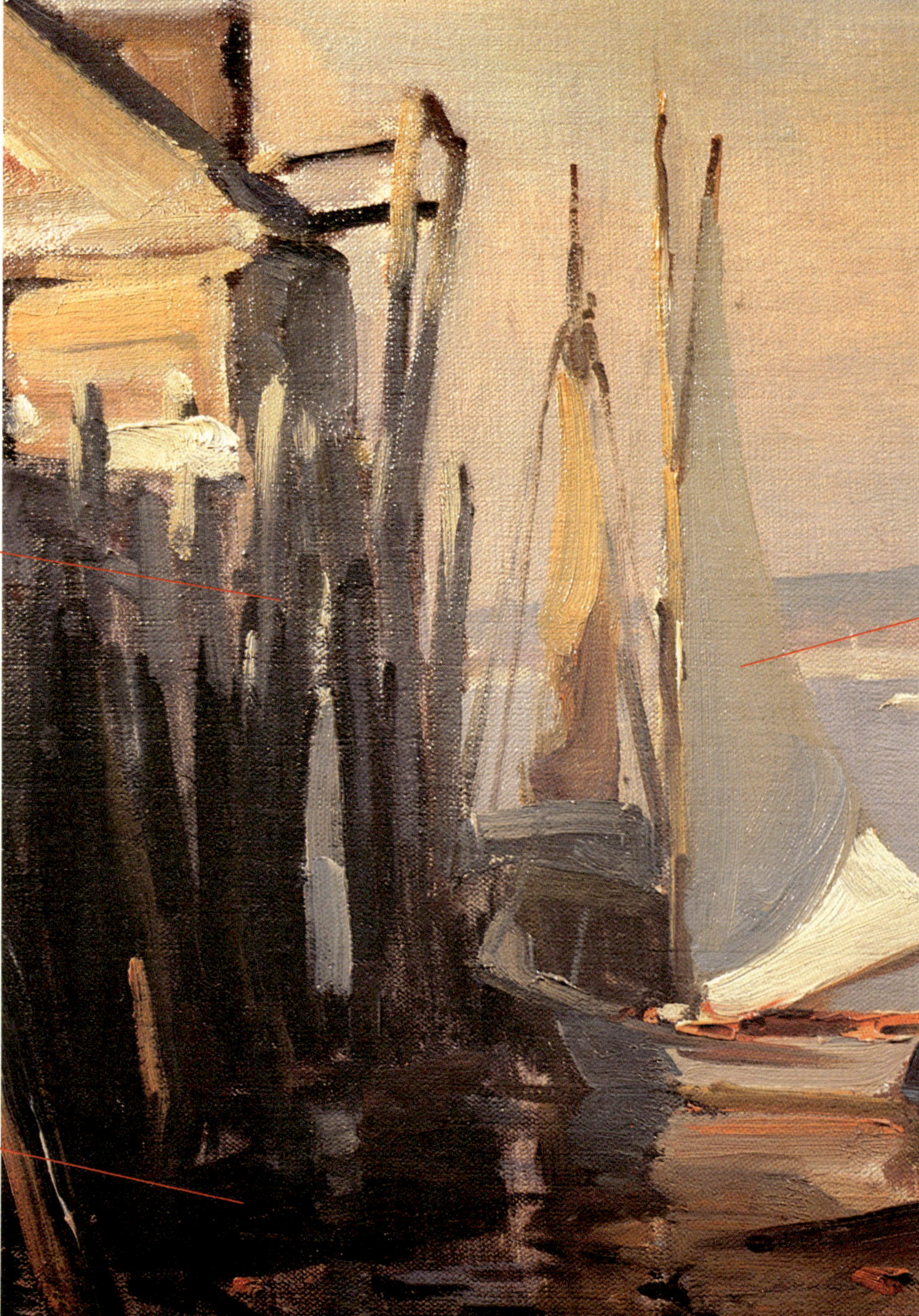

The sail is also flatly done. It's warm where the sun shines through it, but as it curves, it's less affected by the sun. I add a stroke of blue at the base—to echo the color of the sky. The upward curve of the shadow counterpoints the downward curve of the sail.

Darker notes are painted into the preliminary stain.

Boats: Distance

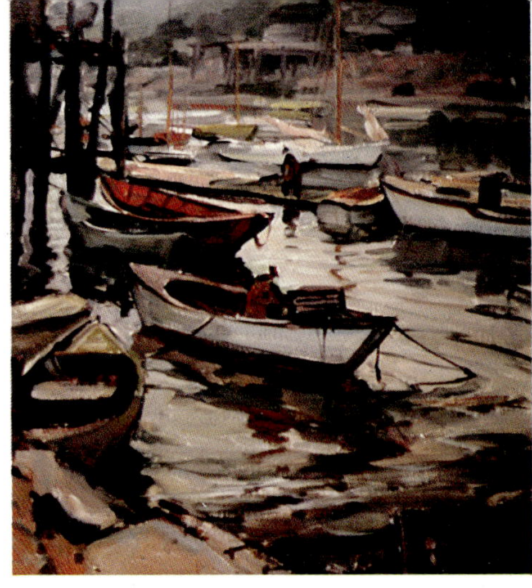

Boats at Anchor
oil on canvas
30″ × 25″ (76 × 64 cm)

To add a glisten to the water, stain the area a warm gray and work horizontal highlights over it. These strokes look rough, but they're very effective in the completed painting.

Since the interior of the gray boat is simple, I can be more descriptive inside the dory. A few strokes suggest wooden supports.

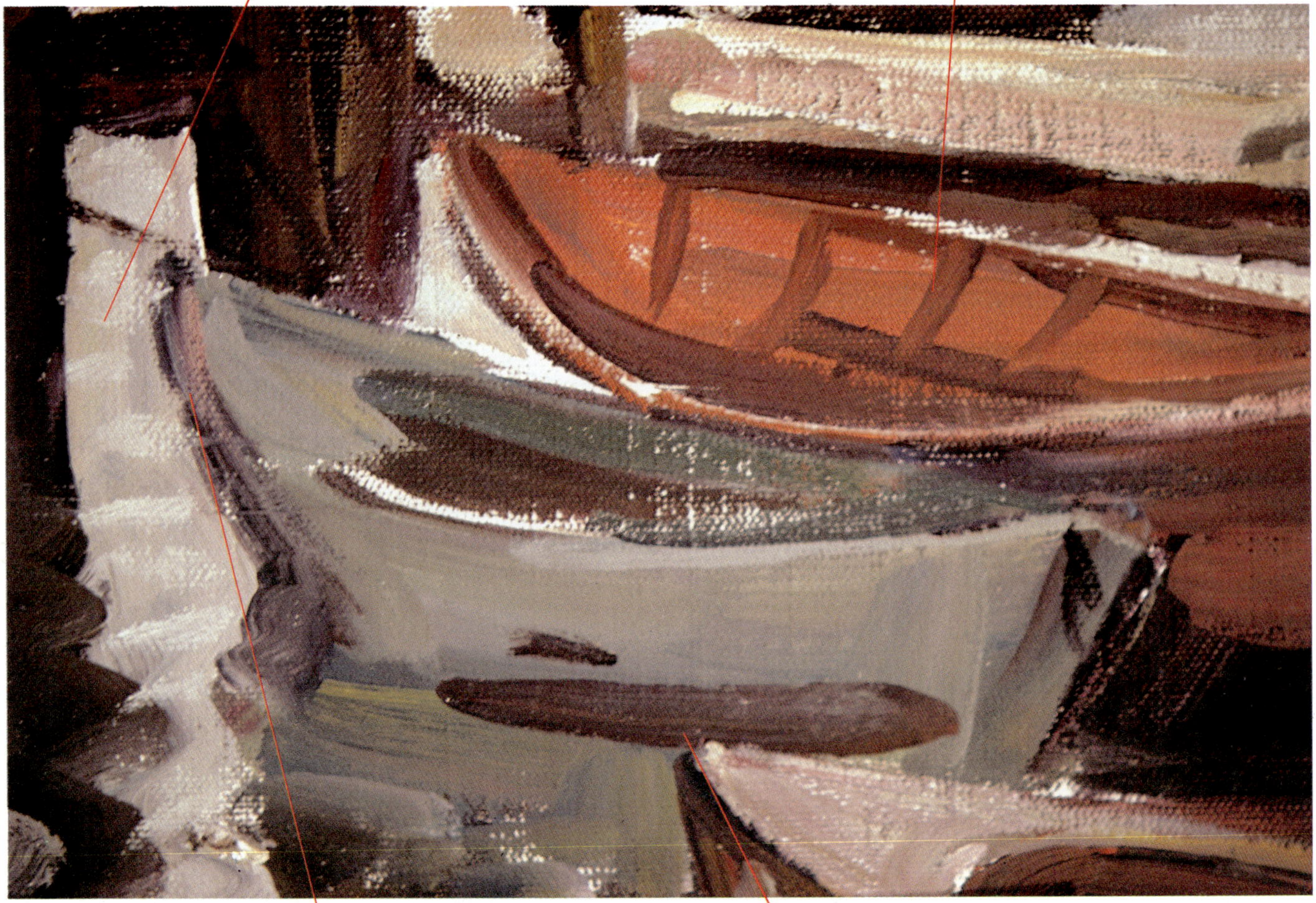

On an overcast day, even light boats silhouette against the bright water. To emphasize the value difference, outline the bow with a dark color. A line is needed to tell the story, so use one.

The dark stroke at the waterline makes the gray boat look lighter. It also explains the shape of the dory.

The foreground boats come together in a large mass. The angle of the dory on the lower left makes the picture; it counterpoints all the other boats. Cover it, and you'll see that everything suddenly seems to slide out the lower right corner. The dark silhouette of the man emphasizes the whiteness of the distant sailboat.

Vertical orange strokes suggest masts and break the dominant horizontals of the picture. Don't bother to add rigging. You can't see it this far away.

In the distance, small boats become spots, both pattern and texture.

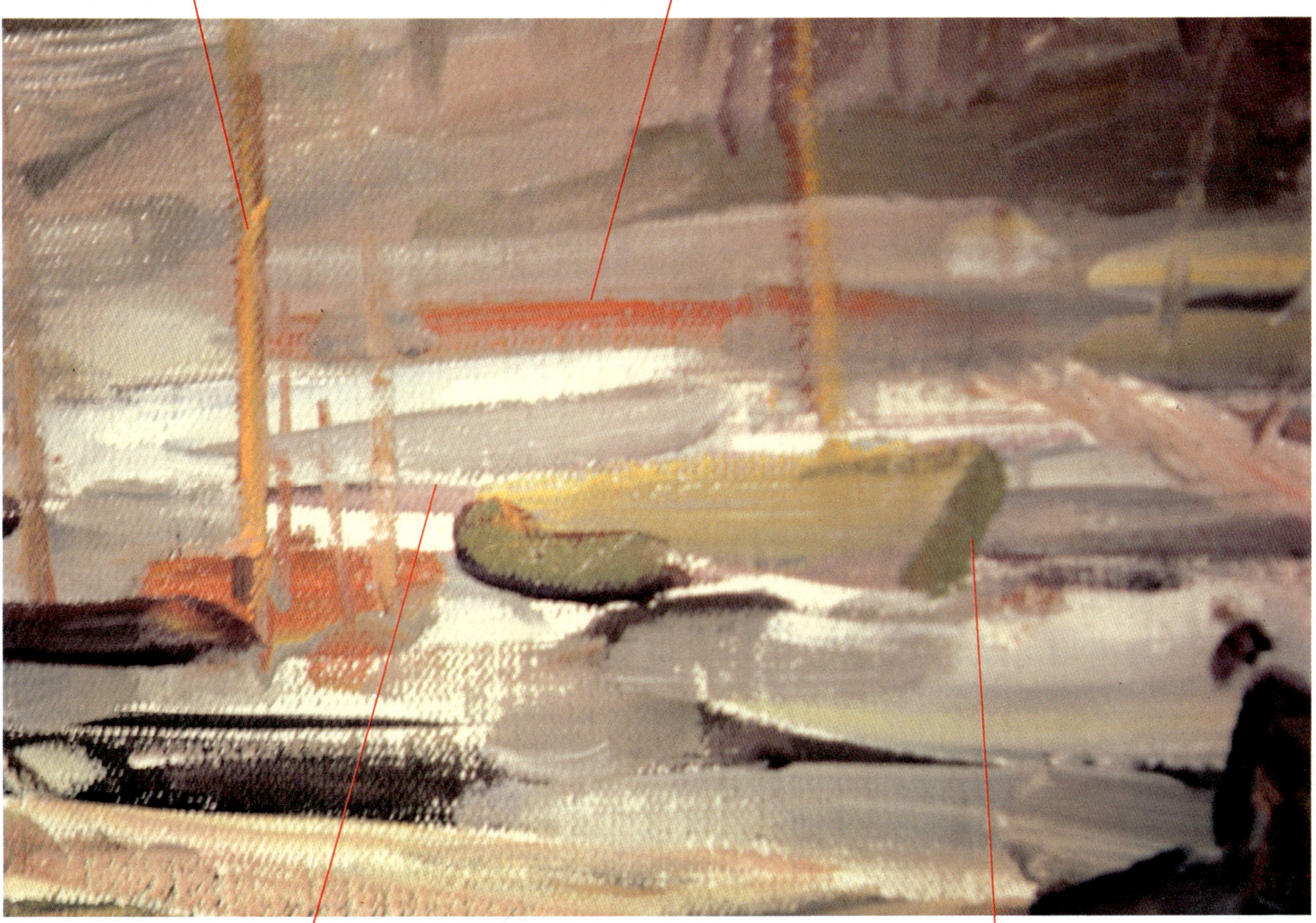

Where the canvas shows through, it looks like light on the water.

Outline a bow occasionally. Such details help you make sense of the more abstract shapes.

Debris

On the Ways
oil on canvas
25″ × 30″ (64 × 76 cm)

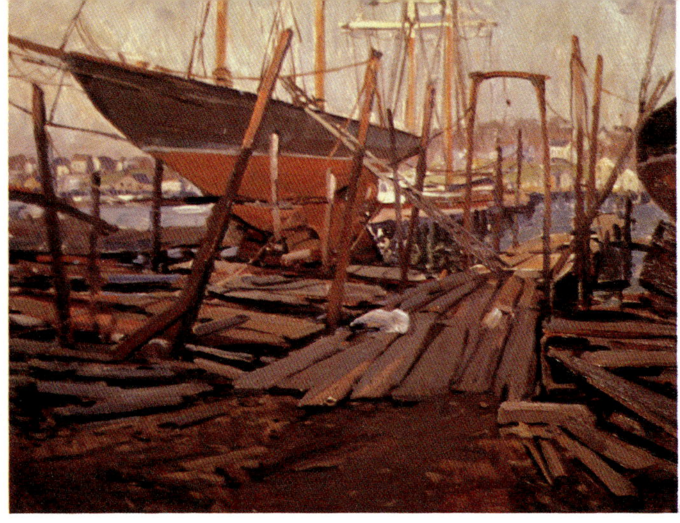

The distant water is a couple of light lavender strokes. There's no detail in this water. Suggestions of ripples would detract from the nearby planks.

A few dots of light color suggest water peeping through the boards. Without these few dots the area would be too massive and visually boring: cover them up and you'll see what I mean.

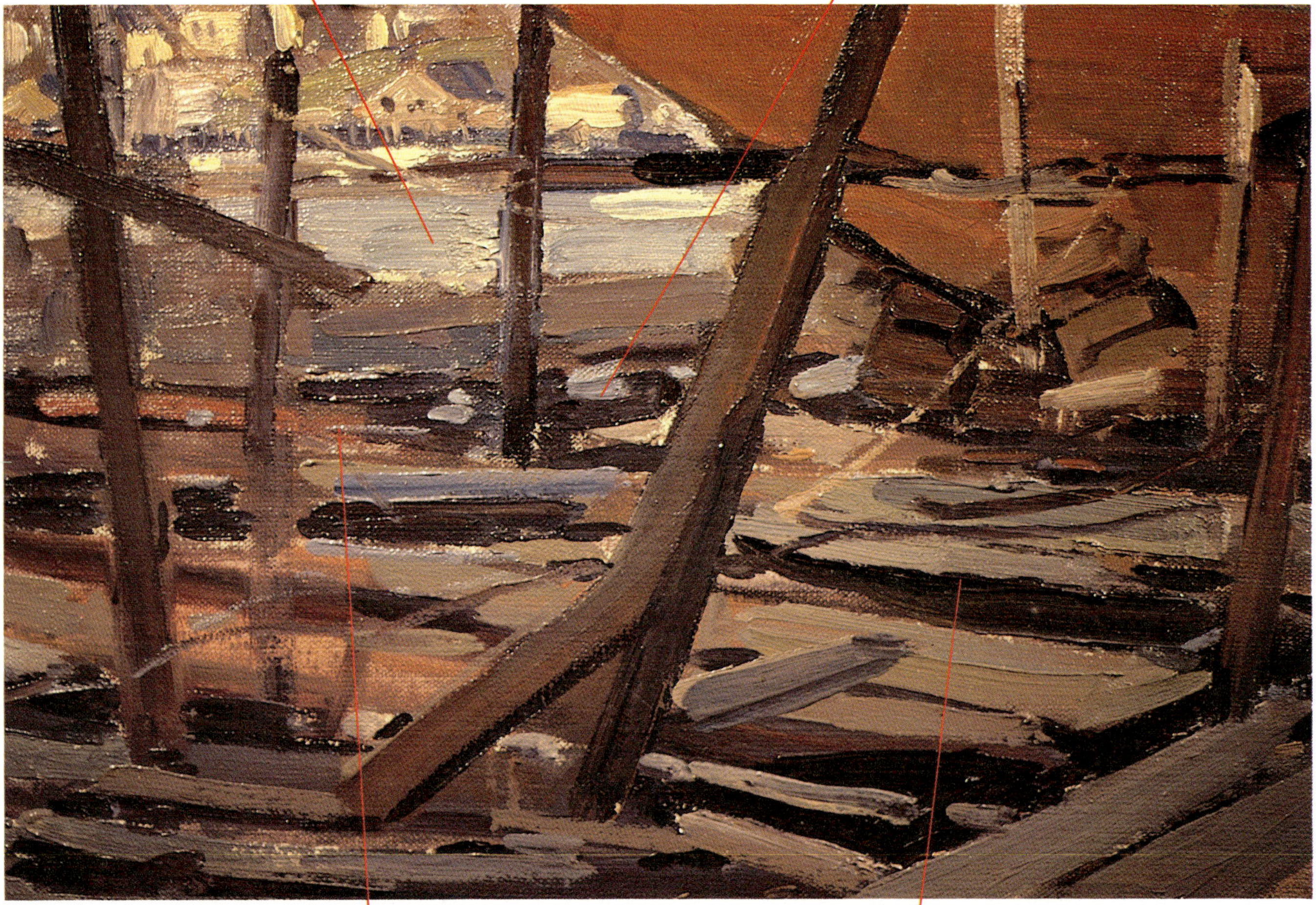

Since the foreground boards are well defined, the farther ones can be suggested by broken slashes of light and dark color. Some strokes blend into one another—just as the boards would appear to merge in nature.

Each stroke indicates a direction of the foreground boards. You can see the dark sides and edges—but not the grain or knotholes. They'd detract from the picture's more important theme of light against shadow.

This picture was painted late in the day. A dramatic shadow is thrown over the foreground, accentuating the sunlit distance. The boat and upright posts are all silhouetted against this high-key background. The subject is the dynamic, contrasting angles of these posts and planks. That's what caught my eye. The boat and foreground earth serve as flat foils to the active brushwork in the center of the picture.

The foreground posts are dark against the sky. They push the sunlit distance back in space. The brilliant sun bleaches the color out of the masts on the left, making them very light.

The distance is a collection of light color notes. You see warm green, pinkish red, and cool purple and read these color notes as fields, houses, and trees. Again: The brilliant sun makes the area into a single, high-key mass.

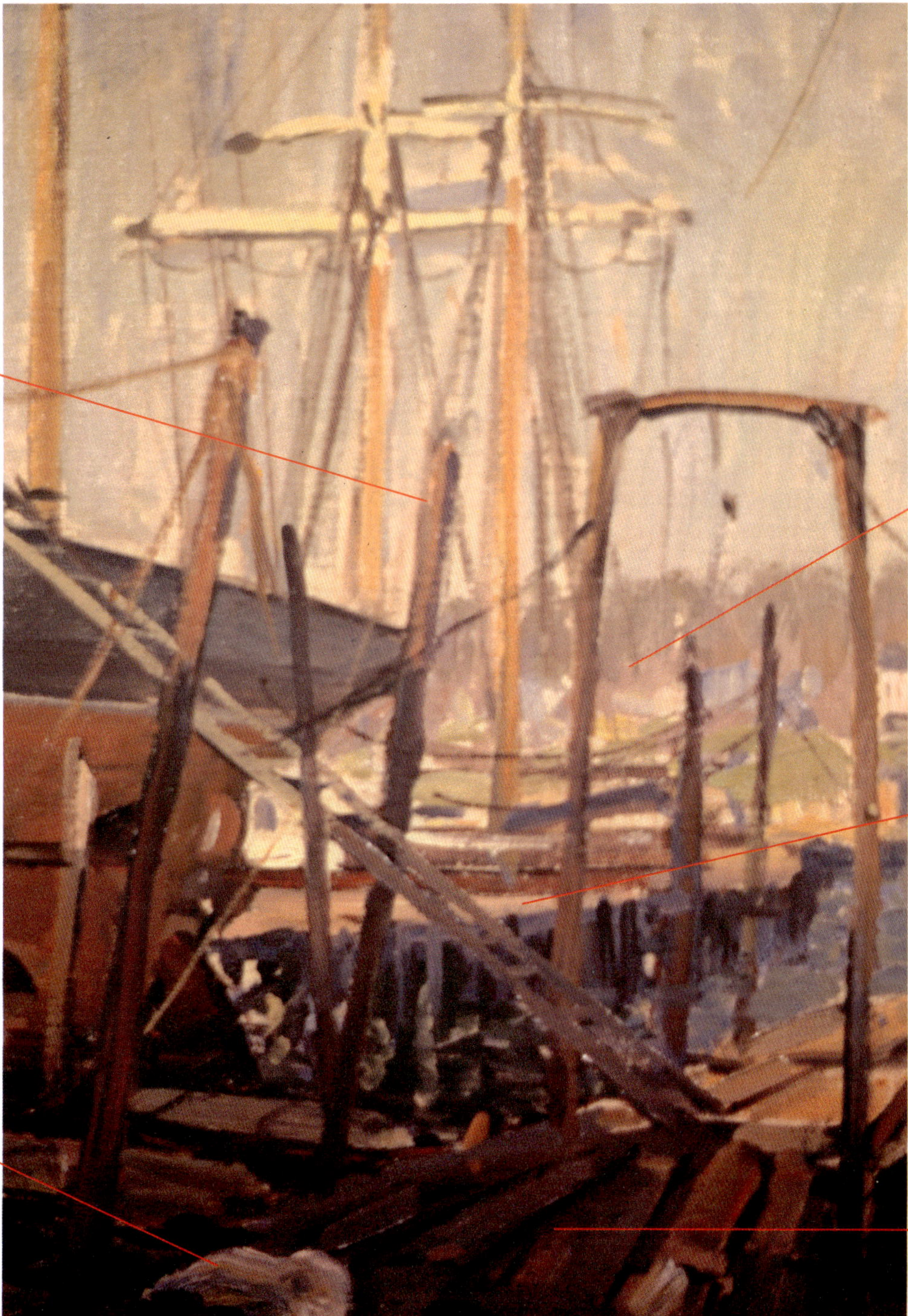

The distant wharf is a stroke of warm color, with a thinly painted area of purple beneath it. More opaque, dark vertical strokes are added to suggest pilings.

The crumpled rag emphasizes the shadow. That light stroke makes the darks look all that much richer.

A flat tone describes the shadowed boards; a few dark strokes separate one from the other.

THE SKY

When painting skies, first determine your light source. Is the sun on your left or right? In front of you or behind you? Maintain that light consistently throughout the painting. The sun moves in the sky, but you have to remember how things looked when you first started to work.

Try to feel the mood of your subject and paint the sky accordingly. If you're working at a quiet moment in the early morning, for example, a bold, heavily textured sky might detract from the peacefulness you want in your picture. A bright, windy day, on the other hand, might impress you with its active, twisting clouds. You feel alive and paint energetically, using rhythmic strokes applied with the whole arm.

Flat skies present few problems to the student, but cloudy days are a different matter. When you paint clouds, you should learn to look for their general movement—then use the ones you think best fit the painting. Remember: Overhead you see mainly the undersides of the clouds. In the distance, the bases flatten out, and you see the billowing shapes of the clouds themselves. Overhead the cloud bases have ragged, diffused edges—they're close to you and you can see how the wind blows them around. In the distance, you can't see such subtle transitions. Background clouds actually appear sharper and clearer than the ones nearer to you.

The student's main problem is getting perspective in clouds. The biggest shapes are overhead; as they recede, the clouds get rapidly smaller. Students draw what they *think* is a big cloud. But "big" in relation to what? They forget that they're designing on a particular size surface, and everything has to be shaped in relation to that surface. So their big cloud, for example, might cover only an eighth of the foreground sky. Clouds like that look like puffballs. Make a cloud base overhead fill half the foreground! Then paint the background cloud base very much smaller. The strong contrast in sizes will pull the viewer into your work. Look up as you paint. Try to feel the full expanse of the sky, not just the part you see under the brim of your hat. When you feel that a thing is big, do everything you can to get that feeling on canvas!

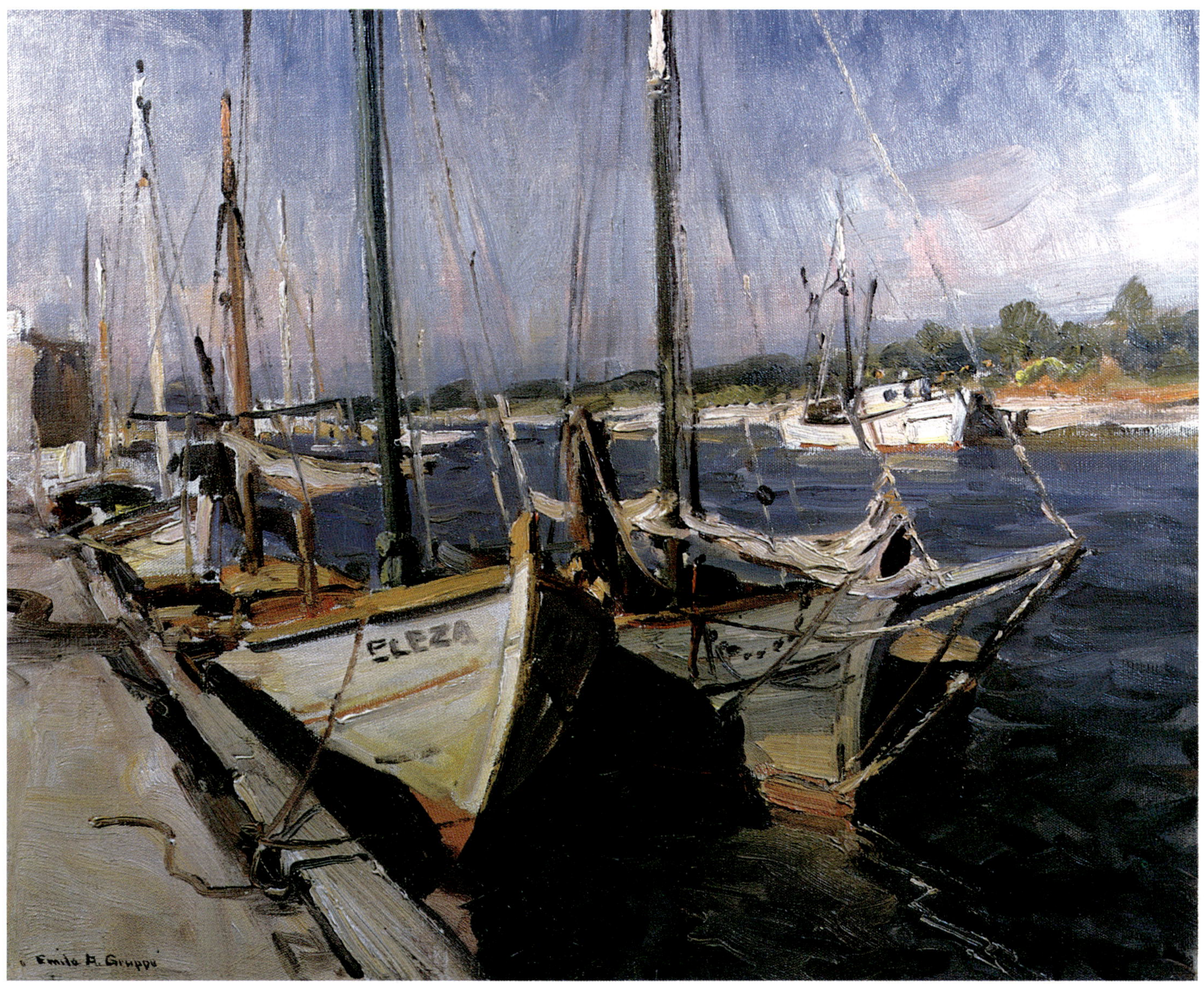

Fishing Boats
oil on canvas
25″ × 30″ (64 × 76 cm)

The day is very clear. The trees remain dark as they go into the distance. The sunlit background boat is clean and white. The sky shows the gradation you usually find when looking away from the sun. It's warm toward the horizon, moves to a greenish band, and near the zenith, takes on an ultramarine blue cast. The sky is very deep and blue overhead; its color reflects into the dark, foreground water. This dark makes a perfect foil for the brighter boats. The water is flat and is painted with horizontal and vertical strokes. To emphasize the height of the sky, paint it with *vertical* strokes.

Cloud Layers

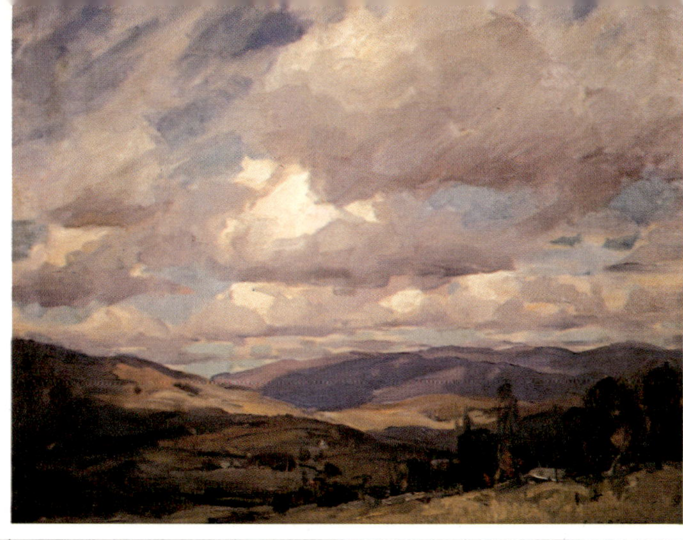

Clouds over Woodstock
oil on canvas
25″ × 30″ (64 × 76 cm)

The small background clouds are painted with rounded strokes.

Above them, the bases of the clouds are contrastingly dark and horizontal.

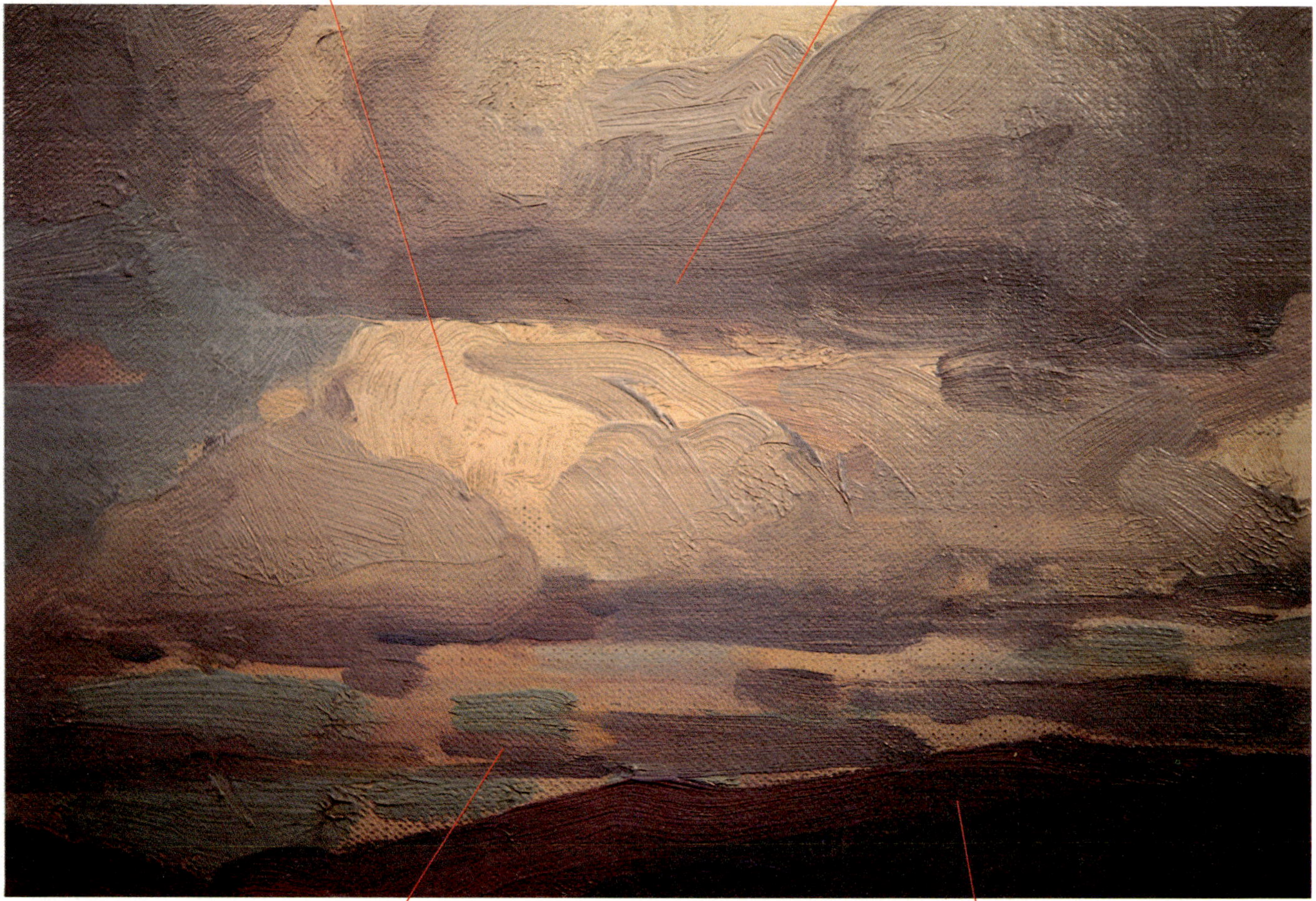

At the horizon, the bases become very thin. Here and there, a dot suggests a free-floating cloud.

The mountains are slightly darker than the bases of the clouds. To give weight to the land, add a few dark lines.

See how the billowing clouds and the light-and-dark pattern of their shadows are reflected on the rolling hillside. Keep the mountain low; the sky dominates. The strong wind blows straight across the land, flattening the bases of the clouds. Greenish patches of sky peep through the distance. Darker, more ultramarine patches are overhead.

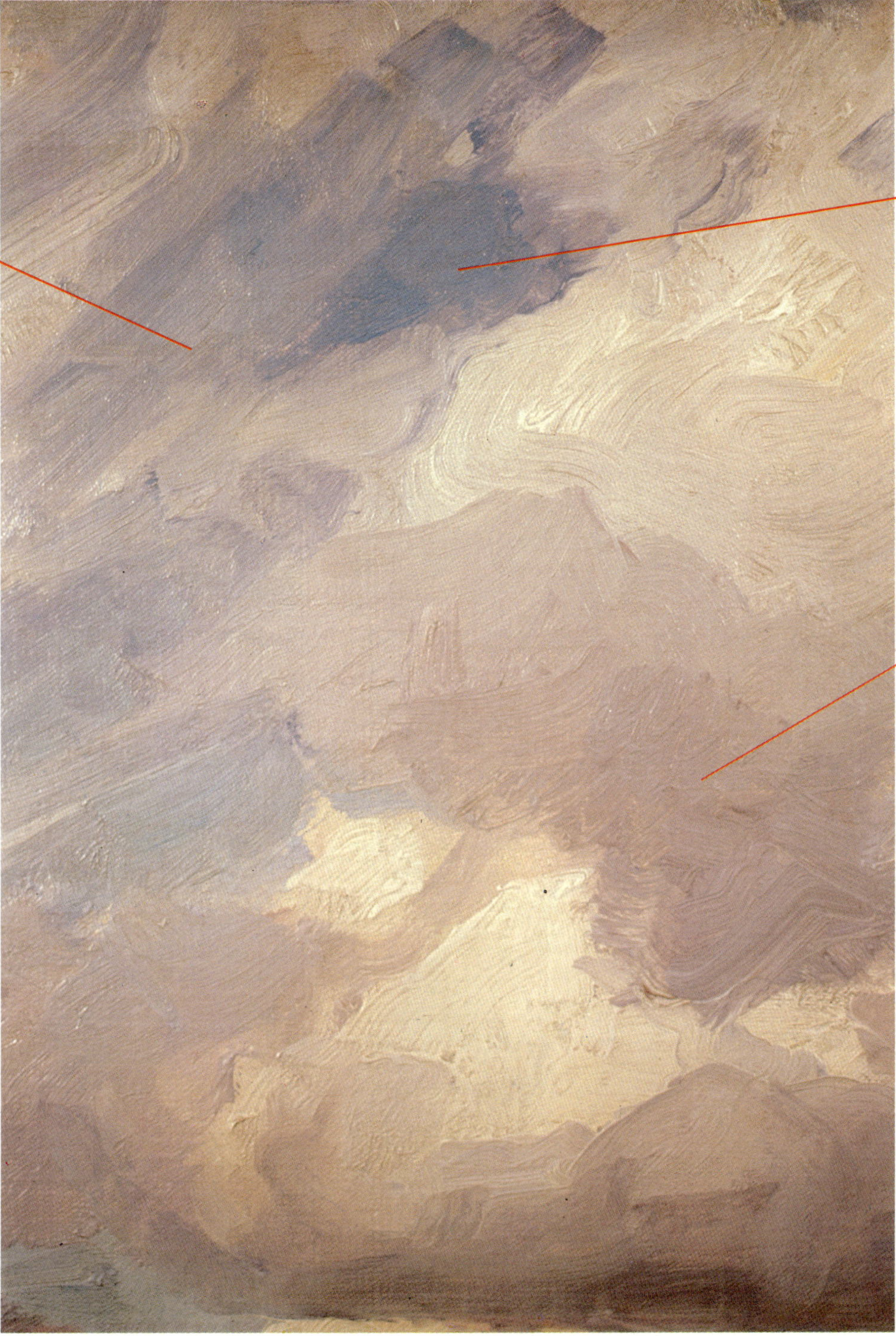

Overhead you can see the effect of the wind on the clouds. In order to achieve it, paint the blue sky into the wet clouds. Where the stroke picks up the lighter undercoat, it looks ragged and suggests wind-blown areas.

The dark sky makes the gray overhead clouds look light and airy.

Active strokes in the clouds parallel the movement of the mass. The base is painted into the wet cloud. Again ragged edges are created where the two layers mix.

Active Sky

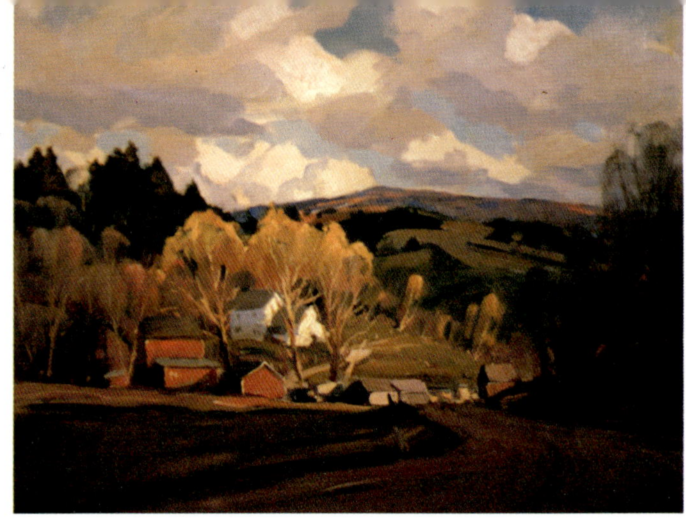

Farm on the Hill
oil on canvas
25″ × 30″ (64 × 76 cm)

The previous illustration had an ominous quality—the result of the low clouds and their insistently horizontal movement. They seem to weigh down on the earth. In this painting, the clouds are much more lyrical and playful. Their upward movement echoes the bright, cheery color of the landscape. Large shadows frame the sunlit hill and suggest the size of the overhead clouds.

Dynamic diagonal strokes form the undersides of the clouds. Paint the lighter bases first and work the darker areas into them.

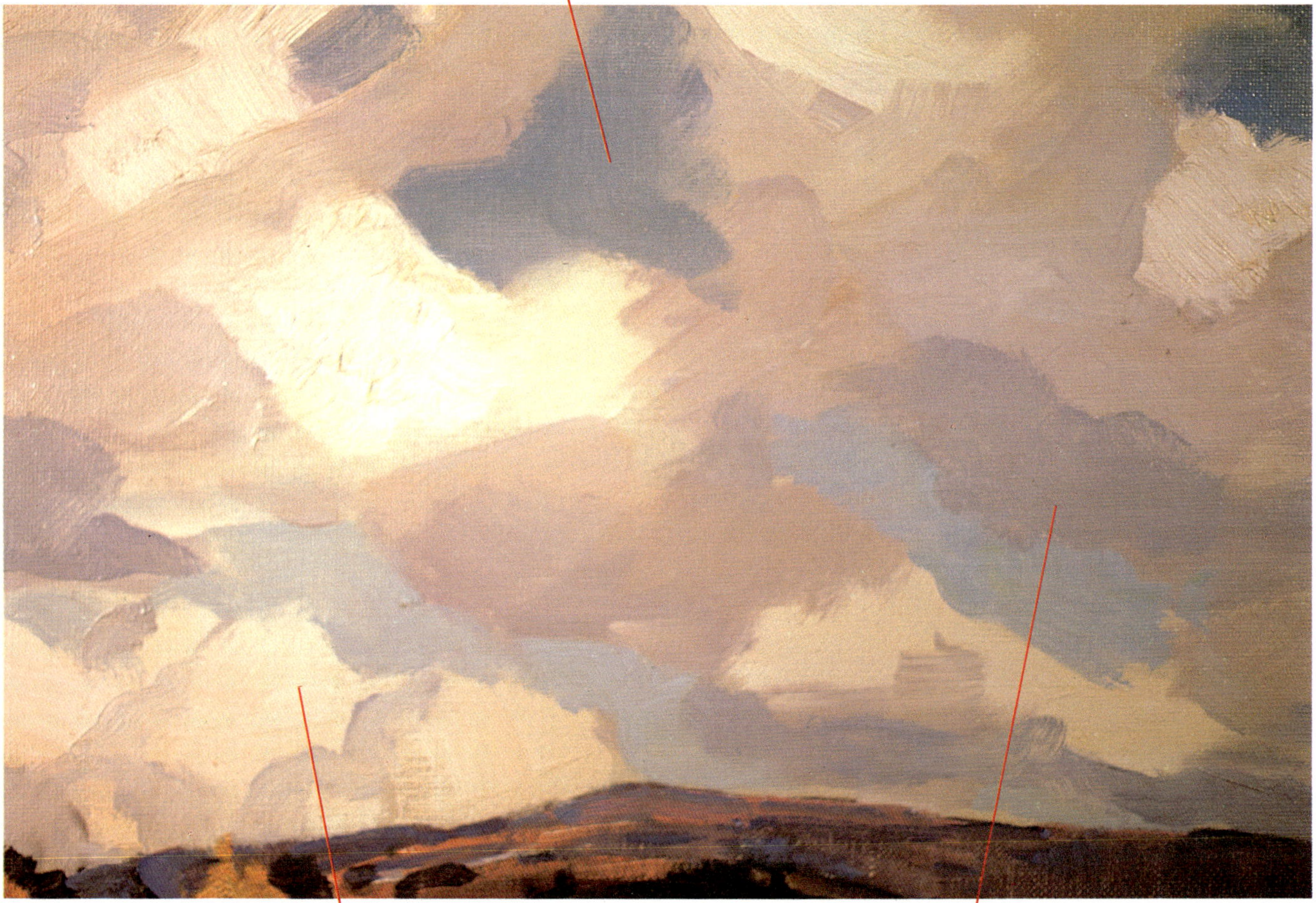

The brightest clouds are again near the horizon. Bumpy strokes accentuate their roundness. The sunlit clouds should be near the center of interest; there's nothing as distracting as a bright cloud against the upper edge of a frame.

To add interest to the sky, paint the undersides of the clouds with a stroke that swings up and to the right. The sunlit clouds are painted with strokes that move in the opposite direction.

Sunset

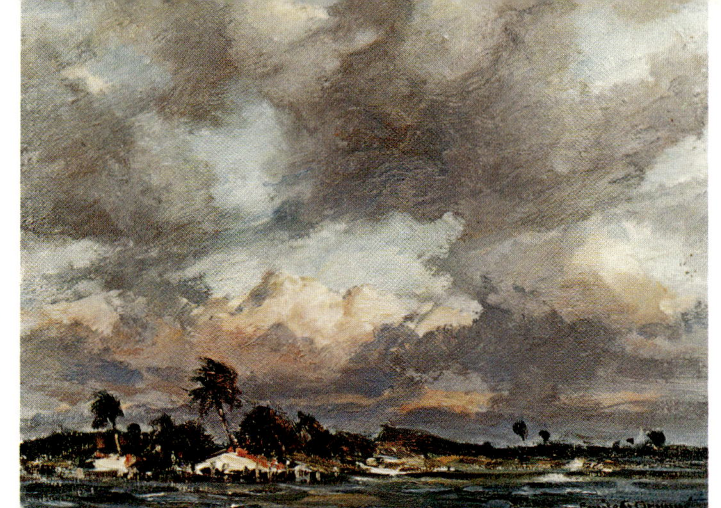

Florida Sky
oil on canvas
20″ × 24″ (51 × 61 cm)

This is an example of the dramatic skies in Florida. Since the effect doesn't last long, you have to paint rapidly. The undersides of the clouds are dark—but they don't look dark against the stronger accents of the distant trees.

These warm, reddish clouds are accented by the complementary green of the sky.

Higher up, you see more of the clouds' warm, red-purple undersides. They get darker as they recede into the distance. The cool atmosphere obscures the red and turns the color of the bases a blue-purple.

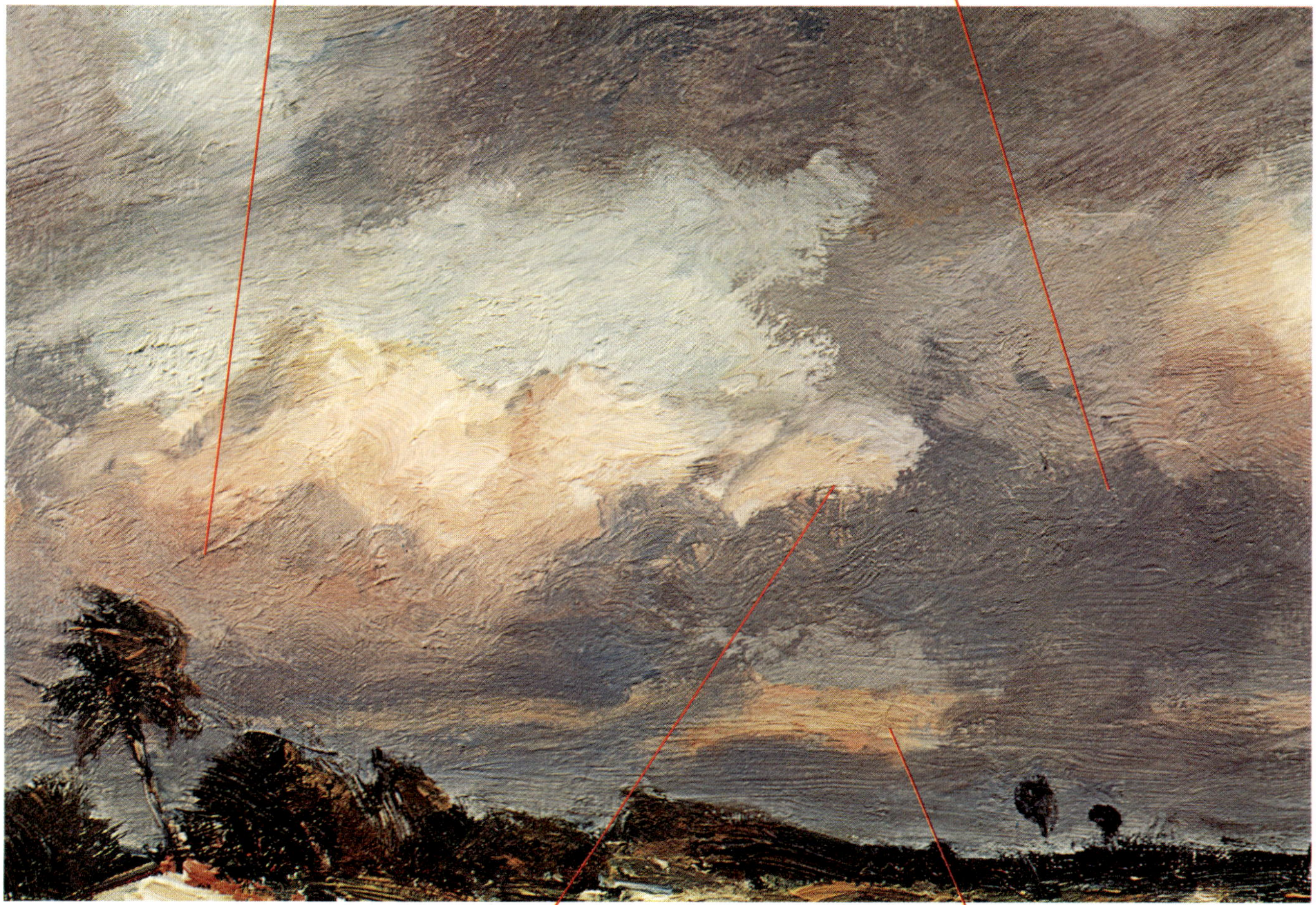

The edges of the farthest clouds are sharp and clear—you don't see subtle, windblown areas.

The warm light of the setting sun hits the fully exposed sides of the distant clouds and makes them a warm red. The small cloud near the horizon is almost carmine.

THE OCEAN

Marine painting is an abstract business: you deal with forces rather than facts. Rocks are angular, weighty shapes. Water, on the other hand, is something that moves. When you look at it, you don't see a lot of edges. Frederick Waugh was a great painter of the sea and a master of thinking up new and original compositions. But, for all his power, he sometimes nailed things down too much. Everything was perfect: a distant wave was as well-drawn as one in the foreground. The picture was like a diagram. When you live with a picture like that, it doesn't grow on you. It lacks mystery. Winslow Homer, on the other hand, used a very eccentric shorthand when he painted the sea. You never see an ocean that *looks* the way he drew it. But those querky, twisted strokes somehow convey the *character* of the subject. A painting by Homer *feels* true. For me, that suggestion is the greater art.

When you paint a marine, ask yourself a simple question: rocks or water? Equal amounts of each would be confusing in a picture; the viewer doesn't know which you want to *emphasize*. What is it you want to *say?* This decision is difficult for the student, who not only likes *everything*, but is also prejudiced by the paintings seen in galleries. It's hard for you to see things with your own eyes. I visited the studio of a friend a while back because he wanted me to give him a critique on a lot of crashing-wave marines. All I could say was, "Kind of cornball, huh?" He was painting someone else's idea of what the ocean should be. I told him to go to the shore and *look*. See what he liked best—and then paint that!

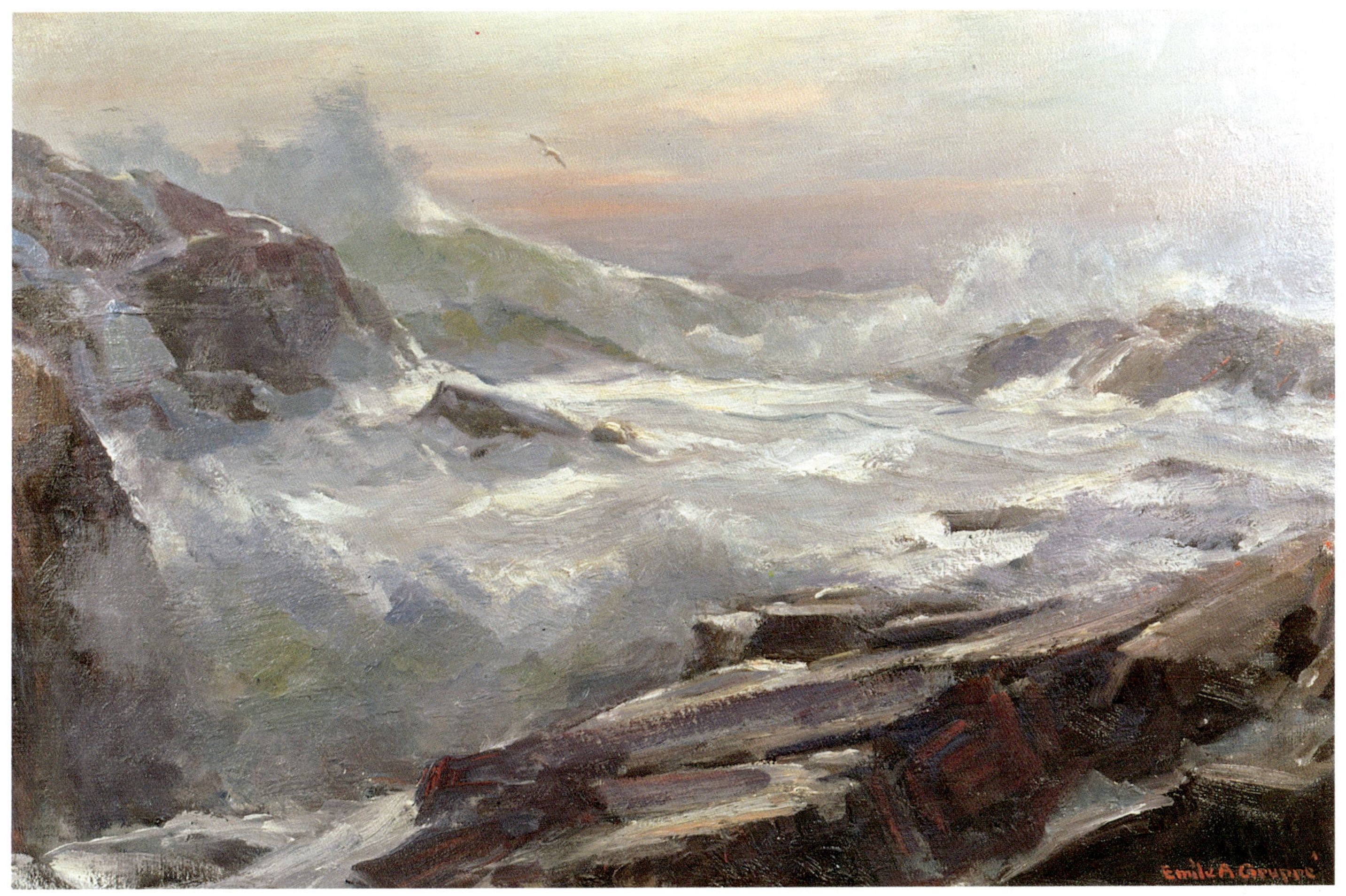

Morning Light
oil on canvas
24″ × 36″ (61 × 91 cm)

The power in this painting comes from the way the large foreground rock acts in counterpoint with the distant wave. Cover the rock, and you'll see that the picture loses much of its force. Although the painting seems full of light, there's little bright white in the foam. The foreground is mostly dark water; when a bit of glare occurs, it *means* something. The foreground rock is painted with big strokes that clearly define its top and sides. As the painting recedes into the distance, the strokes in the rocks begin to merge together. They're obscured by the mist from the ocean. Notice, for example, how simply the rock on the far right is painted.

Foreground Rocks

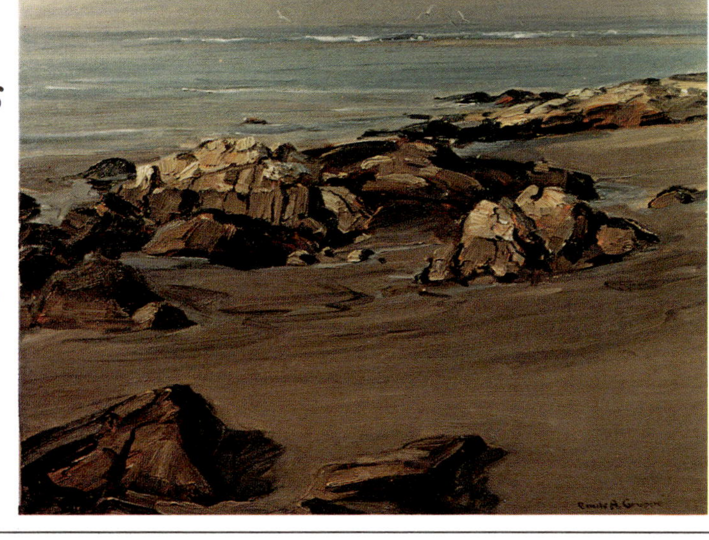

Wingaersheek Beach
oil on canvas
25″ × 30″ (64 × 76 cm)

Here what's interesting is the way the rocks, at low tide, slowly snake their way across the beach and into the distance. The rocks form an interconnected unit, and they're clearly the subject of the picture. The water and distant waves are subordinate elements.

Since the rock juts forcefully out of the beach, apply the paint with heavy, vertical strokes.

Occasionally horizontal strokes create variety within the mass and suggest the different planes of the rock.

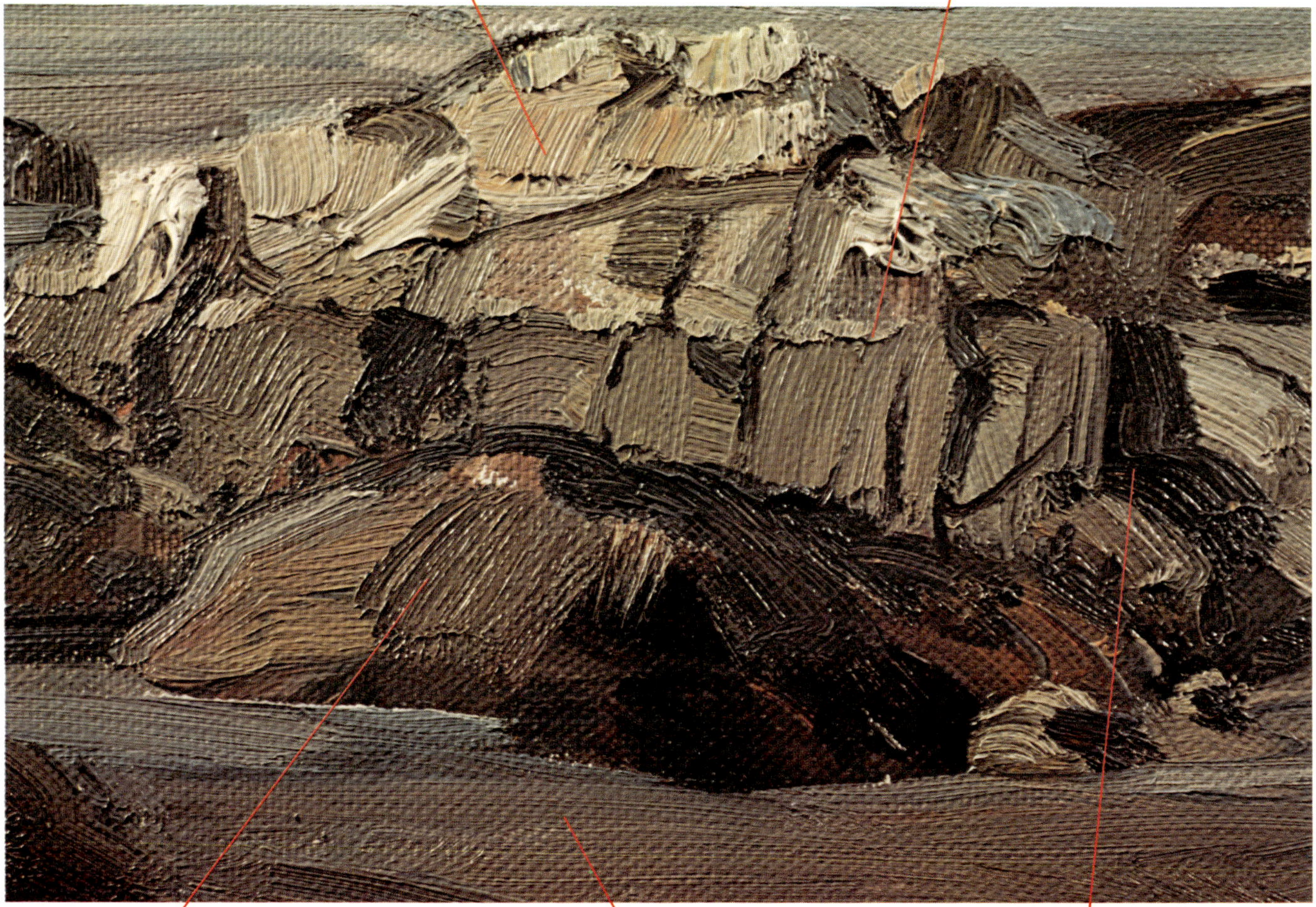

The ocean has the greatest abrasive effect on the lower parts of the rocks. These parts are therefore the smoothest. You can see how curved strokes suggest their rounded shapes.

Paint the sand with broad, horizontal strokes. This horizontal movement contrasts with that of the rocks and thus emphasizes their upward thrust.

The sea stains them, so they're also darker than the upper parts of the rocks, where the sun has a bleaching effect.

Background Rocks

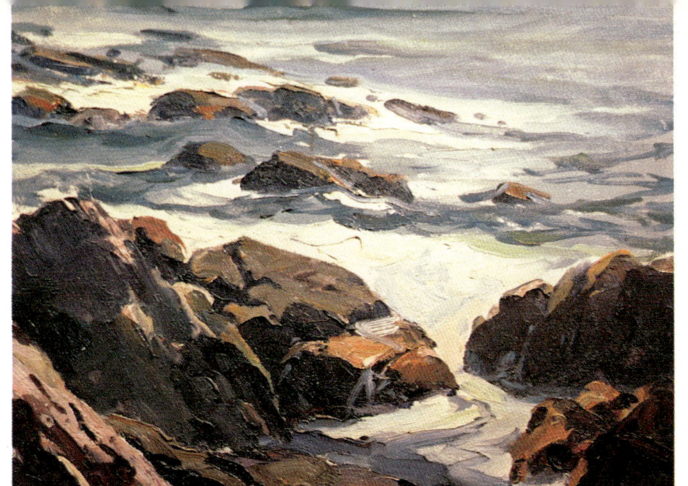

Low Tide
oil on canvas
18″ × 20″ (46 × 51 cm)

Since this is a study of rocks and water, it's fine to omit the sky here. Low tide lets you see the broken shapes of the rocks. The water is only mildly active, so you can get a good pattern of dark, stained rocks against the white foam. These water masses are simple and emphasize the staccato rhythm of the rocks.

Don't worry about distant rocks becoming lighter in value as they recede. They remain fairly dark; it's the *size* of the stroke that creates a feeling of distance.

In the distance, the rocks are short strokes and dots. The small strokes make the foreground rocks look more massive.

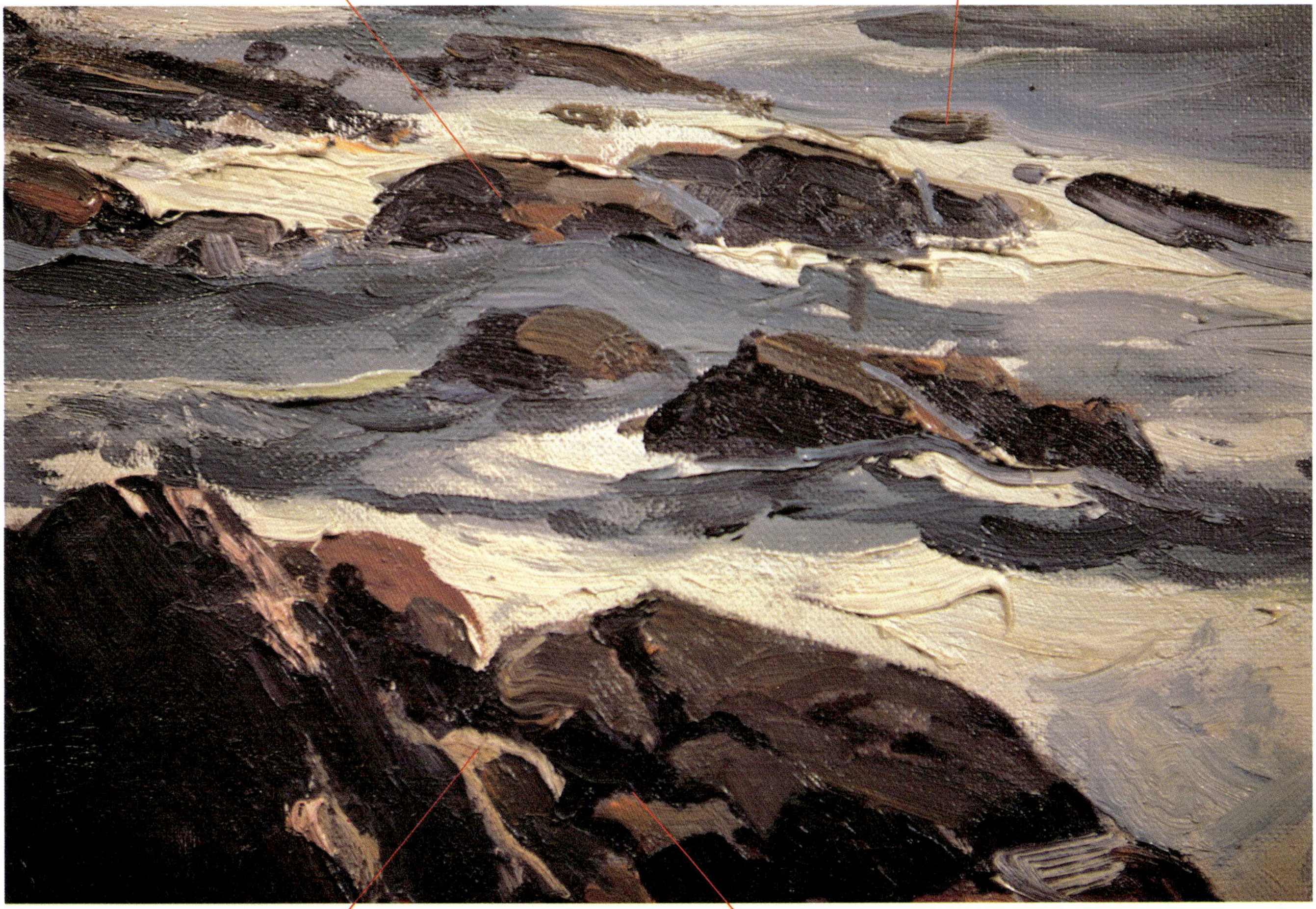

Farther back, there are no crevices. One stroke defines a shadow; another, slightly curved one shows where the rock catches the light.

The nearest rock is painted with some care; you can even see a few crevices. Warm notes help establish a foreground.

Frontlighting

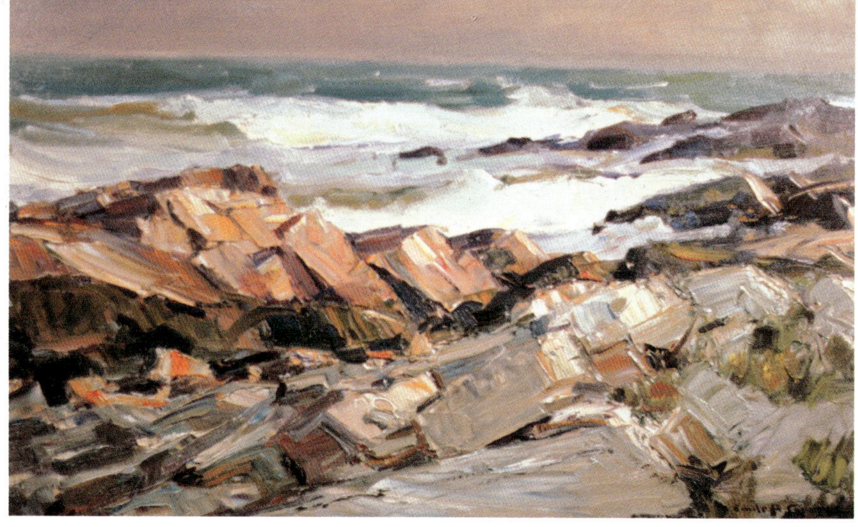

The Back Shore
oil on canvas
20″ × 30″ (51 × 76 cm)
Collection of the
Cape Ann Savings Bank

The dark rocks also emphasize the brightness of the foam. Their simple shapes don't detract from the ocean, while the sharp edges play up the foam's softer ones.

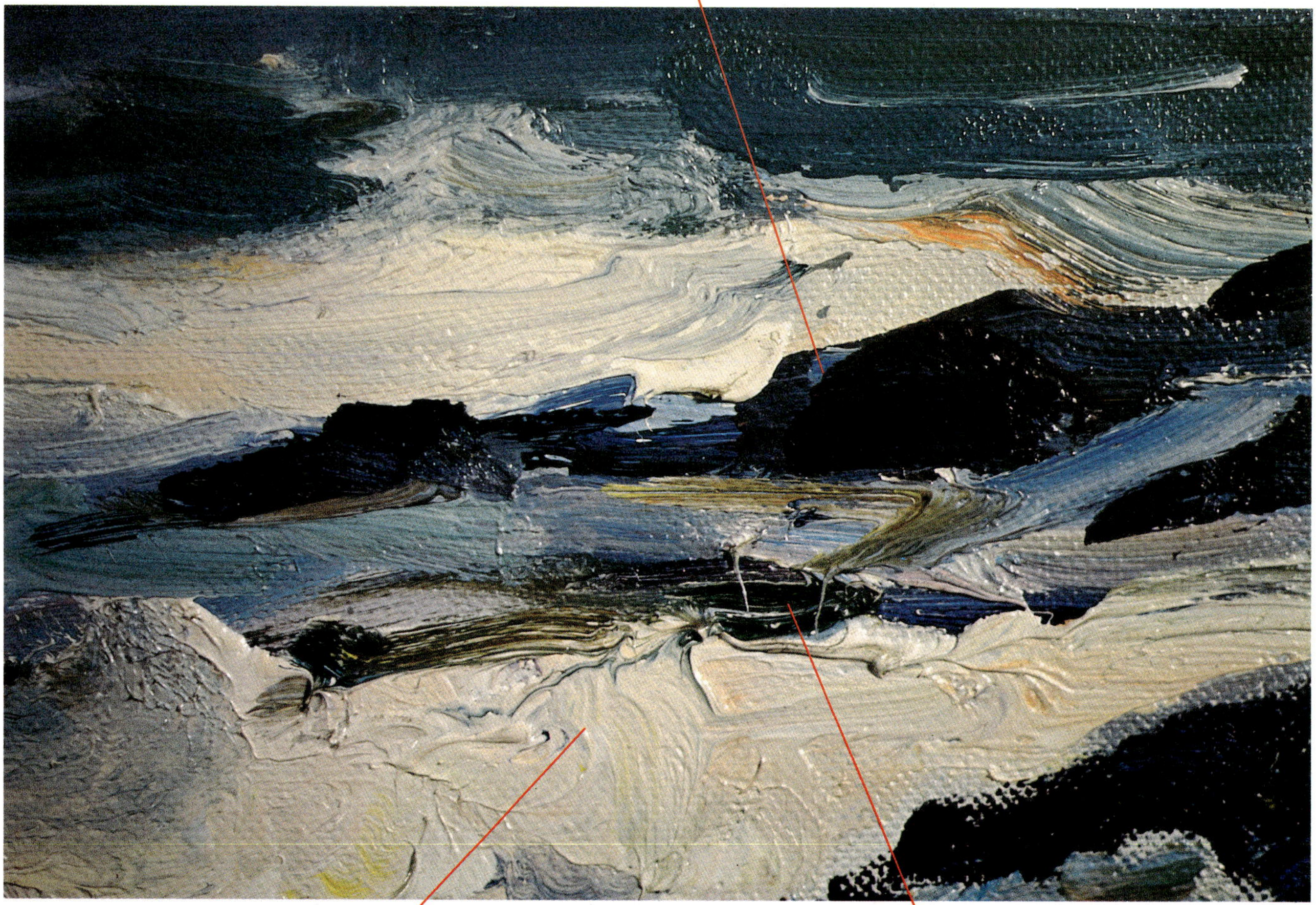

The sun is low in the sky and hits the upright plane of the wave straight on, turning it a brilliant, warm white. There's little visible modeling, since shadows are obliterated by the strong light. Use swirling strokes to show the broken activity of the wave.

The shadows on the water help emphasize the lightness of the foam. They're painted with angular strokes in which the various colors are only partly mixed; the shadows have both green and purple in them.

This area of coast has lots of red granite—a strong color note. The brightest color is again near the shore, where the sea hasn't had a chance to seep into it and stain it. You can see how dark the distant rocks are. This is a *rock* picture. The ocean is the second largest area in the design; the sky the third largest.

Also paint the distant rocks with the brush; they're thin and you can see the texture of the canvas through them.

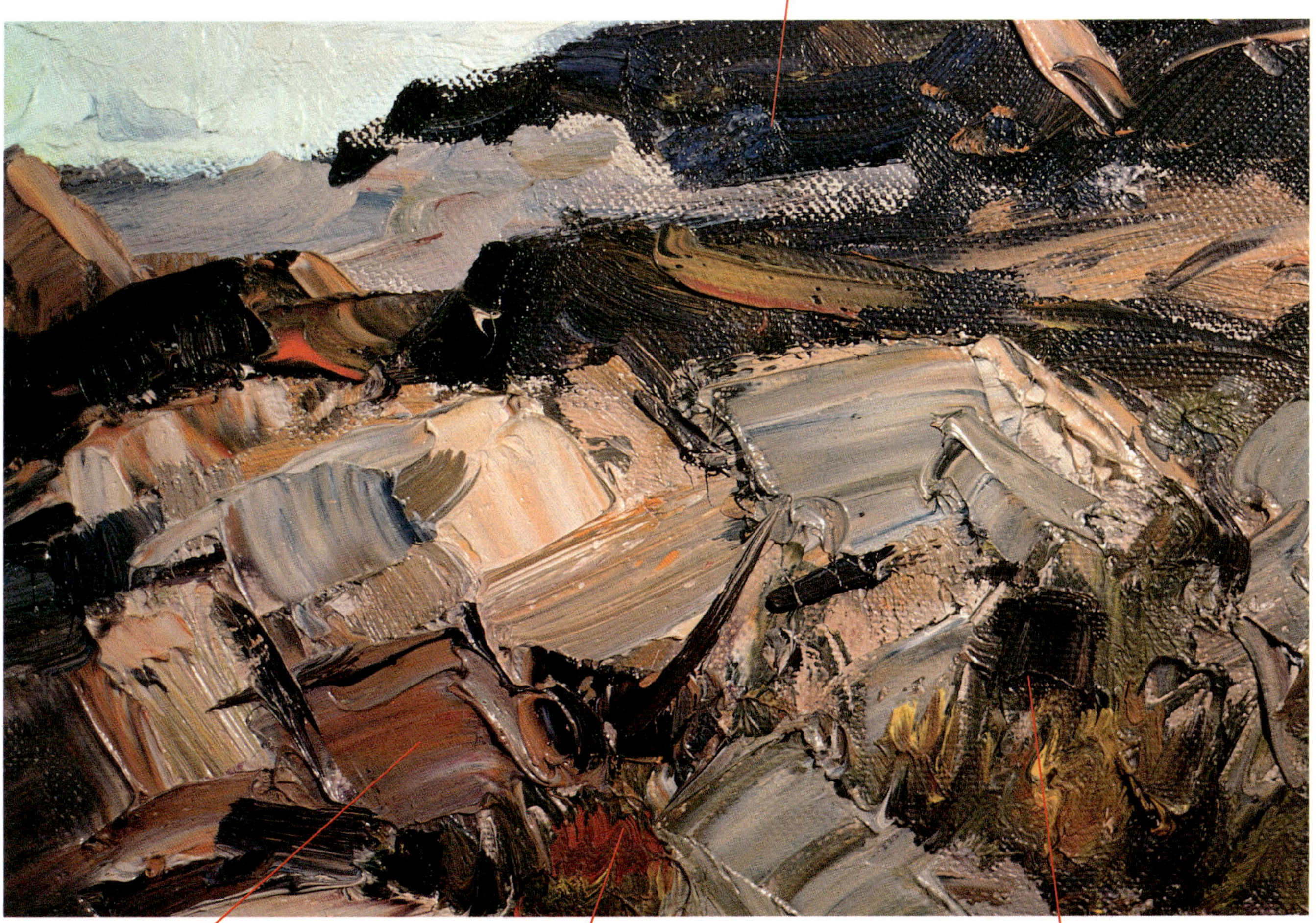

The palette knife obliterates the texture of the canvas, thus making the foreground rocks seem heavy and near to us. It also creates sharp, rocklike edges.

Use a brush for the dark crevices and to suggest clumps of grass and broken twigs.

Use a palette knife to show the sharpness of the foreground rocks—pieces of granite broken by millions of years of wind and ocean. With the knife, you can pick up different colors, mix them, lay them on the canvas, and still retain hints of the original pigment. Here these strands of color suggest facets in the rock. Much of this color is accidental; I didn't know what it would look like till I made the stroke.

Backlighting

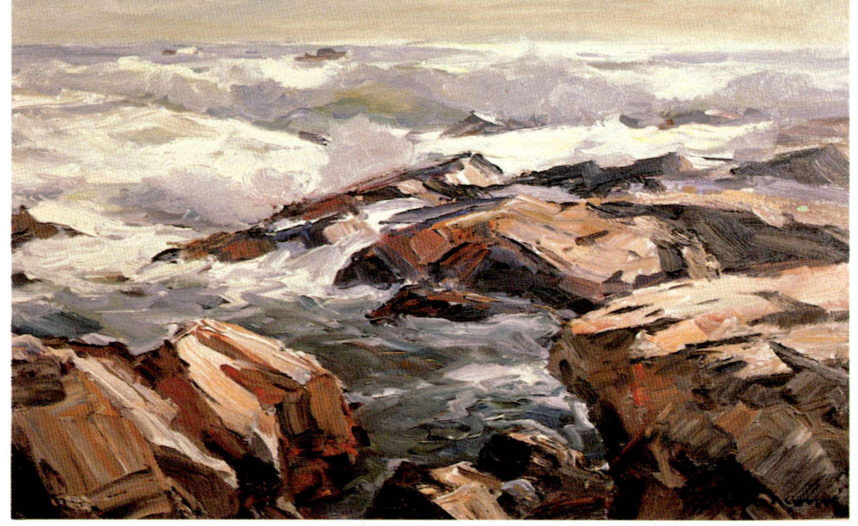

Surf and Rocks
oil on canvas
20″ × 30″ (51 × 76 cm)
Collection of the
Cape Ann Savings Bank

Also paint the distance flatly. The horizon is ragged. Where the canvas shows through, it looks like glare on the water. The dark boat accents the brilliance of the water.

The shadow area of the foam is cool. It catches a lot of blue from the sky and is painted with upward-moving strokes that imitate the vertical face of the wave.

Strokes of warm light are painted into the sunlit foam; they show where light reflects up from the foreground.

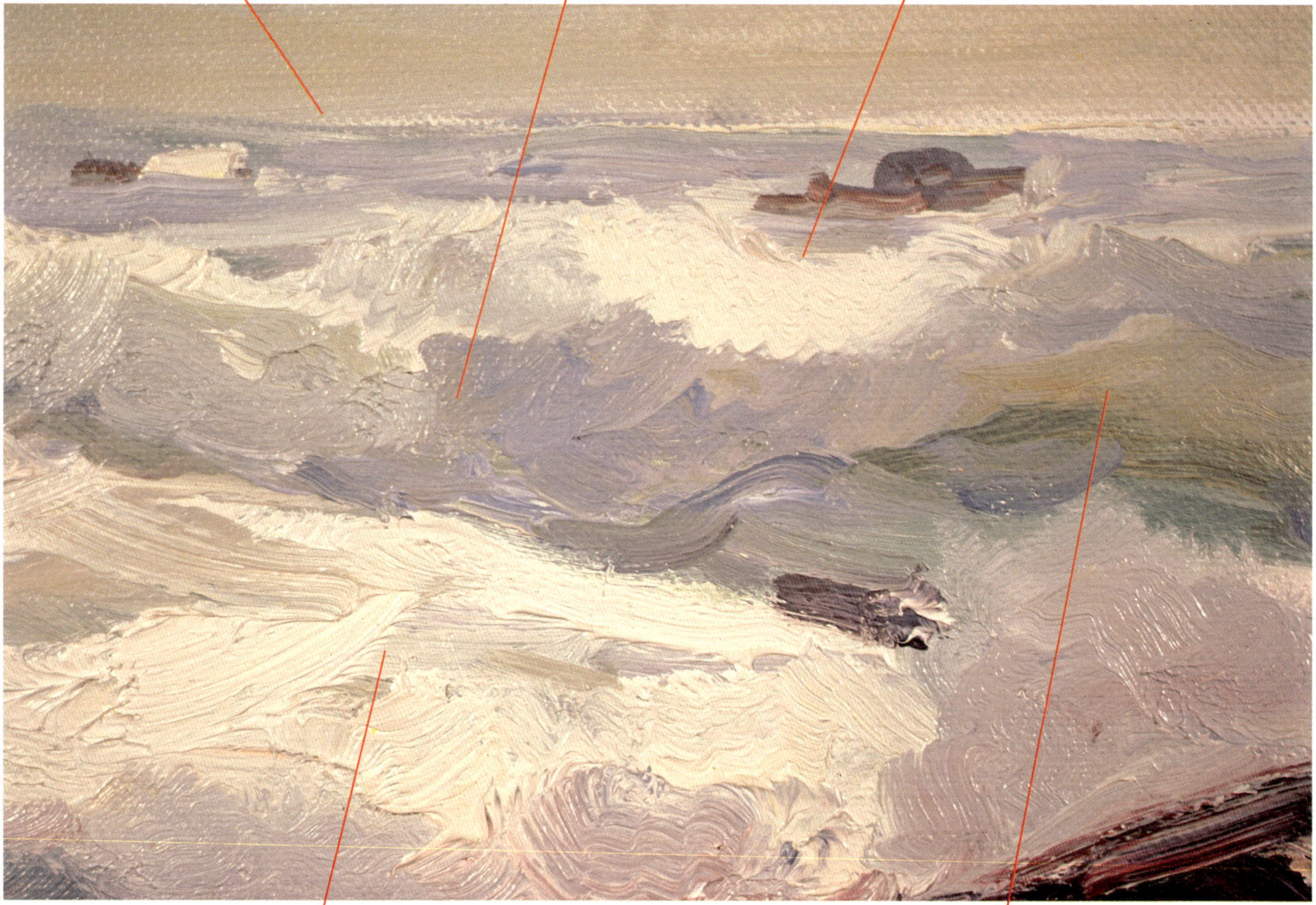

The vertical, nervous strokes of the wave contrast with the less active strokes of the flat area of white water directly in front of it.

Where the foam is thinner, the light comes through it, giving it a warm, orangey look. Where it transmits light less effectively, it becomes darker.

In contrast with the previous painting, this scene is lit from the back. The foam is more broken and interesting in color. The large areas of shadowed rock add punch to the design. In the immediate foreground, swirling strokes suggest an area of backwash; the water, having come into the inlet and hit the surrounding rocks, is moving out again. You can see where it meets the opposing movement of the incoming tide.

Use horizontal strokes for the top of the rock.

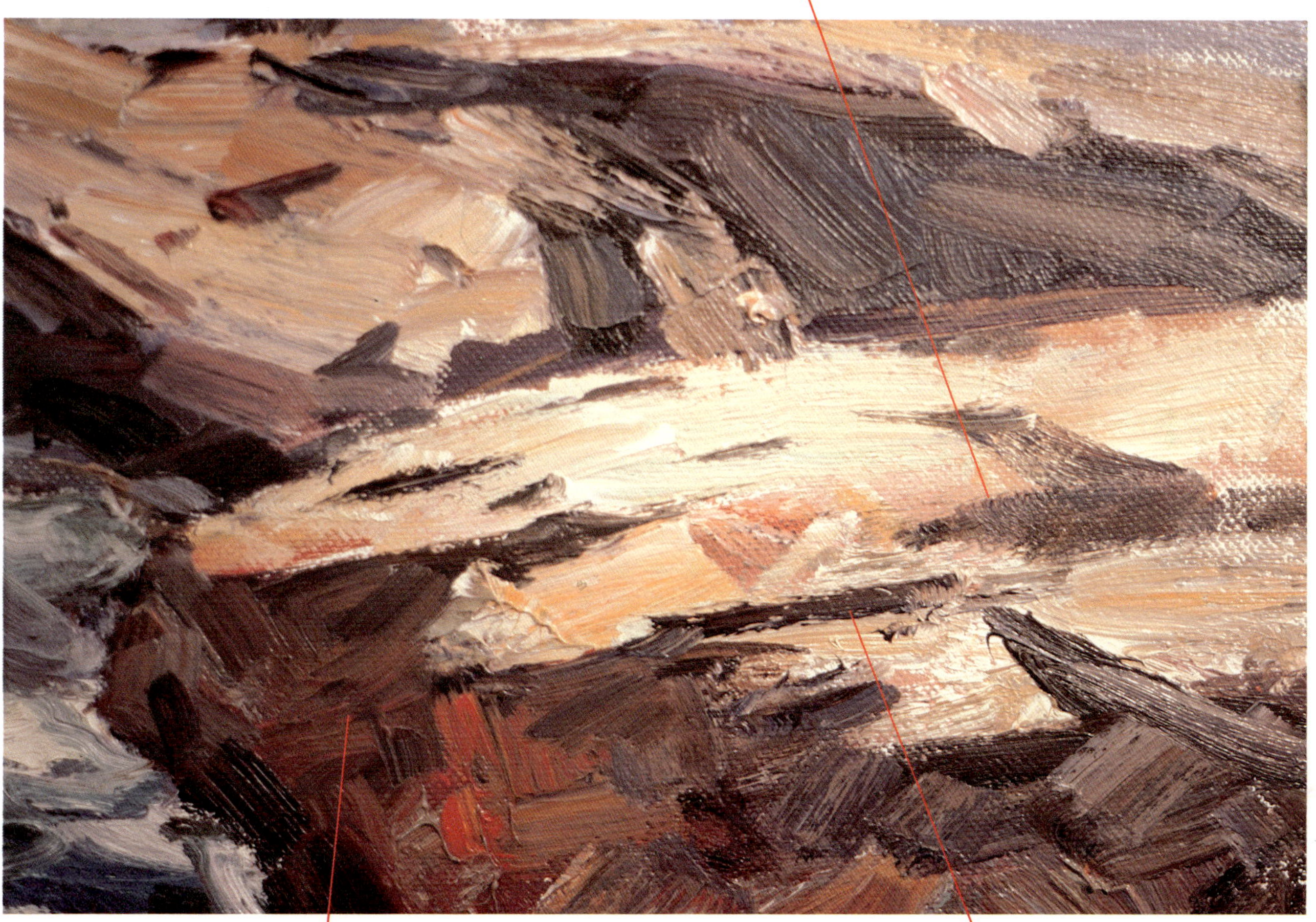

The shadow is painted with contrasting diagonal and vertical strokes; you should feel the crevices in the darks, without actually seeing them. A brush works better than the knife here; you don't want hard edges in the shadows.

Add a few dark crevices, but edit out the hundred unimportant ones and only use those that express the flat plane of the rock.

Highlights

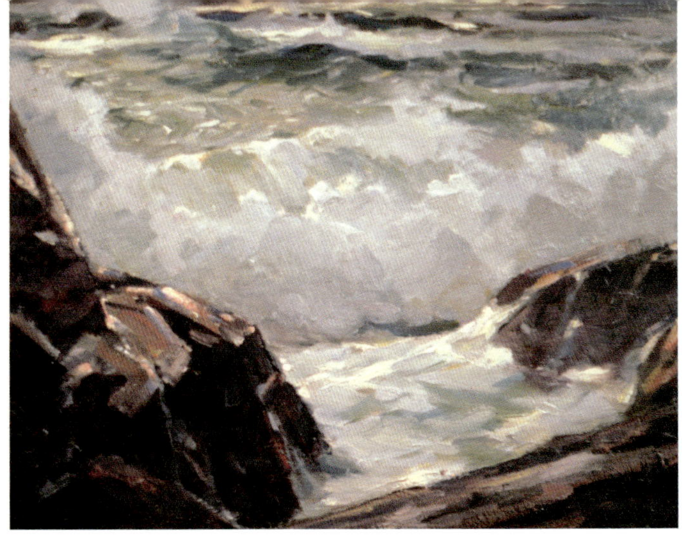

After the Storm
oil on canvas
25″ × 30″ (64 × 76 cm)

The background burst of foam is opaque at the center. Use less paint near the edge, almost "dry-brushing" the paint over the background. It catches the tooth of the canvas and suggests foam blowing in the wind.

Rising water forms a sort of "window" allowing you to look through it into the darker depths. The slanting area is painted with strokes of rich green, worked right over the lighter underpainting. Where the two mix, they form interesting shifts in value and color.

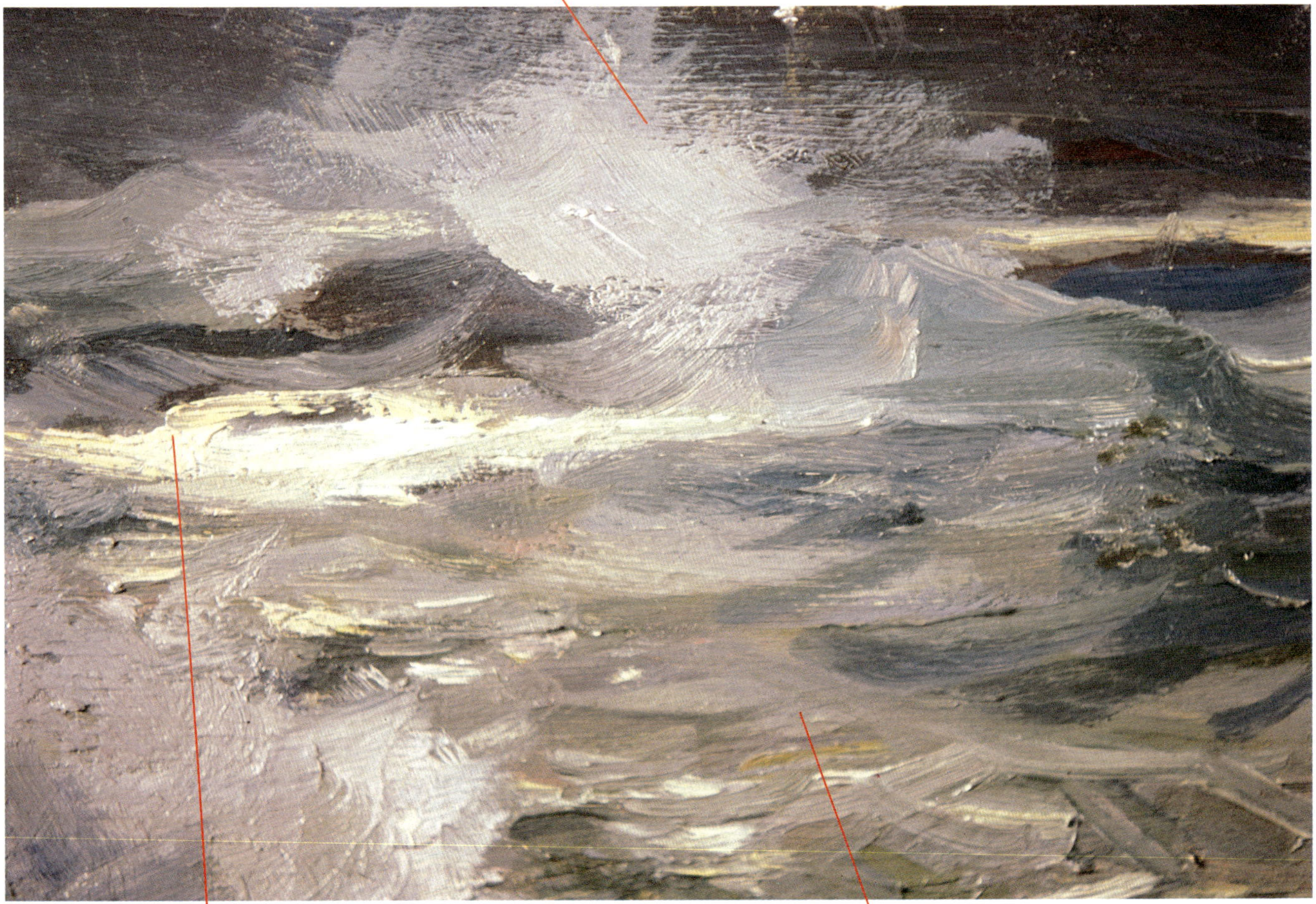

Even thicker strokes suggest the glare of the sun. Some yellow in the white indicates its warm sparkle. Remember: you only need a few such strokes to suggest sunlight.

The ocean is started with a wash of pink—the color of the overhead sky. Thicker strokes are worked into the wash, each stroke representing a bit of foam. These choppy strokes suggest the bobbing surface of the ocean.

People love pictures of big waves—they're so dramatic. But I only half approve of them. When you do a "portrait" of a wave, it seems to stand still. You feel as if it's never going to turn over. Everything comes to a halt, like the sea in a photograph. And a static quality is the *last* thing you want in a marine. In this backlit painting, the drama comes from the large areas of shadow, set off by a few crisp highlights. It doesn't take a lot of highlights to suggest sunlight. In fact, too many of them would destroy the effectiveness of the picture; it would sparkle like a Christmas tree.

The top is a rich, dark brown: The area has been stained by the water. Crisp, angular strokes emphasize the rock's sharp edges. There are a few highlights on the mass—but, as with the water, just a few!

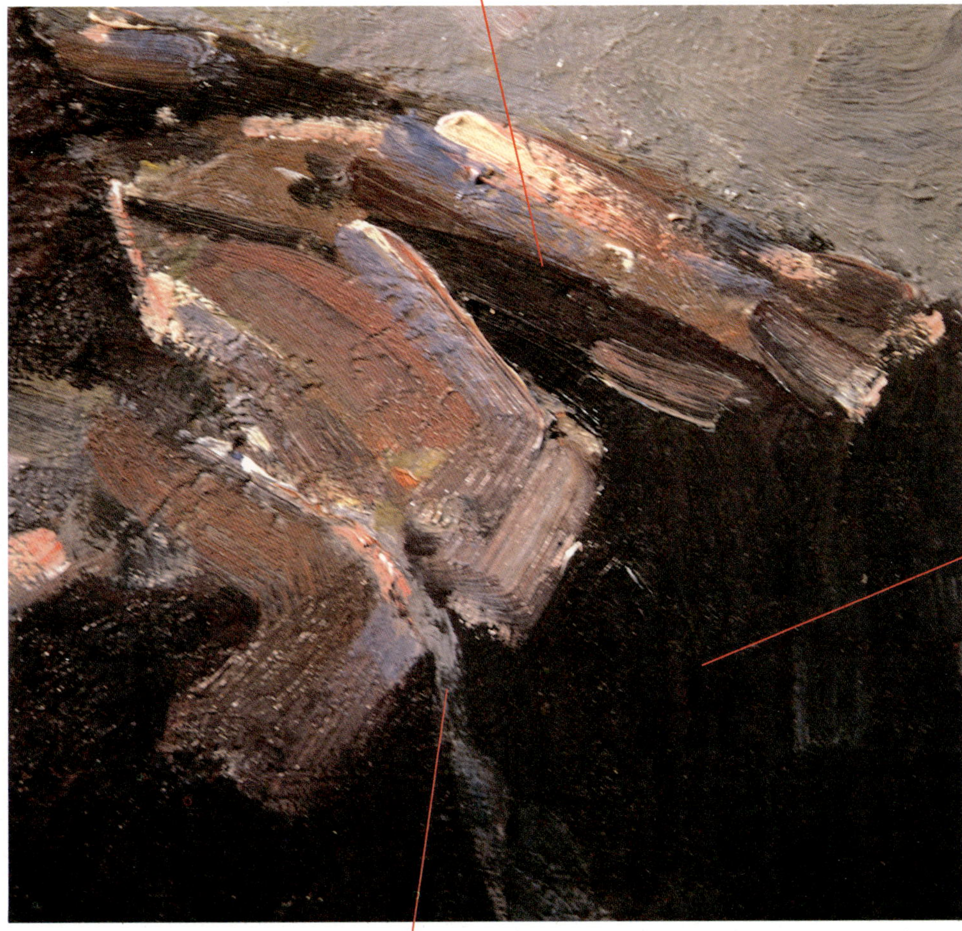

The massive background rock is begun with the dark shadow area. It's flat and simple, so it doesn't detract from the sunlit surface.

In nature, streams of water run down every break in the rocks. If you put them all in, the mass would be so broken that it wouldn't make any visual sense. Here a single stroke suggests water running off the rock. The irregular stroke lets you sense the breaks in the rock, without having to draw each crack.

Overcast Day

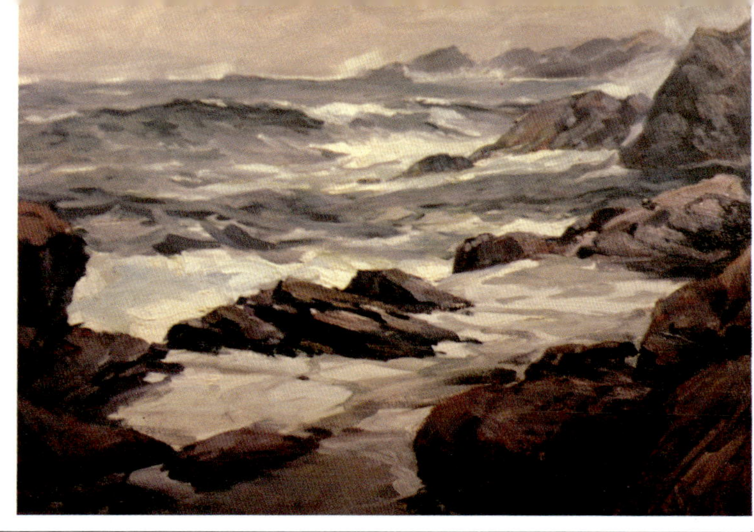

After the Storm
oil on canvas
25″ × 30″ (64 × 76 cm)

The cresting wave is painted with a series of choppy, diagonal strokes. Here and there, a commalike stroke emphasizes the movement of the water along the face of the wave.

The distant water is painted flatly. Use sky color first, to show the effect of the sky on the water. Then work long, wide darker strokes over it. Their length suggests the breadth of the sea.

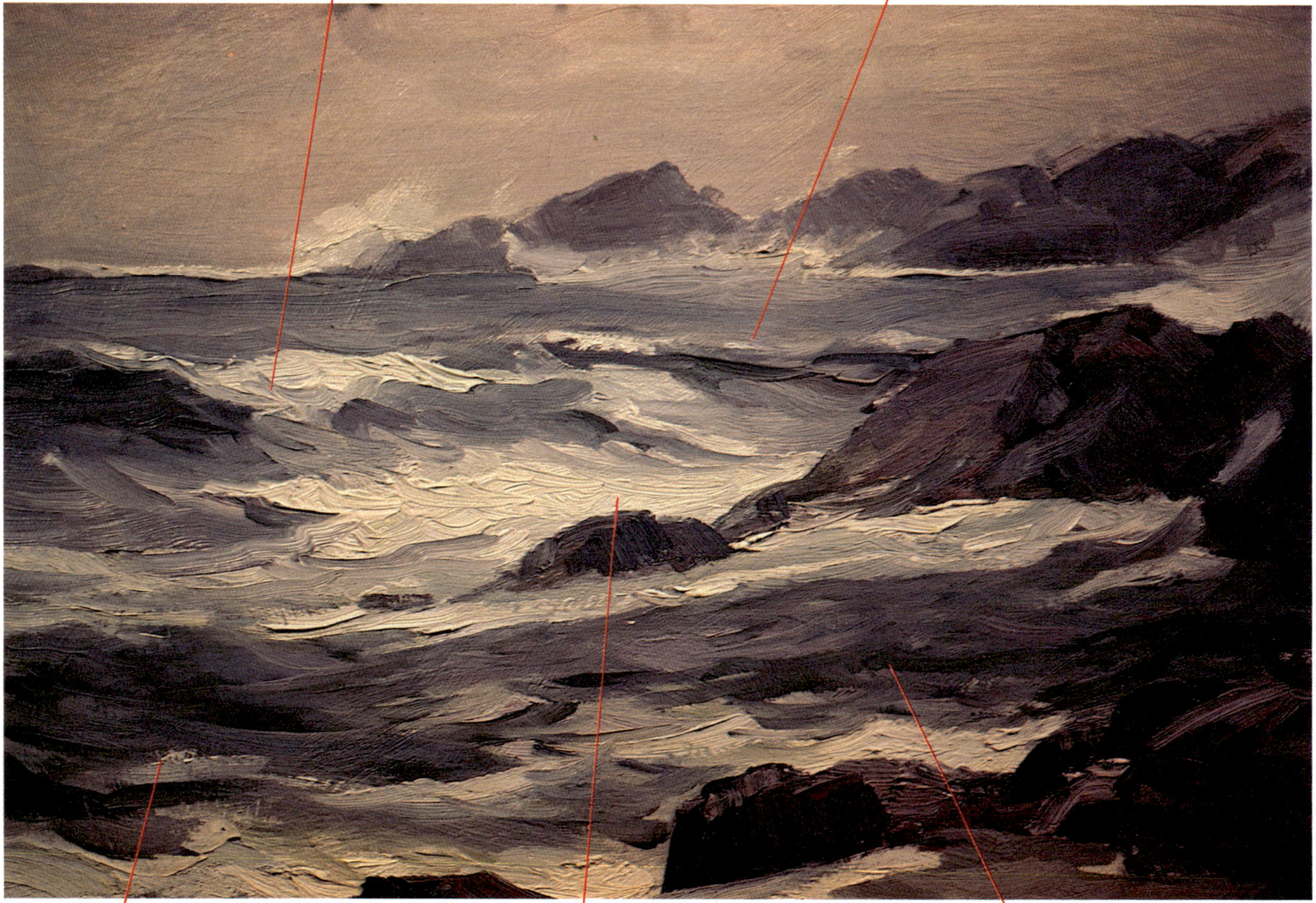

Again use warm sky color as an underpainting; then work darks over it. Since the area is close to us, you can see its texture.

The wave itself is a mass of white paint, with no yellow in it. On a gray day, the sun doesn't have a chance to warm up the foam.

In the foreground, broken strokes move in a diagonal direction, counterpointing that of the distant wave. The strokes are dark, upside-down *V*s, each running into and interacting with the others.

This kind of marine is especially interesting: rough water rather than a "portrait" of one big wave. The large area of sky is free of broken brushwork; it allows you an area of rest from the activity of the other parts of the painting. Because of the gray color of the water, the sky takes on a complementary reddish cast.

The biggest, most broken strokes are the ones nearest to us.

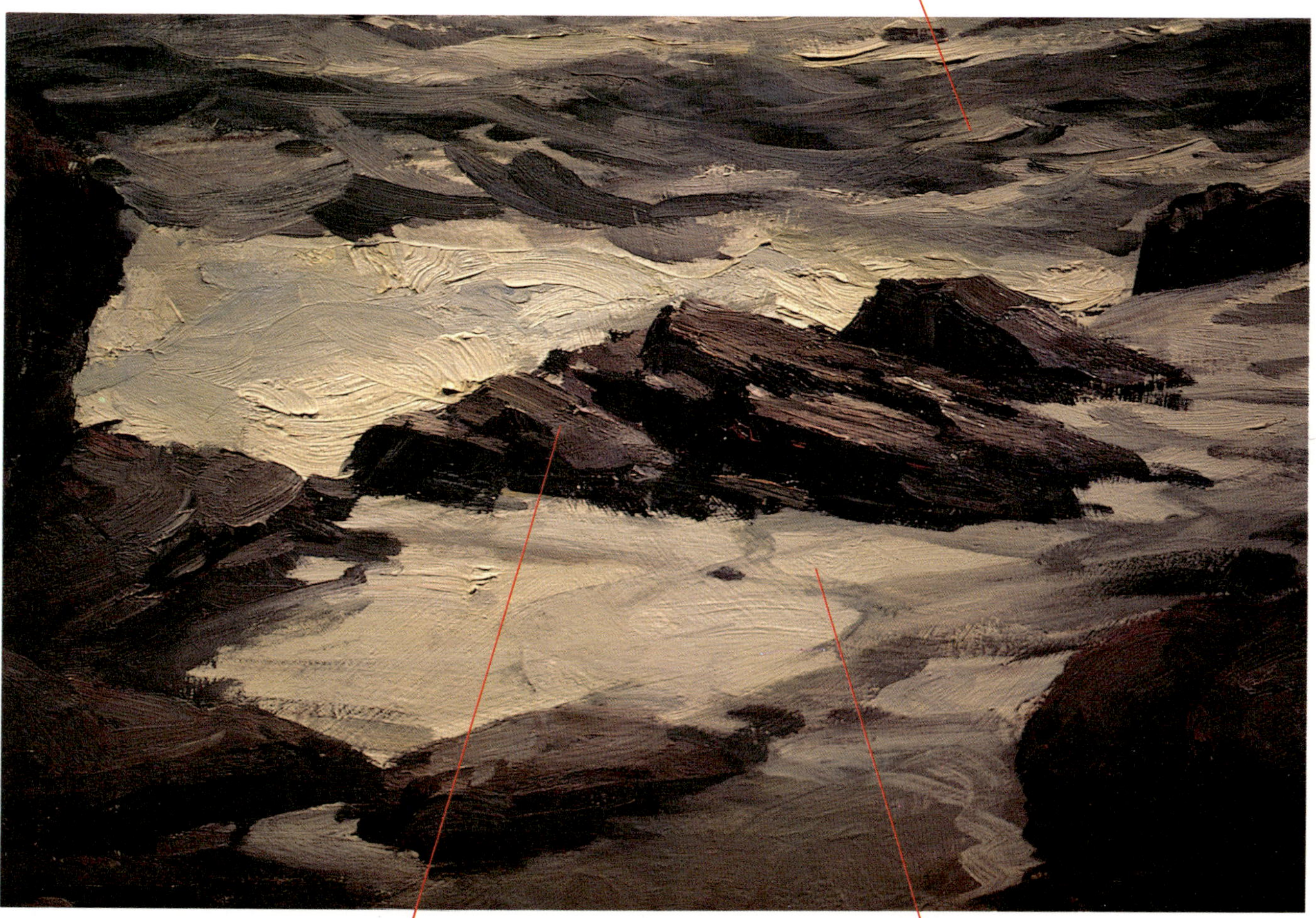

Against the flat mass, the jagged rocks are particularly effective. Since this rock is close to us, you can see its dark crevices and rough texture.

Trapped among the rocks, this water is relatively protected. Use swirling, rounded strokes to emphasize the *flatness* of the area.

TREES AND FLOWERS

If you want to understand trees, you have to paint them outdoors—on the spot. That's where you can capture the accidental quality of nature, the unexpected bits that you could never think up in the studio. Some trees, like the elm, branch far up on the trunk. They're straight and dignified. Others, like the apple, branch close to the ground. They're much more playful in character. No matter where the branching occurs, a general movement characterizes most trees. The lower branches drop down and then move up; they want to get out from under the heavy upper foliage. The middle branches grow horizontally to the sides. The top branches don't have to worry about overhead foliage; they grow straight toward the sun.

There's plenty of variety within this simple framework. The lower branches of a beech tree, for example, drop straight down. The sycamore tree's branches are characterized by stops, breaks, and angles. Maples are knotted and gnarled—they're big and dramatic. A birch tree is more lyrical.

When I started to paint, my father was one of my hardest critics. "Your trees look like telephone poles," he'd say. They went straight into the ground. They didn't have a feeling of rootedness, of a footing in the earth. One day I broadened the base of a tree and even showed part of its root breaking through the soil. I exaggerated the effect, but it looked good. And that was just what my father wanted. Remember, however, to start the flare near the ground—you don't want the tree to look like a funnel.

After you've done lots of studies, you'll begin to sense the rhythm and character of each species. Then you can start to improvise. One day, you'll see a fine movement in the branch of a tree. You may use that movement a week later to enhance a picture painted at a different spot.

Develop your ability to improvise. Be literal at the beginning—and become more selective as you gain experience. I used to go painting with a friend of mine, a really fine artist; and he'd always come over to my canvas and say, "That isn't that tree! If you aren't going to paint it, why don't you stay in the studio?" He was partly right; you need to look and study when you're at a site. But he was wrong too: each painter has his or her own story to tell.

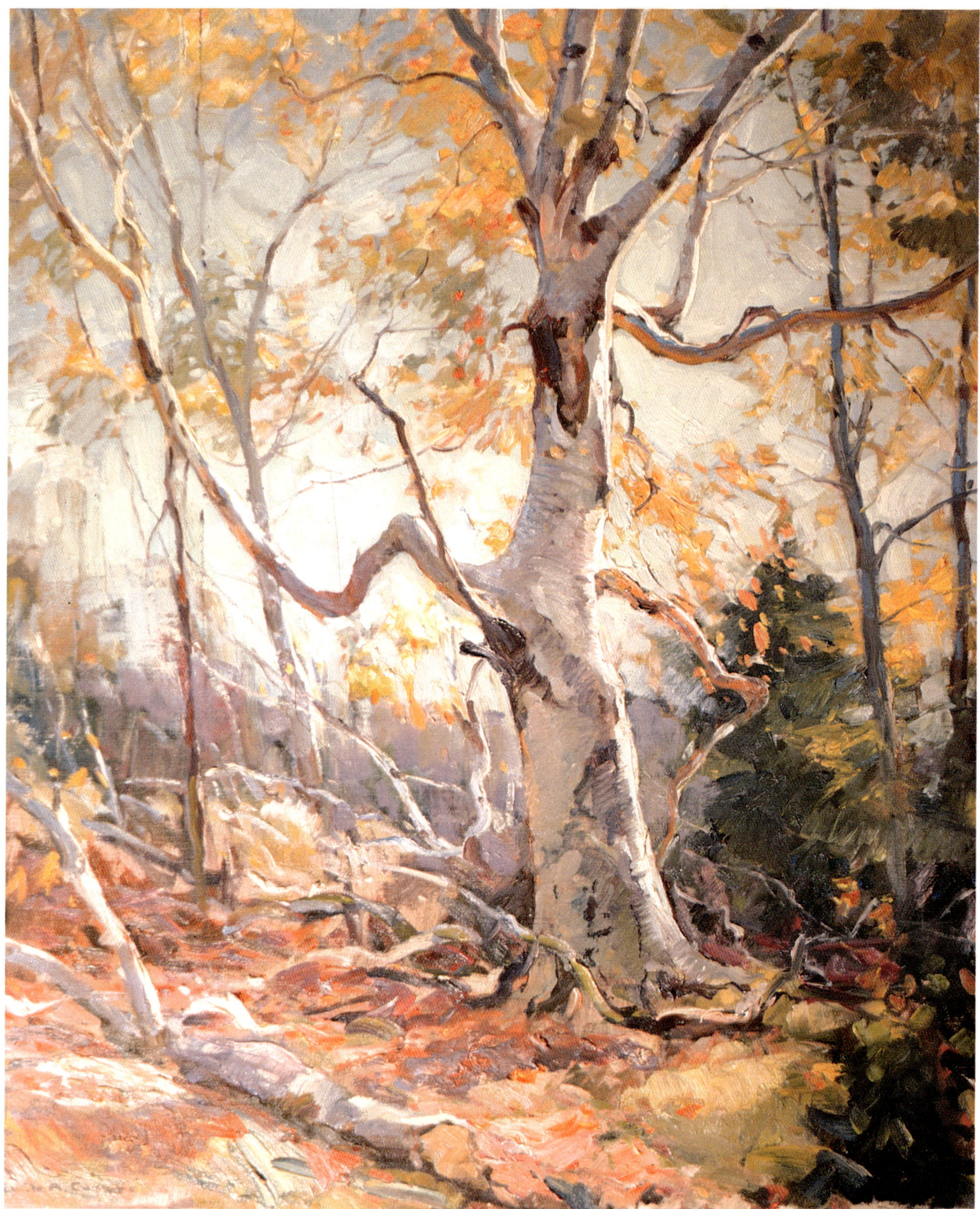

The Old Birch Tree
oil on canvas
36″ × 30″ (91 × 76 cm)

This is a good example of the "truthful" effect that you get only by working outdoors. Make a close study of the old tree's branches, paying special attention to the long branch on the left. In its search for the sun, it goes up, down, up, and finally out of the picture! Birch bark grows in horizontal bands around the trunk, and here the brushstrokes follow the bark's direction. The bottom part of the tree slants to the left, and the diagonal strokes describe the plane of the trunk. The upper part of the tree moves in the opposite direction, as do the strokes. The branches have less texture than the trunk. They're smooth and graceful shapes.

Sycamores

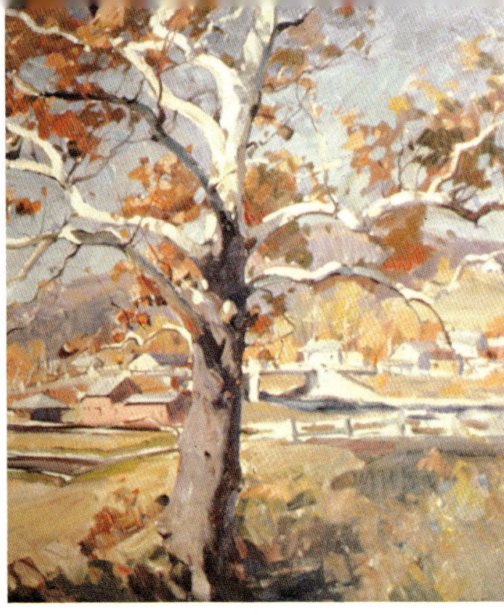

Sycamores
oil on canvas
30″ × 36″ (76 × 91 cm)

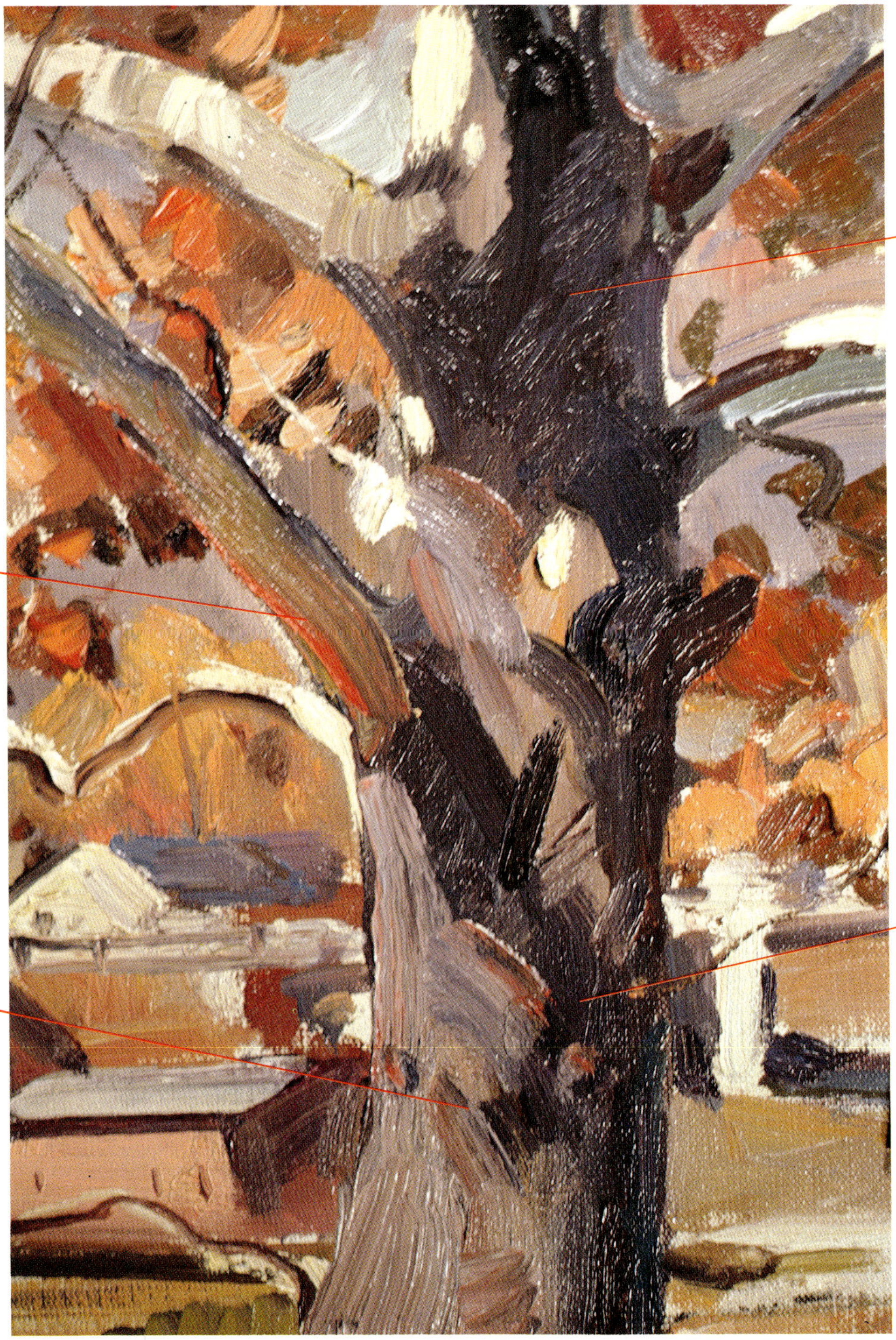

The shadow areas of the tree are a simple stain. Later, opaque paint is added to give the shadow some texture—though not much! The real texture appears in the sunlit areas.

A single, long stroke suggests the movement of the nearest branch. The shadow is warm in color, for it gets reflected light both from the ground and from the sunlit bark beneath it.

In the sunlit areas, you can see broken pieces of bark. The variations are suggested by thickly painted strokes moving in different directions.

Where a light stroke runs into the shadow area, it mixes with the underpainting and creates interesting variations in value.

My years with John F. Carlson made me particularly sympathetic to the nature of trees. He called them "rooted men" and believed that their main characteristic was aspiration. I try to suggest that here by bringing the tree out of three sides of the picture. You sense that it's reaching far over your head toward the sky. The background buildings are a foil for the main tree—the dessert of the picture. Sycamores are a study in contrasts: The lower bark is rough while the upper areas peel to leave a smooth skin. Notice how the angular, staccato movements of these branches contrast with those of the more lyrical birch tree.

The sky is also painted around and over the masses of bright autumn leaves. In places, the paint picks up some of the red color from the leaves. That adds variety to the sky and keeps it from looking flat and artificial. To make it look cool again, simply add a few thick strokes of light blue here and there—without covering all the reddish tone.

Toward the end of the painting process, a few thin branches are pulled across the sky and leaves, throwing them back in space.

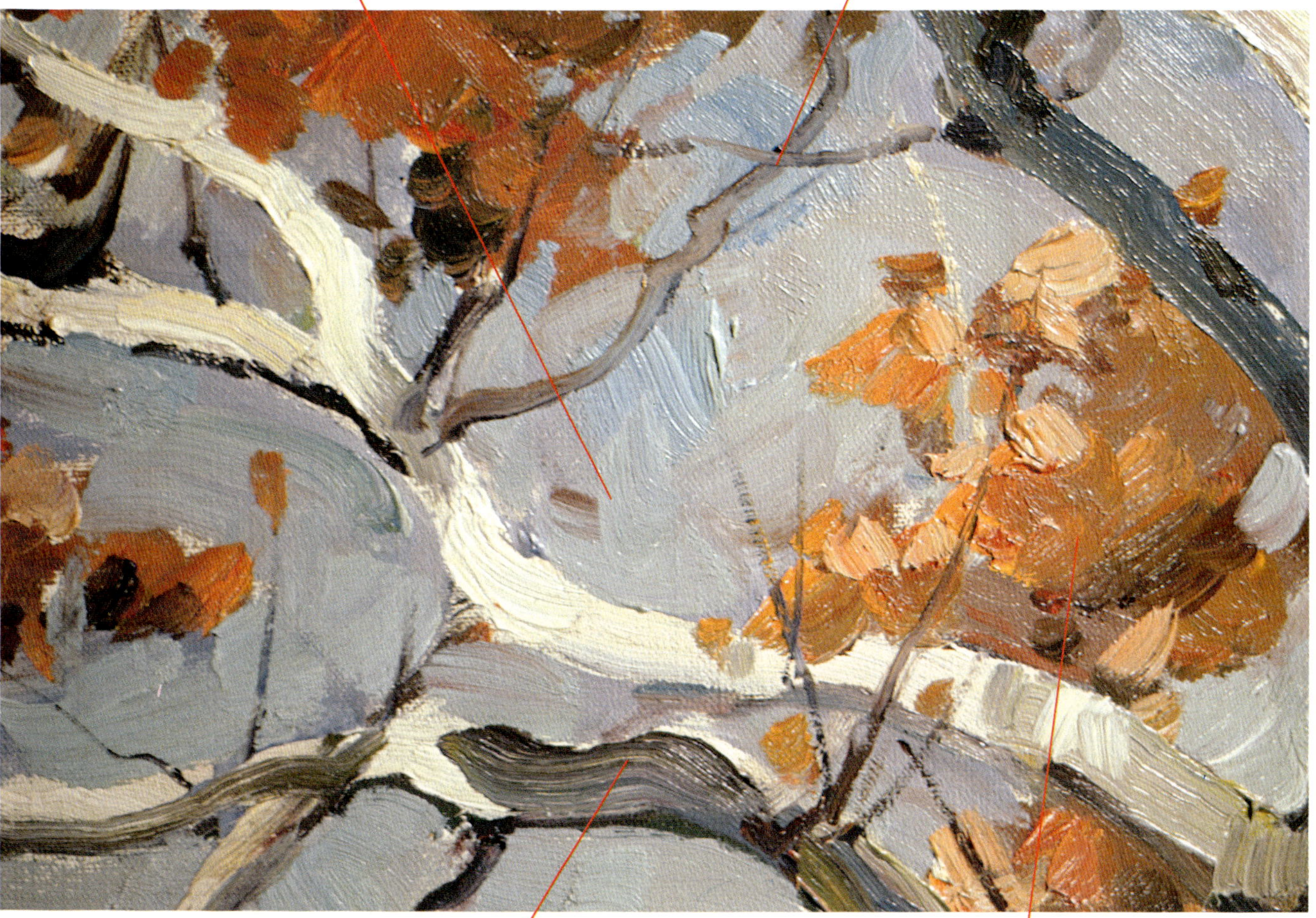

Long, thickly painted strokes show the movement of the branches of the tree. The branches are painted first, and the sky is painted up to them.

The reddish midtone of the leaves is painted first. A few dark accents are added—along with some brilliant highlights. The highlights are very thickly painted: They seem to come off the canvas.

Beech Tree

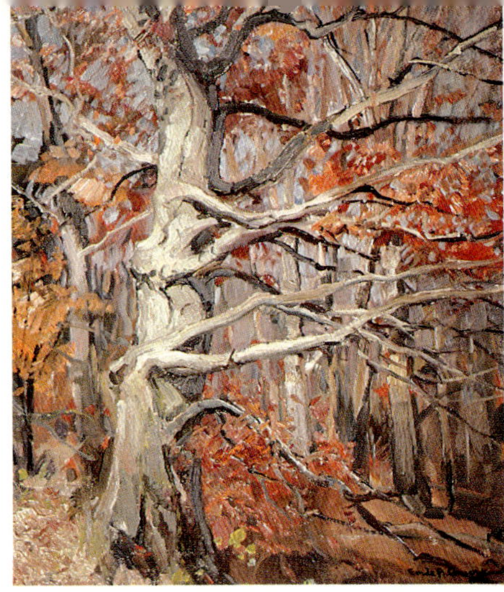

Beech Study
oil on canvas
24″ × 20″ (61 × 51 cm)

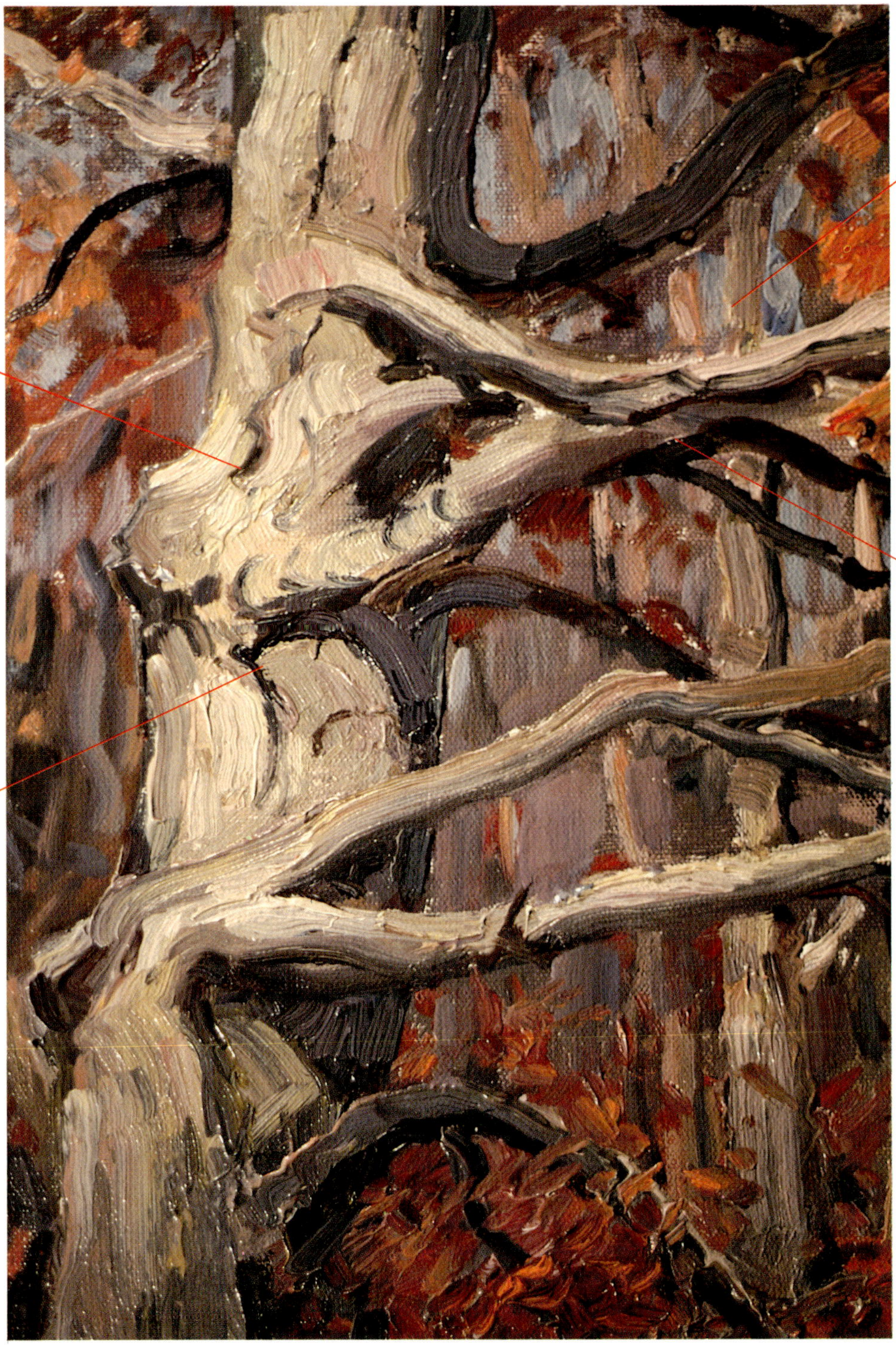

Block the tree in with a thin stain. But after the shape is established, build up the trunk with short, choppy strokes. Bristle marks suggest the texture of the bark. The vertical strokes accentuate the upward growth of the tree.

Thin dark lines add further definition to the trunk. Run these lines along the edges of previously drawn strokes. But watch out! One stroke looks good, so it's a temptation to add a dozen—and cheapen the effect.

Paint the background thinly, so it doesn't detract from the main area of interest.

The branches are long, thick, and fluid. These graceful strokes express the rhythmic quality that attracted me to the tree in the first place.

This beech tree's branches all move rhythmically to the right. A small one moves to the left, counterpointing the main branches. The trees behind the beech lean in an opposing direction, thus helping to balance the picture. The background trees have hardly any branches because I didn't want to take away from the principal tree.

Brush the area of foliage in first. Use a rich, warm red for the background leaves. Dots of orange define the leaves nearest to us.

Apply a few thick strokes over the wet paint of the tree to add interest to its shape.

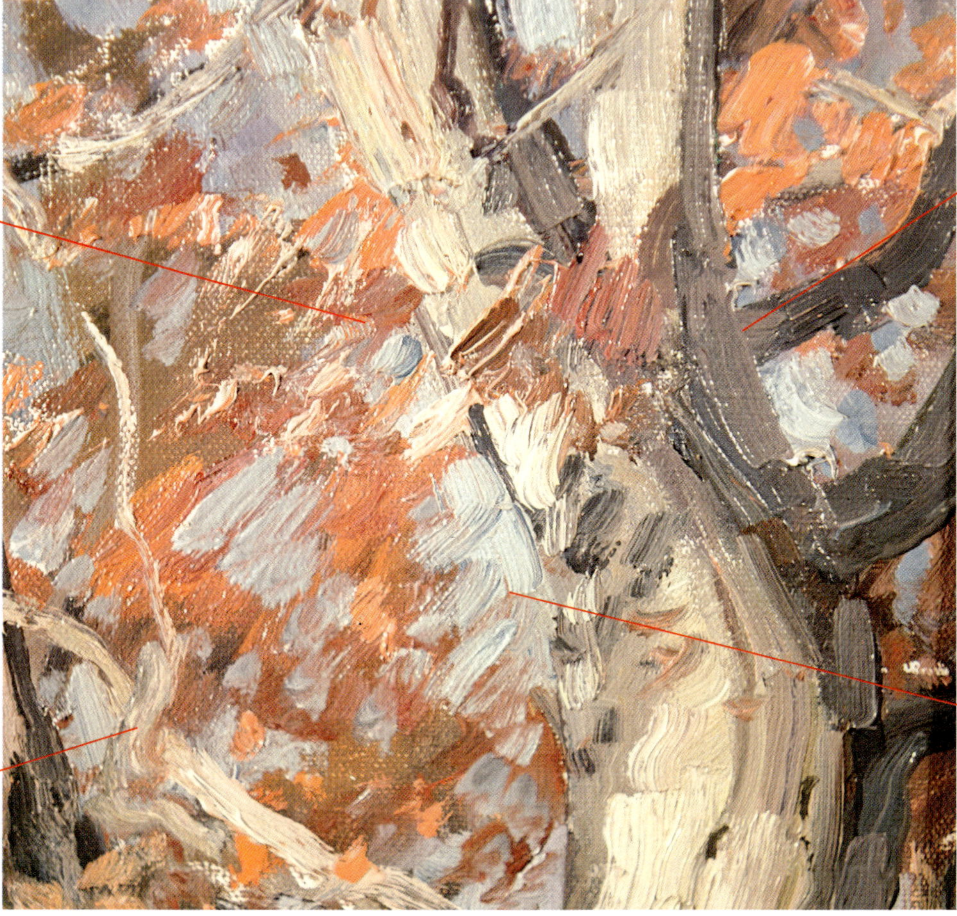

Add thick, fluid branches last, using a broken stroke.

Paint the sky over the red stain, using thick paint and lots of medium so it doesn't mix with the underlying red color. Apply these blue strokes in a diagonal direction. When you look at the completed painting, however, you feel its the foliage that slants, not the sky.

Palm Tree

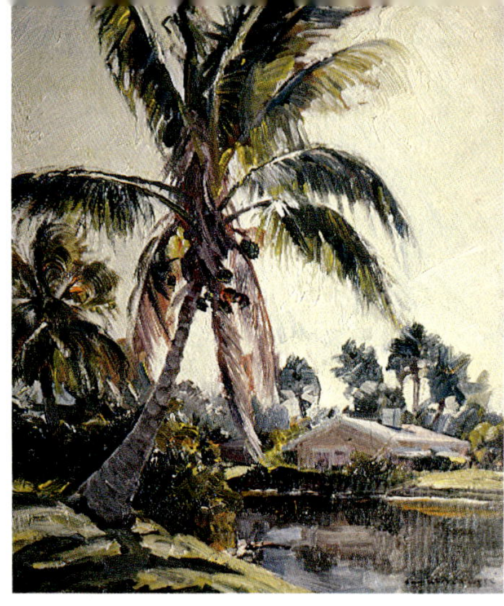

Florida Palms
oil on canvas
24" × 20" (61 × 51 cm)

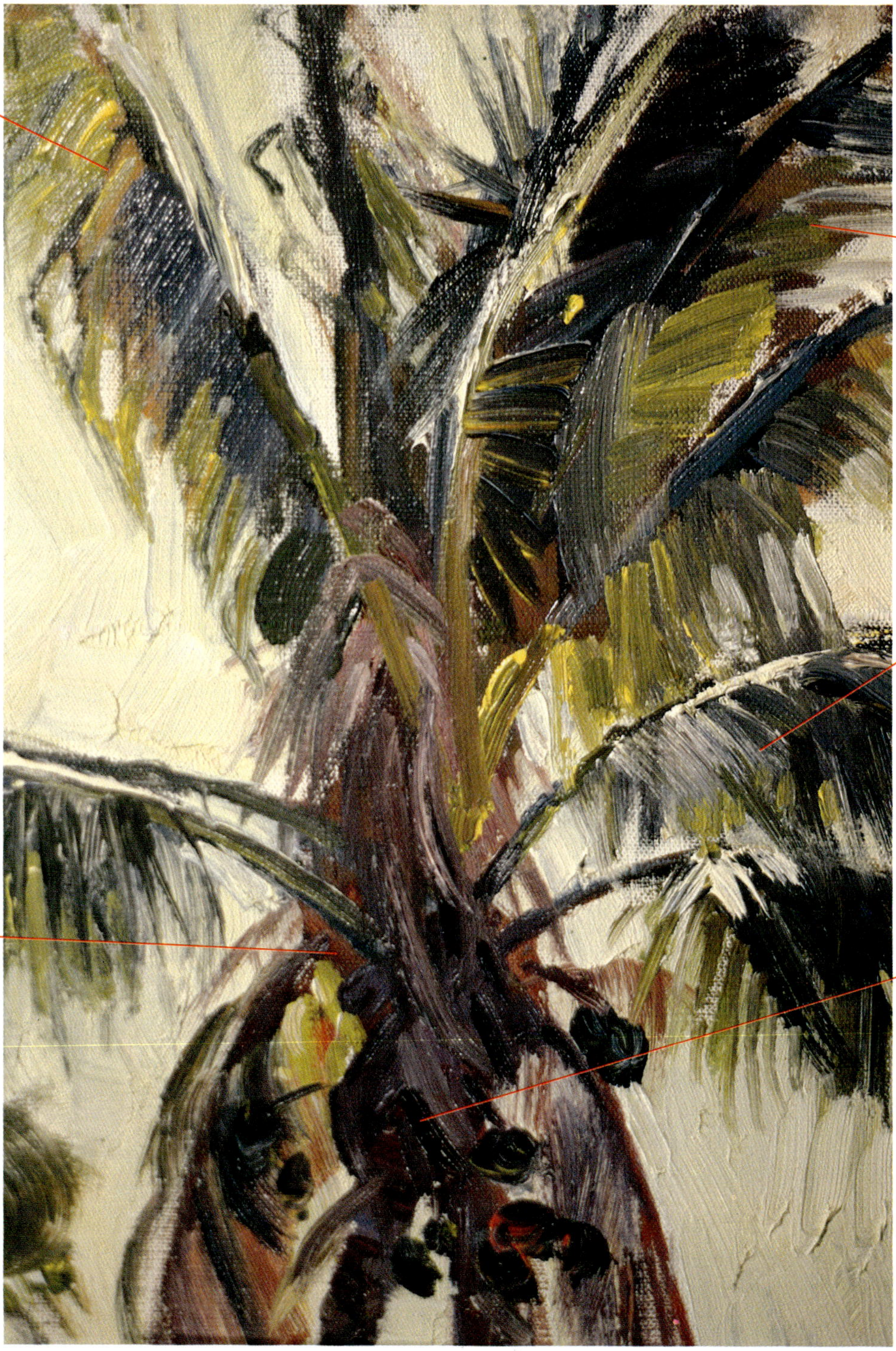

Shining through the fronds, the sun gives them a rich warm glow. Paint some of them with pure cadmium yellow.

Paint darker fronds over the stain. Work back and forth, cutting them into the sky and the sky into them.

On top of some of the fronds, pure white shows where a curved surface catches a glare from the sun.

Before painting the sky, stain the canvas a reddish color, determining about where the tree will be. The stain is visible throughout the detail.

At the top of the trunk, the foliage bunches into a dark spot. A few circular strokes suggest coconuts.

This backlit palm makes a striking silhouette against the sky. Notice how it grows. New shoots come out of the top of the plant, older fronds droop from the sides, and dying ones, red with age, hang limply from the bottom of the tree. The sun turns the sky a warm yellow and shines through the palm leaves. Even the grass has a yellow tinge; the sun lights up each blade. Although the trunk looks dark against the sky, it's relatively light and cool next to the intense dark of the background bushes. In the distance, a hint of cool color sets off the warmth of the dying fronds.

Thick, short strokes suggest the fronds of the palms. Pull the stroke over the wet sky, moving the brush up and out. There's a ragged edge where the brush leaves the canvas. One stroke suggest dozens of fine lines.

In the distance, the palm trees form a simple silhouette against the sky.

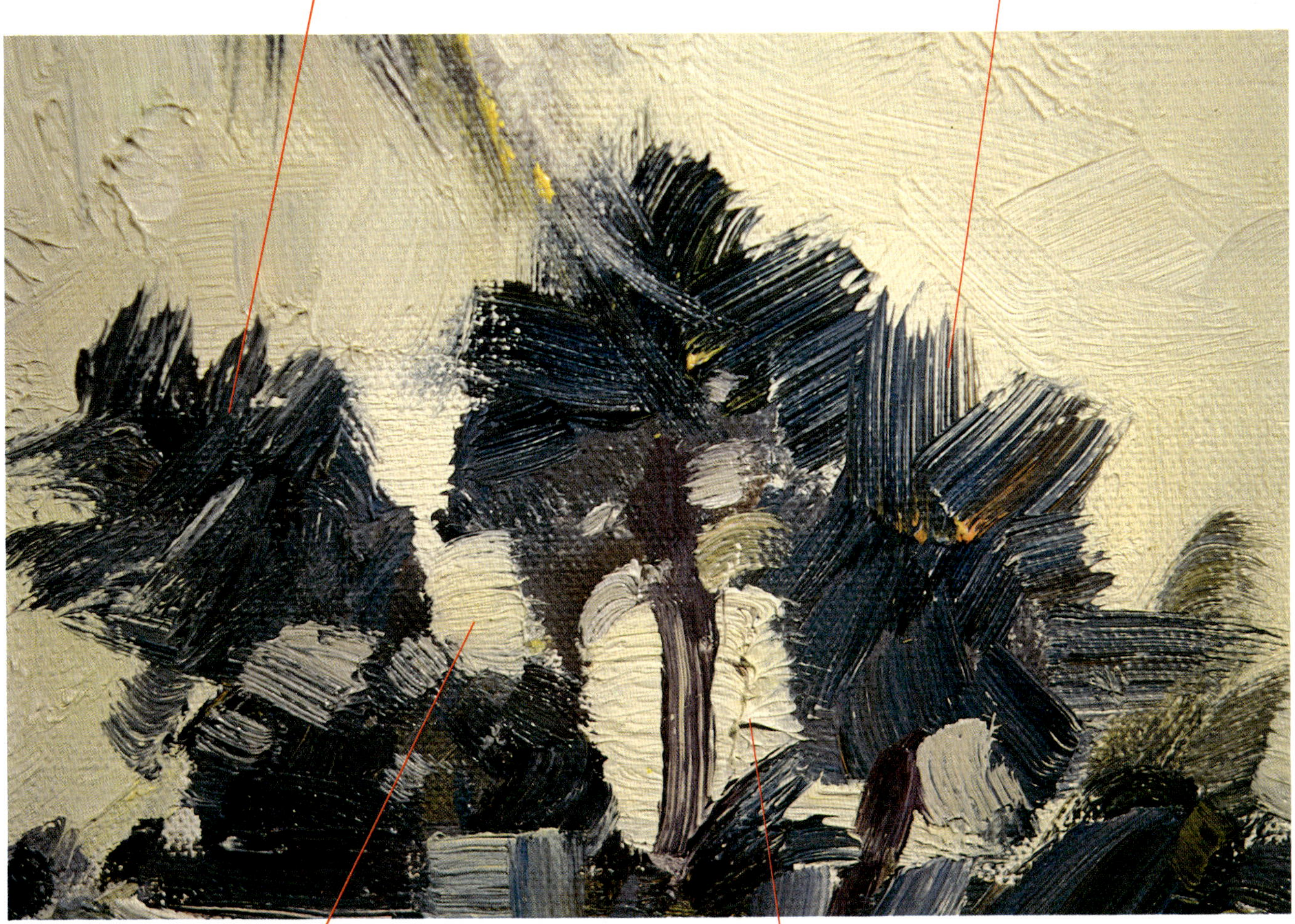

Occasionally paint sky-holes into the wet tree. The paint mixes with the undercoat, making the skyhole slightly darker than the surrounding sky.

Staining the trees first, use a horizontal stroke to paint the area of sky *between* the darks. Then run a trunk over the thick white paint.

Branches: Wet-in-Wet

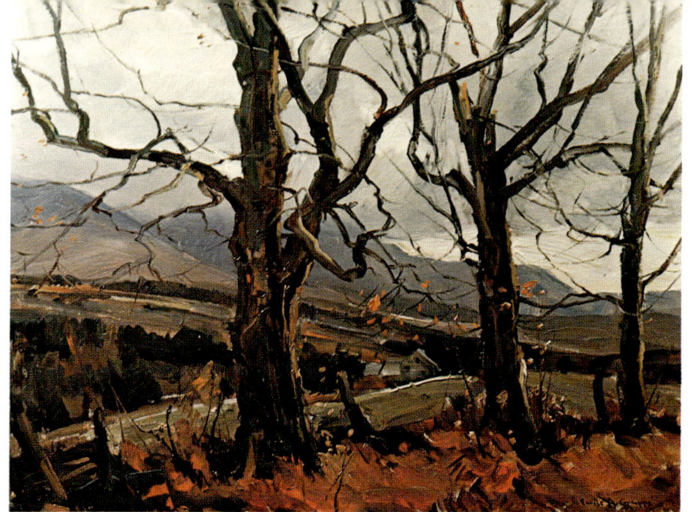

Maple Trees
oil on canvas
25″ × 30″ (64 × 76 cm)

The dark trees make a strong pattern against the overcast sky. The nearest tree is the most important; others get smaller as they recede. The branches of the tree run far to the left and the right, overlapping nearby maples and tying the picture together. The slope of the foreground bank counterpoints the angle of the distant hills. The brilliant warmth of the leaf-covered foreground throws the blue mountains far into the distance.

Make the twisting branches each a brushstroke thick. Since they're painted into the wet sky, they have to be drawn correctly, the first time. The strokes also pick up some light color from the sky, and these accidental value changes suggest shifts in the direction of the branch.

An orange stroke suggests a broken trunk and adds interest to the subsidiary tree.

The branches taper as they grow. They start straight and twist as they search for the sun. Some branches go to the side, while others move straight up.

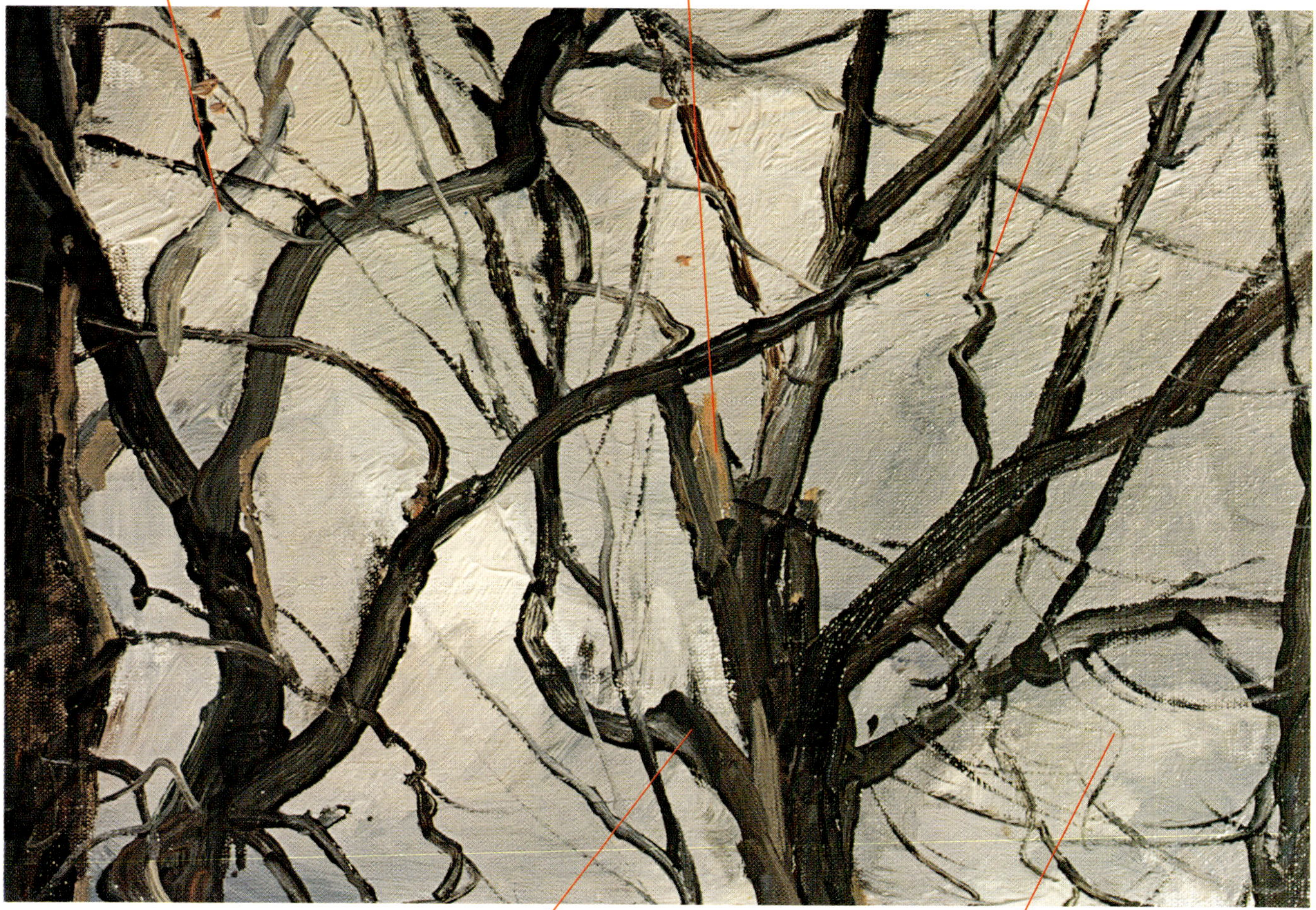

Finding the way blocked by overhead foliage, the branch shoots off along a completely different path. This movement is dramatic and expresses the tree's character and history.

Use a small brush to make a series of very thin strokes. At the site, there are hundreds of these branches; pick only the most interesting.

Branches: Stain and Wet-in-Wet

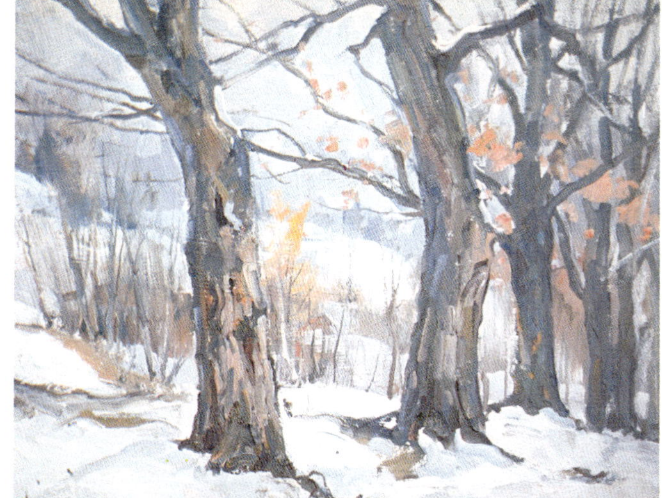

Early Snow
oil on canvas
20″ × 24″ (51 × 61 cm)
Collection of Mr. and Mrs. Donald Grieger

This picture is similar to the painting on the facing page. But the interest centers on the trunks instead of on the overhead branches. These trunks have lots of intricate texture. The branches again tie the trees together; the maples form a dark unit against the snow and the hazy distance. The dark branches at the upper right are a counterpoint to the downward movement of the hillside and fields. The straightness of the distant maples accentuates the twisted ones in the foreground.

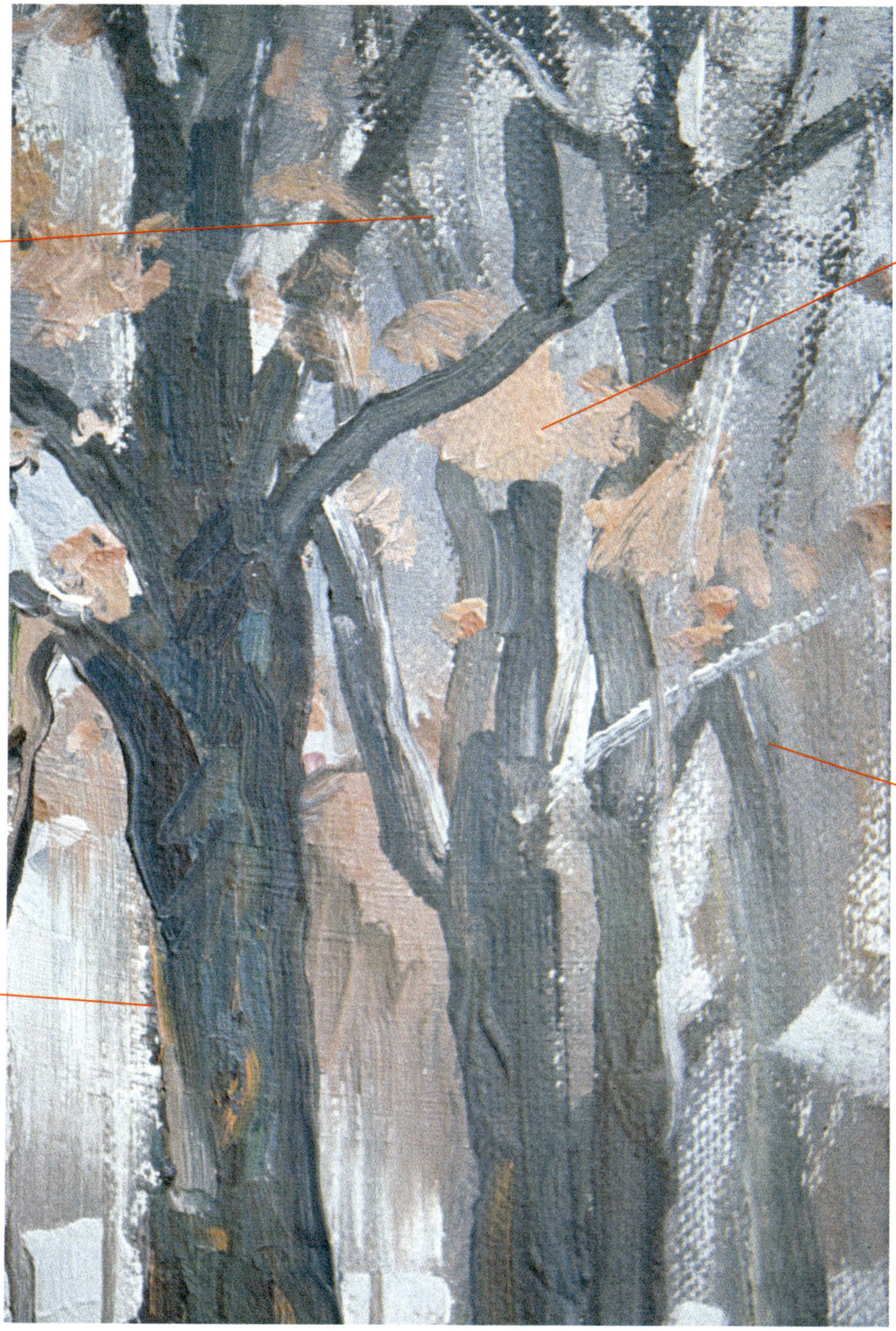

The distance is barely covered. Raw canvas shows through and looks like patches of snow.

Here place the mass of warm foliage first. Then paint the trunk of the tree up to it, skip *over* it, and continue the trunk farther up.

Establishing a darkish tone first, paint the farthest tree into it, losing it occasionally in the wet underpainting. These lost-and-found edges make the tree stay back in space.

Rather than paint this tree over wet paint, stain its general shape and then paint the background around it. You can see where white canvas was left along the edge of the tree.

Distant Trees

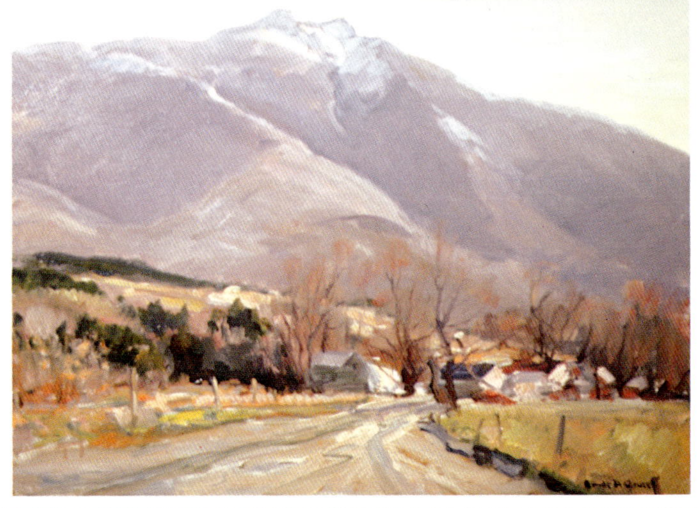

Mt. Mansfield
oil on canvas
30″ × 36″ (76 × 91 cm)

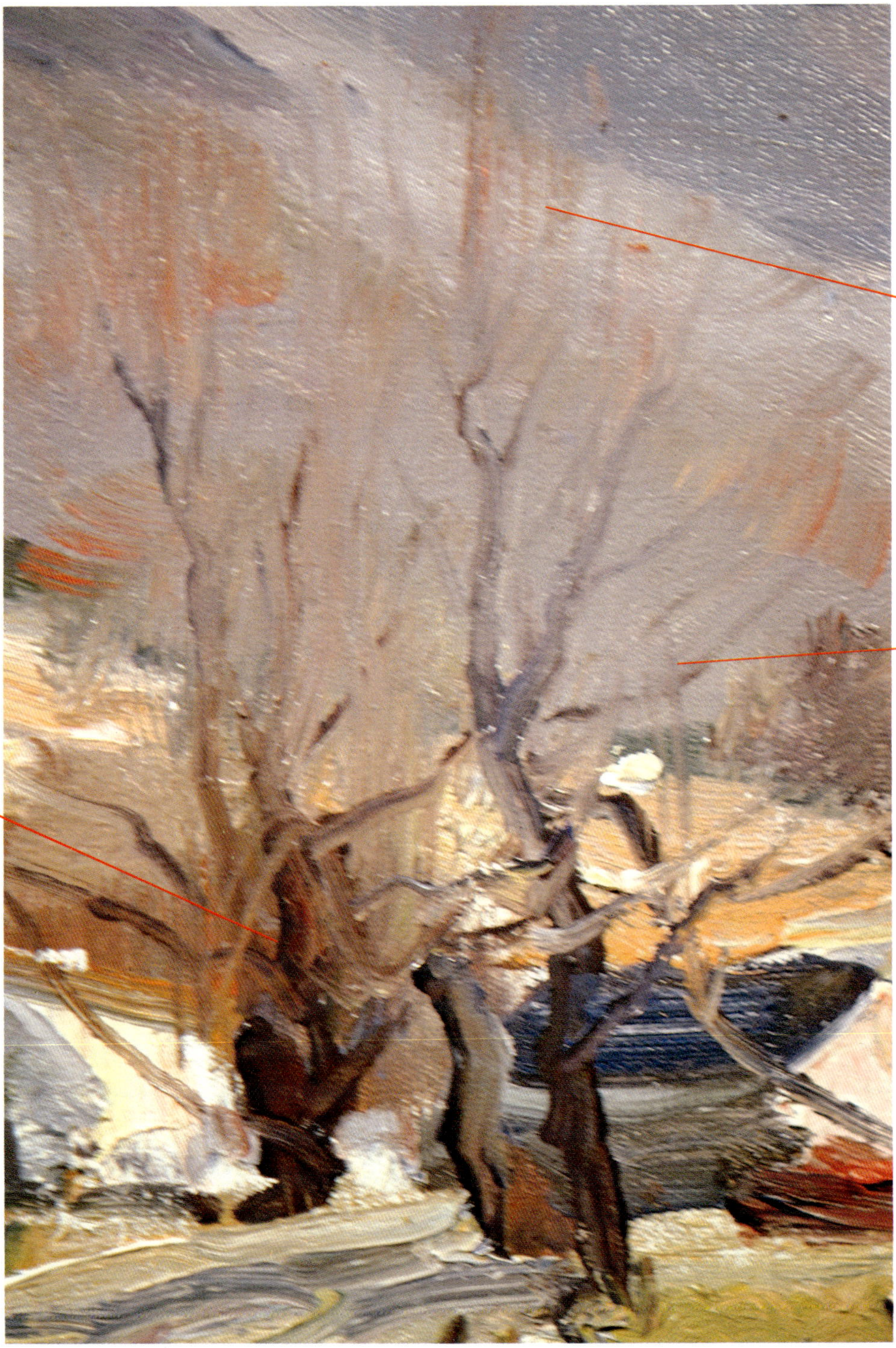

Once you determine the height of the tree, use a few flat, short strokes to suggest the foliage. Paint over the wet background.

The stroke picks up some of the undercoat; the shifts in value suggest the varying thickness of the leaves.

Paint the nearest trees by drawing the trunk and branches first.

This is a *mountain* picture, where everything has been scaled to make the peak seem tall and massive. The dark evergreens on the left establish the foreground. Brought up against the hazy distance, they make the mountain look that much farther back. The line of the road leads you into the picture and acts as a counterpoint to the downward thrust of the mountain. This road is very wide as it nears us; the width adds depth to the picture and propels you toward the center of interest.

Above these buildings, suggest autumn foliage with downward strokes of the brush; the bristle marks look like branches.

Paint the village exactly as you see it: no subtleties—just textured highlights that pull the buildings forward and contrast with the much more thinly painted mountain.

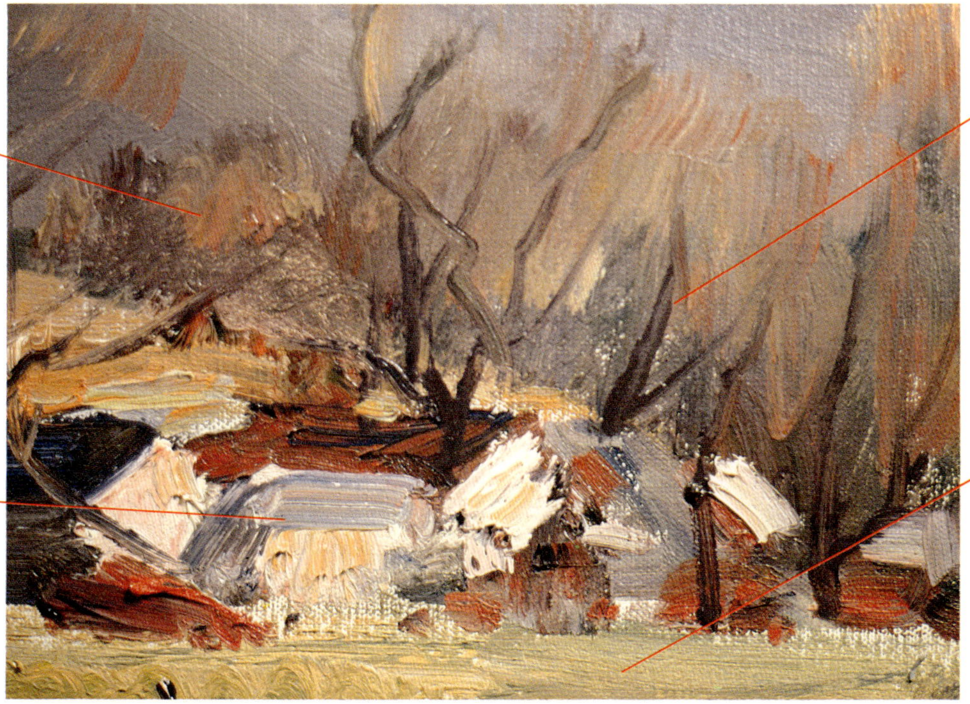

Only draw a few branches. At this distance, all you can see are the trunks of the trees.

Emphasize the flatness of the foreground with long, horizontal strokes. This flatness is important for it contrasts with the height of the mountain.

Paint the hill area with warm reds and yellows to indicate dried fields and bushes. Work thickly to create a strong foreground.

Accentuate this quality by going over the trees with a squiggly line of warm color.

Dark squarish strokes suggest shadows. The dark also accentuates the rich color of the field in the foreground.

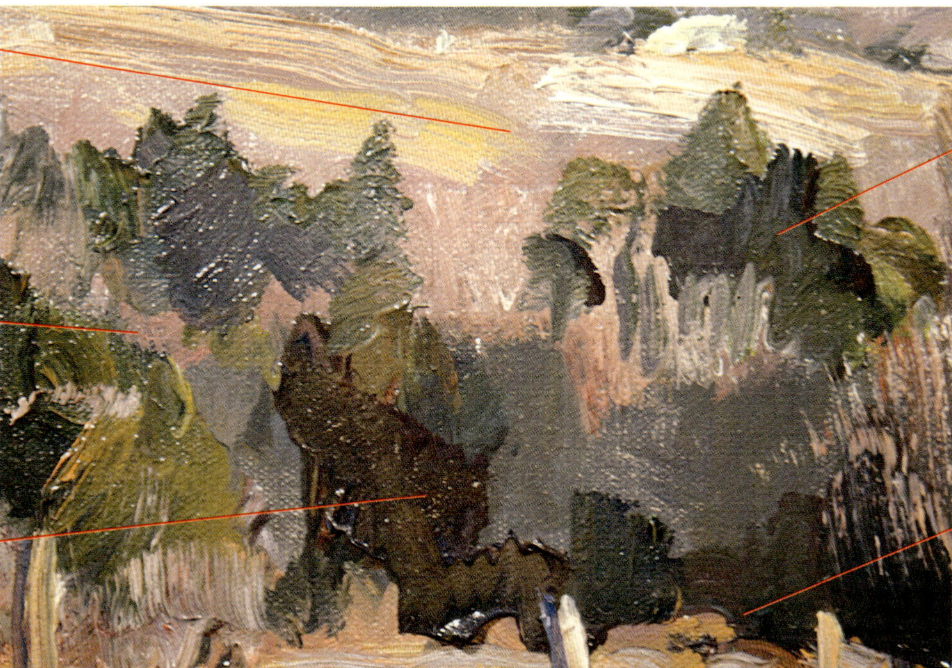

Having established the area, paint dark evergreens over it. Some of the evergreens are painted with diagonal strokes that suggest the direction of the branches; others are made of simple, upright strokes.

Vary the bottom edge of the trees; they look as if they're peeking from behind masses of warm foliage.

Apple Blossoms

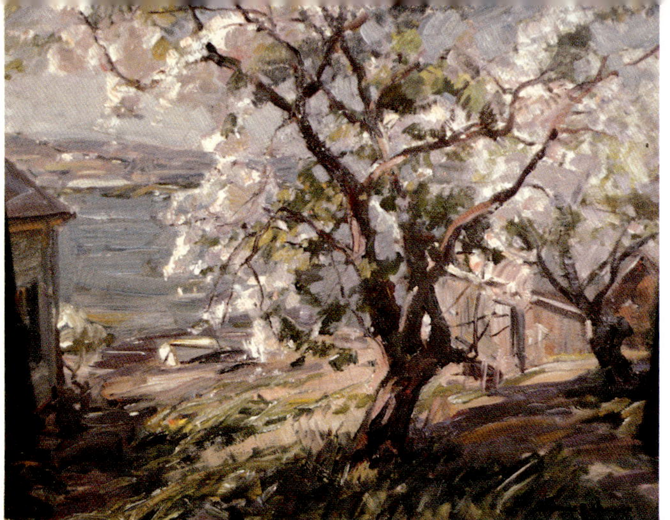

Spring
oil on canvas
25″ × 30″ (64 × 76 cm)

The blossoms near the sun get a strong blast of light. Emphasize the light by "loading" the paint. The whites are thicker than anything else in the area. The paint texture suggests clumps of flowers.

In order for the sunlit textures to show, keep the shadowed areas of blossoms thin and flat. There are different strokes of warm and cool lavender within the mass, but they don't overpower the brighter flowers.

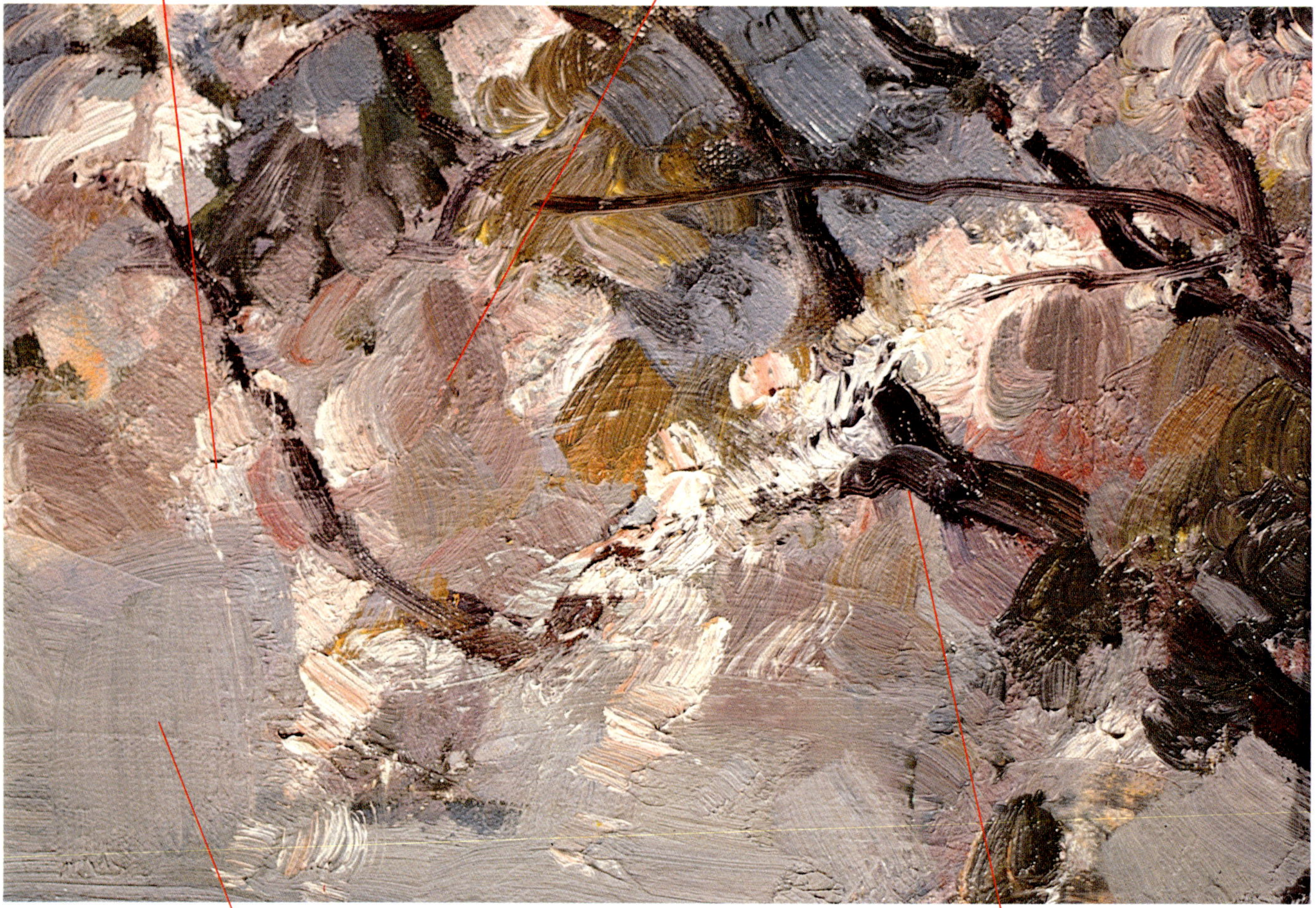

The flat, darkish sky also emphasizes the flowers.

To make the whites seem even whiter, run dark branches among the blossoms, bringing some of them against the brightest areas.

Apple trees have a lyrical quality. When painting them, it's good to accentuate their delicate movement. In the spring, this lyricism is enhanced by the pastel colors of the blossoms. The tree is huge, extending out of three sides of the canvas. Everything else is secondary: the houses, the bit of distant water, the suggestion of a headland.

Where the sunlit flowers are farther from the light, use less impasto; the white flowers are actually bits of unpainted canvas.

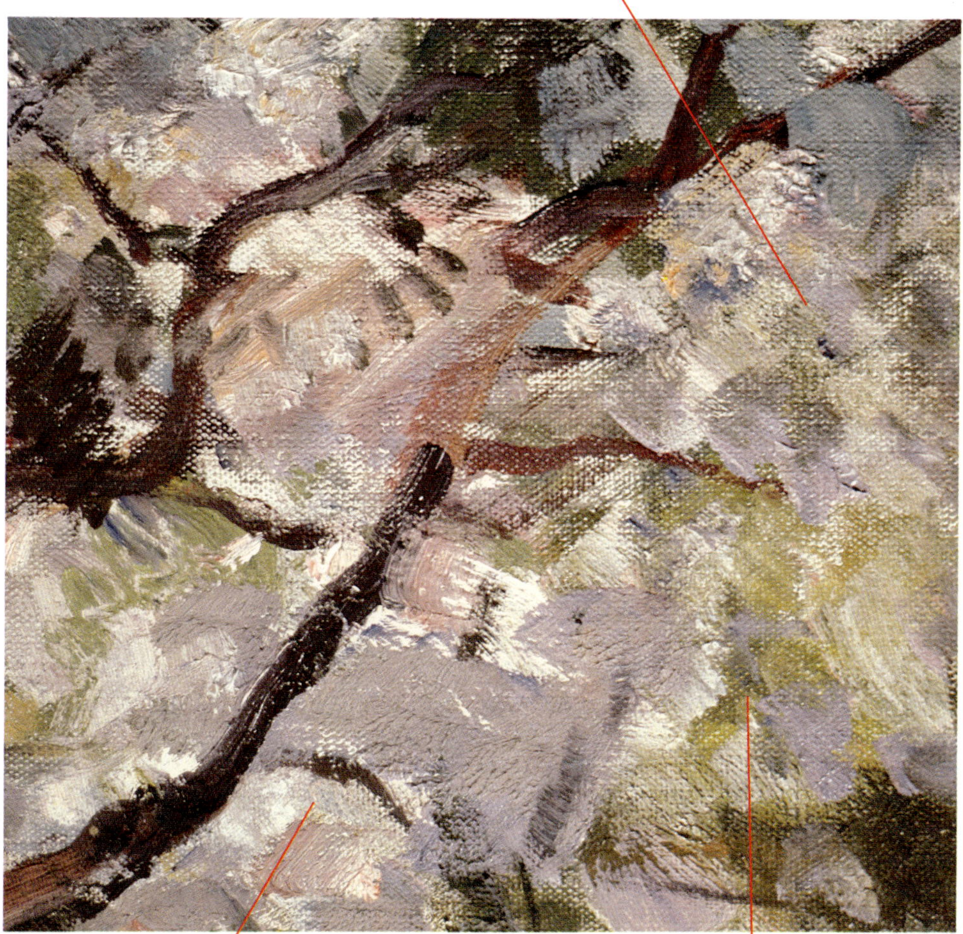

The greens and lavenders are just a stain. You can see the texture of the canvas through them.

Again give visual interest to the area by adding a few dark accents. They suggest free-standing leaves and parts of hidden branches.

Apples

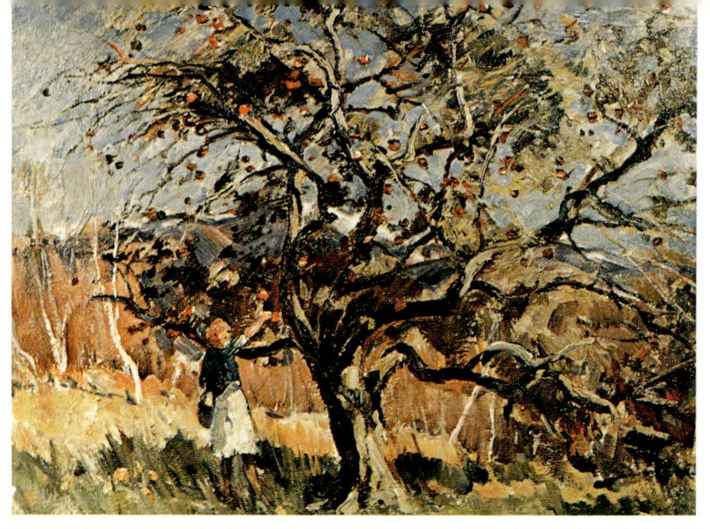

Don't Sit under the Apple Tree with Anyone Else But Me
oil on canvas
25" × 30" (64 × 76 cm)

Note the angular movement of the tree's branches and the red notes of the apples against the green leaves and sky. The tree acts as a screen, through which you can see the fall foliage and the snow-covered peak. Fall is a good time to paint this kind of subject, for the leaves have begun to drop and you can see the anatomy of the tree. The woman's cool blouse contrasts with and accentuates the warm background.

The other apples are darker and less conspicuous. Many of them are hooked onto the shadow parts of the tree. Each is painted with a curved stroke of the brush.

Emphasize only a few apples. The brightest and most detailed have small thickly painted highlights on them.

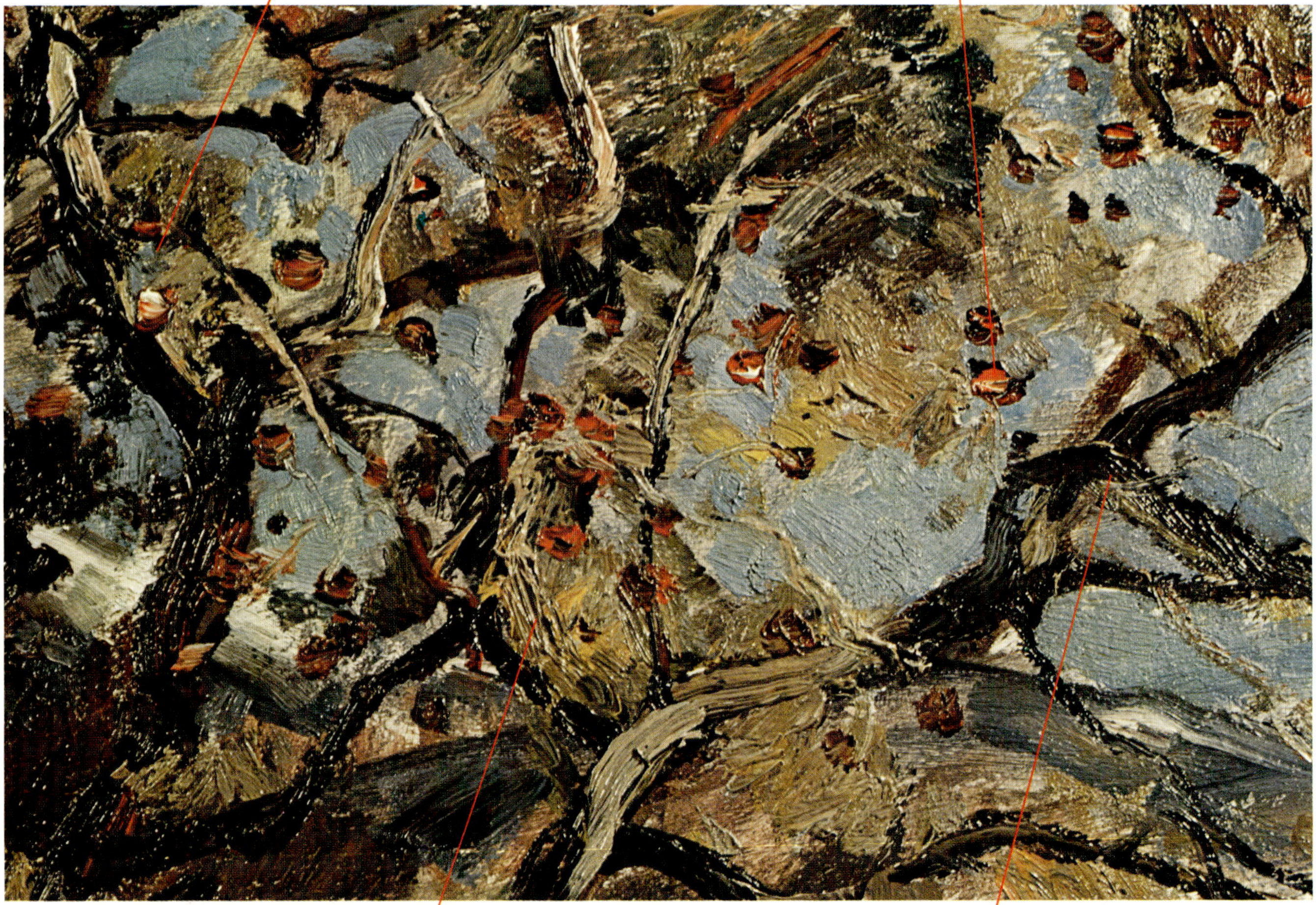

The foliage is treated as a mass of color. Only one or two leaves are visible at the edge of the mass.

The branches are painted with crisp, dark strokes that break and twist in a way that's characteristic of the subject.

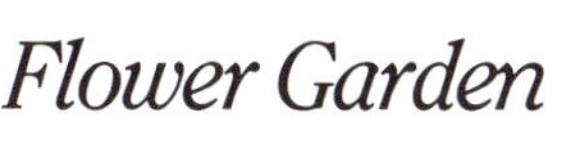

Flower Garden

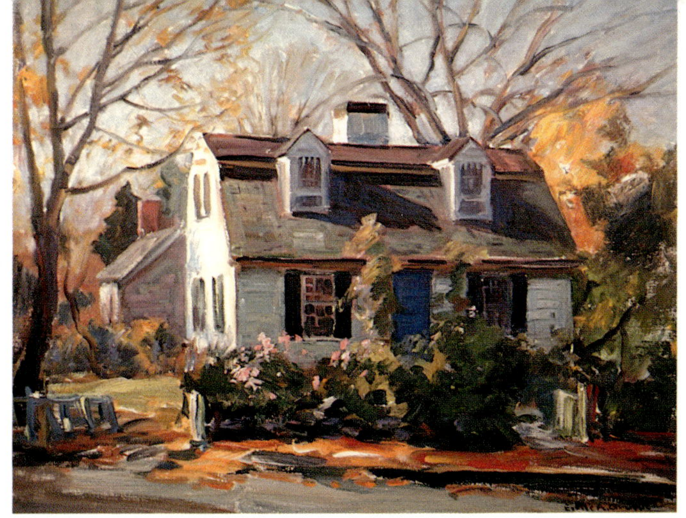

Rockport in the Fall
oil on canvas
25″ × 30″ (64 × 76 cm)

Backlighting is interesting; it creates subtle value shifts in the areas of shadow. To emphasize the house and the roses, use the nearby trees to block out the bright sky. They "kill" that area of the painting—the eye goes immediately to the brilliantly lit house. Every window in the house is painted differently. The door is a rich cool note in a predominantly warm color scheme.

Paint the house and the nearby foliage as a series of simple masses. The shadowed house catches reflected light from the bushes and looks greenish.

The flowers are thickly painted—a stroke for each blossom. Their warm color stands out from the cool surroundings.

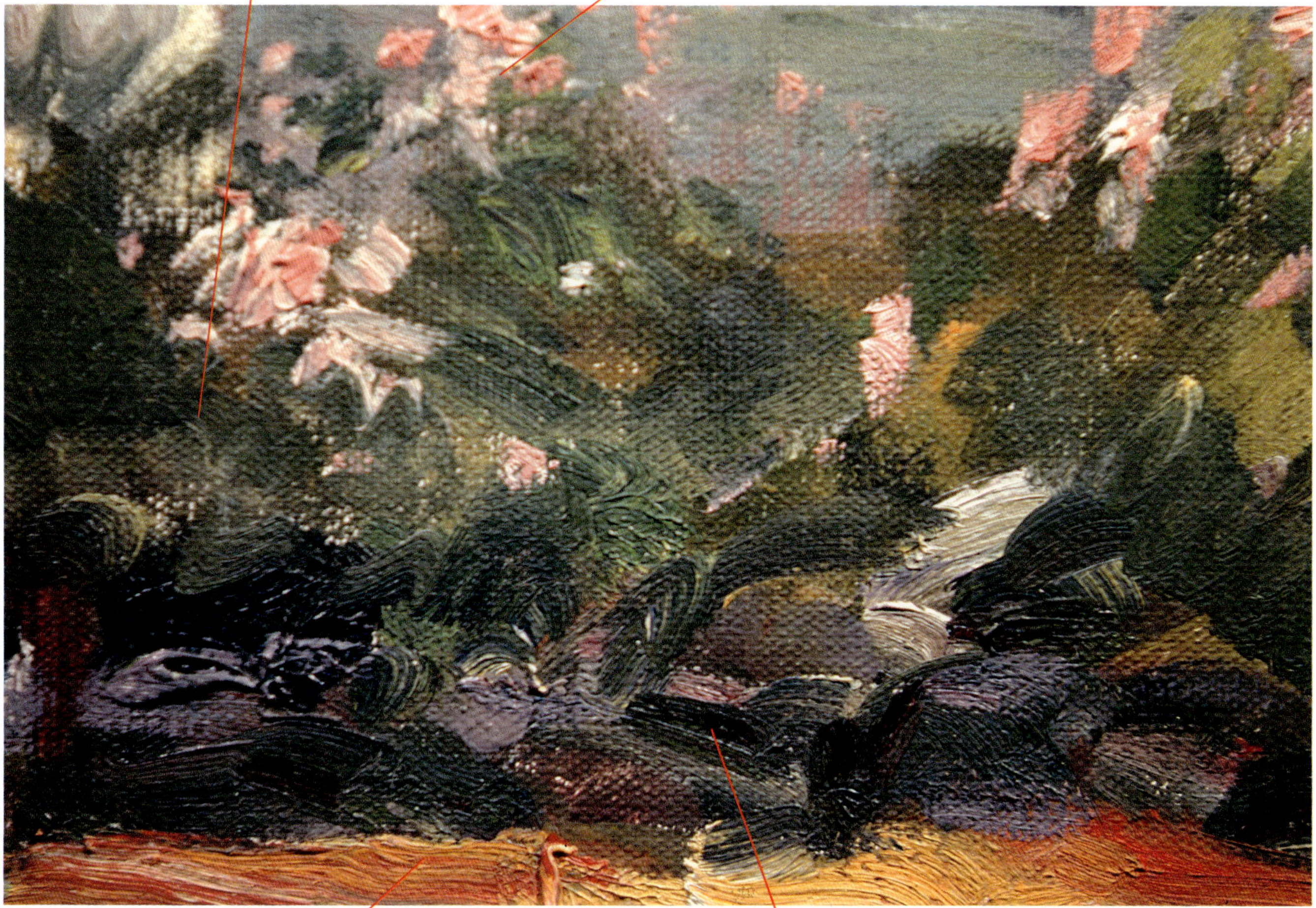

Accentuate the intensity of the greens by running red and orange over the foreground. The area is covered with fallen leaves; but indicate a *color* rather than a texture.

A few staccato notes suggest a wall: a *rhythm* rather than a detail.

Wisteria

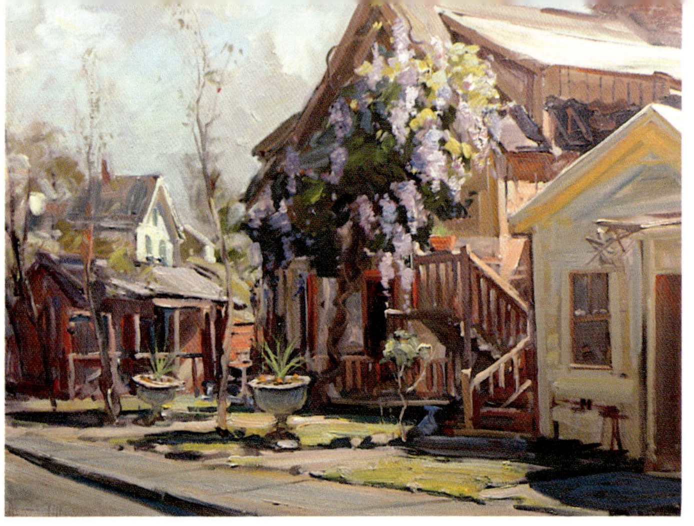

Rocky Neck Studios
oil on canvas
25″ × 30″ (64 × 76 cm)

Note the contrast between the greenish urns and the purple wisteria. Wisteria are like apple blossoms; they're so small that you have to paint them in a mass. Notice the curving vine near the eaves. This stroke tells you how the flowers got where they are; it also breaks the severe line of the roof, making it more interesting to look at. The shadowed white house is a strong foreground element; rich warm color is reflected into the eaves.

Stain the dark leaf area first. Use broad strokes of heavier paint to describe the lighter areas of foliage.

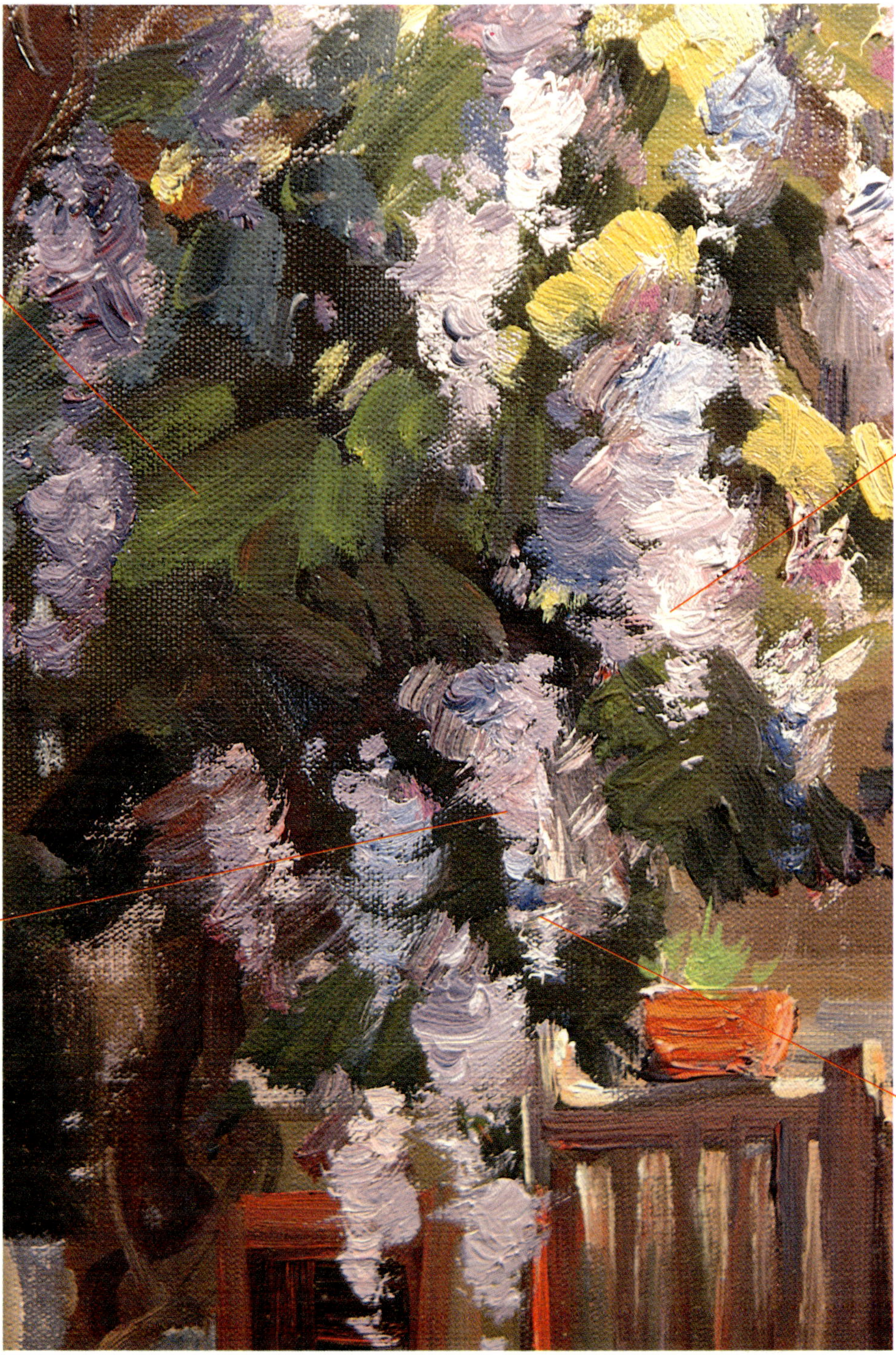

Paint the wisteria closer to you more thickly. The "finished" plants explain the more sketchy, abstract ones.

Use a heavy impasto for wisteria. Work the strokes downward; a few individual marks are visible at the tips of the hanging plants. The short, choppy stroke of the flowers contrasts with the breadth of the foliage.

Intense dark notes give added emphasis to the nearest flowers.

Sunflowers

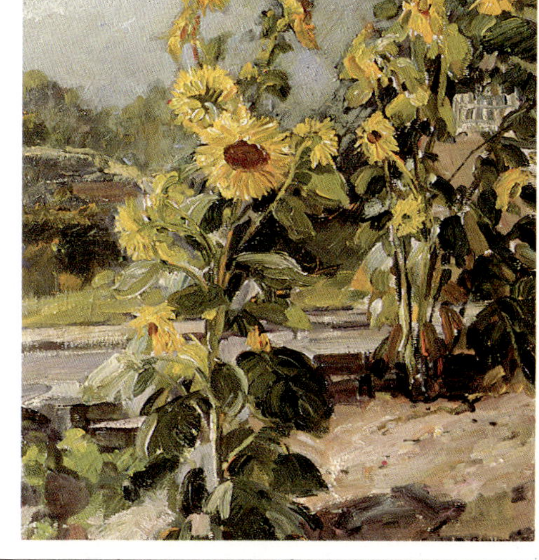

My Sunflowers
oil on canvas
24″ × 20″ (61 × 51 cm)

I painted this picture in my backyard. I like sunflowers, and I admire the lively way Van Gogh handles them. So I decided to try it myself. I emphasize the closeness of the nearest flowers by pulling the stems out of the bottom of the canvas. Since I carefully describe the foreground leaves, I'm able to use simpler strokes in the distance. The sky is a flatly painted foil for the plants.

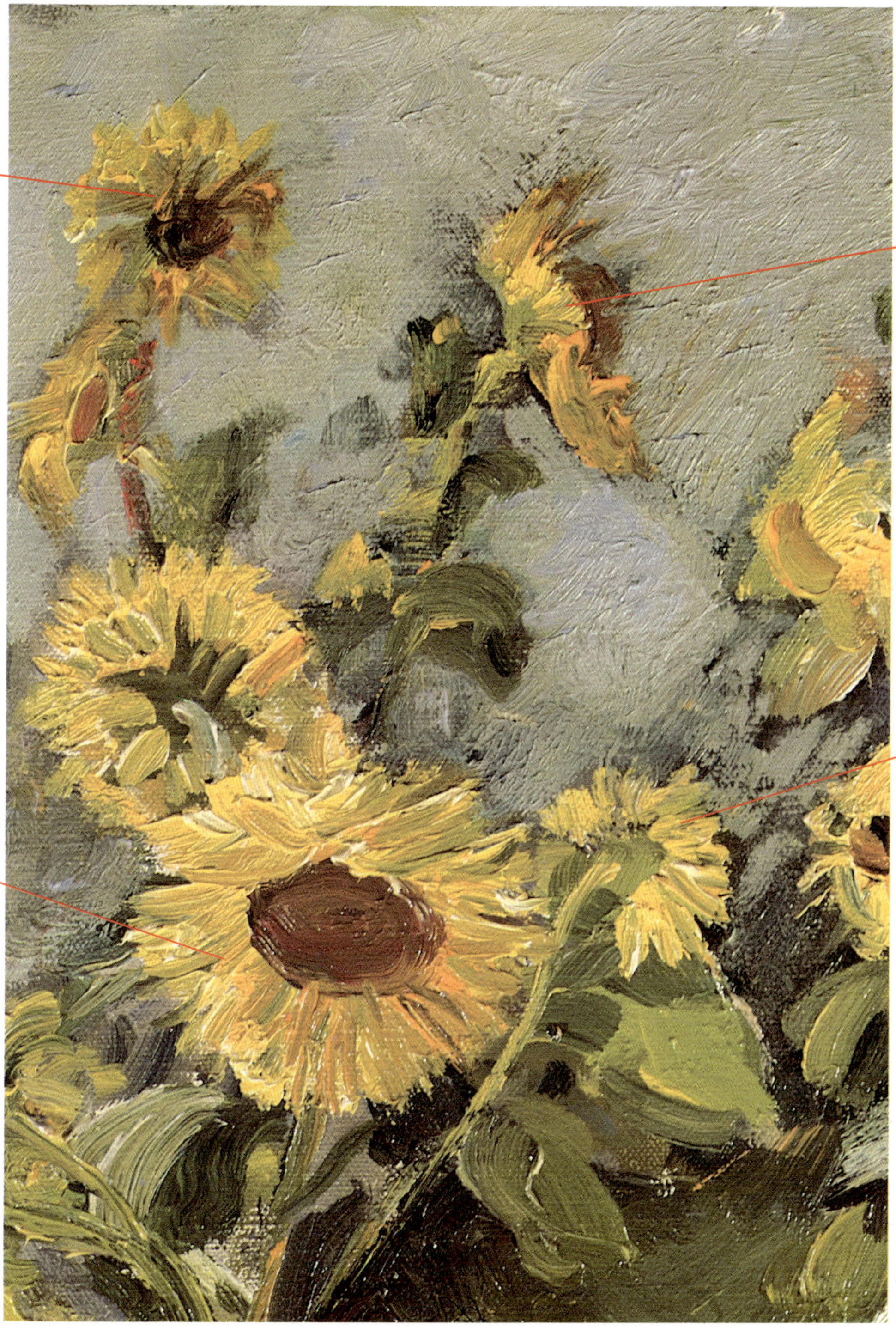

There's a variety of color in the flowers. They're not only yellow, but have touches of orange—and even green, where light is reflected from the nearby leaves.

The background sunflowers are smaller and painted in a broad manner. Each blossom is just a few big strokes.

Only one flower is done in detail. Each petal is a single stroke, with flecks of white for highlights.

The flowers move in different directions: you see the backs of some and the sides and fronts of others. They swing back and forth, moving toward and away from each other.

FIGURES

Before you can paint a figure, you have to know how to draw it. I was lucky; I had two fine instructors. One was a great anatomist. He drew figures upside down for students, and when he turned the paper around, the figures would be in perfect proportion! He made us see the figure; we learned how it moved and worked, where the leverage points were, what it could and could not do.

My other instructor had a more artistic, intuitive approach. He made us draw a dozen lines—then choose the one we liked best. We felt our way into a figure, searching for the qualities that most appealed to us.

Probably the most grueling part of the instruction—and the one of most use—was when the model *didn't* pose. She walked across the floor, bent over, climbed a stand, and then walked behind a screen. As she moved, we picked the pose we liked best and drew it from memory. The instructor said the exercise showed "what you have in your brains rather than in your eyes."

The exercise taught us to catch and record momentary movements. If you paint workers outdoors, for example, they're not going to pose. You have to study them, searching for the twist of the body and bend in the back that fits what you want to say. Your hand has to translate what the eye sees, quickly and with a few shorthand strokes.

Figures are a great asset to a painting; your eye goes right to them. So have them doing things near your center of interest—raking leaves, pulling a net, talking. Also remember to scale them properly. Make them look as if they can go in the doors of the nearby buildings. Small figures in a painting make everything else look large; large figures make the surroundings seem small. Winslow Homer often put small figures in the foreground of his marines; by contrast, his rocks and waves seem more massive and impressive.

The figure's proportions play an important part in how you interpret them. A figure seven heads high looks normal and dignified; one nine heads high looks like a giant. If you make the heads of workers small, you emphasize the strength of their bodies. If the heads are big, you feel you're looking at children.

It's good to convey the idea of a figure—without drawing it carefully. A meticulously finished painting needs carefully drawn figures. But when you work impressionistically, rough figures show a consistency of approach. You feel that they *belong*.

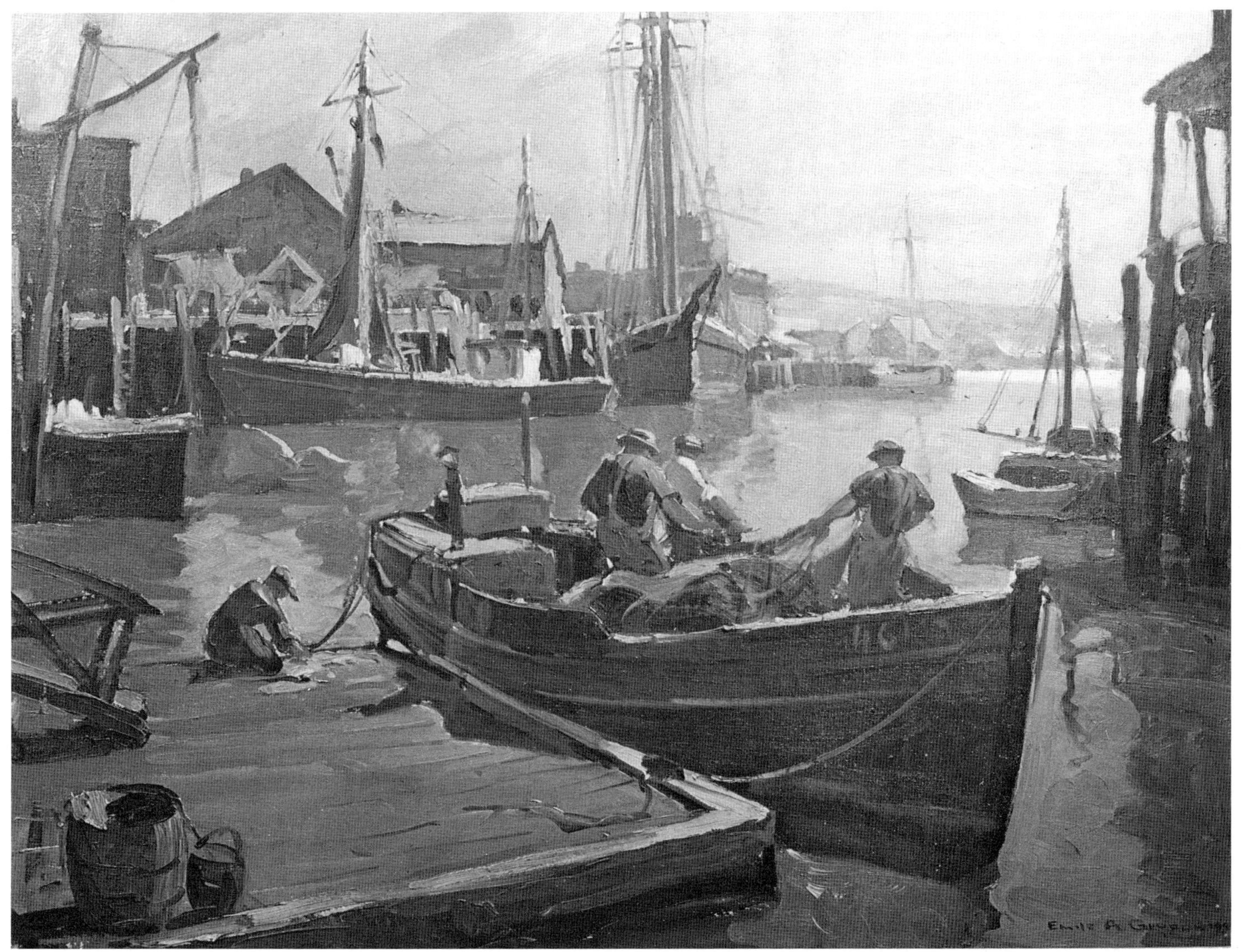

Dock Workers
oil on canvas
30″ × 36″ (76 × 91 cm)
Collection of Paul Clark

In order to emphasize the workers, make them large—and paint the distance, though a complicated area, with very simple strokes. These boats and buildings form large, flat, unmodeled units. Tall masts and derricks add to the dignity of the harbor. The building on the left is done with less than a dozen strokes; it encloses the foreground and makes you feel you're inside a protected slip. The nearest worker is a dark silhouette against the light water. On the left, the dark reflections accent the highlights on the workers' shirts and hats. The kneeling figure blocks the background and leads you toward the men in the boat.

Figure: Close-up

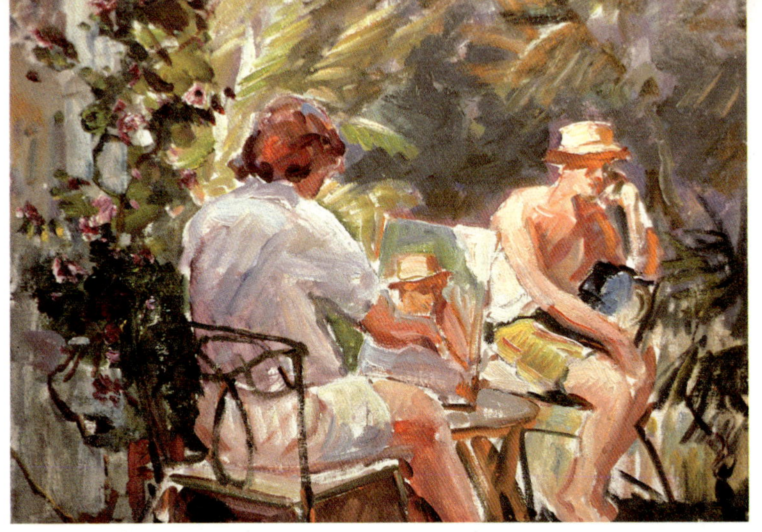

Portrait Practice
oil on panel
16″ × 20″ (41 × 51 cm)

My son is doing a portrait of a friend of the family. It's the sort of thing Renoir liked to do—people in the open air, with outdoor light rather then the predictable lighting of the studio. Notice especially the glow of the warm human flesh against the greens of the surrounding trees.

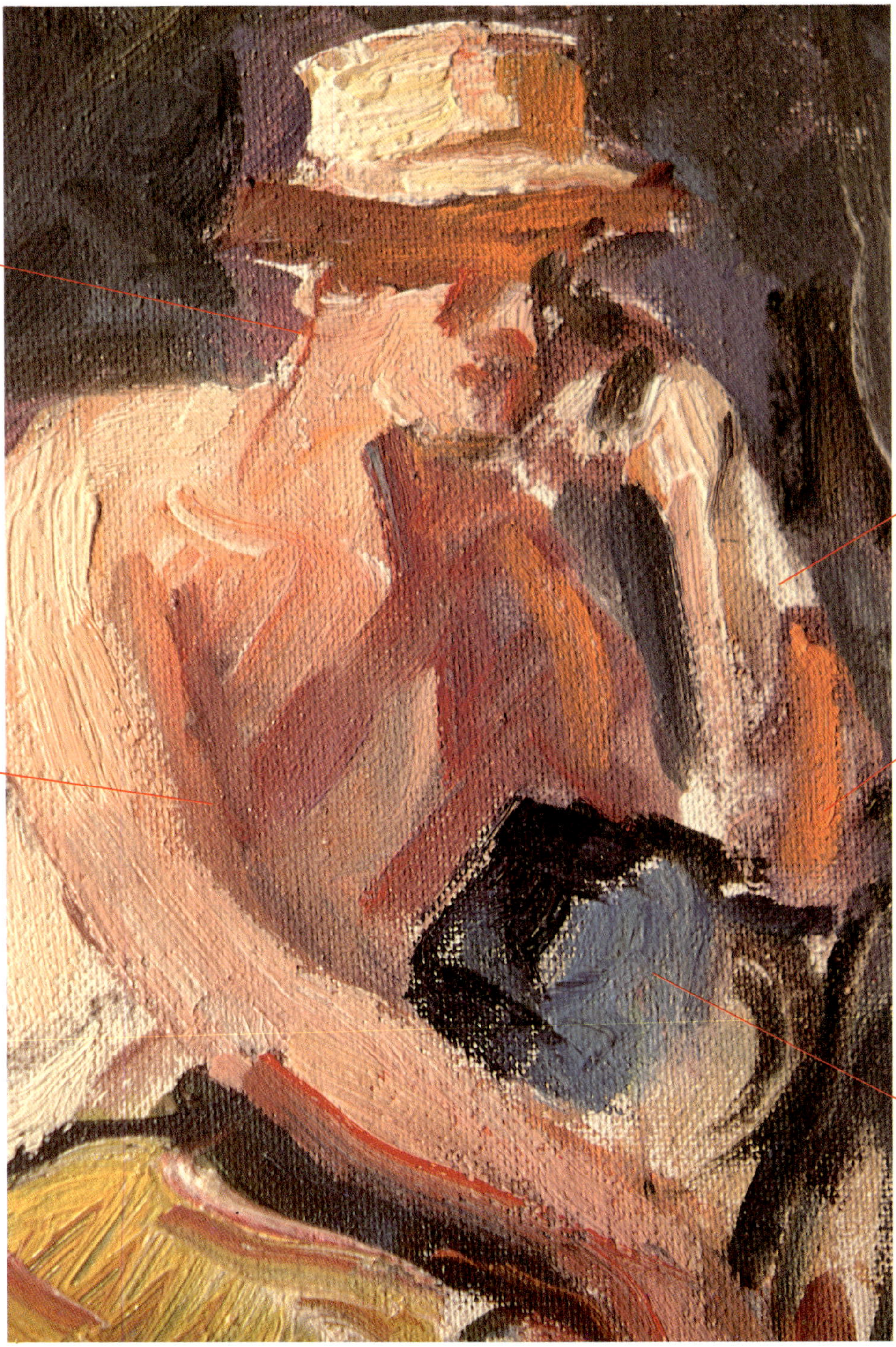

Place the figure with a few lines, and then wash in the darks, leaving bare canvas for the sunlit parts of the hat, head, and torso. The original stain is visible around the head and hat.

A light stroke shows where the arm catches the sun. Cut into it with a few dark strokes for shadows.

Define the chest and arm with contrasting diagonal strokes.

A bright red slash indicates light reflected from the warm surroundings.

A spot of blue emphasizes the warmth of the shadows.

Self-Portrait

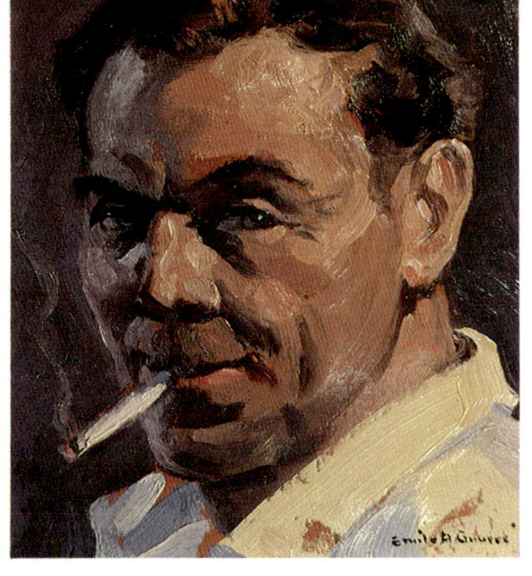

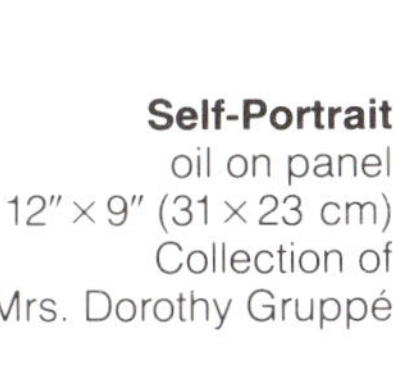

Self-Portrait
oil on panel
12″ × 9″ (31 × 23 cm)
Collection of
Mrs. Dorothy Gruppé

At the last minute, a gallery asked me to do a self-portrait. I grabbed a piece of Masonite and made this quick study. I use a warm light on the face; the shadows catch cool light from my studio window. These shadows are enhanced by the brilliant yellow shirt. I was tanned after a summer of outdoor painting—in places, I let the brown, unpainted Masonite show through.

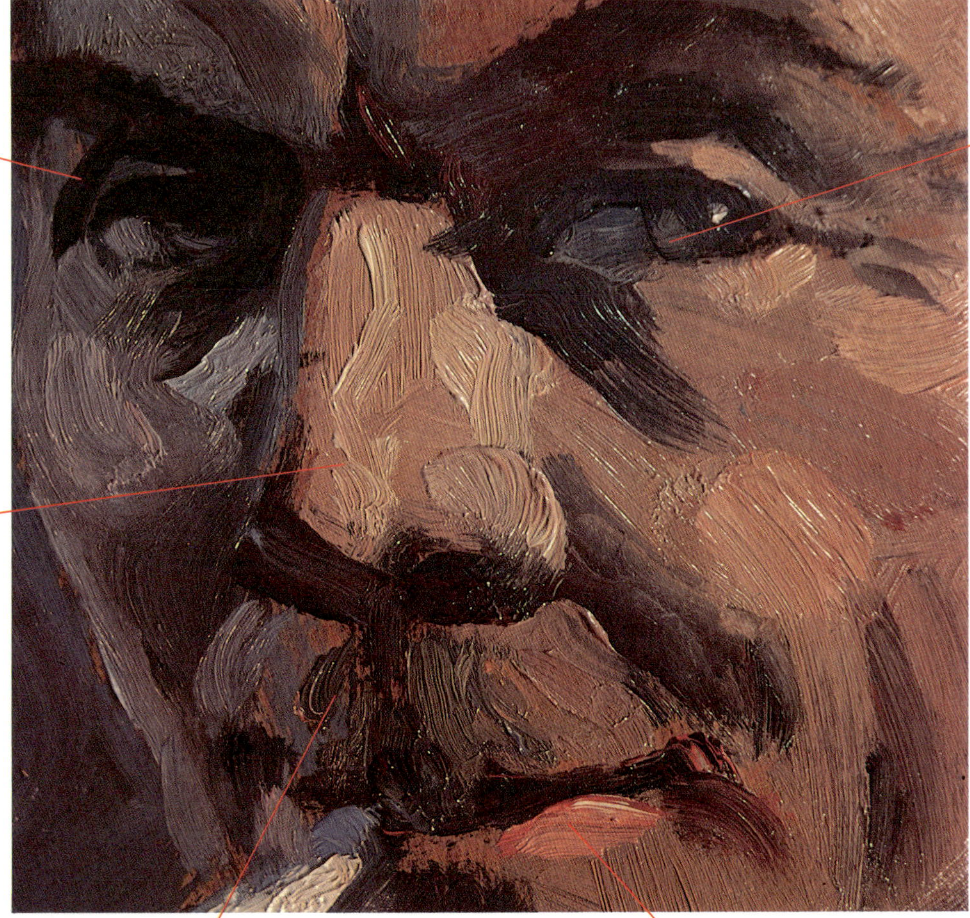

Use dark lines to draw details of the eye socket and cheek.

Keep the white of the eye dark and cool—students always make it too white. The light coming from the right passes through the iris and lights up its *left* side.

Around the eye, strokes define the direction of the lid, brow, and cheek. Note particularly the S-shaped line that shows the bridge of the nose.

The mustache is almost the color of the skin. A few dark, rough strokes separate it from the surroundings.

A piece of Masonite shows at the lip. A red highlight puts the rest of the lip in shadow. The red note also accentuates the green tinge of my mustache.

Figures: Foreground

Mending the Nets
oil on canvas
16″ × 20″ (41 × 51 cm)

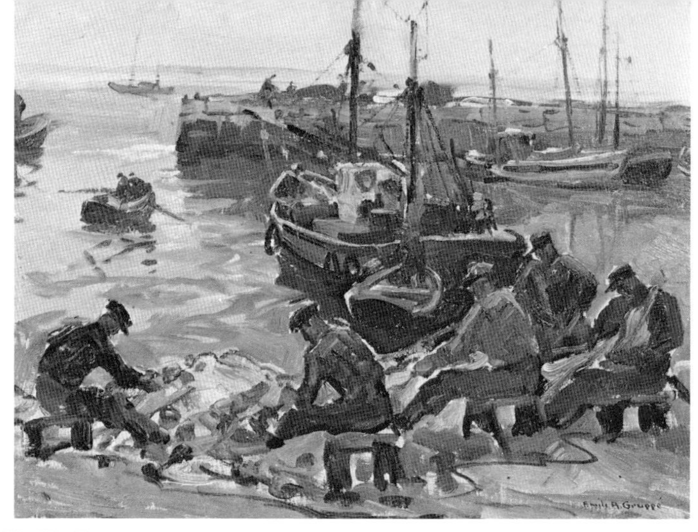

Notice the way the workers cluster around the net. Try to get as much variety as possible in their poses and the angles of their bodies. The boat in the harbor ties the foreground and background together. The small dory on the left blocks your exit from the harbor and keeps the interest in the foreground.

The small dory is an important element in the design. It scales the larger boat, telling you how far away it is.

The workers function as a unit. The group is given a focus by the central figure; he's bigger than the others, is more vividly dressed, and is accented by the dark background boat.

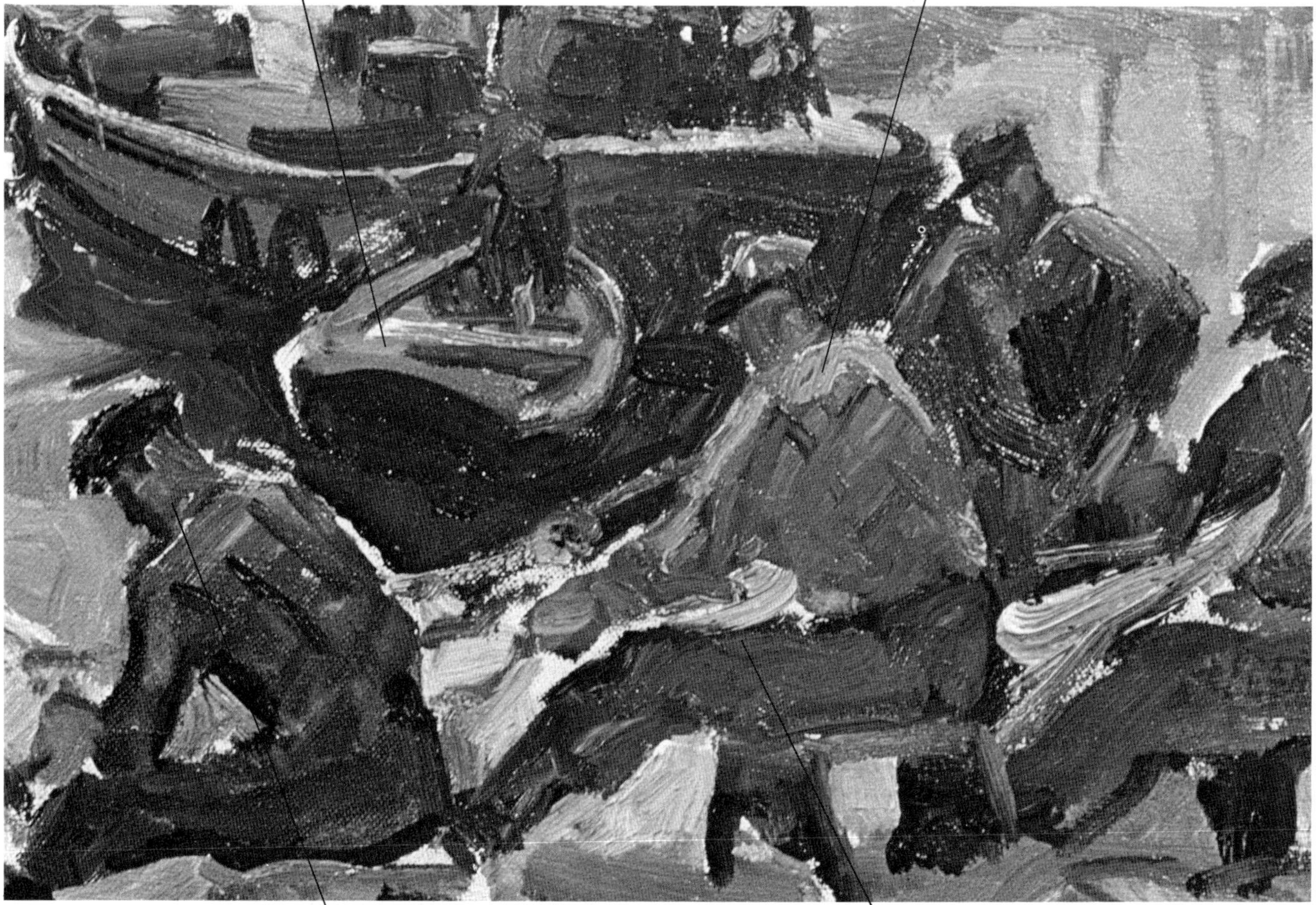

"Draw" the men with masses of color. A hand is one spot of paint; a head another. The rich red suggests their heavily tanned complexions. The green shirt accentuates the reds.

Here and there a dark line brings out a leg or arm.

Figures: Middle Distance

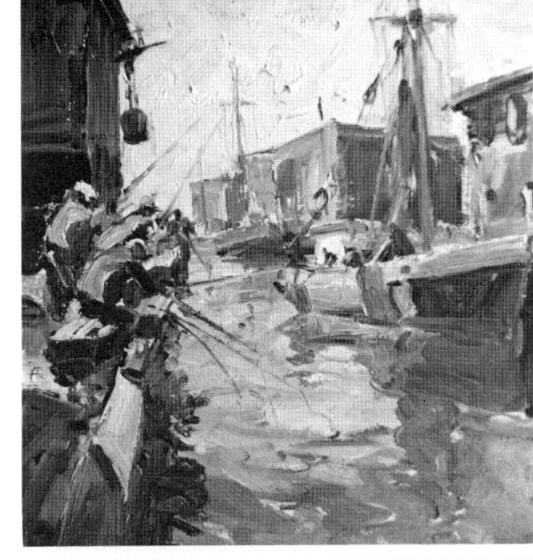

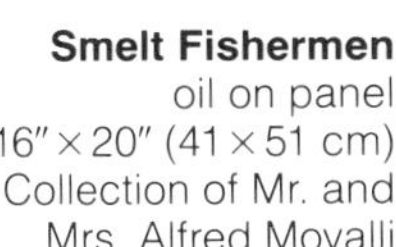

Smelt Fishermen
oil on panel
16″ × 20″ (41 × 51 cm)
Collection of Mr. and Mrs. Alfred Movalli

The fishermen are out on a bright, summer day. The sky at the horizon actually looks yellow. To suggest the lively feeling of the subject, roughly paint the sky, the swirling gulls, the active water, and the bobbing poles. The men move and jostle each other, so you have to work fast.

Spots of unpainted canvas give sparkle and shimmer to the scene.

The lights are heavily painted: a vertical stroke for the back, a rounded stroke for the shoulders, a slanted stroke for the area around the trapezius.

In the distance, the description is even more cursory. A few dark dots suggest heads; a slash of light hints at a back or hand.

Simplify the men into areas of light and shadow, without worrying about subtle half-tones. Paint the darks first, starting with the shadow side of the box and working up the man's leg, shirt, and arm and into the distance. Leave bare canvas for the shirts.

Figures: Near and Far

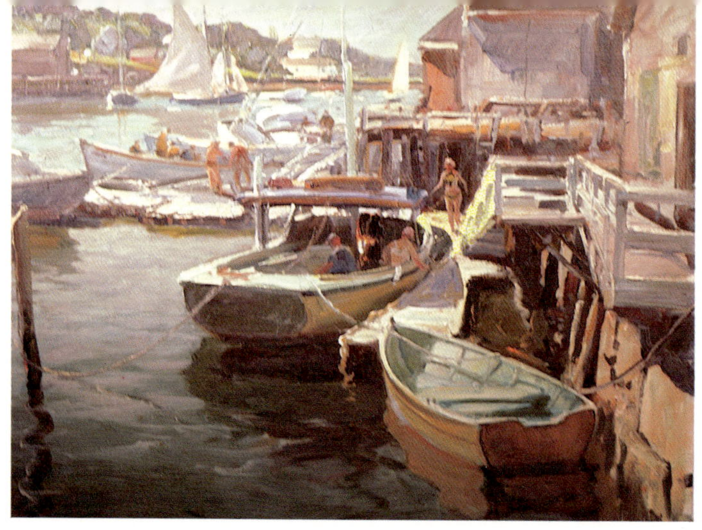

Boats at Rocky Neck
oil on canvas
30″ × 36″ (76 × 91 cm)

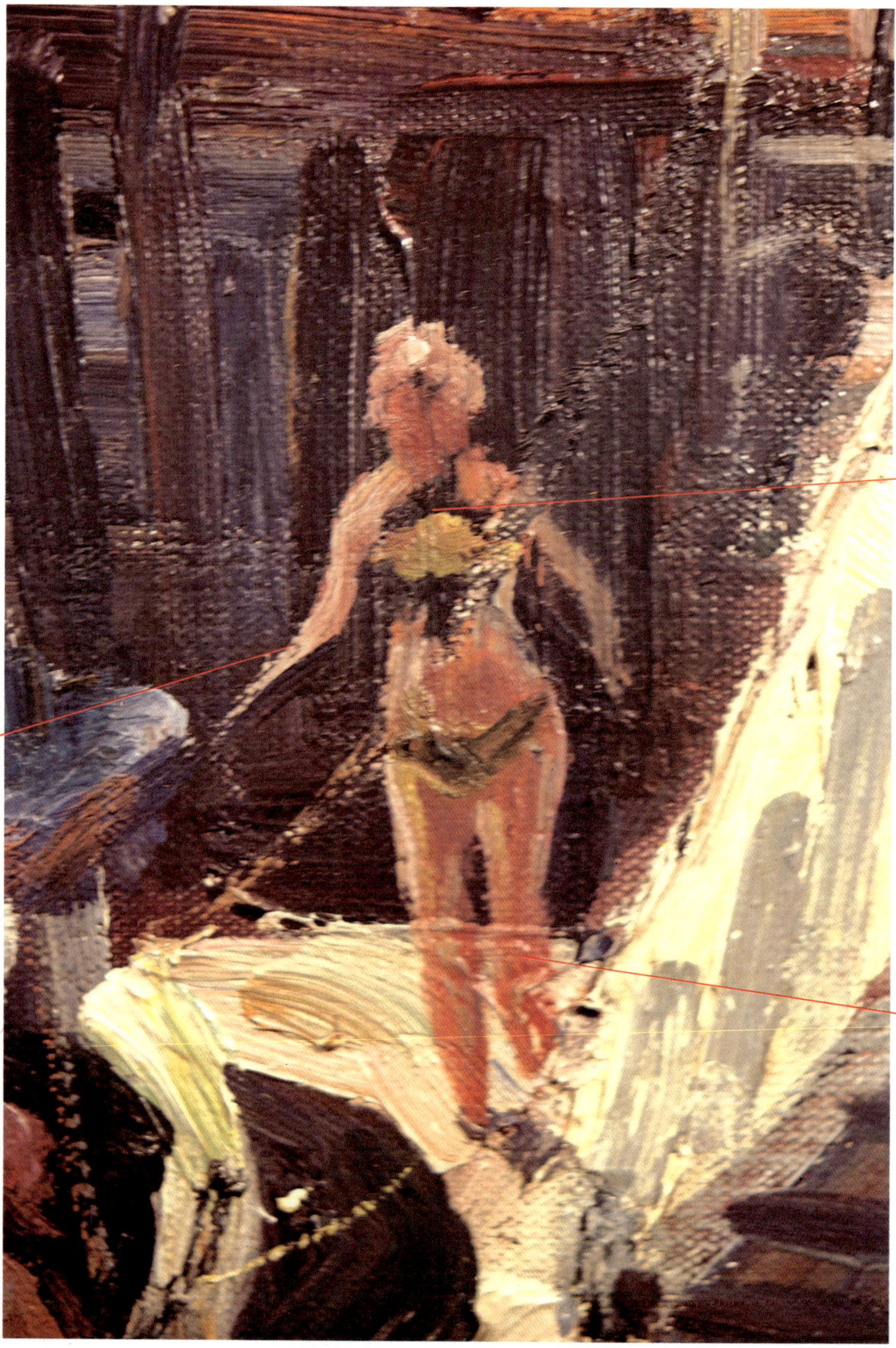

The right arm is a single, tapering stroke. It points you toward the foreground boat.

The bikini is a horizontal stroke, with the original underpainting showing above and beneath it. This underpainting ties the figure to the surroundings.

Bend one leg to unbalance the figure and you feel that she's walking.

The boats move in different directions, one leading naturally to the other. These angular shapes contrast with the rounded forms of the distant hillside. Originally there wasn't a figure on the float. But back in the studio, the area seemed blank. You are led to the spot, but there was nothing to see! The added figure now catches your eye and leads it toward the cabin crusier—the center of interest.

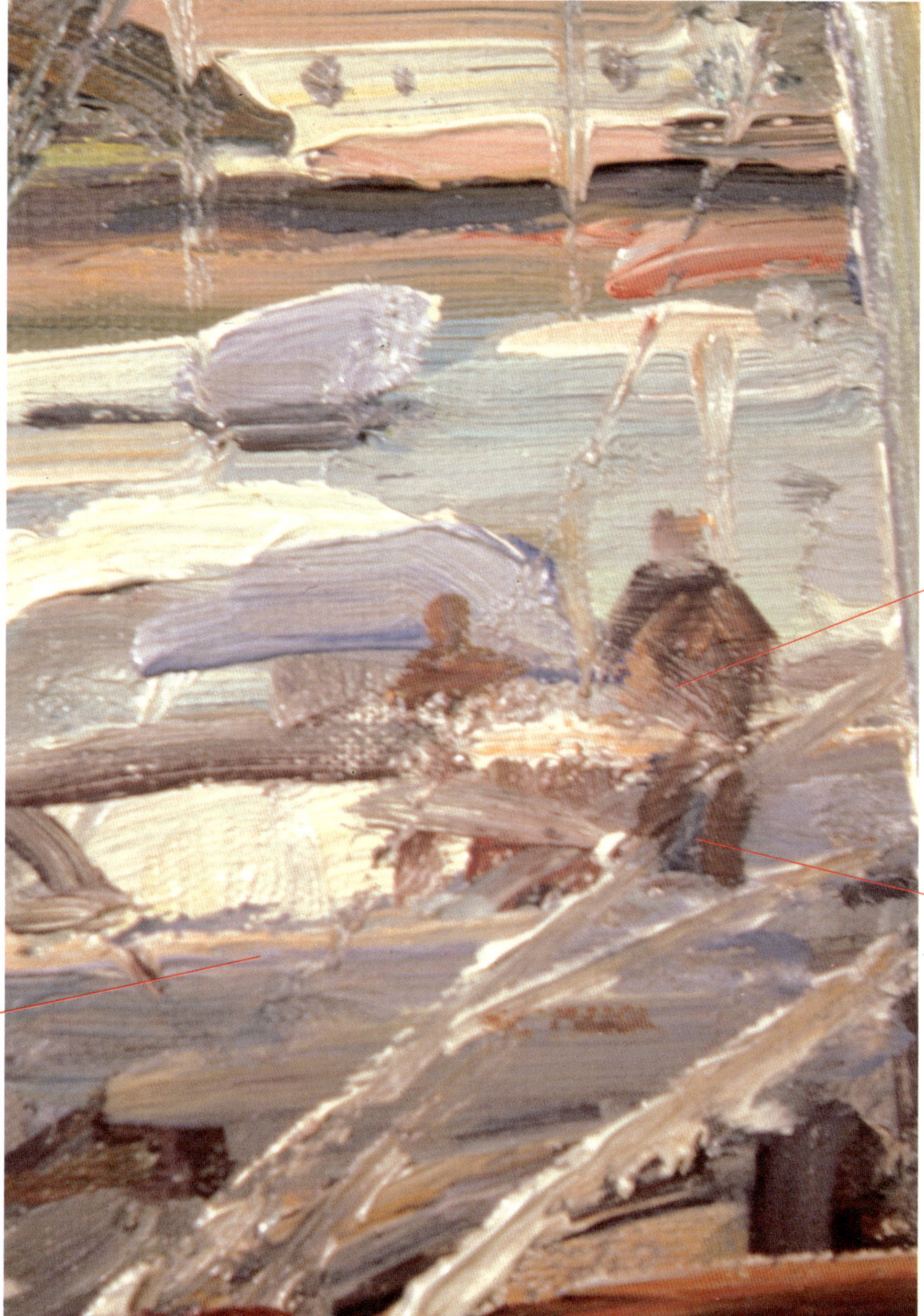

A horizontal highlight sets the figures back among the distant boats.

The distant figures are just dots and rounded shapes. Their warmth accents the coolness of the nearby ocean and shadows.

Upright strokes suggest a pair of legs. These dark notes make the nearby shadows seem more luminous.

CONCLUSION

If you're smart, you'll most enjoy painting the things you know the least about—the things you always fail at. Those are the subjects that keep you from going stale. I knew painters in the old days who only did one picture—the picture the public wanted. They were hooked and spent their lives painting the same tree or the same wave. But there's no fun when you paint like that. It's mechanical, monotonous labor. It's *work!*

When I was younger, I made a name painting nudes out-of-doors. They were sold almost before I finished them. But they were *too* popular—and I didn't want to spend the rest of my life painting figures. So I stopped. I knew another painter who was the rage of New York City fifty years ago. You *had* to have one of his landscapes—just to keep up with the Joneses. And he obliged by turning them out—ten at a time! He ended up with a chauffeur and a Locomobile; but today his pictures are worth only a tenth of what his patrons paid for them. They were what everyone wanted—but they weren't art.

So my closing advice to you is to paint what you like—don't worry if anyone else likes it or not. And study nature carefully, so you know what you're trying to do. Maybe you'll eventually agree with me: if there's a heaven, it must be here on earth. The world is so beautiful! Everyone subconsciously appreciates this beauty. But the painter's appreciation is more conscious—and he spends his life trying to communicate his feelings to others.

Try to do that in your own work. Paint different subjects and different moods. Do all things—but don't abuse any one of them. And be flattered if friends come into your place and ask, "Did *you* do that?" Have a good time when you paint, and people will respond to your pictures. They know you work hard, but they'll also feel that you find painting *fun*. They'll sense that you're doing what you want to do—not what you have to do!

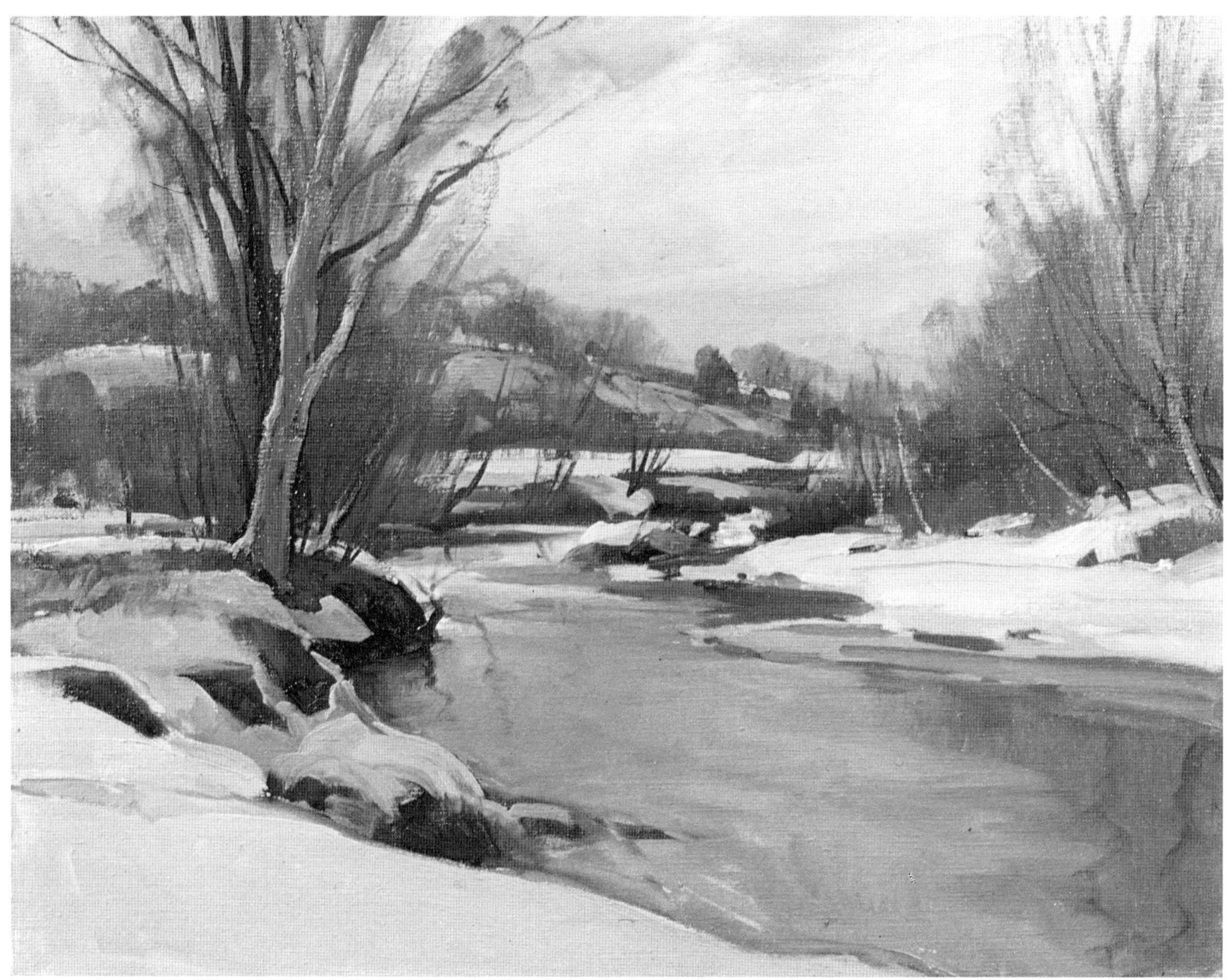

Evening Light
oil on canvas
20″ × 24″ (51 × 61 cm)

Look at the way the stream reflects the delicate, warm color of the afternoon sky. The warmth of the sky and water contrasts with the shadows of the snow and makes them look very cool. First stain the background hill a warm brownish color, over which you should paint blue strokes for the snow patches. The trees on the right are a stain—the same color used in the hills, but a little lighter in value. Lines suggest tree trunks. In the distance, dark accents break the line of the hill. They prevent the eye from moving down the slope too rapidly. They also scale the area; you know from the size of the pines that you're looking at a hill, not a mountain.

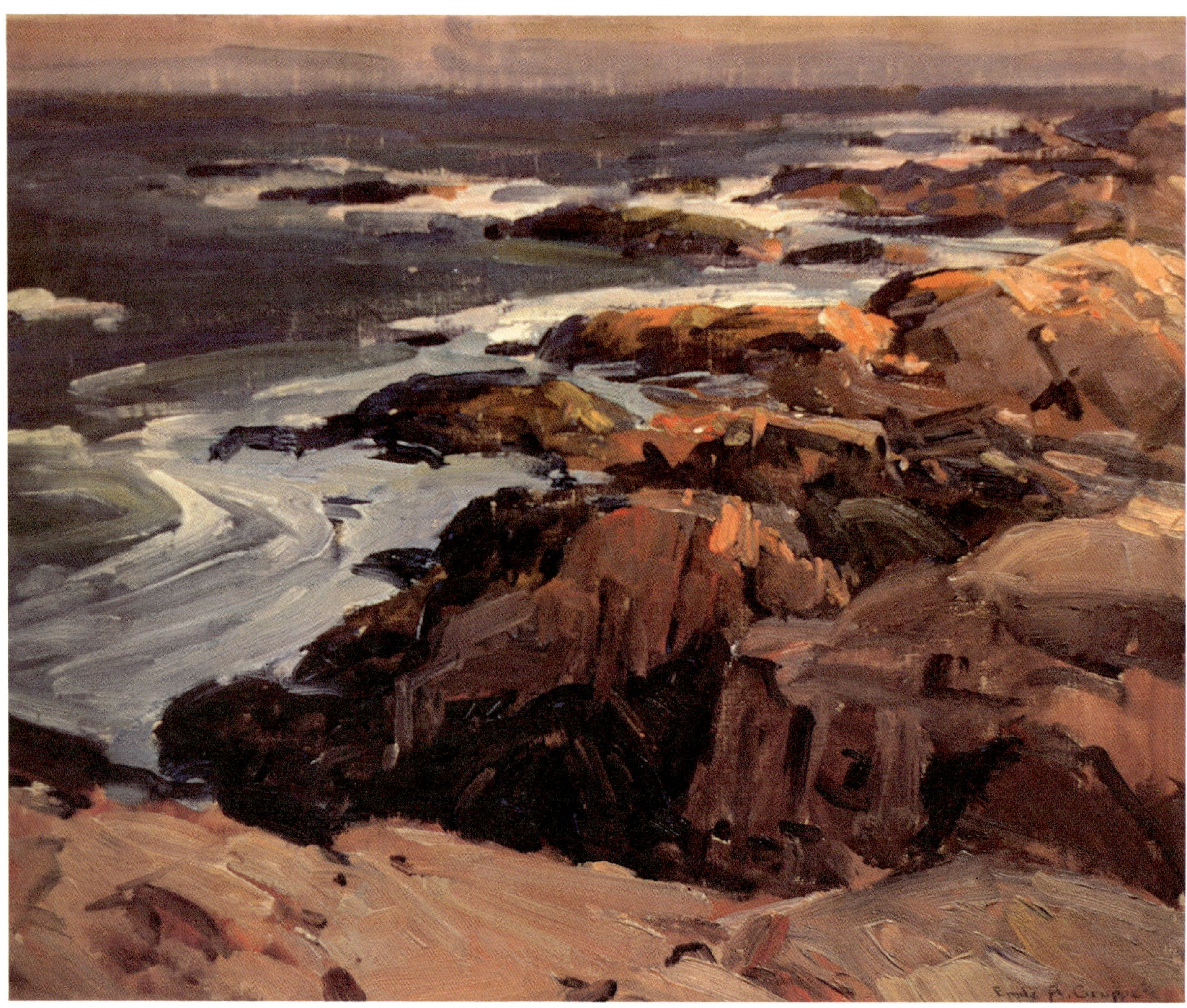

The Back Shore
oil on canvas
25″ × 30″ (64 × 76 cm)

I've always enjoyed painting the broken surfaces of rocks—all the more so since, as a kid, I saw lots of fine painters tackle the subject. Seeing a job done well makes you want to try it yourself. Here the ocean is quiet—but there are enough white notes to set off the darkness of the rocks.

Broad, horizontal strokes again emphasize the flatness of the foreground. The sun strikes this flat plane and makes it very light and warm. The shadowed rocks are painted with strong, upright movements of the brush. The strokes suggest the massiveness of the rocks as they rise out of the ocean. The distant headland is simply a long, slightly jagged stroke. A few diagonals move in different directions and suggest facets in the side of the rock. The distant water and sky are painted with long, flat strokes. These strokes add breadth to the painting and emphasize, by contrast, the upward movement of the foreground rocks. The movement of the foam is indicated by curved strokes. We look *down* on these nearby swirls and see their eliptical shape. In the distance, however, the pattern is hidden. The foam becomes a few horizontal strokes of white paint.

SELECTED BIBLIOGRAPHY

Bridgeman, George. *Life Drawing*. New York: Dover Publications, 1961.

Carlson, John F. *Landscape Painting*. New York: Dover Publications, 1974.

Gruppé, Emile A. *Gruppé on Painting*. New York: Watson-Guptill, 1976.

———. *Color*. New York: Watson-Guptill, 1979.

Hawthorne, Charles. *Hawthorne on Painting*. New York: Dover Publications, 1960.

Henri, Robert. *The Art Spirit*. Philadelphia: J.B. Lippencott Co., 1930.

INDEX

Italics indicate illustrations.

Edited by Bonnie Silverstein and Susan Davis
Designed by Robert Fillie
Graphic production by Hector Campbell
Set in 10 point Times Roman